The Beauty of Living

The Beauty of Living

E. E. CUMMINGS
IN THE GREAT WAR

J. Alison Rosenblitt

W. W. NORTON & COMPANY
Independent Publishers Since 1923

Since this page cannot legibly accommodate all the copyright notices,
pages 325–27 constitute an extension of the copyright page.

For information about permission to reproduce selections from this book,
write to Permissions, W. W. Norton & Company, Inc.,
500 Fifth Avenue, New York, NY 10110

For information about special discounts for bulk purchases, please contact
W. W. Norton Special Sales at specialsales@wwnorton.com or 800-233-4830

Manufacturing by Lake Book
Book design by Brooke Koven
Production manager: Anna Oler

Library of Congress Cataloging-in-Publication Data

Names: Rosenblitt, J. Alison (Jennifer Alison) author.
Title: The beauty of living : E. E. Cummings in the Great War / J. Alison Rosenblitt.
Description: First edition. | New York : W. W. Norton & Company, [2020] |
Includes bibliographical references and index.
Identifiers: LCCN 2019058084 |
ISBN 9780393246964 (hardcover) | ISBN 9780393246971 (epub)
Subjects: LCSH: Cummings, E. E. (Edward Estlin), 1894–1962—Childhood and
youth. | Poets, American—20th century—Biography. |
Cummings, E. E. (Edward Estlin), 1894–1962—Criticism and interpretation. |
World War, 1914–1918—Literature and the war.
Classification: LCC PS3505.U334 Z834 2020 | DDC 811/.52—dc23
LC record available at https://lccn.loc.gov/2019058084

W. W. Norton & Company, Inc., 500 Fifth Avenue, New York, N.Y. 10110
www.wwnorton.com

W. W. Norton & Company Ltd., 15 Carlisle Street, London W1D 3BS

1 2 3 4 5 6 7 8 9 0

FOR C.A.M.F.
in admiration

~

Labour is blossoming or dancing where
The body is not bruised to pleasure soul,
Nor beauty born out of its own despair,
Nor blear-eyed wisdom out of midnight oil.
O chestnut-tree, great-rooted blossomer,
Are you the leaf, the blossom or the bole?
O body swayed to music, O brightening glance,
How can we know the dancer from the dance?

—W. B. YEATS, "Among School Children"

When you and I consult these hearts and minds of ours,what do we learn? That there actually exists a deeper beauty even than the beauty of death—the beauty of living.

—E. E. CUMMINGS, *"Armistice"*

Contents

~

The Beauty of Living

Prologue

"ONLY MY DOOR CLOSING"

—

...it was with a genuine and never-to-be-forgotten thrill that I remarked,as I crossed what might have been the threshold: "Mais,on est bien ici. (But this is fine.)"

A hideous crash nipped the last word. I had supposed the whole prison to have been utterly destroyed by earthquake,but it was only my door closing...

—E. E. CUMMINGS, *The Enormous Room*

E. E. CUMMINGS was imprisoned for two nights at Noyon, a cathedral town in northeast France, in the cell that was fine. It was, said Cummings, "about sixteen feet short and four feet narrow," with straw at one end and an imposing latrine pail at the other. He had by now tumbled to the notion that his arrest was connected to letters written by his friend William Slater Brown. But he had no idea where he was going and only a vague idea why. "I am sorry for you," his interrogator had pronounced, "but due to your friend you will be detained a little while."

"Several weeks?" asked Cummings.

"Possibly."

Or possibly longer. He was soon to find that the efforts of fellow prisoners to contact the outside world had a way of going missing.

From Noyon, he was transferred to a brutal French prison camp in the town of La Ferté-Macé. There he faced malnutrition and disease, dangerous levels of damp and cold, and the threat of transfer to the even more brutal prison at Précigné, where many prisoners died. Life at La Ferté-Macé was a test of mental and physical endurance. Lunch—bread and a few scraps of potato in broth—was "the Soup." Dinner—bread and a few scraps of potato in broth—was, imaginatively, also "the Soup." There was an indigestible piece of meat at lunch three times a week. The meal call, says Cummings, turned the prisoners into animals: a "ferocious and uncouth miracle,this beautiful manifestation of the sinister alchemy of hunger."

It was 1917. Cummings had been serving as a volunteer in the Great War, as a driver with a mixed American-French ambulance unit. It was the fashionable thing to do, and, among his friends from Harvard, he was far from alone in volunteering. They were young men, and they dreamed of adventure.

It was on the *Touraine*, which sailed from New York on April 28, 1917, that Cummings met Brown. Cummings was a Harvard man, Brown a student at Columbia, and they became instant and intimate friends. The journey continued from ship to train; they were lost in private conversation when the rest of their detachment were herded out by a precipitate fellow volunteer, one stop before the last Parisian *gare*. At the next stop, they found themselves alone. They reported to the ambulance service headquarters in Paris, but through the accident of registering one day later than the rest of their cohort, their paperwork and requisitioning forms were separated. The requisition forms for their uniforms were processed on a delay; without uniforms, they could not be deployed; and thus for no reason other than accident of bureaucracy, it was more than a month before deployment to the front caught up with the pair of them.

They, meanwhile, enjoyed five weeks of freedom in Paris, where they immersed themselves in the Parisian demimonde. Here Cummings met and dated the Parisian prostitute Marie Louise Lallemand, the unconventional muse of some of his best war poetry. Cummings's interrogator found this month in Paris most suspicious and was inclined to press the point: "What did you do in Paris?"

"We had a good time."

In the demimonde of Paris and, eventually, posted on the French front to Section Sanitaire XXI of the Norton-Harjes Ambulance Corps, Cummings began to see the world. He saw more of the world than he could freely write about. He tried repeatedly to communicate with his mother: "In this, my fourth letter to you since arriving on French soil, or my fifth including the steamer one, I'm at a loss to know what to say, inasmuch as M. le Censor has seen fit to withhold my past effusions—to judge by your last letter, which I got yesterday. I shall, accordingly, do my best to say nothing at all, trusting that you will understand, given the above circumstances, that any other course would prove futile."

Cummings was a romantic. His letters, poetry, and prose from Paris and the front report regularly on the glow of twilight and the state of the moon. But he also had a certain sound good sense. Brown was his foil. A likeable and intense young man, Brown was also nervous, rash, even hotheaded. He felt the same frustrations at the activities of Monsieur le Censor, but he responded rather differently. From their miserable, muddy posting under an uptight commanding officer, shifting camps around the *départements* of the Aisne and the Somme, he wrote frank letters home about the atrocities of war, the demoralization of the French troops, and the spread of venereal disease in the American army.

Cummings knew nothing of these letters that caused the French authorities to descend upon the pair. The same authorities had no concrete evidence against Cummings, but they were determined to hold Brown. This is as much as Cummings gathered piecemeal from the interrogation to which he was subjected on an otherwise entirely baffling day as it dawned on him that the questions posed by his interrogators centered on letters written by Brown and seized by the French military censors. With only this muddy sense of the cause of their arrest, and no idea at all of their future, his one concern was loyalty to his friend. He had no wish to allow the French authorities to separate their fates.

"Est-ce que vous détestez les boches? (Do you hate the Germans?)"

was the final question posed by his interrogator. It was, as Cummings describes it, a last and desperate attempt to incriminate him.

Cummings was certain of his ground. "I had won my own case. The question was purely perfunctory. To walk out of the room a free man I had merely to say yes."

At this decisive moment in his life, we meet Edward Estlin Cummings. He is perhaps naïve. He has not grasped a fraction of what is in store. He has seen the realities of the front, but he has not lost his taste for adventure. He is determined. Quick-witted. Above all, he is loyal to his friends. He took a dive. Does he not hate the Germans?

"Deliberately,I framed my answer:

'Non. J'aime beaucoup les français.' (No. I love very much the French.)"

And thus his imprisonment began.

PART I

CAMBRIDGE

1894–1911

—

1

BEYOND THE RIVER

E. E. CUMMINGS grew up in Cambridge, Massachusetts, in a house about eight minutes' walk from Harvard Yard. His neighbors were Harvard professors and his childhood was spent in the shadow of the university. His high school, the Cambridge Latin School, sat at the end of his road, and the tops of the grand Harvard buildings are visible from its grounds. Cummings's childhood home still stands today at 104 Irving Street. It is the only house in the area with an 8-foot-high picket fence and a tight, unfriendly ring of evergreen trees, suggesting that its present owners have endured their fill of curious tourists.

Cambridge, Massachusetts is scattered gently along one bank of the Charles River. It bleeds at the edges into its scurrilous twin, Somerville—where (says Cummings) they threw snowballs packed round rocks. Maybe they always packed their snowballs around rocks, but it is hard to escape the suspicion that any Somerville child could spot any Cambridge child from a snowball's distance. In the 1970s and 1980s, Somerville fell into the orbit of the Boston mafia, the Winter Hill Gang, and James "Whitey" Bulger; today it is where Harvard graduate students live when they cannot afford Cambridge rents.

The river itself runs low and flat. It has a dead, blue-gray sheen; it feels fathomless. The line it draws between Cambridge and Somerville together on one bank and Boston on the other is not a line between city and suburb. It divides two worlds, so that from either bank, the other is unreal. In the mind of another Boston poet, Robert Lowell—scion of a conspicuous Boston family that boasted poets and Harvard presidents aplenty—the Charles doubled as the River Styx, with the ancient ferryman Charon presiding, to shepherd souls across to the Underworld:

> ... On the rigid Charles, in snow,
> Charon, the Lubber, clambers from his wherry ...

Boston is a port, indelibly written into history for the Boston Tea Party. At the turn of the twentieth century, it was the fifth-largest city in America. Population: 560,892. But Cambridge held the university. Power lay on both sides of the river.

Cummings was his parents' first child, born on the fourteenth of October, 1894, and named Edward Estlin: Edward, after his father, and Estlin, after the English Unitarian theologian and friend of his father, (Joseph) Estlin Carpenter. He was born into an age of transition. Horse and carriage were the norm—or horse and sleigh, in winter—and motorcars, although not unknown, still seemed a pretentious folly. Cummings's parents acquired an Orient Buckboard, a car that puttered like a dying lawnmower and that looks less like a car than like a four-wheeled wheelbarrow barely scaled up to fit human passengers. The Orient claimed to reach the dizzying speed of 30 miles per hour, although Cummings's younger sister, Elizabeth, remembered its speed as closer to 15 miles per hour. It was manufactured by the Waltham Watch Company (so named because they specialized originally in the manufacture of watches, not cars). The wheels ran on chains like a bicycle, and the engine had to be started around the back by pulling on a strap. Elizabeth also remembered that the local boys would run alongside the car shouting, "Why don't you get a horse?"

Boston was urban, and yet small enough to find a civic identity through its town hall meetings—many of them graced (one might say) with the presence of Cummings's father, the Rev. Edward Cummings, minister of Boston's South Congregational Church.

Cummings's mother adored him.

We have, thanks to her, every physical scrap of his childhood enshrined in the Harvard Library archives. She adored him to the point of absurdity; she saved every piece of paper he touched. There is page after page of baby's first scribbles. Any mother might save her child's first effort at pencil to paper, but Rebecca Cummings saved dozens and dozens: sheets with no more than a pencil scratch across the page, or a gashed zigzag. Some have got as far as a wobbly sort of spiral. There is something endearing but faintly ridiculous in the preservation of these aged and fragile sheets in Harvard's plush archival space, for the benefit of the researcher, who turns them ever so carefully, fingertips on the corners of the page.

The scribbles give way to the usual obsessions and delights of boyhood. There was a trains phase, a heroes from Homer's *Iliad* phase, a phase drawing medieval knights in armor. There is Estlin's Great Animal Arena, exploding with animal life. From the style and sheer volume of the drawings, it is obvious that Cummings sketched and painted swiftly. But he stuck to his topics. His animal arena proceeds methodically through "ungulates" (warthog, babyrousa, peccary, domestic hog, wild boar), "Sirenia" (walrus, seal, sea elephant, manatee, sea lion), "marsupials," and much, much more—all carefully labeled. The zoological taxonomy is obviously lifted from some encyclopedia or book of animals, but Cummings's boyhood imagination was not limited to rote mimicry. Side by side with the methodical copies are dozens of sketches and watercolors in which the animals are recombined into Estlin's own zoo. He privileged his mother with a forceful black-and-red ticket: "Mrs. Edward E. Cummings. Season Ticket. Estlin's Great Animal Arena. Positively Not Transferable. If Presented by Other Person than Party Herein Named Ticket will be Taken Up and Not Renewed. Direction of Mr. Edward E. Cummings."

It would always be like this with Cummings. His work was fed by contradictory energies: it was rapid but focused, instinctive but obsessive. He was known for an urgently spontaneous poetry of "Is" and "Now," but behind these poems lie methodical drafts upon drafts. A poem might evolve suddenly with a change of a line or even a stanza, and then a dozen retypes altering a word or a single comma. Cummings also documented his own life with meticulous care. In introspective moods, he would type page after page of daily thoughts and feelings and memories. But at the same time that he cataloged, scrutinized, and organized his inner life, he would doodle indiscriminately on every scrap of paper within reach. His pencil marks sprawl over every torn-off envelope flap or back of a canceled check that came to hand. In his notes, he pondered the paradox that "chaos" represented—as he saw it—the essence of life; yet, to embody life in art required the imposition of order. He felt that the essential breakthrough of Cézanne was the genius to organize artistic expression without freezing the life out of movement and chaos. Cummings's life and his art were both caught between chaos and control.

To all outward appearances, a childhood could hardly have been more progressive. Cummings's father's father held that it was best for children to start school late, and since this had worked out fine for him, the Reverend took the same approach to his own children. He regarded it as unnatural to force a child of five or six to sit rigidly tied to a desk all day, and both Cummings and Elizabeth started school several years later than their peers.

Meanwhile, there was always company in a household made full by parents, aunts, uncle, grandmothers, and servants, and there were so many places to play. The house was huge and rambling. It had secret hideaways and—Cummings and Elizabeth believed—an even more secret hideaway that they never even saw. This most secret of hiding places lay behind a built-in bookcase on the third floor, and, as far as they understood, it had something to do with honoring the actions of their paternal grandfather, who had offered sanctuary to fugitive slaves on the Underground Railroad. They played in the cellar and the tool room and on the roof, which had a flat portion accessible through a skylight in the loft. In good weather, they used the roof to fly a kite that Cummings had made himself. For cold weather, they had central heating powered by a furnace in the cellar; but as it was a large and drafty house, they kept wood fires burning in almost every room. The house was connected by a series of speaking tubes built into the walls linking room to room and even floor to floor. "Not all the tubes and buttons worked," wrote Elizabeth later, "but some of them did."

Elizabeth was Cummings's only sibling, six and a half years younger than him. They played together throughout their childhood, not only around the house but also roaming the neighborhood. Cummings carried Elizabeth on the handlebars of his bicycle on rides across Cambridge, collecting stones and turtles. About a hundred paces down the street from home, they could escape into a "semi-wilderness" known locally after the Harvard eminence Charles Eliot Norton as Norton's Woods. What was once a nickname is now the official moniker; a small portion of the woods remains, supplemented with a conference center and wedding venue. Apart from a smattering of pines, they are deciduous: mostly maple and American oak. Cummings always remembered the thrill of the threshold, guarded by lilacs, before you crossed into the shock of sudden shade and the sunlight filtering through a high tree canopy. The woods had the tang of adventure, heightened by the delicious memory of having been once chased from the lilac bushes by a neighbor's coachman. It was a child-size wilderness indeed: wild enough to tease the imagination but safe enough to enjoy the thrill of imagined danger.

When you know what to look for in a life, there are always hints of what lies ahead. In his last year before university, at the Cambridge High and Latin School, his marks for English, Latin, Greek, algebra, and Roman history were "Fair" to "Good," with one "Excellent" result in French. But he failed twice—once "Poor" and once, even worse, "Ungraded"—in deportment. Cummings's love of French and his scruffy deportment were to play a more pivotal role in his life than his high school teachers could ever have imagined.

But his robust childhood prepared Cummings in other ways for events to come. When Cummings was five years old, the Reverend purchased a summer home, Joy Farm, near Silver Lake in the mountains of New Hampshire. It was a vast property with a run-down house, outbuildings, enormous grounds, a hayfield, and woodlands as well as pigs, a goat, hens, cows, and a donkey. It became a fixed axis around which Cummings's life revolved until his death, which occurred at Joy Farm itself in 1962.

The property was surrounded by a pine forest, and Cummings and Elizabeth were encouraged to venture as far as they liked, provided only that they carried a compass and a box of matches. The compass was to get them home safely; the matches were an emergency measure. If they were truly lost, they had instructions to build a small fire—safely, on a rock, so that it would not spread—as a smoke signal so that their father could find and rescue them. The risks were real; bad enough for adults. The Reverend and Rebecca and half the local village spent one night searching for neighbors who had gone missing, lost in the pines (and who finally turned up safe but weak the next day). However, Elizabeth trusted her older brother implicitly. She never mastered her own compass, for she knew that he would always get them both home safely.

Cummings felt his sister's trust, and he was protective, tender, and attentive toward her. He was the one to keep an eye on her—as one summer, when the family decided to increase the water supply to Joy Farm by widening the spring-fed water pool from which they pumped water for the house. Drinking water always came from the well for the sake of the taste of the freshly drawn well water, but the Reverend had installed piping and a water tank fed by the pool to meet the other needs of the household. The water pool was rock, and to widen it meant dynamite. They enlisted the local village expert, who rigged up the dynamite in the pool's depth on a long fuse to allow him time to escape. Cummings and Elizabeth and other neighboring children gathered for the event, poised to scarper at the expert's warning shout. Just as he put a match to the fuse, he slipped on a rung of the ladder out of the pool. As he slipped, he shouted, and the sheer terror in his voice caused Elizabeth to freeze. Everyone else ran, and only Cummings noticed that Elizabeth was rooted to the spot. He dashed back, grabbed her, and tugged her into running off together. She (and, luckily, the village dynamite man) escaped in time.

Back home in Cambridge, Cummings and Elizabeth played either together or as part of a neighborhood gang of ten or twelve, of varying ages, more boys than girls. They played makeshift sports, tag, and hide-and-seek. Cummings was a natural leader, and the gang often hung out in his spacious tree house. They governed themselves by a code. "There were," said Elizabeth, "very few fights or squabbles, as I remember it. Perhaps this was because the older children were there to see that nobody got picked on, and the younger ones were ashamed to behave in a babyish way in front of the older ones. If anybody didn't play fair or made a fuss, he was just left out of our games." A very strong sense of honor and of the nature of fair play prevented this policy from turning into mere conformism. Understanding and not judgment was extended to any action taken in good faith. Once, the gang pelted with snowballs a passing adult, who took it unkindly and, turning tables, chased the gang around with a particular desire to ascertain responsibility for the snowball that had clean whizzed off his derby hat. He cornered one of the younger boys, who was terrorized into giving up Cummings as the author of that splendid shot. But no one, says Elizabeth, blamed the boy for ratting. He was utterly terrified and deserved only sympathy.

As well as a leader, Cummings was also a natural storyteller and entertainer. When he and Elizabeth came down with whooping cough and were quarantined in a room together for weeks, he cheered her up the whole time by making up stories to keep her spirits up. Afterward, he formed a "Whooper Club," for which the entry requirements were: (a) to have had the whooping cough, which was rampaging through the neighborhood and (b) to compose a story for the club, so that they could type up a Whooper Club paper on Rebecca's typewriter. It was considered so desirable a club among the local gang that children who had not yet had the whooping cough endeavored to catch it from infectious playmates in order to join.

On the other hand, childhood had its austerities. Rebecca Cummings was a great advocate of the cold bath. She and the children took cold baths every morning in Cambridge, and ice-cold morning showers outdoors at Joy Farm. Perhaps even this played its role later in life. Years of hardening his body in cold showers may have offered some protection against one of the greater dangers of Cummings's imprisonment—the freezing showers imposed on the inmates in the unheated midwinter of a French prison by sadistic guards who regarded their charges as scum, and if they died of pneumonia in prison, then good riddance.

Cummings preferred to remember his childhood as an idyll. There were many splendors of company, and of solitude, and of the gorgeousness of the un-Forbidden Forests of Norton's Woods and Joy Farm. When they could, the family traveled up to Joy Farm in May to see the land at its finest. May brought apple blossom and lilacs, white blossom on the blueberry bushes and wild strawberry, dandelion, buttercup, and muguet (lily of the valley). Irises were in bud and sweet rocket in bloom; then the irises would open, followed by white daisy and white roses. The wildflowers carpeted the expanse under the trees, while the children also thrilled to the lingering woodland hints of earlier settlement. Cummings and Elizabeth belonged to a generation that had little sense of culpability for the destruction brought to America's indigenous Nations by European settlement, and they had none of today's worries about the environmental consequences of deforestation. They took a naïve joy in the idea of Silver Lake's "first settlers," and in the rotting stumps of the largest, oldest white pines that had been cut down to supply those settlements. Among Joy Farm's proudest features were its floorboards, of a magnificent breadth from the largest trunks, unmatched in newer building.

Whether they managed a May visit or not, the family always spent high summer at Joy Farm, and remained through the summertime berries, apples, and the scything of the hayfield. They picked wild blueberries, seven or eight quarts at a time, for jam. At scything time, they supplied the men in the field with homemade "Haymakers' mixture" (switchel) made from well water, vinegar, molasses, and ginger. They had milk from their dairy cows and ate from their own vegetable patch.

The Reverend himself rebuilt most of Joy Farm (preserving its treasured floorboards and fine central brick fireplace). He was a capable and effective man. He had an old-fashioned respect for labor, and he valued the fabric of the building with its great beams wrought by hand and pegged together or nailed with handmade nails.

When Elizabeth looked back, she remembered her father as a handsome man: clean-shaven, with a red-tinted mustache. He had blue eyes and brown hair with a bald spot in the middle, and he spoke with a carrying and persuasive voice. "Somehow he was able to make you know just how he felt when he spoke, and he could make you feel the same way." When Cummings's friend Brown looked back, with an outsider's eye, he remembered the voice of a man who set himself up as arbiter of righteousness and respectability, yet retained license to inflict unease on the others. "At table when he was laying down the law, his voice always sounded as if it were issuing from a deep well and there was always utter silence when he spoke. Yet occasionally he would horrify the family, particularly Mrs. C—, by coming out suddenly with some ribald remark. Once I remember quite a propos of nothing in particular though I think we must have been talking about the fall of Jericho Dr. C—said in a loud voice—'First they blew the trumpets, and then they blew the strumpets.'"

Brown saw through the Reverend's power games. "The old man," he wrote, "was a sort of tyrant in his way and overlorded the family—Grandma, Mrs. C—, Aunt Jane, and Elizabeth all stood in awe of him." Cummings's childhood had a blissful sheen of freedom and safety and security. And yet: "I was always afraid of my father."

2

THE REVEREND

EDWARD CUMMINGS WAS born in New Hampshire, raised in Massachusetts, and educated at Harvard. What some might call the tyranny of moral rectitude, he saw as healthy living; in his own eyes, he was a family man. He extended his benevolence to all human and nonhuman inhabitants of his household. By personality, he was a dog person, but in a spirit of making accommodations, he and his daughter's cat came to mutually satisfactory terms. Fluffy was permitted to drape himself across the Reverend's shoulders at the breakfast table, and received one piece of bacon as his allotted ration in daily exchange for peace and quiet. If the Reverend was a softie at heart, it was to rule even Fluffy with the velvet glove.

The Reverend is the sort of man who likes to control his own story. He is the icon of his age: energy, success, and social progress. He attended Harvard in the 1880s, when it was on the cusp of becoming the kind of institution we would recognize today as an international research university. New subjects—English literature, modern languages, and the social sciences—were rapidly gaining respectability. Academia was moving from the Victorian world of the armchair intellectual into a world of professional research. The star of Harvard's English department in this era was Francis James Child, whose interests lay in popular folksong and whose research perfectly encapsulates that late nineteenth-century moment. His magnificent eight-volume labor of love, Child's *English and Scottish Ballads*, offers an accumulation of folksongs and their variants that falls somewhere in between the world of collecting as Victorian gentleman's hobby and the international research of the modern world. It is still a standard work of reference for traditional English and Scottish folksong. In the course of time, Child's rose cuttings would supply the rose garden at 104 Irving Street, and Child's *Ballads* would become one of the sources of Cummings's simple and straightforward poetic style.

Meanwhile, the future Reverend took his degree from Harvard in 1883, magna cum laude, with a major in philosophy. But he longed for an area of study that would give scope to his searching and progressive mind set. He tried two years' graduate work in the School of Divinity before moving sideways into sociology. Here he clicked, and won the inaugural award of the new Robert Treat Paine Fellowship, which funded a full three years of study abroad. He went to London and to the Continent: France, Italy, and Germany. When he returned, he was welcomed back as a member of the Harvard faculty.

Still unsure of his precise place within academic study, he taught English for a year, political economy for another year, and sociology for a third, before obtaining the first Harvard post dedicated to the study of sociology under the Department of Economics. He remained in this post, as assistant professor of sociology, from 1893 to 1900. But in August of the year 1900, his life took a sudden turn. In spite of the fact that he had never been ordained, he was chosen as minister by the South Congregational Church in Boston—a Unitarian church with a particular philosophy of social engagement. He began as assistant minister under the Rev. Edward Everett Hale, and rose naturally to become the head of South Congregational when Hale retired in 1909.

As a minister, the Reverend finally found the chance to combine his intellectual life with his progressive social convictions. Throwing aside the narrowness of academic disciplines, he poured his learning into his sermons. He served on committees; he spoke at civic meetings. His opinions made news. The *Boston Globe* reported his views on everything from the decriminalization of drunks and debtors to the liberalization of Sunday restrictions, the desirability of world peace, and the evidence for spiritism. The *Globe* even reported the fire that destroyed the small summerhouse built in the garden as a playhouse for Elizabeth. "SUMMER HOUSE BURNED. *Home of Rev. Edward Cummings in Cambridge at One Time Thought in Danger.*" It reads like a local village rag, but this is a newspaper of national standing. Edward Cummings's appointment to one of Boston's major churches turned his only son into the child of a public man.

Reverend Cummings believed in his public self. He would scarcely admit any consciousness of the façade, and he buried deep his feelings of failure. It did not occur to him that his broad-minded flitting from one academic discipline to another was the attitude of a dilettante. He allowed his fortuitous appointment as minister to mask the truth that his academic career had reached a dead end. After seventeen years pursuing the academic life, he had still failed to produce any book, and he had no hope of advancement at Harvard without the capacity for research.

He was lucky to get the job at South Congregational. He was their second choice. They would have preferred Samuel Atkins Eliot II, son of Charles William Eliot, president of Harvard—a man who was also, although it can have been of no significance to the preferences of the church in the year 1900, fourth cousin once removed of the Eliot family's most famous-to-be son: T. S. Eliot. But Samuel Atkins Eliot II turned them down.

Everywhere the Reverend was dominated by fathers. In the eyes of his own father, Grandfather Cummings, he was on a pathway to hell. Inside his home, the Reverend inflicted fathers on himself. In the same year in which he joined South Congregational, he returned from the World's Fair with a great plaster mask of Zeus, which he hung at the foot of the front stairs. There it remained, exuding the patriarchy of the father of the Olympian gods. At South Congregational, he was a mere assistant for nine years to Hale. While Zeus presided over 104 Irving Street, an oil painting of Hale presided over South Congregational. Not until six years after Hale retired did the Reverend finally dare dispose of the painting by way of a gift to a local charity fair.

William Slater Brown hit it on the nose when he described Cummings's father later as a man "whose sense of his own righteousness I always found a bit depressing." Indeed, the Reverend's moral authority was only made all the more tyrannical by his genuinely liberal and thoughtful side: the parade he made of his own righteousness was bolstered by the legitimacy of his claim to be regarded as an upright and progressive man. He was even in favor of the liberalization of Sunday laws—although on the occasion of that particular debate, the wags in the audience got the better of the speakers. When the Reverend averred, "I should like to see a moving picture show in this church," one member of the audience asked why he didn't put one in, then. And when another speaker cited the views of Charles William Eliot—now just retired as the president of Harvard—on the question of playing sports on Sunday, a woman in the back piped up with: "Harvard never won many games under Pres Eliot's regime so I don't think much of his opinion on the subject."

The Reverend's social liberalism masked a deeply authoritarian streak, and the contradictions of his personality pressed heavily on his son. Freedom and control. A crudely drawn turtle, sketched by Cummings when he was four or five, stares out from the headed notepaper of the Mayor's Advisory Committee on Penal Aspects of Drunkenness: Cummings's childhood was surrounded by his father's moral campaigns. The Reverend was "dear Father" when Cummings labeled drawings of his family in early childhood. He was "Dad" by the time Cummings began penning entries in Rebecca's diaries of life at Joy Farm. But this relaxed love that he felt for his father was blended with an unhelpful feeling of awe, an occasional jealousy of his father's indulgence of Elizabeth, and a belief in his own inferiority, which only deepened through childhood and early adolescence.

The adventurousness of Cummings's childhood was, therefore, marred by feelings of vulnerability and shame. He cried, repeatedly, at his first school when he could not manage arithmetic problems at the blackboard in front of the class, and his time at that school was

defined in his memories by "tears and nosebleeds." Poor health in
early puberty embedded his feelings of compromised manliness. He
was recurrently ill in his last year of junior school at the age of twelve.
He already struggled with mathematics, and he missed so many days
in this year that he barely passed the geometry course he needed to
graduate to the Cambridge High and Latin School for his four-year
high school college prep course. When he arrived at the Cambridge
Latin School, he was teased for his short stature.

Among the childhood memories that later struck Cummings as
particularly significant, he recalled that he had thrice fallen climbing trees—twice from a willow tree and once out of an apple. There
is Cummings's childhood in a nutshell: freedom, outdoor adventure,
and liberation, failure and physical vulnerability, and an undaunted
determination to keep climbing.

Cummings did have one male role model who offered escape from
his father's authoritarianism. His Uncle George, his mother's brother,
lived with the Cummings family at 104 Irving Street and spread his
openhearted, generous delight in life. It was his habit to persuade
Cummings's aunt, also in residence, to read after dinner according to
his own taste in literature—for example, a suitably grisly history of
the Tower of London. With a wink at his nephew, he'd call out: "let's
have some ruddy gore!" To build Cummings's physical confidence,
Uncle George taught him basic boxing techniques. Like Rebecca,
Uncle George valued Cummings's poetry and, when Cummings was
about fourteen, gifted him a copy of *The Rhymester*—the popular late
nineteenth- and early twentieth-century guide to the rules of meter,
including all sorts of elaborate verse and stanza forms.

As Cummings grew up, he perceived before he rebelled. While the
marriage between the Reverend and Rebecca appears to have been,
for the most part, a happy one, Cummings glimpsed a cruel side to
it as well. He heard his father criticize Rebecca's management of the
household expenses as a waste of his "hard earned money," while he
rubbed it in her face that she had been penniless at the time of their
marriage. Rebecca was thirty-two when they married; Cummings
was born six years later, and by the time she gave birth to Elizabeth,

she was in her mid-forties. She came into herself with motherhood, growing in confidence as a mother and as a person. In youth, there was an open freshness in her face. She had dark, well-defined eyebrows over bright, slightly merry eyes, and an equivocal but amused smile. She was only five foot four, and after bearing children, she took on a certain stolidity. The youthful brightness in her eyes settled into a heavier face and a large personage, which exuded love and a quality of sturdily downward anchoring. The Reverend told her that she was fat; he nettled her with sarcasm about her "swan-like neck." Cummings saw tears in her eyes, and hated his father for it.

The Reverend's own father, Grandfather Cummings, was a bully. The Reverend fought to keep the bullying side of himself in check, but he did not eradicate it entirely. Cummings was different from his father, and he did not have the same weakness for lashing out. Even as a very young child, Cummings had an instinct to protect. When he wrote about a hunter hunting down a bear—a small child's tale written when he was seven—his sympathies lay entirely with the hunted. The grizzly bear, who was called Jim, saved himself by killing the hunter first. "It was all fair," the story concluded. "The man had tried to take the bear's life from him, and in trying to do so had lost his own."

The same sympathies for the underdog emerge in distraught memories, recorded later, of the childhood sight of a herd of cows led through Cambridge to the slaughterhouse. The trauma lay in Cummings's own inability to intercede. "And gradually I realize they're going 'to the slaughterhouse,' are being driven to their deaths: and I stand hushed, almost unbreathing, feeling the helplessness of a pity which is for some whole world." What struck him most was the cruelty of the cattle drivers, "murderously laying-into the helpless feminine-foolish beings in their care—O this sickens me. The men brutes . . . I wish I could kill them both foreverandever—look at the soft wild eyes of the kine!" This is no ordinary distress. In Cummings's yearning to protect these "feminine" beings and his upsurge of sheer murderous hatred for the male "brutes" who drive them, we see a flash of his intensely close relationship with his mother, his fear of his father, and also his protectiveness toward his younger sister, Elizabeth.

Cummings's painfully intense empathy left him sensitive, delicate, and eager to please. He was a lover of nature and a lover of animals. His most sensitive childhood drawings were made directly from nature, often sketches of very carefully observed birds. Cummings was shy, but his shyness covered a courage both physical and moral. The need to protect lodged itself at the core of his psychological makeup: a need that framed his whole experience to come of war and of prison, and that shaped the role these events would play in his life.

3

THE LAST SUMMER OF
CHILDHOOD

THE SUPPRESSED RAGE and sense of failure that Cummings absorbed without awareness from his father, he channeled inward rather than outward. He entered a phase of tortured idealism, from which both he and his poems suffered. By the age of fifteen or sixteen, he was pouring himself into poetry, and it was atrocious. His poems were loud, forced, and moralizing.

> <u>Can</u> you come up to what is worth your mind?
> You <u>must</u> come up; or tomorrow or to hell.

Above all, Cummings was obsessed with squashing his adolescent sexual desire.

> <u>A FATHER TO HIS SON</u>
>
> It's up to <u>you</u>, my son, to kill this thing.
> You're tempted of the devil which is lust,
> Constantly tempted, strongly, pleasantly.

You've got to fight it out right here and now.
You've got to beat the tempter here and now.
You've got to fight with your whole heart and soul,
To make the devil leave you well alone.
You've got to win, and you are going to win!

Head up, my son; go in and knock him out!
Keep at him till he falters, till he runs.
Keep at him till he troubles you no more.

You've got to make a pure strong Man, my son.
You cannot do it while this fiend is 'round.
Go in to win, with every bit of grit,
And strength, and courage, and resolve you've got!
Go in and win! It's up to <u>you</u>, my son.

This poetic disaster is dated November 6, 1910, one year before Harvard and in the middle of Cummings's efforts to gain a place at the university.

It was a case of knowing you have to get out before you know why.

It was certainly not motivated by an unqualified admiration for the Harvard world. On Irving Street, Cummings lived among Harvard professors. Of particular note were the Taussigs, with their yowling cocker spaniel, Hamlet, and the eminent professor of philosophy Josiah Royce. Cummings found them ridiculous and rather off-putting. This part of him sided with his father. The family at 104 Irving Street, he wrote much later, was "surrounded" by professors, "but not defeated." Cummings did not realize how much he echoed the feelings his father denied. Even ten years after leaving Harvard for South Congregational, the Reverend still carried traces of defensive self-justification. It colors a debate with the new president of Harvard, Abbott Lowell, about the relationship between the university and the city of Boston. While Lowell took an optimistic view of the contribution of Harvard's lawyers, doctors, and architects to their civic surroundings, the Reverend spoke of a deplorable barrier between town and gown. The universities of the West Coast, he said, were superior. Being state-funded, they had a natural integration into their cities, whereas Harvard relied on its endowment money and had no incentive to connect itself to the surrounding community. He might have added that he himself had put his learning at the service of the community rather than stay within the confines of the university, but he lacked the self-knowledge to notice how far his views on university life were shaped to exculpate a departure from Harvard that had not, truly, been his own free choice.

In fact, the scatty Professor Royce did Cummings a very great service. Knowing that his neighbor's son was inclined to poetry, Royce accosted him on Irving Street and summoned him into his own front room for a reading of the sonnets of Dante Gabriel Rossetti. Though Cummings squirmed his way through the afternoon with Royce, he tumbled instantly onto a life-long love of Rossetti. It was the beginning of the end for the moral phase, and it presaged the Decadent sensuality that would make him, in the later words of a Harvard contemporary, one of the generation of Harvard's "fleshly" and "pagan" poets, enchanted with the world of satyrs and nymphs and Bacchus, god of wine, and goat-footed Pan. Nonetheless, and somewhat unfairly, Cummings's abiding memory was of Royce leaving his Irving Street home, regularly chased down by his wife, who waved after him, as he walked from the house, his snap-on necktie.

Whatever his reservations about the professors, Cummings never considered any other route. He took the Harvard entrance exams in June of 1911, having made a trial stab at elementary French the previous year. Harvard had been among the earliest of the American universities to modernize its system of entrance. In 1874, the university added English literature as an option for entrance examination and, in the following year, the examination options were expanded again to include French and German. Serious subjects could be attempted at elementary or advanced level, and the passing of two subjects at advanced level (as well as a breadth at elementary level) was required for admission. In 1887, Harvard took the radical step of allowing

French and German to be taken as advanced subjects—thereby raising them to a par with Latin, Greek, and mathematics.

Cummings entered for English, Latin, French, and mathematics (elementary algebra and plane geometry), as well as elementary history and elementary Greek. He achieved a clutch of C's and D's (between the "honor grades" of A and B and the "failing grades," E and F). One week later, he received a letter of admission, although it seems he had already heard the news of his success through the neighborhood grapevine. He was not given credit for advanced Latin: the letter advised him to retake the exam in September. This he did, and achieved another C. His grades hardly mark him out as a stellar student, but he had managed admission in four years of "College Prep" at the Cambridge High and Latin School, whereas many pupils took five.

Over summer, the family varied their usual plans. Rather than stay at Joy Farm itself, they went to stay down on the shores of Silver Lake. Silver Lake lay a couple of miles due south of Joy Farm. It is a long, thin lake with water still officially classified as pristine and stunning views to its own forested shores and mountains beyond. It stretches over 2.5 miles tip to toe but varies from a mile to only half a mile wide. The Reverend had bought an additional plot of land on the eastern shore and had commissioned the building of a lakeside cabin.

It was an isolated spot and there was no road so far around the lake's perimeter. Most of the lumber for the cabin was brought across the lake that winter, over the ice. By spring, the frame and roof of the cabin were in place, but much of the inside was unfinished. When the family arrived, it was for a summer of boating and swimming and busily helping with the final stages of cabin building. Cummings, with Harvard now securely ahead of him, was just a few months short of seventeen, and Elizabeth was ten.

The Reverend owned a motorboat, two rowboats, and a kind of folding canvas canoe. In his motorboat, he fetched ongoing supplies and furniture all summer, while the two rowboats ferried supplies and workmen. Cummings and Elizabeth were accustomed to using the one boat that remained: the small canvas contraption. Since it was canvas, it would naturally sink if it tipped. However, it was equipped with air bladders to keep it afloat in an emergency. On this particular day, Cummings and Elizabeth had promised themselves an evening outing. When they discovered that the air bladders were deflated—and they took ages to inflate—Cummings intended to call off their outing, but Elizabeth wheedled her brother into taking the boat out anyway, in contravention of their father's rules.

They went with Rex, who had been out on the boat many times before.

Rex was a bull terrier with a short ginger coat and white on his chest, face, paws, and tail. He was a steady and gentle dog, accustomed to being bossed around by Elizabeth's cat, Fluffy, and utterly devoted to Cummings. Although the family had several dogs, Rex had been bought as a puppy and given specially to Cummings by his father. He had an exclusive growl of greeting just for Cummings, and Cummings took him everywhere. One recent summer, they had even traveled up to Joy Farm together, boy and dog, a week before the rest of the family.

Elizabeth and Cummings paddled out across the lake to another bit of shore, explored a bit, and set out to return before dark. Far out onto the lake, a hornet began to buzz around the boat, circling closer and closer to Rex. Finally, the dog lunged at it and capsized the canoe.

They had gone out too far to swim for land. On her brother's instructions, Elizabeth tried to cling on to the boat, but, without the air bladders, the boat sank straightaway. They could only grab the two box seats that had floated free of the wreckage. Elizabeth's seat kept her afloat. Cummings held on to the other seat, but he was heavier and had to kick continuously just to stay above the water. Meanwhile, Rex started swimming for shore. But he couldn't make it, and he turned around and swam back toward Elizabeth. Cummings tried to shout at him to keep swimming for the shore and not to return, but Rex was in an animal panic and could not understand. When he reached Elizabeth, he tried to clamber onto her box seat, thrashing and panicking. He pushed her under. She resurfaced and grabbed the seat, and he pushed her under again. Cummings swam over, wrestled Rex away from the seat, and held him down and drowned him.

In the cold water of the lake, Elizabeth fell far into a sluggish delirium; several times she began to fall asleep, believing that she had only to let go of the flotsam and stand on the lake bottom, forty feet below. Only the shock of the cold water washing over her head brought her back to her senses enough to grab back the floating debris. She cannot have had many minutes left.

Back at the cabin, the Reverend fancied a late evening outing on the motorboat, and so he and Cummings's mother and his grandmother and one of his aunts—also there for the summer—all motored out for the sunset. The Reverend saw in the distance what he assumed were two swimmers and steered over to tell them off for swimming so dangerously far from the shore. To his astonishment, he found his children, clinging on to the flotsam for their lives. Elizabeth was almost fatally fatigued and Cummings dangerously cold and exhausted.

The family enshrined the coincidence of their outing as an astounding moment of sheer good fortune. This is a distortion—because Cummings's decisiveness and realism had actually already engineered their safety. While Cummings used his whole energy to kick and stay afloat, he had kept Elizabeth perfectly cheerful and urged her to keep shouting for help. Mere moments behind the family was another motorboat, with several young men who were camping at Silver Lake and who had heard Elizabeth's shouts. They arrived even as Cummings and Elizabeth were being pulled to safety into the Reverend's motorboat, somewhat chagrined to lose the glory of rescue.

Only now as they were pulled into the motorboat did Cummings allow himself to realize the loss of Rex, not wanting to believe that he could be gone. He begged the campers to dive for him, thinking in confusion that he might still be rescued. The family did find Rex's body when it washed up, stiff and swollen from its time in the water. They buried him and set up a gravestone, and Cummings wrote a long poem addressed to him. He dreamed about Rex from time to time, even many decades hence in middle age.

The Reverend felt it to be a narrow escape. Perhaps his own belief in the value of self-reliance also tipped into bravado in the face of danger. The local villagers certainly thought so. The entire village clucked in disapproval when the Reverend came in the next day to buy Cummings and Elizabeth a new canoe.

Elizabeth said later that she had not herself been frightened on the lake, because her brother kept cheerful and showed no hint of fear. As for Cummings—he never developed any fear of swimming, as perhaps he might have done. On the contrary, he delighted in it as much as ever. He never reproached himself for killing Rex. He knew that he had, in that moment, been faced with no choice. But a deeper sense of guilt and responsibility intensified the protectiveness he already felt for anything younger than himself, anything vulnerable, anything animal or human that stirred his pity.

In early September, he received details of freshman registration for the twenty-eighth of the month. He was notified at the same time about his college adviser. He had hoped for one of the professors who taught composition: Bliss Perry or even the fearsome Dean LeBaron Briggs—a charismatic teacher who was admired and adored by his students, even though he could be scathing when he disliked the style of a student's poetry or prose. Cummings was informed, however, that both Perry's and Briggs's lists were full, and that he had been assigned to Professor Royce and his necktie.

Tuition fees for Harvard came to $150 a year, payable in two installments in advance. The midterm bill for his freshman year shows additional expenses of $36.50 for laboratory fees, membership in the Harvard Union, fees for the infirmary, and rent of a gym locker. Participation in university athletics was strictly regulated by a points system that quantified personal fitness. The calculation was based on lung capacity, push-ups, pull-ups, weight lifted by straight leg and bent leg, and the strength of the grip of each hand. Cummings was small and scrawny. He was five feet nine inches in height, and weighed a mere 114 pounds. The rules were: 700 points as a minimum for university crew, university football, and weight throwers; 600 points for class crew or football, gymnastics, wrestling, or sparring; 500 points for ball nines, lacrosse, or track and field. Cummings scored 486.

Cummings's registration pack included Harvard's rules and regs (academic and disciplinary), an outline of course distribution

requirements, a map of campus, and other sundries for the adjust-
ment to college life. There were various options for negotiating
accommodation and food. Harvard billed separately for "rent and
care of room," "extra services of porter," and "gas burned." For meals,
Memorial Hall advertised itself as providing "the best board possible
at $5.25 per week," suitable for those who preferred a fixed expense.
Randall Hall, on the other hand, charged à la carte. Cummings kept
the registration cards as mementos. Neither the card for Memorial
Hall nor for Randall Hall is filled out.

The Reverend had decreed that Cummings would live at home.

PART II

HARVARD

1911–1916

—

4

TEMPTATIONS

I am a young man living in an advanced and cultivated era, surrounded only by things lovely and of good report. I have a strong mind, a healthy body, resulting from years of careful and devoted watching by father and mother, and a high reputation everywhere I go, as a gentleman. My friends are pure, high-minded girls and clean, manly fellows. My father is a man who has worked out his own success by toil and pluck, who has maintained as a lasting gift to his son a noble soul and well-developed body. He is a man who never allowed the faintest suggestion of temptation to grip him, and expects the high and pure of his son.

—E. E. CUMMINGS,
notebook from the Harvard years

AS A BOY, Cummings was affectionate, family-centered, and eager to please. It had always been taken for granted that he would study at Harvard as an undergraduate, and in this too he pleased his parents. No one—probably least of all Cummings himself—foresaw that the

Harvard years would unleash a full-blown rebellion against child-hood, Cambridge, and, above all, his father.

He began his time at Harvard eager to live up to his new and lofty environment. In a pious exhortation to himself, written out longhand in one of his personal notebooks, he summarized his life prospects. In addition to his father's fine example, he had his mother's "wonderful frame of utter love and endless aspiration." He wrote of his parents' pride and trust in him, and his own desire to be worthy both of that trust and of the God he believed in. He was conscious, too, of the pressure to live up to his newfound friends, and in particular a young teacher of the classics named Theodore Miller who had befriended him and whom he hero-worshipped.

He chastised himself for selfishness. But these rebukes to himself did not carry the anguished self-laceration that came later in the throes of rebellion. There was a psychological security, for now, that came from submitting to the world view of his parents and embracing the thought of his own corrigible vice. "My soul, that is, my thinking and realizing, was brought into the world noble. It is at present beset by a great Sin of Selfishness. The fact that I can write the words proves that the nobility which was first in me is not totally gone. The fact that I must write them proves that it is greatly dimmed." But not to worry. "I am of the aristocracy of this earth.... The world needs me." All that was required in order to rise to his opportunities was to overcome the selfishness standing between him and "immortality's being."

The selfishness that Cummings was determined to root out was not egotism or self-centeredness. It was a euphemism for the sin of acknowledging—not even acting upon, but merely being distracted by—the carnal desires of the body, rather than preserving himself for the spiritual lights of the soul. The body must be held pure for the soul's sake—an aim best achieved through reading improving books, studying seriously but not too much, and taking plenty of physical exercise. This obsession with sexual purity was the legacy of his father, who was tolerant of all things he considered healthy and progressive on social matters, but terrifying when it came to the subject of sexual desire. Years later, Cummings asked himself why it was that thinking of his own fatherhood should "so strangle my heart in guilt-fear?" And finally he answered his question, as a repressed memory resurfaced: "not till tonight do I recall a little story E.C. told me(as a masturbating secretly body)about the danger of lying down under a tree with a girl & waking up with her pregnant!"

Repressive and moralizing attitudes toward sex were reinforced in the early twentieth century by growing fears about the prevalence of venereal disease. Sexually active men and women were vulnerable to crabs (pubic lice) and, in an era before antibiotics, to the much more dangerous possibility of catching syphilis or the clap (gonorrhea). The Reverend himself participated in a town hall debate in Boston in 1914 where he and two medical doctors discussed the advisability of sexual education to combat these worrying threats. The debate—in front of a full hall—was preceded by a piano and cello concert and reported in detail by the *Boston Globe*. Dr. Cabot argued the case for public enlightenment as an enactment of democratic values. Silence on such topics was antipathetic to a democratic society, he said, since democracy is built upon the principle of an informed public. Dr. Cabot's plan was to start early, but in careful stages. It would be going too far to teach sex education in school, but children could perhaps be taught about the reproductive strategies of plant life so as to lay the groundwork for a later appreciation of animal and human biology. Dr. Wilcox then hammered home the medical threat. "If the truth was revealed, the world would be appalled." Finally, Reverend Cummings concluded with the more personal approach, discussing the responsibilities of parenthood and reminiscing about his time in London back when his Harvard fellowship had funded his sociological study abroad. The Reverend lived in Whitechapel during the days of Jack the Ripper, and had even joined a citizens' watch to patrol the streets at night. "They found that a lamppost was worth several policemen in the East End because crimes were committed only in the dark places. 'It is so with this subject,' he added. 'What is needed is more light on it and put an end to the "conspiracy" of silence from which the race has suffered such terrible harm.'"

The Reverend talked a good game about shedding light on the

subject of human sexuality, but at home he had raised his son with a terror of consequences, unspecified and shrouded in a foggy sense of danger, if he were to live as a fully sexual being. Cummings spent much of his life unraveling these threats and fears.

> am almost 62 before it occurs to me that the same Paternal
> Power which taught that
>   "When nature calls,you must not bluff her;
>   If you do,your health will suffer"
> &hence that nothing must interfere with the expression of
> defecatory desires—threatened me with the most awful not
> to say catastrophically mysterious consequences if I didn't
> completely inhibit all my erotic proclivities
>   thus making sexuality un natural,since "nature" was
> exclusively anal!
>   ... & yet I well remember mon père expressing mingled pity
> & scorn re a Harvard professor whose sobriquet was "Picky"
> Everett(if I remember rightly,he picked his nose in class)because
> said prof taught that the pleasures of sex were as nothing
> compared to "a good shit"

When Cummings entered Harvard, he was determined to live up to the expectations of his parents. But from the very start, there were temptations. Cummings regaled his first biographer with memories of his discovery of a library copy of Christopher Marlowe's translation of Ovid during his freshman year: "as the evening wore on, the librarian began to appear more and more frequently to observe the phenomenon of a lone student actually reading for pleasure and unaware of the time." It did not occur to the innocent librarian that Cummings was glued to the page of thrillingly erotic verse.

Marlowe was not the only expansion in Cummings's literary horizons. His reading also blossomed under the guidance of Theodore (Dory) Miller. Dory Miller—the teacher, mentor, and friend whom Cummings specially singled out in his Harvard exhortation to self—loomed increasingly large in his emotional and intellectual life. Miller taught Cummings in his freshman year and began then to shape his further reading. He introduced Cummings to many of the classical poets as well as to Keats and to the Keatsian world of poetry obsessed with beauty and poetic immortality. Miller became the chief reader for Cummings's own verse, and he took Cummings to shows in Boston and introduced him to Boston's Greek restaurant scene. The summer after Cummings's freshman year, Miller travelled up to Silver Lake to stay with the Cummings family. Over the course of their friendship, Miller gifted Cummings several volumes of classical poetry; Cummings returned the favor with a gift of a volume of Tennyson for the New Year, 1913.

Theirs was a highly asymmetrical friendship—not only because Dory Miller was older and a teacher at Harvard, but also because Miller was gay, and Cummings—however much he deeply adored Miller, put him on a pedestal, and hero-worshipped him—was not. There is no doubt, though, that the pedestal was high. "One friend I have of whom I speak out lovingly from my heart at all times. He is a man at the college with me, older, and of perfect chivalry toward woman and man. I love him as I love no other friend; I worship him for good, and imitate him for worthiness. His life, also, has grown into mine. The honor of his friendship he has placed with perfect confidence in my trembling hands; if I do wrong, I commit an unfaithfulness to him whom I admire most of friends."

Miller was, however, a flawed man. When, after Cummings's junior year, he moved from Harvard to Princeton, Miller welcomed that move with an expression of disdain for the diversity (in his eyes) of Harvard's classrooms, where a teacher had to accept the presence of Jews and the Irish. Cummings was highly loath to drop his friends, but he resisted Miller's attempts to stay in touch after junior year. It may be simply that Cummings was growing up, and growing beyond the kind of idolizing hero worship that had defined his friendship with Miller. It might also be that Cummings had grown more aware of his friend's flaws, or that he sensed that Miller's interest in him was not of a kind that he could reciprocate. In any case, the friendship fizzled out by Cummings's choice, and Miller himself died quite young. Later, with decades of distance, Cummings remembered Miller gratefully as the man who had introduced him to Catullus, Horace, Sappho, and Keats, and personally as "a genial lover of good things who'd toiled immeasurably over a PhD thesis on The Old Man In Latin Comedy—at least I think it was The Old Man—only to find that somebody else, maybe a German, had long ago copped that particular subject."

Miller's personal mentorship distinguished his relationship with Cummings from the standard Harvard fare: lecture-hall learning and the imbibing of information dispensed from revered professors, many of them surrounded by their own personal mythologies of demigod grandeur. (Or, as the Shakespeare scholar Professor George Lyman Kittredge replied to a startled "My God" from a cleaner: "Not God, madam, Kittredge.")

Harvard was a self-assured world. Early twentieth-century academia had a taste for organizing knowledge, and Cummings's Harvard course lectures were reassuringly systematic. Cummings took detailed lecture notes, and from these we can reconstruct the chronologies and taxonomies favored by his Harvard professors. He was provided with summaries of the works and styles of canonical authors from classical literature, Anglophone literature, and literatures in languages like German and Russian, which at that date had become the staple of comparative literature courses. He was catechized that there was no period in the history of European literature when any one literary tradition was isolated from the influences of the rest. Moreover, commonality was to be found beyond even the European literatures. He was informed that German scholarship had identified fairy tales whose core was the same in European and in Indian literature.

This particular academic approach to the literary tradition was one of the cultural nourishments of early modernism. Men like Cummings and, just a few years earlier, T. S. Eliot, were educated at Harvard to believe that the great literary traditions were interdependent. A proper appreciation of literature meant an appreciation of the vastness of its history. However, this world of literature, vast though it was, could nonetheless be grasped and tamed—so they were taught—in the confident imagination of the Harvard syllabus. It was this confidence as well as this appreciation of the interdependence of literary traditions that encouraged the modernists to turn to Dante's Italian *Divina Commedia* (the *Divine Comedy*), and to make of it one of modernism's most generative sources of inspiration. Indeed, one of the Harvard professors offered a locally celebrated course in Dante. Cummings took a semester of Italian grammar in the first part of his junior year specially in order to follow it up with the yearlong course on Dante in his senior year.

Thus, at Harvard, Cummings was exposed to an approach to literature that was comprehensive—in a traditional (white, male) European manner—and fundamentally Eurocentric, while it congratulated itself on tidbits of knowledge of subjects like Indian fairy tales. Eliot's *The Waste Land* could be described as the culmination of this Harvard world view: intimacy with Dante, comprehensive allusions to a vast body of literature, and a closing line in Sanskrit, "*Shantih shantih shantih.*"

As well as the history of literature by author, Cummings was also offered overviews by genre—for example, the history of lyric poetry—or overviews by method, such as the allegorical method. And in addition to the study of literary works themselves, he was also exposed to condensed histories of intellectuals and theorists. The emphasis fell on great minds of the nineteenth century like Matthew Arnold, Walter Pater, John Ruskin, and Charles Darwin, but lectures also delved into earlier thinkers like Samuel Johnson or Alexander Pope (studied as a theorist as well as a poet). Some of the ideas to which Cummings was exposed became a part of his early literary vocabulary at a time before he was ready to develop theories of his own. For example, his Harvard notes and essays frequently refer to Ruskin's term "the pathetic fallacy"—that is, the false and sentimental anthropomorphizing of nature or animals. Cummings found it a useful theory to bandy about. But like other ideas encountered through these lectures, the notion of the pathetic fallacy shaped his knowledge of intellectual history more than it shaped his actual poetic self. Ruskin's fallacy did not stop Cummings from romanticizing nature, and throughout his life, his poems ascribe the human condition to bees, mice, ants, cats, and moon and stars and twilight.

Cummings's academic progress at Harvard was powerfully affected by his own medical and academic worries. He did not have a strong constitution and he was self-conscious about his physique and his health. He was inclined to absence through illness, and at least once in his senior year he was off for three weeks straight and ended up penning an apology for the impaired quality of his work. In his freshman year, he managed an A in Greek but only B's and C's in all his other subjects. He began to feel like an academic underachiever. In sophomore year his C in economics elicited, on a handwritten report card, the relieved annotation from his professor: "glad you came thru O.K." In junior year, a D+ in Italian I prompted: "? Now about this?" His grades improved in senior year, but he remained sensitive to assessment. He tried to oil out of exams. As a senior, he petitioned on unknown grounds (possibly connected to his three-week absence) to be excused from his final examination for English 2. It was a major request and had to be authorized by the Committee on Distinction in Literature, above the head of the course professor. But Harvard was a flexible world in some respects, and the request was granted.

Cummings was a young man of exceptional intelligence who cared about his intellectual life and worried about his grades. Some piece of this puzzle is missing. If he were alive today, Cummings would probably have been diagnosed with mild dyslexia. His spelling, even at university, is inconsistent and shows errors typical of dyslexia. He often reversed vowels. He struggled persistently with *ie*, even in basic words (like "feilds" for "fields"); he also made mistakes like "giuded" for "guided" and reversed *i* and *e* even when they could be sounded out as two distinct syllables ("diety" for "deity"). Other persistent types of spelling errors include difficulty with doubled consonants (especially doubled *l*) and the omission of silent letters: "oviosly" for "obviously," "rythm" for "rhythm."

The reversed vowels reflect a mind performing reversals without awareness. That twitch of the mind can also bring an extraordinary facility in handling reversals of other kinds, because the act of reversing can be as natural as seeing un-reversed. Cummings often sketched in mirror image, and he would draw upside down for casual amusement. His papers show other traits that are consistent with dyslexia, including chaos on the pages of his notes and a sometimes-indecipherable handwriting. In the 1950s, he undertook the personal project of sorting through his own earlier notebooks and wrote to a close friend: "I can rarely read my own script." His handwriting skews its relationship to the lines on lined paper, wandering above and below and at angles to the scored lines. Sheets of paper are used and reused in multiple conflicting orientations. He wrote notes over and under sketches. It is an exhilarating visual cacophony and an exploding chaos that characterized his whole intellectual style. He struggled to structure longer, more analytical prose, but he had a reputation for brilliant conversation based on endless streams of astonishing lateral connections. This, too, is a classic presentation of dyslexia.

Dyslexia would have predisposed Cummings to process language differently. It may well have contributed to his remarkable syntax and to his ability to atomize words—that is, to see a word in pieces (letters or syllables) at the same time that he saw the word as a whole. He had an extraordinary ability to arrange and rearrange written language and to pursue the interconnections he experienced between the verbal and the visual. However, in the early twentieth century, the study of specific learning differences was rudimentary. Cummings's spelling errors and his particular combination of intellectual strengths and weaknesses would never have been thought of in such a light. Like many others in this position, Cummings had to live with the frustration of failing, inexplicably, to achieve at the academic level that he hoped for and that would have been consistent with his evident brilliance. This failure became one among various factors that pushed him to seek validation not from his teachers but from his new friends.

5

A WORLD OF AESTHETES

CUMMINGS WANTED TO write poetry. Already before Harvard, he had published five poems in his school magazine, *The Cambridge Review*. Now that he was a Harvard undergraduate, the aim was acceptance into one of the social and literary circles surrounding the university's two rival undergraduate literary magazines: *The Harvard Advocate* and *The Harvard Monthly*. Both papers were keen on Cummings's work, and the editors of the *Advocate* even tried to fast-track his membership. But he held out for the *Monthly*, and was rewarded with membership on the editorial board in his second year at Harvard.

Though an undergraduate magazine, the *Monthly* took itself very seriously. On its own letterhead, it proudly declared itself to be *the* university literary magazine, founded in 1885 and boasting rooms at the Harvard Union. The letterhead likewise paraded the names of its current president, its secretary, and its business manager. The *Monthly* was more aesthetic and self-conscious than the *Advocate*. It was the natural fit for Cummings, who struck his peers as something of an aesthete both in himself and in his poetry. Indeed, in appearance, Cummings was small and fine with hazel-brown eyes and a gentle demeanor, and to acquaintances of a more realist persuasion, his poetry seemed "rather moony."

Also on the board of the *Monthly* was John Dos Passos, the future novelist, later famous for his *U.S.A.* trilogy. Dos (as they called him) was to become one of Cummings's most intimate and trusted friends: the kind of friend who could always cheer him up and the kind of friend of such long standing that he could sign notes to Cummings in late life, "me." The older Dos was friendly, genial, bighearted, and happily married with somewhat rambunctious children. Even when Cummings was middle-aged, curmudgeonly, and grumpy at being forced to receive unwanted guests, he had to admit, however grudgingly, that seeing Dos did him good.

Dos was of Portuguese descent (from the island of Madeira) along his father's father's line, and he stood out from the mostly Anglo-Saxon, Protestant world of Harvard. His face was intellectual, with dark hair, dark eyebrows, and dark eyes under circular, wire-rimmed spectacles. His features presented a jumbled geometry. His eyebrows each descried a perfect parabola, the eyes exactly double-pointed ovals beneath the circular glasses, the philtrum under his nose a deep, ridged triangle, and the lines of his cheeks so pronounced that they drew a line exactly continuing the slope of the side of his nose down to the corners of his mouth. The complete effect would have been that of an early twentieth-century nerd, were the eyes not so mild and sensitive.

Like Cummings, who bore (though he did not use) the first name Edward from his father, Dos too was named after his father, the New York lawyer John R. Dos Passos. Dos, however, came by his name differently, being the illegitimate child of a long-term love affair. His father had made a reputation in high-profile murder cases, then turned to lucrative commercial law: stock brokerage, mergers, and trusts. John R., as Dos calls him in his memoirs, was a flamboyant, extravert type with a boom-and-bust lifestyle. He was a high earner, an unwise investor, and a high spender. He was also an Anglophile, a writer (mostly of legal treatises), and a party political campaigner.

Because of the illegitimacy, Dos did not know his father when he was a young child. As Dos recalled, "I came to know him—through the turbulence of conflicting currents of love and hate that mark so many men's feeling for their fathers—at the end of his lusty climb to wealth and influence." Where Cummings's family embodied respectability, Dos's parents could only appear as a couple in public when they were traveling together in Europe. It wasn't until Dos was a teenager that his father's wife died and his parents married. His paternity was not formally acknowledged until 1916, a year before his father's death. He wrote: "I don't remember exactly how I felt about having my civil status regularized; historical novels had filled my head with the romance of the bar sinister."

Dos was highly precocious, extremely well read, and already familiar with much of Europe from trips that had begun in childhood. He was so young when he passed his Harvard entrance exams that his father would not let him attend straightaway, and sent him instead on a chaperoned European Grand Tour. "As much as any eighteenth-century Etonian I was living in the Roman Forum and the Attic Stoa. I sent home a long Plutarchian disquisition on Alcibiades, his faults and follies." Dos continues, in his memoirs: "My letters got so stilted John R. included in several of his answers a humorous plea 'to forego dogmatism.' I must have been a prime little prig. At home when I came out with some illfounded opinion he had a way—which I found profoundly irritating to the budding ego—of taking off his glasses and staring at me blandly and asking: 'Is that remark the result of experience or observation?'" Dos was still only sixteen when he came up to Harvard on his return from Europe in 1912.

Dos and Cummings would be the most famous writers to come out of the 1910s *Monthly* circle, but among this group of Harvard friends, there were others too who would find a place in the literary world. Robert Hillyer established himself as a poet and won a Pulitzer in 1934 for his *Collected Verse*. S. Foster Damon became a writer and a scholar, spending most of his life at Brown University and specializing in the study of William Blake. "Alas," said another undergraduate at the edges of this literary circle, "intimations of immortality were almost wholly lacking during those few years I spent as an editor of the Harvard Monthly. That Dos and Estlin and Robert Hillyer would become famous, never occurred to me—or, I believe, to them." But it was not humility, exactly, that held ambition at bay for this young circle of friends. It was the breezy self-confidence of men who already felt themselves at the center of things.

For all that this group shared, they still represented a medley of distinct personalities, each with individual tastes within their common literary culture. They could be sharp with one another. One of the group—Cuthbert Wright—regarded Damon's love for Blake as "mental masturbation" and told him so. Each man had his own style. Malcolm Cowley remembered them reading out their poems: "for example, Foster Damon, whose voice became flat and matter-of-fact when he recited an especially outrageous line; and Robert Hillyer, looking like a wicked cherub; and John Dos Passos speaking in very low tones as he peered at a manuscript from behind very thick lenses."

They seasoned the ease of privilege with their adolescent literary anxieties. The systematic Harvard style of learning, and its basis in chronologies and taxonomies, promised the confidence of mastery. The downside of such an exhaustive approach lies precisely there: it also promoted the worry that literature itself was exhausted. Such fears came tinged with the callousness of youth. Damon, the future Blake scholar, told Cummings's first biographer: "We kept saying to each other," (that is, in their first years at Harvard, before the outbreak of the Great War), "that no more poetry could be written, that the best poems had already been written, and all the subjects were used up. There could be no more romantic poetry because there would be no more wars, the nations were so economically interdependent." When war did come, three years into Cummings's time at Harvard, it did not necessarily lessen youth's callow nature. As Dos observed, the world of literature "seemed more important, somehow, than the massacres round Verdun."

It was a struggle for these young men to write poetry that was not derivative, and they failed more often than they succeeded. The fear that literature was exhausted could provoke either a yearning for the new or conversely too much deference to the past, and indeed this circle of friends saw themselves as divided into the "moderns," searching for novelty, and the "ancients," looking to perfect time-honored techniques. Robert Hillyer, the future Pulitzer Prize winner, spelled out this ideological binary, including himself among the ancients and listing Cummings, Dos, and Foster Damon as moderns.

For the moderns, the departure from established aesthetics was fueled by a sense that exciting, explosive ideas about art were pouring out of Europe. One turning point for Cummings was provided by the controversial exhibit of painting and sculpture in New York in 1913 known as the Armory Show. It was called the Armory Show because it was held at the Armory of the 69th Infantry on Lexington Avenue. It took place from the fifteenth of February to the fifteenth of March, and it was open from ten a.m. to ten p.m., including Sundays, before traveling on to Chicago and then Boston. It was all about drawing an audience. To call it an "exhibition" barely expresses the magnitude of the event: it was a phenomenon. There were more than a thousand works of art on display, many imported from Europe. The catalogue was eye-watering. There were eleven paintings and a sculpture in wood by Paul Gauguin; a Kandinsky; eight paintings by Cézanne; two by Edvard Munch; two by Toulouse-Lautrec; seven Picasso paintings and a bronze bust; ten pieces by Henri Rousseau; four by Picabia; and fourteen by Van Gogh. There were also fourteen paintings by Matisse plus a sculpture; two works by Seurat; four by Monet; four by Pissarro; four by Renoir; five sculptures by Brancusi and two by Rodin. Beyond these, there are dozens of other names that would glitter in any lesser company.

The Cubist painter and sculptor Marcel Duchamp entered four works. Duchamp is best known for a piece displayed in 1917: a urinal, which he signed "R. Mutt 1917" and titled *Fountain*, and which has since spawned a hundred years of experimentation with "found" art objects that challenge or transgress traditional ideas about what constitutes art. In 1913, a piece by Duchamp, more conventional in its materials—an oil painting on canvas—became one of the celebrated controversies of the Armory Show. Painted during the pre-

vious year, 1912, and exhibited at the 1913 show, Duchamp's *Nude Descending a Staircase, No. 2* presented an abstract, geometric figure with warm-toned flesh against the planes of a dark buff-brown staircase. The full descent of the staircase is shown. The figure is in motion, painted in a kind of time-lapse, with the geometric limbs and bodies superimposed in sequence on one another as the figure moves down the stairs. Even by Cubist standards, Duchamp's attempt to grapple with motion was cutting-edge. Cubism was not simply one style but a varied and multistrand movement, and the Armory Show brought Cummings into sudden contact with Cubism as a whole world of art.

Among the artists involved with the Armory Show, Cummings particularly admired an American sculptor, Abastenia St. Leger Eberle. Eberle was a feminist and a campaigner for female suffrage, and she believed in the artist's responsibility to act as "the specialized eye of society." She displayed a controversial cast bronze on the theme of child prostitution, depicting a naked, barely pubescent girl pimped by an old auctioneer. Some viewers revolted at the subject matter; others at the idea that such an arresting and affecting work had been created by a woman.

The Harvard of Cummings's era was a highly patriarchal world—peopled, of course, only by male students and staff. Cummings learned from male professors about male writers and thinkers of the past, found himself in a literary circle of aspiring male writers, and was dominated in his personal life by ongoing troubles with his father. It is a point worthy of some note that he reached outside of this male world and was particularly struck by a series of female artists and writers—not only Eberle but also the local poet Amy Lowell and the puzzling nonsense poetry of Gertrude Stein, which fascinated him, although he was unsure ultimately what he made of it.

Modern ideas and the new world of modern art seemed to offer that chance to create something truly original and, as a reward, immortal. However, throughout his first three years at Harvard, Cummings was still socially isolated and poetically stifled. He was improving gradually in technique and control, but he could not find any poetic breakthrough all the while that, at the behest of his father, he was still obliged to live at 104 Irving Street.

The inhibitions felt about undergraduate life, so long as he lived at home, were multiplied by Cummings's sensitivity about his health, his anxieties about his academic underachievement, and his fits of personal shyness. He craved acceptance, but he also retreated from overwhelming company. He fought hard to get his place on the *Monthly*. And yet, once he had joined the editorial board, he held back so much that toward the end of his junior year one of the society's officers wrote a grumpy letter chastising him for his lack of effort and involvement.

Cummings's Harvard friends responded to his peculiar combination of charisma and extreme shyness. Cummings would hide his face in a newspaper when he traveled in streetcars, and he refused to appear in photographs of the *Monthly*'s editorial board. But in spite of his ambivalence toward photography, Cummings was a powerful subject. Photographs of him at all ages convey an intense presence. He had a very gentle face, but a very dominating one. His eyes are so strong that they lock anyone looking at a photograph of him into his gaze. Even at this young age, his eyes both give and demand—they offer and they also measure. Cummings's first biographer, Charles Norman—who knew Cummings as a friend and who was rather too much in awe of his subject—gave Cummings's eye color wrongly in his initial draft. When Cummings corrected Norman's manuscript to say that his eyes were actually hazel or brown, Norman had to admit rather sheepishly that he had never dared in all those years of acquaintance to look Cummings properly in the eye.

Cummings's charisma came partly from his acuity. He could be too soft on the poetry of friends whom he admired, but his judgment about literature was nonetheless far in advance of his age. His aestheticism had a sharp side. As an editor at the *Monthly*, it was his role to read, comment upon, and select poems for the magazine. He could be perfectly withering when he spotted derivative sentimentality. He once took a poem that opened "Thou has faun eyes" and for comment handed it back with a doodling of a mournful-eyed deer. His mis-

chievous, even wicked side shone through and his comments made quite an impression on his fellow editors. What struck his friends most was his knack for cutting right to the heart of the matter. He once observed of another poem: "good but poor," expressing in three words that work could be accomplished and yet lack artistic soul.

Modernity held out the promise of a bold, clean poetic technique, but even modernity had to be learned from predecessors as well as contemporaries. Cummings was in what he himself called his "Keats period." He dissected Keats's poems—for example, copying out many stanzas from Keats's "Lamia" and annotating them with his own observations and stylistic notes. He aimed to scrutinize how Keats achieved his literary effects and to take something from that into his own poetry. But a poet has to learn how to interact with predecessors without mimicking them. Cummings took some composition classes at Harvard, and his professors noticed the influence of Keats's language in some of the poetry he submitted. On the whole, they approved of Cummings's Keatsian tendencies. Keats was classy, stylish, and decorous. Poetry in a derivative Keatsian style was safe poetry. His professors understood it and they were not unsettled by it, as they were by Cummings's self-consciously modern experiments. To find his modern voice, Cummings had not only to reject the literary aesthetic held up for him as a model by his Harvard professors. He also had to forgo the approval offered to his derivative verse by these charismatic and respected men—professors, like the formidable Dean LeBaron Russell Briggs, who were held in awe by their students—and embrace a style of poetry which they openly averred they could not value or understand.

The writers, painters, sculptors, and composers who inspired Cummings during his Harvard years all had one point in common: they were all self-consciously presenting art designed to challenge the notion of what art could do and could be. Even if, as Cummings's classmate observed, it felt far away from these nineteen- or twenty-year-olds at the *Monthly* to imagine that they would end up famous, their relationship with art was still predicated on ideas of artistic immortality. In his first year at Harvard, Cummings drafted a poem contrasting the lot of man with the lot of the poet. Though a man may be "prince over all the human throng," it is a poet, blessed by the Muse, who can dream of "wedding Immortality." In January of 1916, Cummings published in the *Monthly* an experimentation in the classical meter of the Sapphic, exploring with slightly more nuance the same hope that mere human life may be subsumed into the higher calling of poetry.

SAPPHICS

When my life his pillar has raised to heaven,
When my soul has bleeded and builded wonders,
When my love of earth has begot fair poems,
    Let me not linger.

Ere my day be troubled of coming darkness,
While the huge whole sky is elate with glory,
Let me rise, and making my salutation,
    Stride into sunset.

6

REBELLION STIRS

E VENTUALLY THE MORALIZING pressures of Cummings's childhood began to lose the battle against young adulthood, the sex drive, and Cummings's desire to live his life. Staying at home was cramping his style. At least once, he had resorted to sneaking up the stairs in his socks so that his father would not know how late he had come home. Finally, in his senior year, Cummings moved out of 104 Irving Street and into Harvard accommodation, to a room up one flight of stairs in Harvard's Thayer Hall. The move to Thayer Hall brought with it a new freedom to take advantage of the nightlife of Boston. At the center of this life was the Old Howard Theatre, "the Temple of Titillation" (as Cummings called it), where they went to watch burlesque and vaudeville.

The Old Howard already had stature as a venerable theater, imbued with history. In 1916, a local historian spoke to the Bostonian Society on its distinguished as well as checkered past. The first theater building was built as a tabernacle by a doomsday cult called the Millerites, but it lost its purpose when the date of doom passed without the promised apocalypse. It became a theater in 1845. The theater burned almost immediately after opening, was rebuilt, and reopened the following year. These were the days of opera and "legitimate drama," before it became a burlesque venue. Indeed, one of the actors who appeared in the inaugural 1845 season found himself onstage two decades later at Ford's Theatre, on the very night of the assassination of President Abraham Lincoln.

In Cummings's day, the Old Howard staged shows that were as racy as they could get away with, featuring a combination of "house specialities" and traveling burlesque companies. The limiting factor on scantiness of costume was the Boston Watch and Ward Society— a private society that had appointed itself to police the morals of the Boston area, and that numbered among its members the Rev. Edward Cummings. Thanks to Watch and Ward intervention, wrote Charles Norman, Cummings harbored "a regret that has lingered: 'When Miss Gertrude Hoffman brought her lissome self and her willowy girls to Boston, they and she were violently immersed in wrist-and-ankle-length underwear.'" The Reverend's role in this irksome society was a cause of terrific shame for his son.

The Old Howard was embedded in Boston life and reflected the full spectrum of cultural and political interests of its attendees. Shows could be interrupted to include updates on the World Series or the results as they came in of a state election. The theater sat on Scollay Square, which was to the nightlife of Boston what Harvard Yard was to the university. Scollay Square offered young men a different kind of education. Cummings recalled being "greeted by the dispassionate drone of a pintsize pimp, conspicuously stationed on the populous sidewalk under a blaze of movie bulbs and openly advertising two kinds of love for twenty-five cents each." Cummings didn't specify, but two kinds of love presumably meant a hand job or a blow job.

The uptight world of the Reverend and the disreputable world of the Boston underground coexisted in a peculiar tango. Apart from the activities of the Watch and Ward, they could cross paths in the oddest of ways. The Reverend once performed a secret marriage, attended only by himself, Rebecca (as a witness), and the church sexton, for a burlesque star looking to settle to down with her new banker husband into a life of suburban stability. Always a sucker for the lost sheep, the Reverend waited meanwhile for his prodigal son to reform his errant ways.

Even after moving to Thayer Hall, Cummings was not completely protected from the oversight of his father. Hillyer remembered a party initiated by Dos for the whole of the *Monthly* editorial board. Part of the group reunited after dinner in Cummings's room. "It was a Saturday night. We sat up drinking and reading poetry nearly all night, and—I think it was four or five of us—went to sleep where we were on chairs and couches. Early the next morning (or it seemed early) there was a knock at the door. Cummings rightly guessed that it was his father, the Reverend Dr. Cummings, the most famous Unitarian minister in Boston. The room was a shambles. What a to-do there was to whisk bottles and glasses into hiding places and bring some sort of order to the room before admitting the parental divine!"

When the Reverend was a student at Harvard, he had been president of the Harvard Total Abstinence League. Cummings's drinking did not impress him. Indeed, Cambridge itself had passed a local ordinance and was teetotal. Cummings and friends drank privately together or else in Boston. Most afternoons they had "tea," which was to say tea heavily laced with rum while Damon performed Debussy or his own musical compositions on the piano. Damon had a favorite restaurant near the Chinese area of Boston, where they drank dark German beer. Dos favored an Italian restaurant with cheap Italian wine. Meanwhile the Reverend sermonized and spoke out at public meetings on the topic of the appropriate penal treatment of drunkenness.

The Reverend's ideas about public drunkenness were actually progressive. Of the 100,000 men on average who were arrested annually in the state of Massachusetts, more than 60,000 would be arrested for inebriation. The Reverend was against the Massachusetts system of fines and the class and gender injustices it caused. The rich could simply pay the fine for drunkenness and think nothing of it. The poor could not pay and were consequently imprisoned. Women and children suffered. They might forgo food to pay a fine; or a man might lose his job while in prison and the whole family sink into destitution. Instead of either fine or jail time, the Reverend advocated probation as the only just and socially fair punishment and, in his words, the only way to promote reform rather than degradation.

The Reverend spoke his mind and did not shrink from criticism of powerful men. He castigated judges who sent boys to prison with no comprehension of the significance of the sentence. "I wish all lower court judges had to pass an examination in knowledge of the places to which they sentence criminals. I happen to know that some of the Boston lower court judges have never seen the institutions to which they send the defendants who come before them."

Thus in matters of vice and temptation—as in matters of sex— the Reverend maintained a liberal public stance and a moralizing and intolerant attitude at home. The situation was ripe for conflict, and conflict came. Some of the first quarrels concerned girls' hairpins found in the seats of the family car. Cummings would take the car out with friends and with their dates. Rebecca realized and tried to protect him, fishing hairpins out of the car before her husband noticed them. But at least once the Reverend found them first.

A much more serious fight came when the car—with its special clergyman's license plate—was discovered parked in Scollay Square in front of the rooms of a prostitute and towed away by the Boston police.

Cummings was not having sex with prostitutes; in fact, he was still a virgin. He had left the car in search of oranges for his friend, who was quite ill from drinking, and he had returned to find the car gone. He recovered it from the forces of law and order the next morning, but in the meantime the Reverend had been tipped off and it occasioned the worst argument of Cummings's life to date. Cummings would not bend to his father's prejudiced attitude. Instead, he observed that the women who worked in Scollay Square were "as nice as mother" and added that Jesus had kept company with prostitutes. His father threatened to throw him out for good.

Despite his own abstinence, Cummings learned about sex from

his Harvard friends. In a letter from 1916, he writes about having drawn out Robert Hillyer on the tantalizing subject. "Bobby Hillyer wanted to know if I fucked. Now I don't, but wanted to hear about him, so I said, Masefieldically—'not whores.' 'Twas enough. Bobby immediately enlightened me as to the gentleman's sensations during the 69; now I've only got to get the lady's. . . ."

Whatever his father thought, Cummings was not living an irresponsible or louche life. Thayer Hall was one of the cheaper halls of residence—not like Westmorly Hall, one of the so-called Gold Coast dormitories that serviced wealthy undergraduates. Hillyer remembered Damon living the high life in Westmorly, "where tea and toast were served any afternoon upon request." Cummings's expenditure can be calculated to the penny, since he kept a meticulous account book. In his year at Thayer Hall, he spent $94 on his first-term bill, and most of the rest of his cash on basic academic necessities—like course books and paper—and on basic living: 30 cents for a haircut, $3 for a hat, $1.50 for a belt. His luxuries were sodas at 15 cents a pop, occasional car fares, movies for dime tickets, and a few shows. Every penny, nickel, and dime is noted down. It was a full social life, having sodas with friends or seeing shows most days a week, but hardly an exorbitant one.

Cummings found an outlet for his growing sense of rebellion when he was elected in senior year as class speaker and had an opportunity to address the school and the community in a commencement speech at his graduation ceremony on June 24, 1915. He gained this prestigious platform via an essay competition run by his peers, to which he submitted an essay on "The New Art." In this essay turned class speech, Cummings covered the distinction between Cubism and Futurism, the centrality of developments in France in painting and music, and the composer Erik Satie's "truly extraordinary sense of humour which prompts one of his subjects, the 'sea cucumber,' to console himself philosophically for his lack of tobacco." He mounted a clear defense of recent art against the criticism that it was merely arbitrary, unnatural, or incoherent. He built purposefully toward the real scandal of what he proposed to say: he moved on to literature, and devoted the most detailed attention of his speech to the poetry of Amy Lowell.

Amy Lowell was the sister of Abbott Lawrence Lowell, president of Harvard. Her poetry was widely considered a scandal in Cambridge circles, not least because she was a woman, and even more so because she was a lesbian. Cummings's interest in her poetry was completely sincere. Four of Lowell's compositions were among the relatively small number of poems—otherwise including Tennyson's "Come into the Garden, Maud," lines from Keats's "Lamia" and Shelley's *Adonais*, and a poem by Donald Evans—which Cummings copied out into his personal Harvard notebooks. Building on his genuine admiration for Lowell's novel and direct style, he prepared to make his audience as uncomfortable as possible. "Amy Lowell's 'Grotesque,'" he said, "affords a clear illustration of development from the ordinary to the abnormal." He quoted her poem, which begins, "Why do the lilies goggle their tongues at me / When I pluck them." He quoted a second poem, beginning "Little cramped words scrawling all over the paper / Like draggled fly's legs." The "ultramodern" originality of her imagery, he said, was "superb."

It was a triumph of provocation, and a legitimately courageous as well as rebellious act. It takes guts at the age of twenty-one to stare down an audience of well over a thousand. Damon remembered the speech for years: "One aged lady (peace be to her bones!) was heard to remark aloud: 'Is that our president's sister's poetry he is quoting? Well, I think it is an <u>insult</u> to our president!' Meanwhile the president's face, on which all eyes were fixed, was absolutely unperturbed. But one of the Boston newspapers . . . came out with the headlines recalled as 'Harvard Orator Calls President Lowell's Sister Abnormal.'"

For Cummings, the delivery of "The New Art" was a step forward both artistically and socially. Plowing through such a deliberately controversial speech in the public gaze began a lifelong process of navigating the incongruous combination of his shyness with his flair for showmanship. The central place accorded to Amy Lowell at the climax of the speech was a moment of bravura Harvard confidence. Although excluded from some circles on account of gender and sexuality, Lowell was in another sense a local celebrity. She was in close touch with Ezra Pound and with the European developments in poetry. The notion that a local poet could stand among the international cutting edge was an incitement to Cummings and his peers, and the embrace of Lowell, together with Gertrude Stein—American but living in Paris—allowed Cummings to inhabit vicariously the world he longed to join.

7

PAGAN HARVARD

CUMMINGS LUXURIATED IN the seasoned posture of the upper-classman: worldly wise and with a carefully cultivated cynicism. "But look beneath the surface, and you will find that the butterfly is a disappointed idealist. Did he not sit up the first night of college till two A.M., with four friends of his bosom, trying to discover seventeen courses coming between the hours of nine and one, and meeting on the ground floor of the building nearest his dormitory? Did he not triumph, and hand in next day to his advisor the following list: Concentration,–Hypnotism; Distribution–Banking, Hygiene and Sanskrit—only to have that personage insist upon the substitution of Egyptology for Hygiene?"

Cummings enjoyed satirizing the world of Harvard and the undergraduates who crawled over the heart of the campus, Harvard Yard. "Here we behold a well-groomed senior paddling to a perch in some weathered haunt. Now a junior crosses the vision—intent, instinct with the vast interest of something little and perfectly sufficient to the taste. Sophomores, nobly ranked and armed to stamp out the possible impression of σοφο's upon their scutcheon, clamber over 'the square' and its surroundings." (σοφος, or *sophos*, Greek for wise, is the etymology of "sophomore.") "Here and there (and everywhere), emanations of freshman overrun the world with large feet, or flutter excitedly about some sign, like lost adjectives, seeking the subject of their sentence." His professor thought the prose was overcooked and enquired in the margin: "Do lost adjectives act this way?"

Cummings had decided to stay on at Harvard in 1915–1916 for a one-year master's in order to take further courses in English literature and composition. The master's program was organized in a relaxed fashion, and so long as he proposed a reasonably coherent plan of study, he was free to arrange it as he liked. He was growing more confident in his intellectual style and brasher in his attempts to avoid academic assignments that did not suit him. When one of his English professors, Bliss Perry, assigned an end-of-term essay, Cummings instead handed in a "Dialogue of the Dead," featuring George Eliot and Tolstoy among an assembly of dead writers and also the (very much still alive) Amy Lowell. The dialogue is a debate on the merits of various insects, with George Eliot championing the ladybug and Tolstoy standing up for the flea. The piece is not without wit, but it did not convince Perry, who opined that the genre did not suit Cummings's temperament and that such work was essentially ungradeable. He would therefore not grade it, but he would allow Cummings's exam grade to stand as the full grade for the semester.

In his senior year and again in his MA year, Cummings also finally had his chance to take classes with the intimidating Dean Briggs. Briggs taught composition, both verse and prose. His classroom became the social and literary heart of the year for Cummings and his friends, balancing and complementing their evenings at the Harvard Union in the rooms occupied by the *Monthly*. For class, they were expected to read and comment upon one another's work. Briggs had gravitas and his classroom was a demanding forge for aspiring writers. He would happily read student compositions aloud as horrors, *pour encourager les autres*. He had an experienced literary judgment and an excellent ear for the kind of traditional composition he preferred. The new modernist sensibilities perplexed and disturbed him. Robert Hillyer even remembers Briggs approaching him out of some concern for the personal and literary path trod by Cummings.

According to Hillyer, Briggs "felt at liberty to ask me if I knew of anything that was troubling Estlin. He liked Cummings and he discerned his talent, but he could make less and less of the poetry that Cummings was writing. It made him uneasy. . . ." Although Briggs's worry arose partly from his conservative taste in writing, he may also have sensed that the rebelliousness of modernist writing was not always emotionally stable.

Cummings majored in the classics; or rather, technically in "Literature especially Greek and English," because he grew bored of Latin literature and did not care for either philosophy or ancient history as a tactic for satisfying the requirements of the Classics major. He chose to concentrate on the classics in defiance of his father's preference for areas of study like sociology, which were more pragmatically engaged with the modern world. However, Cummings's focus on classical literature did not make him an "ancient" among the "ancients" versus "moderns" of his literary circle. On the contrary, Cummings was the very most modern of the moderns. In an essay written for Briggs's class in senior year, Cummings argued that the Classics are reinvented by each generation of readers. "I believe that the most ultra-modern, the most violently 'Futuristic' ideas, such as translation of an image of one of the senses in terms of another of the senses, are to be found in pristine and full-fledged glory in those classics which are dear to the most conventional as well as the most original of men. When Dante says 'the sun is silent,' he is a poet of the 21st century. Homer and Vergil are far less poets of antiquity than of today—and in this consists their fame. The Greek point of view is to one generation one thing & to another a different and more beautiful." Many of Cummings's modernist contemporaries hoped to achieve a fresh kind of beauty in their own writing through a rejuvenated relationship to the classics.

Modernism sought to harness the prestige and perceived cultural legitimacy of the classics. Classical tropes and tags were ubiquitous. Even the catalogue of the Armory Show in 1913 was fronted by an epigraph, quoted and printed in Greek, from Euripides's play *Iphigenia at Aulis*. Translated (which it wasn't), it meant: "to live badly is better than to die gloriously." The point of the quote vis-à-vis the Armory Show is a trifle obscure.

About himself and Cummings after the Great War, Dos wrote: "In my revulsion against wartime stupidities, as a priest takes a vow of celibacy, I had taken a private vow of allegiance to an imaginary humanist republic which to me represented the struggle for life against the backdrag of death and stagnation. . . . This isn't the sort of thing one talks about, even to intimate friends, but it is these private dedications that mold men's lives. . . . I loved Cummings for his dedication to some similar cult, based, I suspect, in his case on his Greek, a cult that dated back to the earliest Homeric beginnings and stretched forward into prosodies to come."

Cummings's powerfully personal relationship to the classics lodged itself within a shared culture suffused with Classicism. He and his friends construed even their ebullient nightlife as a way to live the world of classical literature. When they went to burlesque shows, they said that they were experiencing the direct heir of Greek comedy: burlesque was the Aristophanes of today. They thought of Amy Lowell as the American Sappho. They wrote poems about Helen of Troy. Most of all, they celebrated the ambiguous figure of Pan, god of the shepherds, bringer of spring, and leader of his horde of goat-footed satyrs.

The world of Pan was a world of sexual chase. Lustful satyrs, half man and half goat and often depicted with an enormous and perennially erect member, pursued shrinking nymphs. This was pagan Harvard, producing a line of Harvard poets described later by Malcolm Cowley—a freshman when Cummings was taking his master's—as "pagans, in the sense that they invoked Greek deities—especially goat-footed Pan—more often in their poems than they invoked Christian saints" and "fleshly poets, in revolt against Christian austerity."

In the early, moral phase of Cummings's poetry, Pan was a force to be resisted. "Not the loud lusting of a bestial Pan / For naked nymph,—no, no, a mans pure love," he wrote in a piece of juvenilia. As he shed the moral phase, however, he embraced the literary enticements of Pan's pagan realm. Pan was "the great goat-footed God of all out-doors," or else he was "the little God Pan" whose eyes would unclose as earth breathed "the first smoke o' Spring." His outdoor world of forests and glades was an eerie and liminal space, in which old gods still whispered. In Dos Passos's "Saturnalia," Dos issued the summons felt by all this Harvard crowd:

> Come old, old ghosts of bygone gods;
> While dim mists earth's outlines blur,
> And drip all night from lichen-greened roof-tiles.

Dos's poem yearns for "the mad gods," the "quaking groves," the "mist-shrouded priests" and their "ancient rites." It was a whole imagination built upon what the Decadent poet A. C. Swinburne called "Pan by noon and Bacchus by night." In the daytime, the panpipes and the stalking of chaste nymphs. In the night, Bacchus the god of wine and his wine-drenched revelry, transgression, and mystery.

Swinburne was the peak and epitome of nineteenth-century Decadent and fin-de-siècle poetry, relishing overripeness and sumptuous decline. This poetry of excess and sensuality openly embraced fluidities of gender, like hermaphroditism, and deviant sexualities—including sexualities like lesbianism that would now be considered entirely within the norm of human experience as well as sexualities that remain outside our norms, like necrophilia. Swinburne sublimated a brutal childhood, in which he was horrifically flogged by sadistic schoolmasters, into a poetry of sadomasochistic eroticism: "exceeding pleasure out of extreme pain." His poems are full of references to blood and wine colors, rich reds and purples, which find their most exquisite perfection in the purple-red bruising of a love bite. He was once himself excoriated by a disgusted contemporary as "the libidinous laureate of a pack of satyrs." Cummings and his friends read Swinburne to one another in their evenings spent in the offices of the *Monthly*. From Swinburne's swirling world of deviance and desire, they discarded some themes, like the motif of the femme fatale, who makes only rare appearances in their poems, while they homed in on others—especially the sexuality of the chase, a central note in their pagan realm of the goat-footed.

"The god pursuing, the maiden hid." (Another of Swinburne's lines.) From their classical inheritance and their Swinburnian leisure-time reading, these young Harvard men imbibed a damaging narrative. The sexual man was a hunter, and so virginal was the ideal woman that, at a last resort, she would beseech the gods for transformation (usually into a tree) rather than succumb to the lechery of her pursuer.

Cummings was mesmerized by the luxurious language of the Decadents, but unlike some of his friends—who tried to replicate Decadent language in their own poetry—his style was evolving into something more delicate and exact. He was conscious that language had to surprise in order to have force. He wrote about a woman he had seen performing at the Old Howard. Utterly smitten, he tried to talk to her after the show, but she shooed him off: "run along dearie run along." Next best was to capture her look in a poem. "I had a hard time making her hair black enough—till I found blue did it."

Cummings's Harvard notebooks have occasional, beautiful flashes of original imagery. "My soul like an old dog lies twitching in the sun." But it was not until 1916 that Cummings began to write poems of real quality. Some of his work came under the influence of Imagism—a briefly flourishing poetic movement engineered from London by Ezra Pound and propagated via a volume of poetry titled *Des Imagistes: An Anthology* (1914), whose contributors included Pound, H. D., Richard Aldington, Amy Lowell, and several more. *Des Imagistes* even includes one poem by James Joyce. From a certain angle, Imagism could be seen as a brand name: a promotional strategy for Pound and his friends. But its brand identity had a wide impact. Imagist poetry prioritized a purity of image, built on language that was precise and stripped down to the essentials. Cummings managed this directness of image in one of his Harvard successes, the twelve-line poem "of evident invisibles."

of evident invisibles
exquisite the hovering

at the dark portals

of hurt girl eyes

sincere with wonder

a poise a wounding
a beautiful suppression

the accurate boy mouth

now droops the faun head

now the intimate flower dreams

of parted lips
dim upon the syrinx

The image of the poem is in fact so boiled down that narrative has been stripped away. Only knowledge of the classical myth—an association triggered by the final word of the poem, "syrinx"—would clue the reader in to the scenario. Syrinx was a nymph: virginal herself and devoted to the virginal goddess of the hunt and the moon, Diana (or Artemis, in the Greek world). When Pan came upon her and gave chase, she ran as far as a riverbed, and then called out with a plea to be transformed rather than caught and raped by Pan. She became a bed of reeds at the river's edge, and thus she escaped; however, Pan still claimed possession. He cut the reeds and fashioned a kind of flute that then bore her name—the syrinx.

Cummings's "of evident invisibles" is a significant poem not only stylistically but also because it exposes Cummings's discomfort with the sexuality of the chase. Cummings embraced the pagan realm of the goat-footed more eagerly than any of his friends, but he worked to change the sexual dynamic within it. His poem offers a different version of the story of Syrinx. Instead of glamorizing the hunt, he sketches a delicate picture of a sexual awakening. He replaces the lecherous Pan with the more innocent figure of the faun. Sexual awakening is mutual, with a parity between the girl-nymph and the boy-faun. In her "hurt girl eyes," the reader perceives "evident invisibles": that invisible something that nonetheless shows itself exquisitely in the eyes, hovering in evidence in those "dark portals" to the soul. The boy-faun is caught in wonder: sincere, not lewd. He is poised, wounded. In the final image of the poem, as the faun lowers his head to play upon the syrinx, the action is given its maximum erotic potential. The flower dreams of the faun playing upon it: the sexual yearning is shared.

The inspiration for the poem is not only the material of the classical world as it passed directly to Cummings but also classical themes in the recent music of Claude Debussy. Damon, who introduced Cummings to Imagism and shared with him a copy of *Des Imagistes*, was an enormous fan of Debussy. Debussy composed several pieces around a Pan motif, including the paradigm-shifting "Prélude à l'après-midi d'un faune" (1894); "La flûte de Pan" (1900); and "Syrinx" (1913). In "of evident invisibles," Cummings used his diction to conjure a vocal lightness like a Debussy flute, as if his words could skim the page. He selected words that open on breathy, flutelike consonants. "Hovering," "portals," "hurt," "poise," "faun," "head," "flower," "parted": three *h*'s, three *p*'s, two *f*'s. *H* is pure breath, and *p* and *f* are both aspirated, meaning that breath is expelled when they are voiced. The breathiness continues in the *g*, *d*, *th*, and *b*, which account for most of the remaining opening consonants. This restriction of the consonantal sounds generates a flutelike, dancing lightness, balanced against the poem's deep sense of longing, like Debussy's quality of nostalgia. Cummings's Imagist compression results in a kind of luxuriousness, like Debussy's recognized sensual richness, as the poem is distilled down to only the most evocative and sumptuous words.

Cummings admired Debussy's style, and especially the way that a Debussy composition (as Cummings described it in a Harvard class essay) "ends abruptly on what the uninitiated call the 'wrong key'— to wit, on a note which leaves them in suspense," and thus controls a musical theme which is "well-founded, cleanly developed to the exquisite moment, and stopped with a *real* suddenness." Cummings achieves exactly this, stopping exquisitely on the moment that the whole theme of his poem falls into place: syrinx.

Debussy's "Prélude à l'après-midi d'un faune" dates from the year of Cummings's birth; his "Syrinx" from only a few years before Cummings wrote "of evident invisibles." The real backdrop to early modernism was not the world of stodgy, whiskered Victorians with their armchairs and their aspidistras. Modernism grew out of movements across the arts that were already shocking. It grew out of the wild poetry of the Decadents and their celebration of sexual license; the painting of Cézanne, which revolutionized the relationships among color, texture, plane, and perspective; and the suspense engendered by Debussy's rule-breaking tonalities. From this aesthetic of the unexpected, modernism learned to prioritize novelty above all. From Debussy's gentle provocations, modernist composers moved on to the dissonant, even unmusical sounds of the 1910s and 1920s, when "music" was no longer limited to the sounds produced upon musical instruments but could include the noise of a typewriter or a siren.

Early modernism was also in a constant tension with form. Free verse did not mean that form was irrelevant. If anything, it made form an even stronger feature by putting the fight against form at the very center of poetry. Behind many of Cummings's apparently formless poems lies a form that is disguised, broken, or violated. Approximately a year before writing "of evident invisibles," Cummings was writing out extensive notes on form and rhyme. He wrote out every possible rhyme scheme that could be used in two, three, four, and five-line stanzas, and tried to define their effects. For example, *abab* creates "doubt, continuance"; if it is followed by *ccca*, this creates a "concentration element" coming from the *ccc* while the final *a* line provides a "harking back."

Cummings used two forms in "of evident invisibles." His poem has three quatrains (that is, four-line stanzas). In an earlier draft, those quatrains were written out straightforwardly: four lines, space, four lines, space, four lines. However, the final version disguises the quatrains with additional spaces between the lines. The lines are spaced in this final version to generate the poem's second form: a symmetry that radiates from the two central lines:

> a poise a wounding
> a beautiful suppression

Cummings places his moment of "poise" and "suppression" at the exact, symmetrical heart of his poem, holding the two halves either side of it in their careful balance.

The double form harmonizes with the mood. A pursuit is linear, and ends when the nymph is caught or else transformed. A sexual awakening allows man and woman to act upon each other. She has the first quatrain. He has the second. They are together in the erotic play of the third. The balance created by the poem's symmetry also suspends them in a parity toward each other. And in fact the poem ends with her. The image of the faun playing upon the syrinx belongs to her: the poem ends not with he who plays, but she who dreams of his playing. In this move away from the hunt and toward mutuality of desire, Cummings gives the last word to the woman.

8

DORIS AND ELAINE

THE WARPED IDEALS of the sexual chase, the male hunter, and the virginal woman complicated Cummings's love life. Cummings had a few early dates and dances with girls he knew, including with one of his childhood friends from the neighborhood gang: "my loveliest playmate," Betty Thaxter. He wrote a couple of poems about Betty, but they are not poems of any significance. They are chivalric poems of admiration for a chaste, idealized lady—a cliché, without the intensity of any unique connection to her.

His first proper girlfriend was a bubbly young woman called Doris Bryan. Doris came from a comfortably wealthy background and was something of a Daddy's girl. She was sporty and loved dances, tennis, golf, swimming, and horseback riding. She had a long, oval face that was pretty but unremarkable, with a soft smile and a direct gaze. Her thick hair was shiny and wavy and cut in a chin-length bob with a heavy fringe. She adored her glossy black Scottish terrier, Scottie, and she was no exception to the rule that there is a certain something in common between owners and their dogs. She and her terrier shared a perky face and a strong brush of eyebrow close to the bridge of the nose.

Doris wrote Cummings almost thirty letters across their six-month relationship. Her handwriting was neat, even, and contained. It marched straight along the page—the antithesis of Cummings's own scrawls. Her oddly squared signature placed the *oris* of her name inside an extended capital *D*, stroked out lengthwise to create a long, closed rectangular frame. Indeed, there was something a little boxed-in about her personality—something she began to sense and fight against as she and Cummings spent more time together.

Her letters begin in the summer of 1915, the summer after Cummings finished his BA and delivered his grand and provocative commencement speech. She was impressed. "I really feel it quite an honor to know the senior, who delivered the oration on the 'New Art': I wonder if you know him at all? He is awfully attractive and very cunning!" With an easy flirtation, it was usually she who invited him for meetings. Did he want to play tennis on Tuesday? Her father had paid for a table at a local club where there would be a pop concert and dancing and had given it to her to organize a party; did he want to come? They exchanged photographs, and occasionally stretched her curfew. Late one evening, she made a mad barefoot dash for her room and got away with it, but theirs was a courtship along the rules for "nice" girls. "Mother did not mention it the next morning. Of course, you are always polite and nice, so I need not tell Mother."

Doris went with her family to spend the summer from mid-July to mid-September at a well-known hotel called the Oceanside in Magnolia, Massachusetts. It was a popular, picturesque, and well-heeled seaside resort where she quickly found a crowd of young people to socialize with. She felt, however, that Cummings was insufficiently attentive in reply to her letters. At points she asked him urgently what the trouble was, and at other points she resorted to long tales emphasizing to him that he had a rival for her affections in the person of one Billy Shaw. "Billy Shaw is really a wonderful boy and very sweet and all that—only I fear it must be 'puppy-love,' which is often very boring. I simply cannot move an inch, without he is right at my heels, just like a darling little dog." He reminded her a bit of Scottie.

Doris also had a mischievous side, to match Cummings's wicked streak, and she and Billy managed to cause one spectacular stir, which she wrote about to Cummings with delighted horror. She and Billy had driven out to the house of his aunt, and his aunt's fiancé had taken them both out in a speedboat. Doris returned cold and soaked through, so—rather than face a cold drive back to the hotel—they spent the night nearby with Billy's grandmother. Billy telephoned back to the Oceanside and left his mother a message explaining where they were, but the message failed to reach her. Billy's parents began to panic, thinking of an accident. Meanwhile, the young crowd at the hotel saw that Doris and Billy had not returned and dreamed up a first-class prank. They sent a telegram to Billy's parents: "Billy and I cannot wait any longer. Please forgive, letter will follow. Doris."

"You can imagine the excitement it made," Doris wrote in squirms of shuddering relish. "Father and Mr. Shaw hopped into a machine and started for Boston to head us off, and Mother was taken upstairs and received notes of consolation all evening, and here we were all the time at Billy's Grandmother's house, as innocent of all this as anything!!!" They returned the next day to find two sets of parents totally distraught at the supposed elopement. The collective parents only accepted Doris and Billy's account of the night when they finally reached Billy's grandmother on the telephone. "Everything is all fixed-up now," Doris promised Cummings, "but it is still rather queer and B. & I are on rather strained terms."

As the summer lengthened, Doris's letters began to show a more self-reflective side. Doris was growing up. She, too, from the other side of the fence, was a victim of the early twentieth-century sexuality of the chase with its idealization of the male sexual hunter and the chaste shrinking virgin. "Nice" girls like her were under pressure to show no sexual side of themselves. Doris was thinking all this through. She wrote to Cummings that people found her "very cold and unemotional, but I guess they don't know me, that's all." In a letter soon afterward she sent him a small, printed clipping. Its text (with context clipped away) read: "I must be an extraordinary individual. . . . Even though I fight against it, I am masquerading all the time. I simulate coldness when I am experiencing the most violent, the most passionate desires. I don't know why. . . ." In blue ink,

she underlined "I" three times at the start, and the word "most": "the
<u>most</u> violent, the <u>most</u> passionate desires." She penned in at the end:
"but it is true."

Doris wanted to let herself out of her box. Around this time, she
changed her signature. Her *D* was still strong and squared, but
she moved the *oris* outside and began to write it out to the right,
as the expected D-o-r-i-s. After repeated requests, Cummings began
to show Doris some of his poetry, and she began to ask him what she
meant to him. Was it merely a physical attraction, "or is there something a little deeper or what?"

Doris had an appealing combination of intelligence and prag-
matism, and she and Cummings had serious and intimate conver-
sations. But it was not entirely an affair of love, or at least not a deep
love. She did profess a love for him and, although we do not have
his letters to her, she writes as if her profession responds to his. But
as autumn wore into winter, it became increasingly clear that what
Cummings felt was an affectionate love and not the passionate love
that Doris craved. Whether she felt more than that for him is difficult to tell. She probably thought that she did. However, her letters are less concerned with how deeply she loves; more concerned
with how deeply she is loved. Cummings's feelings may have stumbled against her own reserve. In a late letter, she talks of being in the
wrong and promises to try to explain to him sometime why she "<u>was</u>
(past) so unresponsive." She wanted to believe that her emotional
and passionate self could break through the controlled surface, but
it seems that the closed surface—at least when they were together in
person—was too strong.

In late December, presumably for Christmas, Cummings gave
her a copy of Oscar Wilde's *Salome*. It was one of their last exchanges.
Doris's final letter to Cummings, on December 29, 1915, refers to a
fuss occasioned by the views of her mother. It appears that her mother's opinion of the relationship had made its way back to Cummings
via someone named Jack, who, Doris said, had no business interfering. Doris's mother denied having spoken to this Jack anytime
recently, but Doris admitted that "Mother did think I was too young

and innocent and all that." In the same letter, Doris made plans to meet, and perhaps this was the meeting at which they broke it off. Her letters cease and that is that. It may have ended because of Cummings's own doubts, or Doris's doubts of his affections, or perhaps in connection with the warning bell sounded by Doris's mother, or all of the above.

Doris suffered from the expectations of a society that required her to be cold in her passion and always in flight from her pursuer. She spent that summer of 1915 caught between Billy, whose dogged pursuit merely struck her as puppyish, and Cummings, with whom she could not fully open up the passion she felt. But while Doris and Cummings both struggled against this unhappy sexual culture, it was embraced to the utmost by one of Cummings's closest male friends, Scofield Thayer.

Cummings had cultivated the influential Thayer, an older undergraduate involved with the *Monthly*, from early in his own Harvard days. Thayer's own poetry had a certain polished accomplishment, but it was old-fashioned and overly contrived. Cummings had not yet honed his critical judgment, and he quite honestly admired it. His first contact with Thayer, initiated when Cummings was a sophomore, was a letter saying so. "I shall feel better when I have made trial of expressing, to you, my admiration of your poem. I shall be very proud and happy indeed when I can say the thing so completely, so purely, and with such a true and fine ring as you have said it. . . ." Cummings's careful approach to Thayer elicited a correspondingly gracious response in praise of Cummings's own lyric abilities; however, Thayer was soon to graduate. He went abroad, to Oxford, for two years, and then returned to Cambridge, Massachusetts, in the summer of 1915. As he left England, he extricated himself from a potentially awkward entanglement with Vivienne Haigh-Wood, who in the immediate aftermath married T. S. Eliot.

Thayer was from textile money in Worcester, Massachusetts. His father had died when he was young, leaving Thayer in control of a considerable fortune. Thayer's wealth and the sheen of worldly experience acquired through his time at Oxford after his Harvard undergraduate years imbued him with a certain glamour when he returned to Cambridge. Most of Cummings's circle bought into him, although the practical Doris thought of him as the one who always said yes yes yes yes yes in a string.

Thayer's Oxford stay had coincided with that of Eliot. Eliot thought Thayer a dabbler, but Thayer regarded himself as the rival of Longfellow. Thayer was blind to his own flaws, and he had no lightness of touch, in life or in art. He could not appreciate anything that was not intensely, almost religiously, heightened. He fixed upon the pursuit of a beautiful schoolgirl, eight years younger than him, by the name of Elaine Orr. Elaine's stunning beauty made her seem a heightened creature, a nymph worth seizing—as intensified in that beauty as the intensity he pursued in literature.

Near the end of March 1916, Cummings met Thayer's Elaine, the woman who would later become the mother of Cummings's only daughter, Nancy. Later, after her divorce from Thayer and when Nancy was four years old, she would become Cummings's first wife. He was enchanted at first sight, struck far deeper than he had ever been by Doris. Elaine was exquisite. But she was betrothed to Thayer, and Cummings convinced himself that he was satisfied to worship her from afar in the self-abnegating style of a medieval courtly lover.

The marriage was planned for June 1916, after Elaine finished school. First, though, Thayer had a little project on. In May, he headed out for Chicago with $10 and the intention of proving to himself that he could have been a self-made man. He spent a month living hand-to-mouth, supporting himself with a sales job that he acquired on the spot. Then, having demonstrated his virility to his own satisfaction, he returned to a life cushioned by effectively limitless financial resource.

Thayer's vast coffers made it an easy matter for him to cut Cummings a check for $1,000, paid as a commission for the poem Cummings wrote to celebrate the occasion of the marriage. The poem was titled "Epithalamion," in reference to the classical genre of the wedding song. It is a highly classicized and idealized poem, full of complicated classical allusions. Pan appears, in highly decorative language, as "the god / from but the imprint of whose cloven feet / the shrieking dryad sought her leafy goal." But Pan's sexuality occupies only these few lines, while six stanzas are devoted to an elevated summoning of Aphrodite, goddess of love. At her "altar," "magnificence conquers magnificence," and under the nighttime cover of a world "clothed with incognizable amethyst," the "inconceivable embrace" of the goddess awaits. Yet again, Cummings shows his preference not for the chase but for mutual erotic love.

Cummings strove in his ornate language to match the adoration he felt for Elaine and the awe in which he held Thayer. Earlier in the same academic year, Cummings had worked on a highly distinctive set of eight drawings, executed with a heavy ink line that evoked the lead lines of stained glass, dividing each subject into shapes that recalled stained-glass cells. His subjects were: clown, prizefighter, poet, Dante, Christ, Saint George, and two versions of Thayer. One of the Thayer portraits mirrors the cheekbones and face shape of the portrait of Christ, and (unlike the others in this series) it is bound in a rectangular ink outline, which makes the idea of a stained-glass window even more explicit. Thayer could hardly be put in more idealized company.

A few days before the wedding, Cummings presented his "Epithalamion" to Thayer. Thayer read it aloud in a restaurant on the spot, with embarrassing gusto. His crude response to the poem's sexual innuendo shocked Cummings, and Thayer took a tumble in his eyes, as Cummings suddenly witnessed another side to the friend whom he had always regarded as the very definition of a gentleman.

The marriage to Thayer would prove to be a catastrophe for Elaine, though Cummings would not know this for some time to come. Thayer had tumbled in his eyes for a moment, but Cummings papered it over and forgot it. His habit of hero-worship, especially felt toward those who were older and seemingly more glamorous and worldly-wise than he, made it too painful to admit fully this sudden flash of insight into the vulgar, even cruel side of Thayer and the disrespect in which Thayer held the woman he was about to marry. Cummings's friends meant everything to him, and he believed in them even to a fault. In his last couple of years at Harvard, as a senior and then as a master's student, he had at last found what felt to him like a fellowship of Decadence, classicism, Futurism, and poetry, along with burlesque, Boston restaurants, late nights, alcohol, and friendship.

9

HARVARD IN NEW YORK

AFTER FIVE YEARS at Harvard, it was time to move on—to New York. Lives were transplanted: the same circle of friends, the same patterns, new haunts substituted for the old. Burlesque at the Old Howard in Boston gave way to burlesque at the Winter Garden in New York. Many young men left Harvard determined to embark on the early twentieth-century version of a city career, but not Cummings and his friends. They were all determined to follow the call of literature and, said Dos: "we were one in our scorn of our poor class-mates who were getting ready to go out into the world to sell bonds."

Though it scandalized his father, Cummings had happily accepted the thousand dollars that Thayer offered him for "Epithalamion." It was a nice nest egg for the move to New York. However, he still intended to sort himself out with proper employment. Bliss Perry—the professor who had caviled at Cummings's dialogue of the dead—advised him against magazine work, on the grounds that it was routine and not truly creative. He said that Cummings would do better to take any old job and concentrate on writing poetry during his leisure hours. Cummings thought perhaps newspaper journalism would be a way forward. He applied to the *New York Evening Post* in September of 1916 and was peremptorily given the brush-off.

He did have, in his favor, a letter of recommendation from none other than the Cambridge poet, star feature in his own commencement speech, and "American Sappho," Amy Lowell. He had met this formidable woman in person when she came to speak at the Harvard Poetry Society in February 1916, sweeping through with magnificently delivered pronouncements about topics like free verse. "I suppose you think that Whitman wrote it; well, he didn't." Lowell sent a warm note to Cummings, enclosing letters of introduction for him to carry to the editors at three significant magazines: *Century, Scribner's Magazine,* and *Craftsman.* Cummings did not get anywhere at any of these magazines, which may or may not be connected to the fact that Lowell introduced him in the letters as Erstline. At the same time that she offered Cummings her support for the New York move, Lowell made a bet with Thayer that Cummings would never achieve any great success as a poet. The bet was $100 and contracted in writing, to be judged on the second of June 1935.

While Cummings was hunting for a New York job, he compromised by basing himself still at the family home on Irving Street. However, his parents felt that he was deliberately alienating himself from them with his increasing insistence upon his privacy and independence, his plans for moving permanently to New York, and his lack of enthusiasm for regular exercise and clean living. Over Christmas 1916, the conflict that had first exploded in the episode of the car parked in Scollay Square came to a head in a second terrible quarrel with his father. It took the shape of an explicit argument about whose life Cummings was leading—his own, or one he owed to his father, his mother, and his family.

The weight of family history hung over the Christmas fight. The Reverend was not alone in his tyranny predicated on morality. It was a legacy that extended back across the generations on both sides of the family, the Reverend's and Rebecca's. On the Reverend's side, that role was inhabited by the Reverend's own father. Grandfather Cummings was a hellfire Christian, in the literal sense: over family dinners, when Cummings was a young boy, he would warn the Reverend, Rebecca, and his grandson of their impending eternity liable to be spent roasting in hell. Cummings both feared and hated his grandfather for heaping abuse upon his own wife (Nana Cummings) and on the Reverend and Rebecca. But his fear did not quash his instinctive defiance. When his grandfather preached his hellfire, Cummings had the wit to chirrup: "I'll see you there, Sir!"

Cummings deeply respected what his grandfather had done during the Civil War when he offered a stop on the Underground Railroad to help slaves escaping from the South. But he also recognized that his grandfather's physical and moral courage during the war was a constituent part of the domineering tyranny: "the child who was I perfectly realized that grandfather Cummings was what adults would call a fanatic, if not a neurotic: I have hated and feared fanatics & neurotics ever since." He added, more facetiously: "Perhaps it was the way his setter dog barked, at table, which gave him away."

The Reverend faced in Grandfather Cummings that pernicious combination of authoritarianism and rectitude that he himself later embodied, and, like his own son in later years, he strove as a younger man to leave that tyranny behind. He tried to embrace the best of his father by speaking out in favor of civil rights for African Americans, and he enrolled Cummings in an elementary school run by an African American woman named Maria Baldwin. In contrast to his father's hellfire, his own Unitarianism represented an attempt to move toward a theology that was loving and not hateful. He had a sincerely gentle side, learned from his mother. Elizabeth remembered him inventing nonsense spells to charm away the pains of childhood scrapes and scratches and playing with the children in snow, when they would build snowmen and snow forts together. He always encouraged the local children's gang to hang out in the backyard of 104 Irving Street, where he was tolerant of damage to the lawn. Elizabeth said, "My father liked to have us play in our yard, and used to say he was raising children and not grass."

But while the Reverend became a far kinder man than his own father, he never quite left behind that authoritarian and patriarchal streak. And when Rebecca chose him for a husband, she was responding to a more benevolent version of the authoritarian patriarchy and

moral tyranny that she, too, accepted as the norm, since it had dominated her own family history.

Rebecca was raised by her mother. Rebecca's father had entered
business together with her grandfather, her mother's father. The
son-in-law forged his father-in-law's name on a check, and when
the forgery was discovered, there was no mercy. His father-in-law
turned him over to the law and established within the family a
damnatio memoriae. Rebecca's father—Cummings's grandfather—
spent ten years in jail, but the family allowed Rebecca to grow up
under the mistaken belief that her father had been hanged for his
crime. That menacing sense of punishment that was ill understood
and out of all measure hung over Rebecca and percolated down to
Cummings's own psyche.

Thus both the Reverend and Rebecca had imbibed an environment where the might of familial disapproval crashed down upon
any individual family member who strayed from the straight and narrow, and they poured this entitlement to judgment into the fight on
Christmas Eve 1916, voicing their censure of the state of Cummings
and of the way he was living. Rebecca pulled out the old aphorism
that cleanliness is next to godliness and added that he ought to bear in
mind the condition in which he would be found, were he to be caught
up in any terrible accident. Cummings objected to their intervention
in his life. He maintained in anger that he "owed nothing to those
who were responsible for my birth,i being helpless at the time,and
having no say." His father dished out a liberal helping of guilt: "look at
your mother . . . she went down to the gates of Death to meet you." He
said: "Remember,this is our adventure,not your adventure." Therein
lay, said Cummings, his father's "whole philosophy." The Reverend
believed absolutely that he was entitled to a stake in Cummings's
own, independent life. Cummings wished to live for himself, and in
the way that he chose. There was no resolution. The fight spilled over
into Christmas Day. His mother urged him: "you have your mother's
reputation,and your father's good name. . . ." They were burdens he
was still obliged to carry.

The extended stay at home produced one result, at least.

Cummings bumped into one of his old Harvard professors, who knew of a job opening and arranged for him to start at P. F. Collier & Son, Inc. in New York immediately come the New Year. Collier & Son was a mail-order book business run out of 416 West Thirteenth Street, and Cummings now found himself answering letters on pay of $50 a week. At Collier & Son, he was underemployed and spent much of his time reading the prose and poetic Edda: the two major works of medieval Icelandic literature. At least, though, he could settle into New York enough to think of making a proper home, maybe even with some decent furniture. He wrote to his father to ask about forwarding blankets and cushions and the large, comfortable chair that he had kept in his Harvard room at Thayer Hall, provided the chair was not needed at 104 Irving Street. His father, however, regarded it as too expensive a piece to part with. Cummings's next letter, on Collier's headed notepaper, is addressed "Reverend Sir:— Yours of the —th inst. received: we beg to say that we had no idea of the value of the furniture left behind us in our hither-journey. . . ." It is a parody of the letters that Cummings was writing in his day job, and it is clearly tongue-in-cheek. But it suggests at the same time that Cummings was still smarting from the Christmas fight, further stung by his father's stingy attitude toward his new adult life, and hoped to sting just a little in return.

One difference arising from New York life was that from now on the Harvard crowd saw much more of their New York–based friend, Edward Nagle. Nagle was another "modern," who was keen on D. H. Lawrence and Dostoyevsky and also followed developments in Paris and the early poetry of T. S. Eliot. Nagle's interest in Paris was facilitated by his mother's second marriage to the French sculptor Gaston Lachaise, now also living in New York. Lachaise was a powerful presence on the American art scene. He worked in bronze and marble, adopting a modern style with clean lines, which he deployed especially in the creation of his simplified and exaggerated female nudes, heavy with sensually enormous breasts and hips. In the 1910s and 1920s, Lachaise represented the meeting point of French and American modernist art in New York. Nagle's European proclivities and his connection with Lachaise brought Cummings and Dos ever closer to feeling the pulse of the artistic world of Europe.

Cummings stayed in the job at Collier's for less than two months before he chucked it in. There were more interesting things to do, including plans for a book to advance the literary ambitions of himself and his friends. They had left the days of the *Monthly* behind, and left that cherished magazine to an unanticipated fate. In less than a year, it would perish when the editorial board found itself split down the middle, four against four, on the question of America joining the world war. Unable to resolve their differences, they folded up. Their rival, *The Harvard Advocate*, survives today.

For Cummings and his circle the *Monthly* had fulfilled its purpose, and it was time to look for a wider readership. Cummings, Dos, Hillyer, Damon, and four other friends clubbed together for a volume titled *Eight Harvard Poets*. The prosaic title testifies to the value of the Harvard name in their early strategies for self-promotion. Dos took the lead in the endeavor, together with another of the eight named Stewart Mitchell, and Dos persuaded his father to guarantee the costs of the publisher against sales.

Most of the work in *Eight Harvard Poets* is juvenile. Indeed, the volume is hard to obtain nowadays, except in facsimile edition, in part because one of the contributors—William Norris—in later life so regretted his youthful poetic misadventures that he set about to buy up and destroy as many existing copies as he could find. According to Dos, they all regarded Dudley Poore's verse as the best in the volume, which says more about their predilection for Decadent themes and language than about their literary judgment. Poore's imagery draws on a Decadent vision of nature inflamed with desire. Such imagery was entrancing when it was fresh, but lacks authenticity when it was recycled:

> Some strange and exquisite desire
> Has thrilled this flowering almond tree
> Whose branches shake so wistfully
> Else wherefore does it bloom in fire?

The rhyme itself, *desire/fire*, is derivative of the nineteenth-century poets and the poem as a whole is self-conscious and overworked. Even Cummings's more traditional verse was better than this. In contrast to Poore's wrought-up almond tree, Cummings's own poetic garden, in *Eight Harvard Poets*, comes alive with "Frail azures fluttering from night's outer wing."

Cummings's friends did not yet realize that he was the standout poet among them. Even the "moderns" did not fully appreciate what he was trying to achieve. When the publisher for *Eight Harvard Poets* was annoyed by Cummings's small *i*'s and idiosyncratic typography, Dos replied—behind Cummings's back—never mind about the *i*'s. He could capitalize them if he wanted to. And another of the eight, Cuthbert Wright, advised that if Cummings was determined to be difficult about the capitalization or punctuation of one of his poems, then that particular poem could simply be dropped. Later Dos had a fit of conscience about Cummings's typography and consulted him. Cummings dug his heels in, and regarded his own intransigence—which, he said, came spontaneously and as somewhat of a surprise to himself—as the moment when his commitment to his developing style became absolute. The printers still ignored him and changed the lowercase letters to capitals.

Eight Harvard Poets was in process when the question of war became urgent. The atmosphere in the country had shifted. No matter how dimly, to borrow Dos's word, the din of the war had sounded in the offices of *The Harvard Monthly*, by now the military mood was ubiquitous. Even the character of their beloved, escapist world of burlesque and vaudeville theatre was changing. Acrobats were in shorter supply, since they were commonly brought over from Europe and harder to come by as the Great War took its toll. Entertainers and chorus troupes were varying their usual popular fare with patriotic songs. Links to the war were advertised in promotional material: such-and-such performance brought to America a production that had been seen in France in the trenches. Plot lines for plays began to hinge upon devices connected to the war, and the newspaper's "news, notes, and gossip" contained items like news of an actor who had volunteered as a stretcher bearer because a dickey heart had prevented him from joining the ranks.

No able-bodied young man was immune to the hovering question about his own intentions. Damon wrote to Cummings in February to complain about it. "'What will you do if we go to war?' I am so sick, So SICK, of that eternal question. 'Enlist, I suppose.' A pox o' both your houses."

Ambulance service was the fashionable course to take, and Cummings was considering it even before America declared war on April 6, 1917. When the declaration came, there was a new pressure. Cummings did not want to be caught in the widely anticipated draft. He had no desire to be shipped off to the trenches, and that seems fair enough. One can hardly blame a man for wanting to do his duty but also, ideally, to survive doing so. Nor was it only a question of the fear of trench service. The Reverend had been looking into the question on his son's behalf, and he explained that voluntary enlistment currently entailed a minimum of six years' service: the first three on active duty and then another three years in reserve. There were unofficial promises that volunteers would be released regardless at the end of the war, but no way of knowing if such promises could be relied upon. Cummings did not need long to think about it. He replied immediately: the ambulance route was the answer for him. "It will mean everything to me as an experience to do something I want to, in a wholly new environment, versus being forced to do something I don't want to + unchanging scene. I only hope I shall see some real service at the front."

Cummings wished to escape not only the draft but also the upsurge of propaganda and judgmental patriotism. The Reverend—though very patriotic—was actually far more balanced on the subject than most. He had become a trustee of the World Peace Foundation in 1910 and its general secretary in 1916, and his church sermons at the outbreak of war emphasized the ideals of democracy and human brotherhood. His approach contrasts favorably with other local ministers, some of whom went full force with sentimentalized anti-German propaganda. "There is a power loose in the world that is murdering, outraging, madly killing and plundering helpless women and children. That is why America is at war. That is why Jesus would go ahead and carry the flag for us." Others went full force with judgmentalism: "We have had a sad spectacle of hundreds of young men hastening to be married, apparently in order to escape military duty. The wonder is that there could be found so many young women who would accept as husbands men who are made of such stuff." Even before Cummings arrived in Paris and found himself bewitched by the French, his tolerance for his fellow Americans was growing thin.

Dos also enlisted in ambulance service. "I was all for an architecture course," as his own father desired, "but first I wanted to see the world. The world was the war." Many of the Harvard men—Hillyer, Malcolm Cowley, and more—did the same.

Cummings was booked on the *Touraine*, due to sail from New York on the twenty-eighth of April, 1917, along with twenty-three other ambulance volunteers. It was largely a northeastern crowd, with seven men from New York and eight from Massachusetts among the twenty-four. They were given a list of items to bring, including clothes, bedding, basic equipment (knife, electric torch, wristwatch, whistle), playing cards, soap, and toilet paper. And thus: "Being neither warrior nor conscientiousobjector, saint nor hero, I embarked for France as an ambulancedriver."

Five months earlier, Cummings had made an ambitious approach to *The Seven Arts*—a short-lived but prestigious literary magazine. Appearing in *The Seven Arts* could make a reputation. The poems that he submitted were rejected, but with kindness. The editors told him that he had "a great gift," but he needed a bit more experience of life— "the experiential element which must help you to put the gift to larger uses." Now, in April, he prepared to take that advice.

PART III

MONTMARTRE

May 8, 1917–June 15, 1917

—

10

ACROSS

April 28, 1917

LA TOURAINE SET sail from Pier 57 at the end of West Fifteenth Street, New York. "Looking back, one saw the reel that was New York a leonine uproar of rose in the unpuncturable stupidity of heavenless heaven."

So Cummings wrote in one of his notebooks as he searched for that intensity of expression that was prized among the modernists and, above all, by Scofield Thayer. What Cummings began to find through his scraps of notes was what Picasso found in his painting: that ability to be wholly accurate and exact and yet wholly idiosyncratic at the same time. The modernist aesthetic called for evocative language, but not language that simply spun off into itself. No word was allowed simply because it sounded good: everything had to convey an element of meaning in a direct relationship to the experiences and realities of the world outside. Thus Cummings translates into words the New York that receded from his view, as *La Touraine* pulled away from the harbor, roaring up like a lion and unfolding like a film reel as the essence of technologically thrusting modernity, awash in the emotions of rose-pink with a pun on the "uproar of rose." Yet there

was something foolishly stupid in the fact that, for all its skyscrap-
ers, it could not dent or punctuate the sky, and such a stupidity of sky
must be empty of any heaven, a "heavenless heaven," for its failure to
return any feeling to the roaring lion of the city.

In the eight months to come in France, Cummings filled more
than a dozen notebooks with such tiny images of buildings, people,
animals, streets, and skies. Each exact observation sharpened him. If
Harvard had been a release into a world of pagan sensuality, France
was a disciplining of the self.

The Reverend was keen to put his own spin on Cummings's venture. He sent a valedictory telegram to the ship on the day of sailing, couched in twee rhyme. "As said in advance, I envy your chance
of breaking a lance for freedom in France by driving and mending
an ambulance. Best love and luck a soldier ever had, from Betsy,
Mother, Jane, Nana and Dad." Signed, Edward Cummings. The Reverend warmly approved of Cummings's patriotism, and he felt that
volunteering for ambulance duty showed the proper chivalric spirit.
He took it for granted that his approval (or disapproval) remained
relevant, and so in his heart did his son, in spite of the Christmas
fight and Cummings's protestations that he wished to be his own
man. Cummings had turned to his father repeatedly during the process of enlisting in the ambulance service, and not only because he
needed assistance with the relevant paperwork—birth certificate,
passport, and so on. He had also sought and welcomed his father's
advice as he weighed the prospect of volunteering for ambulance
duty against the growing expectation of a general conscription into
the army. The decision to volunteer in France preserved a delicate
psychological compromise. France offered freedom, and it was a
freedom that Cummings felt to be his own choice and on his own
terms, but at the same time they were terms of which his father
approved. It was defiance without actual defiance, and without the
pain of alienation that would come from more truly severing his
own life from his father's.

The exuberance of sailing out from New York did not last long. A
nor'easter hit—with it, seasickness. By the end of his first day at sea,

Cummings was thoroughly ill, and he spent the next four and a half days below.

The *Touraine* was a large ship with a fine pedigree. It was a twin screw express steamship, with three decks: promenade, upper, and saloon. It had been in transatlantic service for just over twenty-five years. None of this impressed Cummings after nearly five days unable to keep down a bite. "The 'boat,'" he opined in a ship-board letter to his parents, "is a funny thing, made of wood and stone, with a few bricks loose in the hold." It shook at every touch of the rudder in a manner that did not inspire confidence. "When the 'boat' wants to whistle, 'she' shuts her eyes, stops her heart-beats, buttons her vest, and goes off with a heart-rending scream that reminds you of Cambridge policemen at busy traffic-corners. 'She' has a way of dying in the grip of a fair-sized wave, which is heartily amusing."

The Atlantic crossing was dangerous. On the first of February, 1917, the Germans had moved to a policy of unrestricted submarine warfare around the waters of Britain and the coast of France, and April 1917 was the very peak of German U-boat success, before the Allies turned to traveling in convoys and naval losses began to fall. It took some nerve to sail out in late April—but what the risk really was, no one could have said. The naval situation was too much in flux and, anyway, newspaper reports were more interested in striking the right patriotic tone than in providing informative statistics or risk assessments. No casual American ambulance volunteer had the facts needed to approach the crossing with realism, and therefore each man responded to the danger according to his own personality. Cummings responded with bravado. After his five days of seasickness, he penned imprecations upon *La Touraine*. "Should the blond captain of a U boat consent to waste a torpedo on thy torpid bowels, I'd grasp his Hunnish hand."

Once they were through the nor'easter and the seasickness had passed, Cummings cheered up enormously. It was an eleven-day crossing, which meant that even after losing half the voyage to seasickness, he had five days ahead. He spent them pursuing the friendship struck up on the very first evening aboard, before the seasickness drove him belowdecks, when he had met "a wholly possible boy from Worcester" named William Slater Brown.

Brown's own story begins some generations back in an act of industrial espionage. Samuel Slater, his great-great-grandfather on his mother's side, was an apprentice in the English textile industry at a time when no one in America had mastered the workings of the spinning machine and no one in England was lawfully permitted to exit the country with that knowledge. But Slater snuck out, and took with him the secrets needed to break England's industrial monopoly. This piece of enterprising criminality earned him the names "Slater the Traitor" back home, and "Father of Industry" in America—so-called by no less than the president of the United States, Andrew Jackson.

And so Brown was descended from an American textile baron. Indeed, the very town he grew up in—Webster, Massachusetts— had been personally named by his ancestor. By Brown's own time, the descendants of this pioneer industrial *espion* were quite dysfunctional. Brown's mother died when he was sixteen. Brown's nephew, James Lincoln Collier, reconstructed later the collapse of the Brown family as follows: Brown's father, a medical doctor named Frederick Augustus Brown, turned to alcohol after his wife's death. Meanwhile, the brother of his father, who was employed at a local bank, was found to have embezzled a very large amount of money and Brown's father paid it back as a debt of honor, impoverishing his own family in the process. Family resources were stretched even further by an act of gross cruelty and social snobbery. Ruth Slater, a sister of Brown's dead mother, was found out in a love affair with the Slaters' farm manager. He was paid to disappear. Ruth was broken by it, and spent the rest of her life taking cocaine. And capping it all off, while the family crashed out around the alcoholism of Brown's father, the crimes of his uncle, and the callously interrupted love affair of his aunt, Dr. Brown was sued for malpractice after the death of a patient—a death for which he may well have been culpable, as his drinking was out of control. His medical practice virtually ceased and the family was left to subvention from the already-depleted finances of the Slaters and to creditors.

A friendship such as that between Cummings and Brown is not uncommon among young men. It is the friendship of a dominant personality, like Cummings, who has yet to come into himself and a more gregarious, outrageous, and unstable personality whose dynamism at first seems dominant. It is often some years before it is evident that the more quietly charismatic friend is actually the alpha male of the two. And as was indeed the case here, the other will never fully understand how that friendship has played out across a lifetime.

We shall call him Brown. To some he was William, to others Bill Brown or Slater Brown or Brown or Slater. The instability of his social self is not multifacetedness so much as unease and a certain shifting quality throughout his life. Cummings usually thought of him as Brown, and addressed letters to "W.S.B."

Both Cummings and Brown were rebels. Cummings's rebellion was productive; Brown's, destructive. But only hindsight sees such things clearly. Like Cummings, Brown was in rebellion against his father. As his nephew later observed, "he was rebellious from youth. His sister Joyce...said that their father was always saying, 'I just don't know what to do about that boy.' They battled constantly, father and eldest son." After Brown's mother died, Brown went to stay with relatives in Cambridge in order to attend Cummings's old school, the Cambridge High and Latin School. Brown was staying barely a few houses away from the Cummings family, but he was two years younger than Cummings, who was by now already at Harvard, and their paths did not cross—although they realized later that Brown's cousin had been a friend of Cummings's sister, Elizabeth. After Cambridge High and Latin, Brown moved on to Tufts, another Massachusetts university. But he stayed only a year, and then left Tufts for the Columbia School of Journalism in New York. "I wanted to get the hell out of New England." Even this provided no satisfaction. The School of Journalism was "phony," and so he switched to Columbia University proper. Still restless, he took leave from his studies and signed up for ambulance service.

When Brown and Cummings met, Cummings had stopped on their first evening on board *La Touraine* to ask Brown's companion for a light. The three men ended up going together for a drink, and Brown remembered later being terribly impressed that Cummings was drinking cognac, when he himself was drinking a gin fizz. They clicked instantly. They shared a dry, sardonic take on the world. Brown was fascinated by Cummings and awestruck by his flashy conversation and the endless, seemingly effortless, streams of language and ideas. Cummings was famous for his conversation, and that fame outlives him, but only as the testimony of those who knew him. For us now, there is something that always dies with the man, and—like an admirer wrote to one of his friends after Cummings's death in 1962—we might think: "I envy you having known him. I heard many times that he was a brilliant talker, that he seemed to be able to go on forever, the glittering words tumbling out, fixing his listeners completely."

However, when Cummings was not taken by a fit of outpouring conversation, he was reserved, almost retiring. It took time for Cummings to come to terms with the strength of his own personality. Meanwhile, others sensed it and were fascinated by it, but they did not understand it. Like the other seven Harvard poets who could not see that Cummings was the truly great poet amongst them, Brown was compelled and enchanted by a character that he could not fully take the measure of.

To their later ambulance unit commander, Mr. Anderson, Brown and Cummings appeared to be two peas in a pod. To many of the officials involved in their case, Brown seemed the dominant figure and Cummings the follower. The official view, in the end, was that "Cummings's only fault was his friendship for Brown," "under whose influence he seems to be." Brown was the driver of events: it was his impulsive letters that prompted their arrest. He was the more outward and daring of the two. While Cummings was a quiet man leavened with extraordinary fits of conversation, Brown was a genuine talker with a "high-pitched, almost musical" voice and a laugh that was "a dry chuckle." But Brown's extravert sociability masked a much deeper angst, and he was far more fundamentally troubled than Cummings.

It worsened back in New York, after the war. Brown was now a part of Cummings's old circle, and he socialized with Cummings's Harvard friends, including Elaine. He wrote Cummings once that he'd been on an outing with Elaine, "although I had to drink 3 ales to get up enough courage to telephone. I wish I weren't afraid of people." And so he drank. He would spend three decades down the bottle before sobering up and living to the age of one hundred.

But all this lies ahead, in the future. For Brown and for Cummings, the thrill was the sudden aliveness of the present. The threat of the U-boats added a frisson to the last days on board. "Tonight we enter the mythological danger-zone. This only means that we can't sit on boxes of Pathé (movie) film (the stern is heaped with them) and smoke,—hoping for something to happen,—as of yore. Also, all lights will automatically plonk into nihil." As Cummings pointed out, it was dubious what would be achieved by the blackout given that the moon was full. The precautions at which he scoffed were less extreme, however, than the policy encountered subsequently by Dos Passos, who found the windows of his own ship shuttered in iron.

Those who were not inclined to such flippancy became more and more nervy, the closer they came to France and to danger. Two nights out, many slept on the deck in their clothes, and one man slept in a life jacket. On their final night, an official shipwide notice was issued for sleeping in clothes for rapid evacuation if the ship were hit. They were near enough to the coast by now to hope for rescue in the event of the worst. They could already see lights. On deck, "a seven-foot Arab danced, and a Turk played, and Greeks sang their songs—'to pass danger-time.'" They were boarded overnight by the French authorities for passport checks. At five a.m., Cummings found himself gazing at France, and a few hours later, the ship docked safely at Bordeaux.

Cummings had very little time in which to jot down first impressions: "hobgoblin buoys," blue men, "toy boats at toy angles," and slanting houses in lilac and old pinks. By ten thirty in the morning, on the eighth of May, Cummings and Brown were already on a train to Paris.

Dos Passos also landed at Bordeaux, later the same summer. In his memoir, *The Best Times*, he writes of having a grand old trip across the Atlantic, thinking little of the threat from U-boats, and then, hungover from a party-hard crossing, arriving where the Gironde met the sea. "There we had a chill reminder that war was a serious business: floating debris, the spars of a recently sunk steamer standing up out of the water and redfunneled launches towing boatloads of survivors into the estuary." The French, Dos said, cheered their walk from the landing to the train station. "Pretty women clapped. A Frenchman came running up and put his own hat on the head of a boy who had none. My, we puffed out our chests."

Dos painted a fuller picture of Bordeaux when he fictionalized his experience in a novella, titled *One Man's Initiation: 1917*. There, he writes of the newness of Europe for the American volunteer, encapsulated by "the new, indefinably scented wind coming off the land." Like Cummings, who saw Bordeaux in pastels of blue, lilac, and pink, Dos also saw a gentle city—a city of "mellow houses," with fabulous ironwork balconies "carefully twisted by artisans long ago dead into gracefully modulated curves and spirals."

It was ten hours to Paris by train. Cummings gave his mother a perfunctory account of the mix-up about stations. "At the Gare d'Austerlitz the leader and everyone save B. and me got out—signals were badly crossed." Cummings and Brown alighted at the Gare d'Orléans. They went straight to the Rue François 1er to register at the Paris headquarters of their ambulance service, found the office closed, searched around the corner and ferreted out lodgings at the Hôtel du Palais, failed to find any supper, returned to the hotel at one in the morning, and fell asleep, on this, their first night in France.

MARIE LOUISE LALLEMAND

May 8, 1917

"THESE SPRING DAYS," Brown wrote to Cummings's widow, two years after Cummings's death, "I long for France or Italy. May 8th forty-eight years ago Cummings and I landed in Paris and soon forgot all about the war going on. I wish I could be as carefree today."

After crashing out at the Hôtel du Palais, Brown and Cummings woke the very next morning, the ninth of May, to Parisian newspaper headlines of "L'Affaire Slater." Brown had a second cousin in France, Samuel Slater, who was all the news on the ninth. Samuel Slater's housekeepers, husband and wife, had sequestered Slater under lock and key in the attic of his own house and were cashing extorted checks. When they were found out and arrested, a news reporter came to the house, only to find Slater dressed up as a Wild West cowboy, pistols and all. On grounds of human interest, the story even made its way back to one of the New York papers and to the *Boston Globe*.

After digesting the entirely coincidental news of the misadventures of Brown's second cousin, the most urgent task for Cummings and Brown was to report to the Norton-Harjes Ambulance Corps headquarters, since they had arrived too late to register the previous

evening. Enrollment in the ambulance corps was a multistep process. The initial stage of signing on in New York gained them passage to France at a discounted ticket price. However, in order to
begin the next stage of enlistment, they still had to present themselves at headquarters in Paris, bringing with them a letter of introduction issued by Eliot Norton who was operating stateside (brother
of the Richard Norton who ran the service), together with further
letters of reference. For purposes of deployment, they were entitled to a uniform, poncho, blankets, bedroll, lantern, and duffel bag
at the expense of the ambulance corps. But because of shortages in
France, they had been advised to purchase all except the uniform
for themselves in New York and obtain reimbursement. As for the
uniforms, however—these indeed could not be issued until arrival
in Paris. Once everything was in order, deployment would follow.
Meanwhile, Cummings and Brown were at liberty to make the most
of their time in the city.

It was never intended that they should remain in Paris for as long
as they did. But this was not army enlistment, with call-up dates,
roll calls, barracks. The various American volunteer ambulance
services operating in Europe during the Great War were individual creations, driven by the personal energies of men—in this case,
Norton and Harjes—who saw that France was underequipped for
ambulance transport and decided that they themselves would do
something about it. These ambulance services survived off of personal networks, intense fundraising, and ad-hoc arrangements that
interacted—sometimes collided—with the structured world of the
French military. In the case of Cummings and Brown, when they registered in Paris separately from the rest of the expected cohort from
La Touraine, their paperwork went one way rather than another; the
requisition of their uniforms hit a delay somewhere along the line.
Weeks passed on a happenstance.

Paris in wartime was a world of men in uniform or wounded or disabled and a world of women, many of them widows dressed in mourn-
ing black. Airplanes and dirigibles flew overhead. It was also a world
of prostitution. "We were astonished," said Dos Passos later, "by the

crowds of prostitutes. Many were young and some were pretty." But for Cummings and Brown, it was first and foremost a world of art.

At Harvard, the opening up of an artistic world came in part through a drip feed of European painting, literature, music, and artistic ideas. In an era when the phonograph was still relatively new and pointedly "modern" technology, physical access to art was a precious and finite resource. While, on the one hand, Cummings's literary circle turned to the classical past, the "moderns" among them also sensed that an incredible stream of innovation was pouring out of Europe.

The preface to the catalogue for the New York Armory Show of 1913 had voiced a troubling thought for American artists: "The less they find their work showing signs of the developments indicated in the Europeans, the more reason they will have to consider whether or not painters and sculptors here have fallen behind...." The aim of the show was access for both artists and the public; its promoters argued that both groups needed the chance to see for themselves. Cummings saw for himself when the Armory Show traveled via Chicago to Boston, exhibiting the work of Cézanne and Picasso and the techniques of Cubism and Futurism. Much of the excitement of his literary life at Harvard came out of this new access to European artistic movements—but there was always the question of how exactly knowledge of them could be transmitted. Access to Debussy was mediated via sheet music, which Foster Damon was able to acquire and play. The literary cutting edge reached him partly in the form of the slim volume of poetry edited by Ezra Pound, *Des Imagistes*, which brought the poems and the ideas of the Imagists. Cummings also acquired one of the two editions of the avant-garde literary magazine *Blast*, which briefly embodied the manifesto and ideas of Vorticism. But none of this could match Paris: suddenly, unrestricted access to the very heart of artistic change, as it happened, in real time.

Cummings and Brown attended the premiere itself of Erik Satie's ballet *Parade* on May 18, 1917, at the Théâtre du Châtelet, a swishy theater a stone's throw from the bank of the Seine. *Parade* was the artistic event of the Parisian decade. It featured the music of Satie and a scenario devised by the French poet Jean Cocteau. The choreography was by the Russian dancer Léonide Massine with set and costumes by Picasso. It was performed by Diaghilev's Ballets Russes. With Picasso at the pinnacle of Spanish art and Massine and the Ballets Russes bringing the finest of the Russian ballet tradition in flight from political upheaval in Russia, this unprecedented collaboration brought together the artistic luminaries not just of France but of Europe. In the course of rehearsal, Picasso also met the woman who would become his first wife, the ballet dancer Olga Khokhlova, who danced with the Ballets Russes.

Parade represented a staggering break with the traditions of ballet. Cocteau said in an interview many decades later that it embodied all the injustice of youth. Youth, in the view of Cocteau, is necessarily unjust because it seeks always to overthrow its inheritance and to dethrone the greats of the preceding generation. The *Parade* collaborators sought to dethrone Debussy and Ravel: "to them we opposed Satie who is not more thin . . . who is . . . how can I say it, who has a less expansive orifice, but I said that through a keyhole one can see everything." Before moving to Paris, they rehearsed in Rome and drew inspiration there from Italian Futurism. They wished to translate into dance the artistic leaps that had been made in the visual arts. "I asked him," that is, the choreographer Massine, "to raise the gestures of real life into dance, to deform them into dance, just as Picasso was copying objects from real life and transporting them into a world which was his own where people did not recognize them but where they kept their volume and their force."

Picasso's cardboard costumes for *Parade* were clunky, even awkward: for some of the dancers, it was literally ballet from inside painted boxes, within which or through which they had to create their dance. Massine's choreographic ideas rose to the challenge with notes like (for a dancer whose head was not inside a box): "flex your cheekbones." The poet Apollinaire wrote the program notes, and here, in his notes, was the first appearance of the word "surrealism" in the world of modern art.

For Cocteau, a living public remains a child: ". . . each individual is an adult, but taken together the public is a child. One can make it laugh or one can make it cry." *Parade* made it angry. The audience booed and whistled, and a crowd went for Cocteau and Picasso. They absconded safely thanks only to the presence of Apollinaire, whose head was bandaged from a shrapnel war wound and whom the crowd therefore would not touch. Cummings meanwhile began cursing out the show's detractors in his developing street French, ready for it to come to blows. Punch-ups in the audience were a lifeblood to the avant-garde composers and playwrights of the 1910s, whose reputation depended on their ability to stir controversy. Cummings had clicked with the local spirit. This is Paris in the year after the invention of Dada, on the way toward the grand, public stagings of artistic nonsense and anarchy that were to come when Dada peaked three years later. In Paris, Cummings found a symbiosis of art and life that went far deeper than the Harvard crowd's fantasy that Greek comedy could be relived in burlesque theaters. Even so, Parisian life still struck that Harvard crowd partly through the Greek lens. According to Dos Passos, the excitement of the Ballets Russes lay in the thought: "The ballet would do for our time what tragedy had done for the Greeks."

Even if it seemed that some modernist artists or movements stirred controversy for its own sake, these were not empty controversies. Art was a public concern. At stake was the self-image of society. *Parade* was political in the sense that it asserted the right of the transgressive artist to play a fundamental and determinative role in deciding what French society was, what ideas and values it shared, what aesthetic it embraced, and how it communicated itself to itself. In 1917, in Paris, some 70 or 80 miles from the front of a world war, it was no small matter for artists to claim this right to determine society's selfhood. It was war at the front, said Cocteau; but revolution in Paris.

A more dangerous audience brawl for Brown and Cummings was only narrowly averted at the same Théâtre du Châtelet at a showing of the ballet *Petrushka*. They had just had their inoculations, including a jab for typhus fever, in Paris and all in one go. They were at a matinée performance afterward, and when the orchestra started to play the French national anthem, "La Marseillaise," Brown found suddenly that he was too weak to stand. People began to stare. He grabbed a pillar on his left and managed to haul himself up out of his seat, within a breath of a serious thumping.

The Théâtre du Châtelet was a private venue, but all space in Paris had become public space. To be out and about meant moving through a city where everyone was subject to the judging gaze of a populace at war. Soldiers who were in Paris on leave—which the French called *permission*—normally wore their uniforms. Young men who were neither visibly disabled nor in uniform were objects of suspicion and hostility. For Dos, the uniform was top priority on the day after his own arrival in Paris. "The immediate thing we had to do was get ourselves uniforms. Young men out of uniform were liable to arrest on sight and to be put through embarrassing interrogatories." To cover the few days of waiting for the uniform, Dos was issued with a pass that identified him as a member of the ambulance service and therefore not an *embusqué*—that is, a "shirker." Cummings and Brown had no uniforms; indeed, it was the very absence of uniforms that held them happily in Paris. However, Cummings had no intention of wearing his uniform, even had it been in his possession. He stood by his nonconformist instincts and the principle that his own life was nobody's business.

In the midst of this world of art that was so absurd, so much against all the rules—which changed the horizons of the possible in art—Cummings's world expanded also in another direction. He met the first woman he ever truly fell in love with: Marie Louise Lallemand, who was working in Paris as a prostitute.

Prostitution was ubiquitous in Paris and everywhere else where there were soldiers. For many volunteers or conscripts who were shipped out to war, one of the first experiences of military life was the encounter with prostitution. The writer Robert Graves, best known as the author of *I, Claudius*, captures a sense of the banality of prostitution in the memoir of his wartime experiences, *Goodbye to All That*. Graves did not sleep with prostitutes (and faced the derision of his peers for his abstinence, which he could only justify to their satisfaction by claiming that he was worried about contracting a venereal disease). When he was shipped out to France, he landed at the port of Le Havre, where boys pimped for their sisters—or at least for girls they described as their sisters. Whenever a company of soldiers was rotated for rest behind the lines, the presence of brothels was assumed. At one brothel near Béthune, a hundred and fifty men had queued for the services of three women. That oversubscribed brothel served the rank and file. A distinction was normally drawn between facilities for the officers and facilities for the men. In the war zone around Amiens, the men attended the Red Lamp while the officers were welcomed at the Blue Lamp. "Whether, in this careful maintenance of discipline, the authorities made any special provision for warrant-officers, and whether the Blue Lamp women had to show any particular qualifications for their higher social ranking, are questions," said Graves, "I cannot answer."

Prostitutes on the pick-up in Paris tended to congregate in theaters and at shows, in restaurants, and, of course, on the streets—especially on the grand Boulevard des Italiens on the Rive Droite, the right bank of the Seine. Walking out on the Boulevard des Italiens from the Place de l'Opéra, away from the river, a right turn at the end of that boulevard reaches the Boulevard Haussmann just before it becomes for one block the Boulevard Montmartre. At the end of that block, offering a sharp left turn, the Rue du Faubourg-Montmartre leads farther north, farther away from the river, straight into the Quartier Pigalle and the lower area of Montmartre below the hill on which the Basilica of Sacré-Coeur was, in 1917, but newly finished. Here in Montmartre and the Quartier Pigalle was the red-light district of Paris.

We do not know on which day, or how, Marie Louise and her friend Mimi met Cummings and Brown. From a comment that Cummings made to Brown later about looking for the old crowd, we might guess that they met at the Algerian couscous restaurant that, once discovered, became in May their instant favorite: Sultana Cherqui's Oasis, situated in a small court off the Rue du Faubourg-Montmartre.

Mimi lived nearby on the Rue des Martyrs in the Quartier Pigalle, perhaps about ten minutes' walk from the restaurant. Marie Louise lived some distance south and east, at 9 Rue Dupetit-Thouars, not far from the Place de la République. On the back of one of Cummings's notebooks, in a woman's handwriting, is the address for Marie Louise and a date and place for meeting up: Saturday, noon, Place de la République, at the statue. It may be their first date.

No photographs survive of either Mimi or Marie Louise, but Cummings sketched them both in pencil in his notebooks and in words in his published poetry and in other unpublished drafts. Mimi was darker than Marie Louise. She was Jewish through her mother and Spanish, supposedly, through her father. In Cummings's pencil sketches, her eyes hold a strong gaze within a heart-shaped face, which is echoed by her small, heart-shaped mouth. Her hair gestured toward the androgynous: she wore a pixie cut with a smart yet louche quiff. In one of the sketches, she is chewing a piece of straw. Montmartre before the war was famous for its nightclubs and cabarets, including Le Chat Noir and Le Moulin Rouge. Mimi, "*à la voix fragile*" (with her fragile voice), had been a singer. Now Cummings said that she sold on the street "her small smile."

There is no evidence of any feeling deeper than friendliness between Brown and Mimi, although—unlike Cummings, who held back from sex with Marie Louise—Brown had no qualms about sex with Mimi. Of Mimi's own attitude, we know very little. She and Marie Louise were the best of friends, and Cummings liked her and was at ease around her.

Unlike Mimi, who was a bundle of energy, Marie Louise was graceful and languid. We can know her more directly than we know Mimi. In fact, her handwriting alone gives a strong impression. It was an even, assured, and feminine hand. Its size on the page was judged to aesthetic perfection. The letter forms were distinctively European, and the writing confident, grounded, and with flourishes that added elegance but never obscured legibility. The hand as much as the words conveys a straightforward and open person, and one who cherished herself in spite of what life had brought: her most exquisite letters are the uppercase *M*'s and *L*'s, as in her signature, Marie Louise. Her handwriting was beautiful, as she was.

Like Cummings, Marie Louise loved poetry. She introduced him to the nineteenth-century French Romantic poet Alfred de Musset, and in particular to his mournfully elegiac poem "Lucie," in which the speaker recollects his lost, dead love and begs his friends to cover his own future grave with a weeping willow tree. Marie Louise rather fancied the notion of dating a poet, and often referred to Cummings as "mon petit poète," my own little poet. When she called him by his name, she called him Edward—or, rather, "Edouart." To everyone else in his life, Cummings was always known by his middle name, Estlin. Only to Marie Louise and Mimi was he ever Edward. It affected him. He even experimented with signing sketches in his notebook as "Edouard C."

Cummings's excursions into Somerville during his Harvard years had already planted the idea that writing about prostitutes might offer the kind of exquisite, hardened realism for which he was searching. Now, such writing finally began to take shape. For these months and for years afterward, he wrote about the prostitutes of Montmartre and America. Almost every prostitute is written about by name, and these poems stand out for their vitality. In his later American portraits, Liz yawns and observes that "Business is rotten." Mame has "a mellifluous idiot grin" as she tells her customer that she had her tooth pulled without gas. Fran has an erotic allure that the customer cannot fathom: she is not beautiful, but "her tiniest whispered invitation / is like a clock striking in a dark house." But no portrait is as haunting as the memory of Marie Louise, "the putain with the ivory throat," who asks:

> n'est-ce pas que je suis belle
> chéri? les anglais m'aiment
> tous,les américains
> aussi ...

(Am I not beautiful, darling? The English all love me, and the Americans too.)

It was not simple for Cummings to fall in love with a prostitute, or for her to love him. Five years later, when Cummings was advising his sister in a letter to make up her own mind about life, he wrote: "e.g. I am taught to believe that prostitutes are to be looked down on. Before believing that,I will,_unless_ I _am_ afraid _to_ do it,make the following experiment:I will talk with,meet on terms of perfect equality,without in the slightest attempting to persuade,a prostitute. Through my own eyes and ears a verdict will arrive,which is the only valid verdict for me in the entire world—unless I take somebody's word for something,which(because I desire to be alive)I do n_o_t." Cummings was defiant, in 1917 and beyond, writing to his sister of what he would do in the sense of what he had in fact done. Equally Cummings had more of his father in him than he liked to see, sometimes. The son who would damn well socialize with prostitutes was not so far from the father who would damn well visit prisons to see the conditions for himself. Nor is the Reverend's scorn that he poured on those who would determine prison policy from an ignorant distance so far from Cummings's sermon that a person who cannot look at the world for him- or herself is not even alive.

But there is no denying the atmosphere of prejudice around Cummings and Marie Louise. As Dos wrote—not in his own voice, but to parody a judgmental soldier—" 'Well, I was at the Olympia with Johnson and that crowd. They just pester the life out of you there. I'd heard that Paris was immoral, but nothing like this.' " Dos's characters talk of venereal disease and being disgusted with the women they sleep with. Dos himself saw things more honestly, and he exposes for his reader the soldiers' own lechery and hypocrisy: " 'Looks like every woman you saw walking on the street was a whore. They certainly are good-lookers though.' "

Surrounded by prejudice against sex workers, what did it mean for Cummings to make up his own mind about Marie Louise? He did not reject what she did. Some modernist poets and painters fetishized prostitutes. He did not do that either. His desire for her blended her in his eyes into prostitute, queen, virgin. She was a *putain*, a whore, and she was also the "Reine des femmes de noces" (the queen of brides) and the "Pucelle aux yeux bleus" (the virgin with the blue eyes). She had "queenly legs" and the face of Cleopatra. In the only published poem that names her, Cummings slips from thoughts of her to thoughts of the Virgin Mary, "Marie Vierge Priez Pour Nous" (pray for us). In another poem, unpublished, he uses those same language rhythms, "Marie Louise, dis-nous" (Marie Louise, speak to us)—rhythms that are instinctively recognizable to anyone who has seen *Vierge Marie priez pour nous* on the numerous inscriptions and statues erected to the Virgin Mary at the crossroads before so many French villages. At the same time, the language and stanza form of that unpublished poem draw on Cummings's beloved Swinburne, and specifically on Swinburne's "Dolores," his sadomasochistic fantasy of the femme fatale: "O bitter and tender Dolores, / Our Lady of Pain."

On the ninth of June, Cummings, Marie Louise, Brown, and Mimi went together for a day's outing to Nogent-sur-Marne, a bathing spot on the outskirts of Paris on the River Marne just before it flows into the River Seine. Cummings spent a portion of the day sketching both Mimi and Marie Louise. He drew Marie Louise twice, in profile. Even in a black-and-white pencil sketch, Cummings manages to suggest the ivory throat and snowy complexion he describes in his poems. He saw both her strength and her fragility. In the first portrait, her look is softer, her eyes glancing down, her lashes long, although her pre-Raphaelite tenderness is balanced by a mouth that is almost hard. In the second portrait, her Roman nose is sharp, more classical. She wears her hat and holds her head straight and strong, and yet her mouth is softer and younger. She signed the pages of Cummings's notebook, writing the date and the place and all their four names. She looks deeply serious in both of Cummings's sketches, but it must have been she who added to the signature page a silly cartoon face popping oddly off a squiggly worm-wriggle of a body.

Cummings would not have sex with her, perhaps partly for fear of the clap or, worse, syphilis. But that day on the Marne she did get him off. She referred to this sexual encounter in a letter, but not to its explicit details. Presumably it was oral sex. She was irked that he neglected, on this occasion, to offer her any payment. She was with him because she wanted to be, but she also expected him to respect her livelihood. Perhaps she was also hurt that he did not—it can be inferred—reciprocate. Cummings was fascinated by the idea of female pleasure. In the 1920s, he drew endless sketches of men pleasuring women and of women pleasuring themselves. But he was still very inhibited, and he struggled to trust his connection with Marie Louise. She raised the point of payment with him, but gently. Just as it was not simple for Cummings to know how to love her, it was not easy for her to know how to work and love at the same time.

All the time he was in Paris, they grew closer, although each struggled to be certain of the feelings of the other. What Cummings loved most about her, apart perhaps from her beauty, was her kindness. They shared a great deal, including a sexual connection that Cummings had never shared with any woman before. It had its points of awkwardness, but it was a love affair.

12

"a twilight smelling
of Vergil"

"THE ONLY VICE is Imitation," wrote Cummings in one of his 1917 notebooks. The search for novelty preoccupied his generation. But art also has to be anchored, or it loses its meaning and its ability to communicate. The challenge, then, is to create art that possesses the genius of originality and yet retains contact with its artistic environment. One idea Cummings had was to focus on translation from one medium into another: to pay homage to the music of a violin in a painting, or to capture a sunset in music. He was in that optimistic phase when it seems that theories of art, theories of knowledge, even metaphysics can be unified into grand and coherent theories of everything. He reinforced his aspiration to cross artistic media with the thought that such crossings are natural to the senses: for example, he argued, "You know what kerosene tastes like, from the smell—altho You never tasted it." He wondered if taste could therefore be defined as the combination of smell and touch.

He was never more confident. Under the heading "Εγω" (that is, *ego*, Greek for "I"), he wrote with triumph and conviction: "while Pound is angling for new atmospheres, I am pumping toward a vacuum."

This boundless theorizing was balanced out by meticulous observation and a hunger to consume the new environment of Paris. He wrote pages of notes on the streets, parks, and monuments of the city. Although his notes are stylized, he pushed himself to observe the atmosphere and capture his honest response, not just the expected response. At Notre-Dame, he watched "the solemnity of mass attacked by prettiness of candles." He also pushed himself to observe synesthetically, to put into practice his desire to translate across artistic genres or across art and nature. The organ at Notre-Dame was "like a locust in great summer of columns."

Cummings responded to Paris as much in drawing as in words. He sketched on the Boulevard des Italiens, at restaurants, at shows. He drew waiters, beggars, soldiers, prostitutes, widows, the war wounded on crutches, a boy selling the French newspaper where they got their morning news, *La Liberté*. Each avenue had a distinctive character for him. He drew boat workers down by the Seine and their boats and cranes. He drew the caricatured puppets of the Grand Guignol and the acrobatic performers at the Olympia.

Mostly he drew people, although the trees in Paris and later on the front made a deep impression. Two things he always associated with France: *la guerre*—the war was always *la guerre* for him, whenever he remembered it—and the poplars.

He did not only watch people; he also listened. His notebooks are full of snippets of conversation that he either overheard or invented out of the attitudes and types he encountered. His own sardonic take on the world dictates his choice of material, as he shaped a vision of the world that was both caustic and deeply human. Cummings had already encountered T. S. Eliot's earliest work, which he always rated above later Eliot and even above *The Waste Land*. He sensed the complexity of Eliot's poetic speakers, who push the reader away and yet elicit sympathy as well. Cummings too was striving for this complexity of tone, and his notes capture scraps from speakers who might be targets of satire, but targets tinged with plausibility, pathos, or the kind of humor that sparks empathy. Cummings wrote down (with forward slashes, suggesting that it represented poetic lines): "I bought some goddam Cubist stuff/you never can tell,it may be valuable/some day. I don't believe in taking/chances. It's not fair to your/children."

Cummings and Brown were themselves busily buying as many Cubist prints as they could afford. Cummings wrote to his parents that they walked ten or more miles a day, and bought books and photogravures of the work of Cézanne and Matisse. In addition to its demimonde restaurants and nightclubs, Montmartre was known for its printing industry and art shops, such as the famous shop of Père Tanguy, who dealt in the work of Cézanne, Gauguin, Renoir, Van Gogh, and more. For Cummings, the encounter with Cézanne was transformative. Cézanne was obsessed with the achievement of three-dimensionality. For his still-life work, he would even prop up fruit using coins so that the fruit tipped forward, thus exposing more of its roundness. Under the influence of Cézanne, Cummings began work on theories of roundness that would define his art for the next decade or more.

Cummings would come to feel that classical art was deficient, even in its highest (to him) expression, Greek sculpture. He theorized that roundness could only be appreciated when it was in tension with flatness, and so Greek freestanding sculpture never truly achieved the round—or what he preferred to call, the bulge. Cézanne achieved bulge because he understood the flatness of planes. Against the flat, it was possible to see the actuality of bulge.

He was electrified at the thought of achieving the same fullness in poetry. Under the heading *ego*, after his swipe at Pound, he added:

art is <u>The Verb Cold</u> ——— [translated] ———<u>The Bulge</u>

He asterisked his insight and double-underlined it. It is a condensed statement of the essentials of his theory of art: a breakthrough in his search for a credo. Vitality, aliveness, movement, and chaos are all comprised in the verb. But in order to make art, the verb must be frozen cold, because the verb itself is ephemeral. Movement and life are in constant flux. It is, pragmatically, the condition of art that it freezes movement, life, chaos, and everything represented by the verb—whether it does so on a painter's canvas or in the words of a poet. But by freezing the verb, art translates vitality into bulge. Bulge is the measure of art. It is the capacity to see simultaneously what is seen and what is hidden: to feel what is behind as well as what is in front. It is truth.

The search for truth is always subject to the possibilities of disappointment, and the desire for novelty is fragile. It awaits disillusionment. The joyous belief in originality hovers precariously ahead of betrayals to follow. Cummings would find betrayal later in Picasso's words, which he summarized somewhat unfairly as: " 'we know now that art is not truth. Art is a noble game.' " "When I saw those words," said Cummings, "I felt that the person who wrote them was no longer alive . . ."

Among the Harvard crowd, Malcolm Cowley was a particular connoisseur of anecdotes of betrayal. He copied out for Cummings's first biographer, Charles Norman, the observations of the writer James Kern Feibleman on the avant-garde composer George Antheil, whose radical approach to music in the 1920s involved modern, mechanical sounds like airplane propellers. "Those of us who in the nineteen twenties in Paris gave ear to the compositions of George Antheil thought we were witnessing the birth of something important, and not until some years later when Antheil tried to write in the accepted modes did we discover how very unoriginal and derivative his work is."

But that is nothing compared to Eliot's The Waste Land. The problem with The Waste Land, as Cowley saw it, was that the poem represented everything that his generation believed that literature and poetry should be; but: "At heart—not intellectually, but in a purely emotional fashion—we didn't like it." The Waste Land undermined their sense of purpose and value. It was a slap in the face: ". . . we felt the poet was saying that the present is inferior to the past." Cummings was particularly stung. Cowley writes, "When The Waste Land appeared, complete with notes, E. E. Cummings asked me why Eliot couldn't write his own lines instead of borrowing from dead poets. In his remarks I sensed a feeling almost of betrayal."

At this early and optimistic moment, however, not only did the betrayals lurk far ahead but there was no consciousness even of their inevitability. For now, it was an explosion of experimentation and ideas. It was easy to throw oneself into fabulous new modes of art.

That is not to say that everything came easily. In spite of his artistic breakthroughs, Cummings tried many things during these summer weeks in Paris that did not work. He had radical ideas about the physical presentation of texts. Perhaps one could have a book where every page had a different shape. It was not a practical idea. But it fueled future experiments in the layout of text on the page. He thought: perhaps a poem about rain would slant as the rain slanted. Later, he would distribute his lines, words, and letters on a page to suggest the crescent of a moon, the scattering of birds in flight, or (most famously) the jump of a grasshopper. He also, later, took one opportunity to challenge the traditional layout of the print book format. His collection *No Thanks* (1935) was privately printed: "no thanks" to the fourteen publishing houses who turned him down, whose names are listed on the dedicatory page in the shape of a classical funerary urn. The private printing gave him an opportunity to have the book bound at the top rather than at the side, so that the force of the poem strikes readers more immediately and directly as they flip open to a page rather than turning pages through, side to side.

Some of Cummings's exercises were too mechanical. He was interested in assonance and consonance—the repetition of words with the same vowel or consonant—and so he compiled lists of words for each alphabetical letter. He wrote out *A* to *Z* across the top of a two-page notebook spread. *S*: squid, sponge, Sallust. He realized quickly that this project was not going anywhere, and abandoned it after fewer than forty entries.

For the short while that Cummings pursued it, the entries have a random quality. In addition to the Roman historian Sallust for *S*, Cummings came up with Jugurtha for *J*—the name of the Numidian king who challenged Roman power in the late second century BCE and became the subject of Sallust's second historical monograph. Cummings and his peers took for granted the knowledge of a shared pool of classical ideas, people, and places. These classical items jangling about in the mind did sometimes become mere vocabulary, detached from meaning. Classical references are pervasive in Cummings's notes, but often trivial. The loudness of a voice relates to Solon in the Athenian assembly; a scarlet-clad cardinal at Notre-Dame has a face like Caesar. At other times, the embrace of the classics went far deeper. All of art or all of history might be comprehended in its juxtaposition to the classical world. Cézanne had achieved the roundness that had escaped the Greeks, and Virgil's epic *Aeneid* was the poetic prism that refracted and clarified the great watersheds of history.

Virgil himself aimed to create in Latin an epic poem that could cope with and even rival the legacy of Homer in Greek. His *Aeneid* embodied the aspirations and ambivalences of the Roman Empire in the age of Augustus. In his *Divine Comedy*, Dante had made Virgil his guide through Hell and Purgatory. Dante's *Divine Comedy* was an obsession for the modernists, and, via Dante, Virgil stood as guide in the largest sense—a guide to history, to literature, to humanity. For a generation of modernists, the *Aeneid* stood for empire, the stormy shaking of the world, and the twilight of an era. Ezra Pound, Dos Passos, T. S. Eliot, and others each carved out their own individual take on Virgil. Pound figured Virgil as "Phoebus' chief of police," the bureaucratized enforcer to Phoebus Apollo, god of the sun, who was associated with the very most ordered kind of classicism: proportion, decorum, and humane elegance. The Great War was the crashing down of that Virgilian world order. For Dos Passos, the epic order of the *Aeneid* barely contained its own chaos, in which the storms and threats of the natural world mirror the brutal carnage of war. Caught once unprepared in a small boat on the Mediterranean, Dos found that it was Virgil who came to him in a perilous moment: "Suddenly it seemed like one of those windstorms in Vergil's *Aeneid* when the winds blow from all directions at once." Eliot found Virgil abundant in intellectual value but short of compassion. Virgil offered "a civilized world of dignity, reason and order," and in Virgil's poetry, "the world made sense . . . history had meaning." Yet Virgil lacked the fullness of love. "If we are not chilled we at least feel ourselves, with Virgil, to be moving in a kind of emotional twilight."

Cummings too sensed an end of something Virgilian, a twilight of an old order, which he wrote about in one of his most brilliant war poems. The fresh voice he sought through the combination of synesthesia and exact observation brings to life a wartime Parisian evening invaded by "a twilight smelling of Vergil." The poem is written as a broken-form sonnet, and Virgil's Latin hexameters—the meter of his epic poem—trample through the broken English form just as his unpleasant, militaristic twilight marches through a room above the streets of Montmartre.

> through the tasteless minute efficient room
> march hexameters of unpleasant
> twilight,a twilight smelling of Vergil,
> as me bang(to and from)
> the huggering rags of white Latin flesh
> which her body sometimes isn't
> (all night,always,a warm incessant gush
> of furious Paris flutters up the hill,
> cries somethings laughters loves nothings float
> upward,beautifully,forces crazily rhyme,
> Montmartre s'amuse!obscure eyes hotly dote
> . . . . as awkwardly toward me for the millionth time
> sidles the ruddy rubbish of her kiss
> i taste upon her mouth cabs and taxis.

Cummings has captured the distinctive architecture of South Pigalle, where many women lived in rooms just such as this. High buildings permeated with the smell of a dive offered floor above floor governed by long, dirty corridors. A shared toilet was a tight squeeze, with terrible plumbing, and too small to keep legs and arms out of contact with the dank walls. Each rented room might be barely large enough for a bed and, perhaps, a sink, a basic dresser, or a chair. A woman alone might live in—and in the case of a prostitute—work in such a room.

Against these dingy interiors, light streams in from the huge rectangular windows that are typical of the quarter. The gaping window utterly dwarfs the room. Shutters open wide, allowing a block of light uninterrupted by windowpanes. Only across the bottom of a nearly floor-to-ceiling window would an ironwork grille interrupt the ivory-bright light, which bounces off the white walls of buildings opposite, across narrow streets. From such streets, the sounds and smells and air float upward just as Cummings describes. The street itself seems to disappear, as the gaps are too narrow to see anything of street-level unless leaning out of the window to look right down. The white light is so bright and penetrates a dingy room with such power that it seems to carry the voices in with it, almost as if the light were the vehicle of the sound. Then as night falls and the voices begin to rise through the dark, they seem disembodied, airy—things in themselves.

Although Cummings wrote his broken sonnet later, from memory, in 1918, it echoes the notes he made in his notebooks in May and June.

> striding the rising boulevard in warm silent darkness of the evening filled with smiles in cafes,drinking and smoking and loving,huge heavy feet of little perspiring soldiers on perm [*permission*] with great sticks and musettes and capotes and crazed faces, assaults of floating softness and little perfumed voices just brushing the heart

For Cummings, the vitality of Paris bulges in the face of the war. That bulge, that three-dimensionality he aspired to, is shaped in the poem against the backdrop of the classical world. The woman of the poem herself exists as a synesthetic blurring of language, sex, and war. Her "white Latin flesh," which her body "sometimes isn't," but therefore by inference also sometimes is, makes a living, fleshly Latin embodiment of the Latin language in which Virgil wrote his hexameters. On her mouth, which tastes of the "cabs and taxis" of Paris, Cummings

1. Cummings as a baby with his mother, Rebecca Haswell Cummings.

2. Cummings as a boy with his father, Rev. Edward Cummings, and his sister, Elizabeth.

3. *A Heading for February. By Edward Estlin Cummings. Age 9.* Ink over pencil, by E. E. Cummings.

4. Cummings with Elizabeth on the family's donkey at Joy Farm, New Hampshire.

5. Cummings with his sister, Elizabeth, and his dog, Rex,
at Joy Farm, New Hampshire.

6. Boating on Silver Lake, New Hampshire.

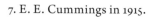
7. E. E. Cummings in 1915.

8. Cummings's first girlfriend, Doris Bryan,
posing with Cummings's rival for her affections, Billy Shaw.

9–10. Advertisements for volunteer American drivers for transport and ambulance services during the Great War.

11. Postcard (from 1918) of *La Touraine*, the ship on which Cummings crossed the Atlantic to France in April–May 1917.

12–13. Two sketches of
Marie Louise Lallemand.
Pencil in a notebook
from France, 1917,
by E. E. Cummings.

14. Sketch of Marie Louise sleeping.
Pencil in a notebook from France, 1917, by E. E. Cummings.

15–16. Two sketches
of Marie Louise's
friend Mimi. Pencil
in a notebook from
France, 1917, by
E. E. Cummings.

17–18. Marie Louise Lallemand to E. E. Cummings. Letter of July 8, 1917 (*above*). Letters of August 31, 1917, and September 7, 1917 (*left*).

19. E. E. Cummings at the front in the summer of 1917. Photograph taken by William Slater Brown.

Brown asleep

20. *Brown asleep.* Pencil sketch of William Slater Brown in a notebook from France, 1917, by E. E. Cummings.

21. *Germaine*. Pencil sketch from the front in a notebook
from France, 1917, by E. E. Cummings.

22. *La marche*. Pencil sketch of soldiers on the march in a notebook
from France, 1917, by E. E. Cummings.

23. An example of the monitoring of correspondence by wartime censors. Pictured here is the envelope of a letter sent by Estlin Carpenter from Oxford (England) to Rev. Edward Cummings at 104 Irving Street.

LA FERTÉ-MACÉ. — *Le Petit Séminaire*   *Collections ND. Phot.*

24. Postcard of the seminary that became the prison at La Ferté-Macé. The "enormous room" occupied the top floor of the wing to viewer's left.

25. Cummings's color palette. Notebook from La Ferté-Macé, 1917.

26. E. E. Cummings in 1918.

27. *Untitled* [Sexual embrace].
Pencil sketch by E. E. Cummings.

28. *Untitled* [Sexual posture].
Pencil sketch by E. E.
Cummings.

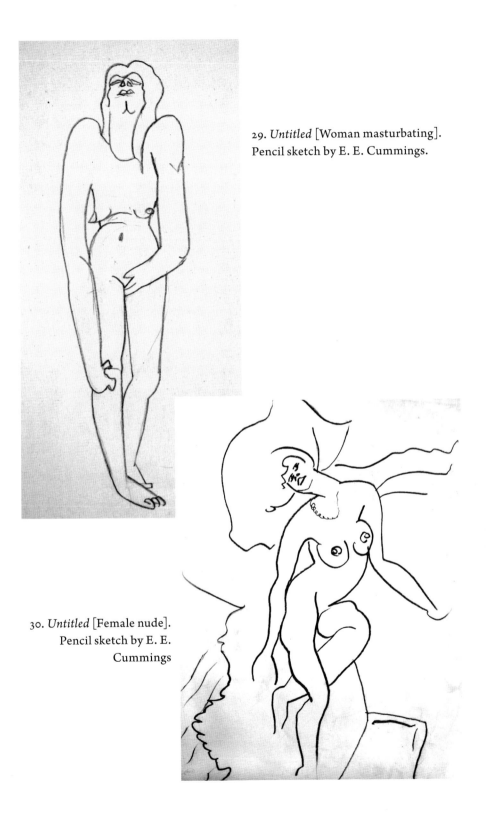

29. *Untitled* [Woman masturbating].
Pencil sketch by E. E. Cummings.

30. *Untitled* [Female nude].
Pencil sketch by E. E.
Cummings

31. *Untitled* [Scofield Thayer]. Pencil sketch by E. E. Cummings.

32. *Untitled* [Scofield Thayer]. Pencil sketch by E. E. Cummings.

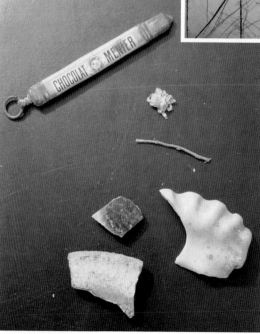
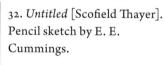

33. Mementos kept by Cummings from La Ferté-Macé: a pencil stub, a daisy head separated from its stem, and three pieces of broken glass.

puns also on the Greek word *taxis*: a broad word for form or order, encompassing everything from the order of ancient battle formations to literary form. It is the root of the English word, "syntax." A taxi has a long *i*, but the Greek *taxis* is a short *i*, and rhymes with "kiss." The rhyme scheme of the poem slowly tightens to pull the reader inexorably into the final pun. The rhyme of the first two quatrains is loose: *a b c a*, and the *a* is only half-rhyme (room/from); then *d e d f*, using another half-rhyme (flesh/gush). But the last six lines move into full rhyme along one variant of an expected sonnet scheme: *g h g h* (float/dote, rhyme/time); and the couplet, *i i* (kiss/*taxis*). It is this tightening of the rhyme scheme that pulls the *i* short, and creates the pun on the Greek—indeed, on the Greek word for "order" precisely as it pulls the poem into the ordered rhyme. Cummings's sonnet leaves his reader, on his final word, with the thought that the kiss of the woman contains both the taste of syntax and the taste of war.

The poem is literature, not autobiography. It goes further in sexual experience than Cummings ever went with Marie Louise. There was one night together though—a night that Cummings called at the time the best night of his life. What form of sexual encounter they shared that night is not known, but we do know of an intimate conversation about themselves and their pasts.

Marie Louise thought that Cummings was young, and after all a man, and impervious to the pain of love and life. She thought that he would forget her. 'I have suffered much all my life," she told him. "It's always been men: *alors, ça ne fait rien* (never mind, it makes no difference)." She told him that he had not suffered.

He tried to write to her afterward, to say what he had been unable to say at the time. He wanted her forgiveness, but he also said that if he had hurt her, then he suffered too. It was not possible to cause suffering without feeling it. He struggled to draft his note; probably he never gave it to her. He wrote, in French: "you say you suffer and that I have never suffered in love. And I replied nothing. I knew you were right. But I also suffer perhaps a little. You say, no. You are right; but you are also wrong. You are right: I am not worthy to say I have felt that pain. You have said it: nothing is equal to your sufferings.

O joyous young girl! But if the pain lies in knowing that you have lost your right to a life. . . ." Then Cummings's French grammar failed him: "One cannot lose what does not exist"? Or "one does not lose except by existing"? Or "to exist is to lose"? His French by now was excellent, and it disintegrates only where he most struggled to know what he wanted to say. Through him, we also hear her. "I have lost my right to a life."

It is clear that Cummings did not know how to respond to such pain. Throughout his letters to Marie Louise, he says again and again how *gentille*, how kind she has been, and how he is cruel, *méchant*. He transmits his own fear that he did not know how to be a lover. He refers to something thoughtless, hurtful that he once said to her, and how she had told him that he would regret that remark someday, and now he does. But more deeply, his persistent fear that he was cruel, had been cruel, held him back from opening himself up fully to her.

He could not find a way of expressing to Marie Louise how absorbed he was by her. His life in America was falling away from his mind. Everything for him was alive in Paris: with her, with the beautiful Parisian summer days, the long walks, the world of art and cafés and restaurants, and the people to observe and to draw and to overhear.

13

SIN

CUMMINGS AND BROWN had plenty to do in Paris. Calling in at the Norton-Harjes headquarters for updates. Obtaining full identity documents. They both had to have photos taken for their ID cards. "Cummings reacted so violently to the magnesium flashlight held by the photographer that he had to be photographed again in a calmer mood," said Brown. Cummings could afford this time living at the Hôtel du Palais, dining in cafés and restaurants, seeing all the shows, and buying books and art prints, because his father had supplied him with funds in the form of a letter of credit. It was a merited gesture of support for a young man undertaking wartime service on behalf of his country. It was not made free of strings: the Reverend expected, in exchange, a certain access to Cummings's life. He hoped, too, that Cummings would connect with his godfather, the Reverend's old friend Estlin Carpenter, in England.

Fulfilling his duties as godfather, Carpenter used to write to Cummings from time to time, in a kindly and old-fashioned manner. When Cummings had been a child of six or seven, Carpenter rather sweetly wrote to him in block capitals, so that he could read more easily for himself. Now that Cummings was an adult, he used his natural hand: the hand of a man who took delight in the formalities of an era already passing. He formed his *s*'s in the archaic or German manner, with the first of any double *s* penned like an *f*. He called his godson and namesake "Estlin minor" and sometimes signed himself as "Estlin major."

Carpenter's attitude toward the Great War is by now such a cliché of the home front that it seems almost a parody. He wrote to the Cummings family at Irving Street and congratulated Cummings's mother for having "shed no tear" as *La Touraine* sailed. He commended both Rebecca and the Reverend: "You give gladly of your best for the cause of liberty." And he was certain that their son would be improved, "the richer & more capable for this new experience of helpfulness." Meanwhile, Carpenter also wrote directly to Cummings, c/o the Norton-Harjes headquarters at 7 Rue François 1er, offering energetic platitudes about the entry of America into the war, excusing himself for not having located (at the Reverend's request) a suitable pair of light field glasses, and urging Cummings to visit in England, where he lived in Oxford at 11 Marston Ferry Road, before the European sojourn was over.

Carpenter's address was one of the only entries in a nearly empty address book that Cummings took with him to France. Cummings did not, however, bother to get in touch. Instead he crammed the tiny, leather-bound address book full of even tinier micro-drawings, a few centimeters in dimension, irregularly cut from stiff paper and jammed in for safekeeping.

He did write home to his parents when he could, but not enough to satisfy his father—although the censors' interference with some of his letters leaves him hardly to blame for insufficiency of news. These vagaries of transatlantic postal service and censorship left father and son communicating on a significant delay. The Reverend wrote the following tart missive on the twenty-eighth of June, replying to a letter from his son dated to the seventh, and he wrote in ignorance of Cummings's departure from Paris in the interim.

Rev. Edward Cummings to E. E. Cummings.

June 28, 1917.

Dear Chub:

I am thankful to say your letter of June 7th came this morning as I was about to send a brief note to you by Sibley Watson. Sibley telegraphed yesterday that he was going to sail on Saturday, the 30th of June, and offered to take letters to you. Unfortunately your mother is at Martha's Vineyard visiting Gay Schuyler Webb, so she probably won't be able to avail herself of Sibley's good post offices. I am also giving Sibley a letter of introduction to Richard Norton, stating that you and he are inseparable friends, and therefore ought to be put together for the satisfaction given to you and Sibley, and incidentally your respective families. It would certainly be great good fortune if you two fellows could work together. Possibly we might hear from you indirectly now and then by way of Watson's family.

You will be sorry to learn that Professor Langford Warren died unexpectedly yesterday. Jimmie and all the rest of the family, except Arthur, were there when I called this morning. Fortunately Jimmie had not been called to the Naval Reserve at Newport, but Arthur is at Plattsburg.

I suppose Mother told you of the engagement of your neighbor, Betty Thaxter, to a classmate of yours named Hubbard, the son of Old Mother H. no doubt. Wedding some time in August. Wear your uniform if you decide to come.

By the way, before you spend the last centime of that letter of credit (it seems to be slipping through your fingers like the proverbial sands)—be sure and buy another set of pictures of yourself in uniform, full length. No matter if the cap does do some injustice to your noble countenance. In fact, while you are about it you had better get a good picture and send it over.

Incidentally, drafts on your letter of credit are as regular and frequent as your letters are irregular and infrequent. The fourth one came this morning. Evidently you do not find a letter of credit as superfluous as you thought it would be when I urged one upon you. Perhaps you have been taking my advice, making the most of your preliminary freedom to get acquainted with contemporary France. The genial Mr. Riddell in charge of Lee, Higginson's letter of credit department, whose acquaintance you made, comforts me by saying, "they won't come so fast after he gets into the field. There is very little opportunity for using money there."

Your letters, with that fine disdain of financial affairs which characterizes the aristocrat, have never referred to any of these letter of credit drafts, but I take it for granted they are all right. May I suggest, however, that letter of credit communications are not as interesting reading when they come alone as they would be accompanied by letters of the ordinary sort. If you purpose keeping up the present rate of draft for a few weeks longer until the letter is exhausted, kindly let me know so that I can leave adequate deposits to meet the payments.

If you had been more communicative so that your devoted family knew whether you liked your letters best with or without socks, cigarettes, chocolate, and other alleviations, Watson would probably have been loaded up with a lot of additional plunder. Perhaps the censor has abstracted the socks and the cigarettes and the chocolate. If so, word to that effect with directions as to the method of circumventing him would not come amiss.

We think of you constantly. Think of us now and then and put your thoughts on a post-card and direct it to your mother. Time does not go so fast at this end of the line as it does at yours. You say you have lost all sense of time and space, but ours has been correspondingly intensified and exaggerated. VERBUM SAP!

I am glad Estlin Carpenter has written to you. Be sure and let him hear now and then. If you get a furlough bye and bye, arrange to go to him in England if you can. I am told it is difficult going across the Channel and that it takes a good many days to get the necessary passport and opportunity for transport, but it will be worth trying. Anyhow, send him a line now and then.

Take the best care of yourself. We are all well, and all send a great deal of love.

With best wishes,

    Affectionately,

    [Signed] E Cummings

    D D

[Handwritten]
Have a Heart!
Be a sport!!
Write!!!

The Reverend's drily critical tone was felt much more sharply at the receiving end. The relationship between father and son juddered against delays of communication and belatedness of news, but it is clear that the Reverend's persistent complaints and undermining attitude continued to gnaw at Cummings. At some point Cummings drafted a long, mock letter from father to son, laying out in painful detail the respects in which he felt himself to be a disappointment in his father's eyes. The letter is written into one of Cummings's French notebooks and it was composed either during his time in France or immediately afterward; if the latter, it reflects the emotions of this earlier period. It is full of chastisement of Cummings's life at Harvard and before the war, making no mention of what was about to come— his time at the front or in prison.

This mock letter pulls no punches. Mimicking his father's biblical register, Cummings writes: "had I known a son of mine would turn out so I'd have spilled my seed upon the ground rather than beget him." The letter outlines the fall from grace of a charmed child. As a boy, he was sensitive and idealistic. But he went wrong. He went to college and he succumbed to selfishness, laziness, drink, tobacco, and bad company. He neglected himself physically and ignored his father's prayers. His father begged him to give up alcohol for his mother's sake and—adding an almost comic (from the outside) instantiation of the principle of a healthy mind in a healthy body—to spend more time at the gym. A man is, after all, judged by the appearance he presents to the world. In the imagination of the letter, his father piles on the emotional blackmail. "I threatened, I begged . . . You spiritually spit in my face. I cried to you: Treat me like a dog, me your father . . . but for God's sake remember your mother, who went down to the Gates of Hell to get you. . . ." These words echo the fight of Christmas 1916, which was still clearly raw. "You answered in your cavalier way that it is not your fault that you were born." But "<u>you do not belong to yourself.</u>"

The letter also reveals Cummings's awareness of the Reverend's controlling relationship with Rebecca as well as his determination to control his son. "Your mother wanted to have more children, but I said to her, we will have only 2 children, but they shall be Eagles." On and on the letter goes, citing the sacrifices made by the Reverend and Rebecca for him and excoriating his dissolute lifestyle and dubious friendships. It chastises Cummings further for cutting himself out of his parents' life. The Reverend had offered him nothing but patience in the face of his criminal laziness, and yet he withdrew from the family. He would not afford his parents the pleasure of partaking in his life or grant his father the pleasure of the companionship of a like-minded son. The litany of disappointment ends in threats. If he fails to renounce his unmanly, lazy, and worthless ways, the fate in store for him is "blacker than any man-enriched Hell, which the human mind has ever been able to conceive."

This viciously ventriloquized "letter" from the Reverend distils the head-on crash of Cummings's rebellion and his self-blame. That same struggle is mirrored in his relationship with Marie Louise, where Cummings wavered between guilt and the deliciousness of transgression. He began work on a poem, "cherie, I suggest we've sinned / against the world." Although he abandoned these lines, he returned to their imagery, some years later, when he reworked and polished the idea into a light imagining of himself doomed at Judgment Day to the same circle of hell as the famous lovers Paolo and Francesca in Dante's *Divine Comedy*. That poem (which was only published posthumously) has a frothy nonchalance about the Day of Judgment:

(when all the clocks have lost their jobs and god
sits up quickly to judge the Big Sinners)
he will have something large and fluffy to say
to me.

He draws the sting from the fright of hell, with perverse embrace of the realm where "fiends with pitchforkthings / will catch and toss me lovingly to / and fro." The prospect of eternal punishment offers a joyful frame for celebrating the thought of two lovers pitted against the world. Cummings toys lightly with damnation. But he was descended from a hellfire tradition, and the mock letter shows how deeply Cummings could feel the weight of moral condemnation at the same time that he advertised his own defiance.

PART IV

THE FRONT

June 15, 1917–September 21, 1917

—

14

CALLED FOR SERVICE

THE TIME WITH Marie Louise in Paris was nearing its close. The rest of the Americans who had come over on *La Touraine* had long since moved on to postings. The processes of the Norton-Harjes ambulance headquarters were something of a mystery, arguably even to itself. Cummings had no eagerness to leave Paris, but he and Brown dutifully called in at headquarters from time to time. They met only the repeated assertion that uniforms would arrive soon and that they could not be deployed until then. Around the fourth of June, the arrival of a uniform for Brown heralded the beginning of the end of their Parisian freedom. Then the second uniform arrived for Cummings: a khaki affair, in good quality, heavy cloth, fleeced inside the coat for warmth and comfort. The puttees (leg wraps) and the leather belt that should have accompanied the uniform were still missing, and Cummings had to buy these at his own expense—a considerable one, given the wartime shortages. And now, at last, the bureaucracy of the ambulance service swung into action. In the arbitrary way that the bureaucrat has of characterizing his victims as miscreants, the powers that be construed the delay as the fault of Cummings and Brown, and the director of the service in Paris expressed himself personally as most unimpressed with the pair of them. "Mr. Harjes himself called us in and had us on the carpet," said Brown. "He asked us, in so many words, whether we had been having a good time in Paris, and kicking up our heels for an entire month, and we replied, in so many words, yes. The next thing we knew, we were driving ambulances together at the Front."

In fact, when they left Paris for the front, they did not really believe that they were going for good. After so many delays, they assumed that they would, as like as not, be back within a couple of days. So Cummings left without waking Marie Louise. Mimi was awake, and he said his goodbyes to her. He left a little money and he voiced the insecurities that plagued him throughout his time with Marie Louise. He said that he would understand if she was through with him, and that Mimi was to look after her for him, that night especially, for he did love her. Mimi tried to reassure him that Marie Louise loved him as well, but he brushed it off. Not possible, he said. Mimi was a sweet liar.

At the Red Cross in Paris, they left a part of their luggage, including their precious prints of Cézanne, Picasso, and Matisse, which they never imagined were left behind only to be mislaid and lost forever. Then they boarded their train almost due north to Creil, and then from Creil north and east to Noyon, in the *département* of Oise.

Noyon would come to be one of the most fateful places in Cummings's life, although on this, the first time he passed through, it seemed a merely incidental location.

Noyon was more municipal than anywhere that Cummings had yet encountered in France. A love of midlevel bureaucracy and small power can be felt distinctly in the architecture of the central municipal building, the Hôtel de Ville. This civic edifice today exhibits an only moderately successful marriage of a frilly central Gothic façade with wings built in a cleaner, squarer style at either side. These square modern additions replace a narrow annex that once clung to the building on the right and a hodgepodge agglomeration once extending forward at 90 degrees on the left, both destroyed by German bombs in 1918 but still standing in 1917 when Cummings arrived. The Hôtel de Ville, which now services a town population of around 15,000, has been in all eras but a pale relative to Noyon's genuinely grand cathedral, where Charlemagne was once crowned king of the Franks.

Noyon had fallen under German occupation on the thirtieth of August, 1914, merely weeks into the war. When the Germans invaded, they were operating according to the so-called Schlieffen Plan. The brainchild of the German field marshal Alfred von Schlieffen, it had been conceived about ten years before the outbreak of war itself. Schlieffen's plan of strategically ideal invasion projected a rapid march across Belgium and through northern France, so that the Germans could then swing around the western side of Paris and finally turn 180 degrees upon a French Army now trapped from its natural rear and pinned back against its own defensive structures at the French frontier. There it would face another portion of the German Army that had marched directly to that frontier, and in this way the French Army would find itself sandwiched and could stand no chance. However, when the Germans adopted this plan for action in 1914, they conveniently deleted Schlieffen's own stipulation that German manpower was insufficient to execute his grand plan.

The German Army, overstretched, indeed failed to encircle Paris. Instead, they were met by the French Army, whose reinforcements reached regions to the north and east of Paris more rapidly than the Schlieffen Plan allowed for. And so, entrenchment began and the western front coalesced in northeastern France. When the German lines settled, Noyon fell just inside the perimeter of a salient—an arcing bulge outward in the German line. Though not even ten miles from French-controlled territory and the French side of the front, to be occupied was to be cut off. Throughout occupied France, the Germans forbade contact between the occupied population and the French Army. Only smuggled letters could bring news of sons, husbands, brothers who had already left to join the army in the weeks before northeastern France was taken. Food in occupied Noyon was rationed. The Hôtel de Ville was confiscated and turned into a headquarters for the German entourage. A new sign in the German language, "Offiziers—Kasino," hung over one of its arched entranceways and designated the German officers' mess.

In 1916, after two years of war, the Germans and the British each undertook a major offensive. In each case, it was ultimately disastrous. The German offensive at Verdun and the French counterattack lasted from February to November. The Germans sustained casualties of over 300,000 and cost the Allies the same. Meanwhile, on the British section of the front, the offensive at the Somme in the summer of 1916 led to more than 400,000 British casualties and more than 200,000 German casualties. This year of brutal fighting ended without strategic gains on the western front for either side, and both sides lost faith in their overall commanders. The British commander, General Haig, kept his command but no longer enjoyed the confidence of the new British prime minister, Lloyd George. The generals at the top of both the French and the German Armies lost their commands. The top job in France went to General Robert Nivelle, who was deemed to have acquitted himself well in subordinate command at Verdun, while overall command in Germany was handed to two generals promoted from the eastern front: Erich Ludendorff and Paul von Hindenburg.

Under the new command of Ludendorff and Hindenburg, the German Army on the western front gradually withdrew from strategically insignificant bulges of occupied territory, reducing a meandering perimeter, profligate of German resources, to a straighter front line with far stronger defenses: the new Hindenburg Line. Among the abandoned bulges was the Noyon salient. Thus, on March 17, 1917, after two years and six and a half months of occupation, Noyon was restored to the French. It was scarcely three months later that Cummings arrived in the town.

In keeping with his new habits, Cummings sketched to capture the essence of Noyon in his notebook. His sketches of Noyon are rigid, with a tense and terse quality to the pencil lines. There is sorrow in the gentle and flowing sketches that Cummings made subsequently from the front itself; but at Noyon, anger. He sketched a small stone house with such a sharp and abrupt back wall that it looks as though a normal house has been sliced in half. He sketched a man sitting on a bench behind a hut and a tree, drinking wine from a teacup, viewed coldly from the back, turned away. At the Hôtel de Ville, Cummings sketched the imposing archway that led onto the pissoir. Below his sketch, he made a careful note of the graffitied record of a French prisoner—his name, his father's name and his mother's, his date and place of birth, his appearance, black eyes, average nose, and his sentence: two years for refusal of obedience and desertion. From the stairway at the Hôtel de Ville, he assiduously copied another piece of graffiti. This one depicted two tonsured monks. One of the monks is pictured from behind, though his obscenely grinning face twists around toward the viewer. He stoops forward and his monastic habit is wrenched up around his waist as he defecates profusely into the outstretched hand of the second monk. Cummings observed it with detachment, and added in his notebook the query: "was other monk pissing?"

But for all the heavy atmosphere of the place, there was no harbinger of the role that Noyon would play in the lives of Cummings and Brown in another three months' time. For the moment, their relationship with the town was perfunctory. A considerable number of American volunteers had been instructed to report to Noyon. They were assembled on arrival. From amongst those who had trained out, five were to be sent to the front and the rest would return to Paris to wait again for another call-up. Selection was arbitrary; Cummings and Brown landed among the five. Cummings was chagrined at how unprepared they were for deployment, lacking even tobacco. But there was nothing for it now. They were formally enlisted in the ambulance corps, in the French *section sanitaire*, in the unit designated as SSU XXI.

15

AT THE FRONT

THE REALIZATION THAT he had left Paris for real, and not for a boomerang return to that glaringly vivid city, was a wrench long remembered. Years later, in the autobiographical lectures he gave at Harvard in the 1950s, Cummings talked of having come truly alive in Paris for the first time. "While (at the hating touch of some madness called La Guerre) a once rising and striving world toppled into withering hideously smithereens, love rose in my heart like a sun and beauty blossomed in my life like a star. Now, finally and first, I was myself: a temporal citizen of eternity; one with all human beings born and unborn."

The momentous nature of deployment to the front was beginning to sink in: Cummings, who almost never dated his sketches, drew in his notebook five men lazing in a field and penciled in 6/15/17—the exact date of his deployment, the fifteenth of June, 1917.

Following the selection at Noyon, Cummings, Brown, and the others who had been chosen were conveyed by military truck straight to the camp of their new unit. Here, under the command of an American named Mr. Phillips, were the twenty cars and the manpower who comprised SSU XXI—roughly (give or take those who left and those who arrived) forty Americans, two per car, and eight Frenchmen who assisted the unit as mechanics and cooks.

When Cummings and the others arrived at camp, they arrived either to the primary encampment near Ham—a settlement about one-third the size of Noyon and lying twelve miles further from Noyon toward the front—or to Germaine, one of the unit's more forward positions. In any case, they were at Germaine by the eighteenth of June. The unit moved every few weeks, and Cummings's itinerary can only be reconstructed in approximation. Exact records violated the need for military discretion. In fact, Cummings's letters to his parents are obliquely coded in an effort to satisfy their anxiety as to his whereabouts without triggering the censor's pen. He found himself in "a place hardly germain to my malcontent nature" (Germaine) and then subsequently "a place SO quiet that Dickens' 'little Nell' might be read as daily work" (Nesle).

These villages and hamlets that Cummings came to know over the summer months all lay in the region so recently recovered in early 1917 from German occupation. When the Germans completed their strategic withdrawal to the new Hindenburg Line, they ceded an area of approximately 1,000 square miles, or, around the size of the state of Vermont. As they retreated, the German Army adopted a scorched-earth policy. SSU XXI operated within this scarred territory, serving the new French front line.

The very next morning after his arrival, as soon as he had a moment, Cummings's thoughts turned to Marie Louise, and he wandered out alone past the edge of the camp in order to write to her.

Cummings's correspondence with Marie Louise is worlds beyond his playful attachment to Doris or his careful letters to Elaine. He had not forgotten Elaine: he toyed with an epistolary poem to Scofield Thayer (another of his compositions in French), in which he imagined himself and Thayer reunited and nodded to the pleasure of seeing Elaine again. But in this distance from his American circle, his whole emotion now centered on Marie Louise.

In his letters to her, Cummings often reproached himself for cruelty. It is never clear whether he is referring to the inequality in the sexual aspect of their relationship or to his generally cynical take on life. He still dwelt remorsefully on that thoughtless remark (whatever it was) that he once made to her. Perhaps, too, he felt that his struggle to express his own emotions was a kind of cruelty. He was working in his notebooks on a delicate poetry of cruel love, including beautiful, lyrical poems like the one that opens:

> cruelly,love
> walk the autumn long;
> the last flower in whose hair,
> thy lips are cold with songs

What was poignant in his poetry was more self-loathing in real life. There were barriers between Cummings and Marie Louise, and one of them was his fixed belief that he was too cruel to deserve her love.

Their relationship began across a social barrier. His love for her broke every taboo of Cambridge society, and her love for him complicated her life as a working prostitute. As their relationship deepened, they faced other, more emotional barriers. From that night together when they spoke of her past and his, it is possible to see much of what stood between them. The very fact that Cummings could say so little at the time, and tried only later to write out what he had been unable to say, speaks volumes. From her perspective, living with her own history of damage at the hands of men and supporting herself as a sex worker during the war, she saw reflected in Cummings much that had been denied to her. He was a man. He was young. He had his whole life ahead of him and a chance to live it as he wanted.

Her own unhappiness and anger at her life clearly left Cummings unable to believe that she could be serious in her feelings for him. But while he agonized about her feelings, nonetheless, he did not retreat; he plunged forward. He took his notebook, found a field full of those red poppies that are the iconic imagery of the Great War, and wrote from the heart.

My Marie Louise, my precious darling.
You will excuse me, I write to you on a page from my notebook
because I have no more paper for writing.

   You must understand that we did not take the train at 8:00 this
morning because of the stupidity of the unit's sub-commander. So
I had to wait until 1:00 in the afternoon in Paris. I lie down under
a willow tree with exquisite leaves, on the bank of the Seine, and I
think of you and of Mimi, and I hope that you sleep well, both of
you. At 1:00 we took the train for Creil, it's a bad train, not direct,
and always sluggish. We waited more than two hours at Creil for
the train to Noyon, where we arrived at 7:00 in the evening. A truck
brought us from Noyon to here. Was I ever hungry, and did I ever
eat! I promise you, I'm still embarrassed by it. Afterwards, it was
9:00, I take a little stroll away from everyone. The day closed with the
rain which I love, and I think of another rain, and of that night when
we three curled up in one bed.

   The next day, that is to say, today, it is beautiful, I walk in the
field, with constantly trembling poppies which weep butterflies. In
the brutal sky, larks invisible chatter: my heart, which grieves for
the contentment which is gone, remembers mysteries. It seems to
me that we were lost in a great, strange wood, a funny and curved
wood, which leads to lakes where the snowy swans swim, and where
the earnest chaps fish, and where the joyful and innocent children
dance. And I hear a voice which says: "You know well the small, chic
recesses, don't you?"

   I told you that we will leave here soon and while I write, an old
man who smokes an enormous pipe mows the field with the scarlet
poppies, and he tells me that this is to make a road, and that the
eleventh infantry corps is expected; in other words, the corps for
which we drive is going to depart immediately. And now they say to
me that we will be leaving at 5.00 in the morning for Nesle, where we
will stay for several weeks in reserve with nothing to do, or perhaps
several days only—no one knows.

   Darling, you know well that I cannot write those things, precious
and extravagant, which Love puts in the heart of the lover. Darling,

> *Marie Louise, you who are more to me than the scarlet poppies which are mown, more than the yellowing evenings which we see die, more than the silence full of stars, the completely white silence of night, only awaiting dawn, — take the kiss which I give you, that kiss, without value, because it comes from a soul which loves you.*
>   *Edouard*

He wrote, of course, in French, which he could manage fluidly though with some minor errors. He always drafted his letters several times, partly in order to find what he wanted to say and partly to work out how best to say it in French. It is these notebook drafts that now survive.

Cummings's unit operated a three-day rotation: one day on post, one day on call, and one day off. To be "on post" meant a day (and a night) in a forward position away from the camp and nearer to the trenches, usually sitting (and sleeping) in a parked car, waiting to act if needed and otherwise waiting to be relieved in twenty-four hours by the next rota. The normal daily schedule was simple: they rose at 7:15 a.m., they had three meals a day, and they turned in for the night at 10:00 p.m. On their day off, they were at their own liberty.

Cummings and Brown spent their free days exploring. On one occasion, they nearly walked straight into no-man's-land. They did not realize that the sound they heard overhead was the sound of the machine guns, and they were only saved by the timely intervention of a Frenchman who shouted them back. This near miss must have been early in their time at the front, because Cummings soon recognized the sounds of the war and the whistling of the shells.

It was a little while before he saw his first bombs, for once falling thrillingly close—about 50 meters from his car. He told Marie Louise that this first shelling had pleased him immensely, bursting like small birds all above them, and he reported to his father that the bomb closest to the car had left a crater 2 by 3 meters wide. His excited reaction was not unusual. Many found their first sight and sound of guns enthralling and stimulating. Wilfred Owen, although he is responsible for the most famous poetic indictments of the war in "Dulce et Decorum Est" and other wrenchingly scathing poems, thought when he heard the guns for the first time: "It was a sound not without a certain sublimity."

Cummings returned to the sound of cannon in a war poem that he finished after his return from the war and signed Xmas '18:

> the bigness of cannon
> is skilful,
>
> but i have seen
> death's clever enormous voice
> which hides in a fragility
> of poppies. . . .
>
> i say that sometimes
> on these long talkative animals
> are laid fists of huger silence.
>
> I have seen all the silence
> filled with vivid noiseless boys
>
> at Roupy
> i have seen
> between barrages,
>
> the night utter ripe unspeaking girls.

It is noticeable that the cannon and the nocturnal barrage are brought within the poem's lyrical tone, not excluded from it. For numerous war poets, one of the complications of their war experience was the feeling of awe. Shelling had a perverse beauty. A night barrage would flash the sky. The cannon and the poppies, the talk of the guns and the silence are poised in intimate communion.

Not only did guns talk in the war; they could even sing. Cummings wrote of the "shell-song" to his mother. Robert Graves wrote of a different "singing," shared between the British and the German lines. "There was a daily exchange of courtesies between our machine-guns and the Germans' at stand-to; by removing cartridges from the ammunition-belt one could rap out the rhythm of the familiar prostitutes' call: 'MEET me DOWN in PICC-a-DILL-y', to which the Germans would reply, though in slower tempo, because our guns were faster than theirs: 'YES, with-OUT my DRAWERS ON!'"

Cummings was caught in a gas attack early in July, and he wrote to Marie Louise about the sight of the wounded and about shelling and the sounds of war. He also wrote to Thayer and to his mother about coming under fire at Jussy, where he was posted sometime in late July. The shelling at Jussy tested the nerves: the Germans were dropping bombs daily into a field just over 200 yards distant from the ambulance camp. It seems that Jussy was less conducive to the reflection and sketching that were Cummings's passions that summer. Of all the main places where Cummings's unit was stationed, only Jussy is not sketched: other locations appear in his notebooks, distilled into the images that capture what each place meant to him. At Germaine, a dark and poignant stone cross commands the center of a field. At Nesle, sloping canvass tents are clustered in amongst the trees in their tall columns. At Roupy, the wind blows through a mishmash of trees that tower over a small, flat bridge along the road.

In this region of Picardy, as in Paris, the French poplars defined the land. Two kinds of poplars filled the treescape: white poplars, whose leaves in the wind flap their underside, bright white almost like a little man came around regularly to polish them, and Lombardy poplars, the tall paintbrush trees that draw the eye no matter what other foliage surrounds them. Graves regarded it as "fun to see the poplar-trees being lopped down like tulips when the whizz-bangs hit them square." If literary history had gone a different way, it could have been the poplar rather than the poppy that embodied the destruction of the Great War.

Cummings's notes are full of scratchy ideas about poplars.

poplars are,
talking to the
sunset of my love;who
is perfectly walking

shivered—Fields where,
light abstains
from the unwieldy blossom!

Or, instead of the famous poppies blowing in Flanders Fields, the
Great War could have been troped by the orchids blowing in the
French copses in which some of the worst fighting occurred. Another
of Cummings's abandoned poems speaks of orchids in the darkness
of the forest and the hollow:

I'm [....]

going to bury
Orchids where Orchids

Blow.

But the orchid was a fin-de-siècle flower, with its Decadent, over-
wrought exquisiteness, and perhaps it could not adequately trope a
world that all felt to be changed and changing. The human cost of
the war was felt everywhere. Roupy—the place that features most
by name in Cummings's war poems—was a tiny settlement, barely
a village and more accurately just a cluster of houses along a single,
straight road.

along the justexisting road to Roupy
little in moonlight
go silently by men
(who will be damned if they know why)

From its cluster of houses along this barely existing road, Roupy lost twelve men in combat and three civilians in the Great War. Ham, where the ambulance unit had its main encampment, saw ninety-two deaths in combat and seven civilian deaths. Losses can be counted on the civic monuments that are found in almost every village, town, or city in the region.

The most emotional letter among those that Cummings sent home from the front is a letter to his mother, which he chose to write in French. (Rebecca was entirely comfortable reading French; years later, Cummings's third wife opened a chest that had lain undisturbed for decades at Joy Farm and discovered a stash of French novels that had once belonged to her.) He dated the letter August 9; he had now been at the front for exactly eight weeks. One of the passages, translated, reads: "As for the Germans, there are those who imagine them so barbarian as to be strangers to any feelings of pity. I tell you straight, Mother: do not give any credence to such talk. The French, those who have suffered everything for three years, have for the most part only the most respectful feelings toward the bosches. But the War—for the French, for them it is an abominable charade, which has consumed their friends (men and women), all those whom they loved and for whom they lived. For example: a mechanic who is attached to the ambulance unit was saying to me that in the course of a fortnight of war he lost his father and his two brothers. His mother is dead. 'I am a patriot,' he says, 'but not like that. The war—no, no.' Do you suppose I said to him: Monsieur, your feelings dishonor you? Mother, I took his hand, and said: friend, you are right."

16

DRIVING CARS AND
CLEANING MUD

FOR AN AMBULANCE driver, the job was to receive and collect those who were wounded or ill, and transport them from the battle lines to the nearest field hospital. As one advertisement for the American Field Service (AFS) put it: "You drive a car here—why not a transport in France?" In reality, it was not that simple. The men who volunteered were amateurs: gentlemen drivers. Their level of skill and suitability for the tasks at hand varied considerably. Roads were churned into mud and pockmarked by shells. Sharp turns and small bridges over streams were not necessarily well lit, and at night it was often necessary to drive without headlights so as not to reveal one's position to the Germans. Heavy and large military transport trucks might be coming the other way, toward the front, and an ambulance trying to pass such a truck at the edges of a damaged road without room for two-way traffic could easily wind up tipped into a ditch. The gasoline was often of very poor quality. On roads that were muddy when wet and dusty when dry, cars would frequently stall or run into other mechanical trouble. There were specialist mechanics attached to the ambulance corps, but these mechanics serviced cars at the base and a driver needed a sound understanding of a car's engineering in order to cope with emergencies en route. A good sense of direction was also essential: it was easy to get lost, especially at night. Occasionally an ambulance driver had to drive under shelling, and that took nerve.

Cummings took some delight in the rudimentary conditions of camp life. "One fine thing," he wrote to his mother: "I never have to wash. I changed my socks the other day because it rained hard. It was the première fois." (First time.) Cummings's nonchalant attitude (shared by Brown) to appearance, hygiene, and regimentation left their commander, Mr. Phillips, with a deep prejudice against the pair. However, Cummings appears to have been in fact an excellent driver. In one of his notebooks, he sketched an extremely sensible, personal route map for one of the areas they served: a triangle of land between Saint-Simon, Cugny, and Flavy-le-Martel, two-thirds of the way from Ham towards Jussy. The map notes the better routes for day and for nighttime, the key landmarks, lanterns, a crater and other hazards in the road, sharp turns, gradients, bridges, and train tracks.

Cummings valued his own competence and was scornful of the incompetence surrounding him. There were two drivers per car—a lead and a secondary driver—and Cummings was assigned as a secondary to a lead driver for whom he had no respect. This man he regarded as "a tight-fisted, pull-for-special-privilege, turd," who had already caused an accident by running into a stationary car on the other side of the road. "I learned a day or so since that he is the man who poured essence in his radiator and water in his gasoline-tank—this is a fact."

On another occasion, as second fiddle to a different lead driver who was particularly anxious to get back to camp before the loss of the moonlight, Cummings drove successfully at speed for half an hour on roads full of sharp bends and strewn with shell holes before his lead driver took the wheel, missed sight of a bridge until the last moment, panicked, swerved, and drove straight into a central division. He blew two tires, wrecked the rear axle, and lost in the tumble all the tools they kept in the car for such emergencies. The car had to be abandoned on the road and Cummings and his driver were lucky to catch a ride from another passing ambulance car. The practical and emotional relationship with roads that characterized the life of an ambulance driver surfaces in Cummings's poetry in the glimmer of that "justexisting" road to Roupy, a "slouch of silver" in moonlight.

The most dangerous times in ambulance service came during the day and night spent on post. These posts were not right in among the forward trenches, but they were in areas around the rear of the trench maze that were still highly susceptible to shelling. For a number of reasons, major cannon bombardments were not aimed exclusively at the enemy's frontmost trench. First of all, they might be aimed toward the rear of the trench formations in an attempt to destroy the enemy cannon and the enemy infrastructure—including roads. And secondly, shelling was still highly inaccurate. The distance traveled by any one particular shell was subject to a wide margin of error, since there was only very limited capacity to correct for the variable weight of individual shells, wear and tear on cannon barrels, wind resistance, and air temperature (affecting air density). Guns were therefore often aimed long in order to hit distance targets, and shelling might fall on those targets or far rogue of them. The location of ambulance posts behind the lines was no guarantee of safety.

In his memoir, Dos quoted passages from his own 1917 journal, realizing in retrospect that the detailed self-scrutiny of that war journal had been his coping mechanism. "Dissecting the sensations of danger and fear was my way of making them tolerable: 'In myself,' I noted on August 26, 'I find the nervous reaction to be a curious hankering after danger that takes hold of me. When one shell comes I want another, nearer, nearer. I constantly feel the need of the drunken excitement of a good bombardment. I want to throw the dice at every turn with the old roysterer Death . . . and through it all I feel more alive than ever before . . . I have never lived yet. You can still see the marks of the swaddling clothes. Tomorrow I shall live to the dregs or today I shall die.' "

Cummings coped in a similar fashion on those occasions when he came under bombardment, although he relied less on the self-scrutiny and more on the unexamined cavalier excitement. Most of the time, when there was no present danger, he coped by adopting that same cynical and sarcastic detachment with which he had approached the risks of the Atlantic crossing. In those moods, his complaints of boredom, inactivity, and pointlessness reflect both his own state of mind and the realities of the front in the early to mid-summer of 1917.

To understand the front as it was when Cummings arrived mid-way through June, it is necessary to understand the history of the war during the first half of 1917 and the horrifying nature of those events for the French.

While the Germans, during their gradual withdrawal over the first months of the year, busily fortified and strengthened the Hindenburg Line, the new French commander, General Nivelle, hatched plans to leave his own mark on the course of the war. Like so many others on both sides, Nivelle was convinced that if only he picked the right spot in the lines and conducted the attack in the right way, he could ensure the sort of strategic gains that would change a war of attrition into rapid and clear victory.

Nivelle launched his offensive in April of 1917, with the primary aim of seizing the Chemin des Dames, a road along a ridgetop whose insurmountable defensive advantages of terrain and command of the view below made the French strategy a folly from the out-set, even before the Germans managed to compound their advantage by procuring in a raid the complete French plan of attack. The French knew that their plans were exposed, but changed nothing. The Germans prepared in detail, emptied artillery and men from areas that they knew would come under French bombardment, and concentrated forces against the French advance, using their own untouched cannons to fire down upon the French troops as they attempted to take a ridge that, at its worst points, was almost a cliff face. The catastrophic fighting at the Chemin des Dames has not lodged in Anglo-American cultural memory in the same way as the Somme offensive of 1916. However, it was of enormous significance for the French, who lost over 100,000 men at this one battle site during three April days with no strategic gain of any kind. Nivelle refused to face the facts; the offensive had to be called off, above his head, by the French government.

After such losses and promises of victory betrayed, soldiers mutinied all along the French lines. They did not abandon their posts, but they stated that they would refuse any orders of attack. Nivelle resigned, and his place was taken by General Philippe Pétain, who promised that no further offensive would be undertaken without the addition of American troops. Therefore, when Cummings and Brown were deployed to the front, the policy all along the French sector was to minimize engagement while waiting for the slow buildup of American troops from high summer onward.

Cummings and Brown knew all about the mutinies and about the anger still simmering in the French Army. Cummings disliked the "typical" and boorish Americans with whom he was posted, and he and Brown socialized mostly with the French, who shared with them all the news and rumors from the French perspective. They even chose to bunk with the French cooks and mechanics, who made a space for them in one of the French tents, and they spent a portion of their free time at a café favored by the French soldiers, the *poilus*, where they traded gossip and songs. The pleasure of cultural exchange was mutual. The *poilus* were keen on English tunes, and, as Brown always remembered, they once prevailed upon him and Cummings to sing "It's a Long Way to Tipperary." "So Cummings and I got on the table and all we knew was the chorus, but Cummings thought we ought to be able to do more than sing the chorus. So he began. He made up all the words leading up to the chorus—impromptu and all in rhyme too. I remember that the last two lines that he sang were 'And to her maidenhead I softly, softly send.' And I joined in the chorus, 'It's a long way to Tipperary. It's a long way to go.' I'm sorry I can't remember the other passages because it was all as neat as that. And quite, you know, ad-lib. Cummings could always do things like that."

Cummings's growing sympathy for the *poilus* also left him angry at the propaganda that severed the civilian perspective from the experience of men at the front. It was an anger felt frequently by those who served and it was often vented as dark humor. The *Wipers Times*, a satirical newspaper published by and for British soldiers, offered one version of the trench perspective. "Making the Trenches 'Comfy'":

"The mothers, sisters and sweethearts of the men in the trenches will be delighted to hear of the latest instance of the solicitude of the military chiefs for their comfort and good health. Every yard of roofing felt that can be found in the United Kingdom is being commandeered for the lining of the trenches on the Western Front." This kind of article satirized the growing gulf between those at home, and the ways in which they channeled their cares and worries, and the world of the soldiers.

In Cummings's view, soldiers had one thing on the mind, and that was sex. As he put it in a poem published in his 1926 collection, *is 5*:

> my sweet old etcetera
> aunt lucy during the recent
>
> war could and what
> is more did tell you just
> what everybody was fighting
> for,
> my sister
>
> isabel created hundreds
> (and
> hundreds)of socks not to
> mention shirts fleaproof earwarmers
>
> etcetera wristers etcetera,my
>
> mother hoped that
>
> i would die etcetera
> bravely of course my father used
> to become hoarse talking about how it was
> a privilege and if only he
> could meanwhile my

self etcetera lay quietly
in the deep mud et

cetera
(dreaming
et
   cetera,of
Your smile
eyes knees and of your Etcetera)

He was not wrong about soldiers and sex. Since Cummings served during the period of the French policy of no offensive engagement, he ended up transporting as many or more of *les malades* (the sick) as those injured and wounded, and amongst the *malades* was a notable prominence of venereal disease. Some soldiers even sought out the infections. A self-inflicted wound could bring a long prison sentence or even execution; syphilis might be the better bet.

300 in this hospital sick of syphilis. Stay here 6 weeks, cured; every six months. If no drink and smoke. Many drink, smoke all day all night; say: Better be sick all time than in trenches.

Go to Paris, stay with bad girl, pay good money to get; come here—bon! When get permission, go back, get again!

See that man? He has it. You saw those 3 officers there? They too. When I was Verdun, 1700 soldiers. 45 % Fr. army

The French Army was not alone in facing this problem (or opportunity, depending on the perspective) of sexually transmitted disease: it affected every army in the field. When the United States joined the war, the incidence of venereal disease within the American army more than doubled. According to the first serious mid-twentieth-century investigation of sexual behavior during the Great War, the percentage of soldiers in the US Army suffering from venereal disease, which had stood beforehand at 16 percent, now reached 40 percent.

Official versions of the Great War suppressed some of its bodily realities—not only sex and venereal disease but also, for example, the importance of latrines. Latrines all over France offered one of the best means to gauge the cultural pulse or to keep up with unofficial news. Cummings and Brown had joined their pen to the graffiti on Parisian toilets, registering antipathy to the war and to the president of France, Raymond Poincaré: "A bas Poincaré! A bas la guerre!" (Down with Poincaré! Down with the war!) The toilet was the place to observe humanity in action. "Water Closet / woman - / shouting tits (Magdalen)." Intimacy with the latrines of France separated those who served from those who only knew of the war secondhand. Latrines were not a suitable subject in the days when censors still held considerable power. The first American translation of Erich Maria Remarque's *All Quiet on the Western Front* censored three passages: the first to do with prostitution and the third concerning sex between a soldier and his wife; the second passage, omitted from the American edition, described soldiers playing cards on the latrine.

The latrines were the place where soldiers swapped rumors; the first news that Dos heard about forthcoming offensives came via latrine rumors. On his days off, however, Dos luxuriated in his escape from those communal latrines. He and Robert Hillyer and another of their Harvard friends, all posted together, on one of their excursions discovered a treasure. Behind a shelled and abandoned villa, they found a luscious garden that remained, in spite of it all, replete with roses and phlox and honeysuckle and neat garden paths—and an outhouse. "We had found the latrines the most hideous feature of the wartime scene, slippery planks over stinking pits. The Boche seemed to have an evil intuition about them: as soon as you squatted with your pants down, he would start to shell." The three kept their prized outhouse secret. "To sit there, looking out, quietly and reflectively, into the weedy garden was a halcyon contrast with the crowded choking scramble of our lives on duty. Not rack nor thumbscrew could have torn its location from us."

About three weeks after Cummings and Brown arrived at SSU XXI, the despised Mr. Phillips departed. The rumor was that he had been fired, although the official version was that he had left because he wished to enlist in the armed forces. Cummings hoped for improvement when Mr. Anderson took over, but instead found worse. The general attitude of Cummings and Brown, which had irked Mr. Phillips, positively enraged Mr. Anderson. Mr. Anderson was a narrow-minded man who thought that the Americans under his command should disassociate themselves from the slovenly French. He could not understand why any American would be so fond of French company. He punished both Cummings and Brown, who had finally obtained their own car together, by separating them and reassigning them as seconds to other drivers, and eventually minimizing their driving time altogether and retaining them on miserable, menial cleaning duties at camp. They spent a great deal of time cleaning mud from returned ambulance vehicles.

Cummings did not budge from his open comradeship with the French. That is not to say that he was simply a fool for French society. His prose scraps offer sarcastic perspectives on both American and French political cultures. In one, he varies the famous motto of the French Republic, *liberté, égalité, fraternité,* as "Liberty, Equality, Fraternity, or Death." However, his deep sympathy with the French was connected to their suffering in the war, the general desire for peace, and the generosity of French perspectives on the Germans (in contradistinction to the insanities of American propaganda). In one pen portrait—presumptively combining observation and imagination—he describes a French woman as if she were the goddess of love, Venus, alluding ("drawn with loves") to the tradition of painting the goddess in a chariot drawn by winged "Loves" (Cupids).

The Woman --
has a face drawn with loves and/quartered with dreams.
the nervous marble strength/of a Greek Venus,the smile of a
searing Spanish/primitive Maria. Behind her she held/secretly
a obscene sickle. When you ask her if/the huge Bosches were

mauvais here,she tells me not par ici,/I lost 2 fils et un frere.
Nothing is left me. And how many like that? The war is terrible.
It must be made to cease le plus tot possible.

(When you ask her if the huge Bosches were cruel here, she tells
me not in these parts, I lost two sons and a brother. Nothing is left me.
And how many like that? The war is terrible. It must be made to cease
as soon as possible.)

Drawing literary ideas out of the war experience meant combining observation with Cummings's own literary world and with all the store of images and meaning that he had built up over his last six years. At Harvard, in one of his most famous poems, he wrote about the balloon man whose arrival heralds the season of "Just-spring" with his whistling "far and wee." In notes on Paris, Cummings saw another keeper of balloons, "the fat great Baloon-woman" in "torchlight." And on the front, where shells whistled as they flew down from the sky, he found a new meaning in the sound: "when the big <u>ship</u> Death comes, with his <u>high</u> <u>white</u> whistle and whistles the worms into you and me." It may have been partly this recurrence of imagery from his most iconic poem about the coming of spring that led Cummings to associate *la guerre* so strongly with springtime, even though he himself experienced the war in summer. In the idea of spring, he saw the collision of winter's death and the New Year's rejuvenation, destruction and life's determination to reassert itself, which was so poignantly juxtaposed at the front.

For propaganda in these days, Cummings chose the "propaganda of sunset." He dissected its colors.

white/colour of separture   colour of colour   (of colours)
green /   colour of gold,colour of twilight
orange/   c of love c of ambition
yellow/   colour of nothing
blue/   colour of peur? [fear?]

No other propaganda was of use to him. Even a critical mind could not know which news to believe. Cummings had long since discarded the most outrageous stories about the Germans, such as the story that German soldiers hung the vaginas of Belgian women on the door-knobs of their homes. Skepticism was the only way to retain a liberal and humane mind. When it came to World War II, Cummings at first doubted the veracity of accounts of the Holocaust, because so many stories of German atrocities had been so blatantly fabricated in World War I. And what of atrocities on the Allied side? Rumors of these circulated in France. Cummings left them alone. Brown, however, could not, and he began to write ill-advised letters home.

The following letter was among the correspondence confiscated by the French authorities and used in evidence against Brown.

William Slater Brown to Charles Francis Phillips.

September 4, 1917.

Dear Charlie,

I find myself writing you again. Whether you have received the five letters which I have mailed you during the last month and a half, I do not know. In this letter I will try to say nothing which may be censored, so that at least you will receive one letter from me.

As soon as the Americans arrived in France, people at once began telling stories about them which of course have not the slightest ground of truth to them. One of them is that syphilis in the American training camp is spreading like an epidemic, and of course this is laid to the work of spies. It is said that the syphilis is of the virulent variety and is contracted through cuts and open places in the skin. There is another story of less truth than this one however, and you know Americans too well to consider the story of the slightest truth. It is said that the Americans are already considering shooting of the officers whom they do not like. From what I hear, the French who are in their camp have taught them this. It is a well known fact that this has happened to a large extent in the English Army, due to the fact that the superior officers used to charge "over the hill" with their men, which gave their men a good chance to shoot them if they felt like it. It is rather easy to shoot the officers, or at least so I am told. It would be the simplest thing to follow out Bernard Shaw's advice on this matter it would cure all.

A propos of this story a French soldier told me the other day that in his company there were two officers whom this soldier did not like and one night they were both found dead. When the doctors examined them they found French bullets in their backs. I guess the man was a liar. The French soldiers adore their officers, as any one with a little observation would see.

This French soldier also told me that once the French made a gas attack on the Germans. After this gas attack, as is customary for humanitarian purposes, they send either black men or French soldiers over into the German trenches with knives to clean up the rest of the Germans who have not been killed by the gas. One night a French priest went over with these "cleaners" and came back some time later. "I finished 18 of them" he said. "I don't believe that" said the Lieutenant. The priest then pulled out 18 ears which he had in his pocket and proved it.

This incident only proves to what a state of bravery and self sacrifice war leads men. If it is not true, it matters little, the man who told it to me admired the act by the priest, and admiration of brave and fine deeds of course leads other men to an emulation of them.

I have heard many other thrilling stories of valor here in France, and it all leads me to an intense admiration of those men who have the power and the brains to lead men to the ways of valor and bravery. If I come back to the States soon, and it is quite possible that I may, I will tell you many other things which you may use to prove that war is a great purgative—the great purgative. It robs men of selfishness and makes them do great deeds for the common good. I do not think that the American people realize this enough. Perhaps if they did they would be more enthusiastic for the war.

At times it seems that the war will never end, such at other times it seems that it will end in a few weeks. It is all so terribly complex that one simply decides it with the emotion and little else. Germany is far from being defeated but as I read in a French paper the other day, a German General admitted that the allies were more eager for the war than were the Germans. A rather important statement or at least it seems to me. Tell Ed. Meyer to write to me, that is if you see him, I should like to hear what he is doing.

Give my love to all and your friends. I miss you and my good friends in a way far more than I miss my family.

I suppose Estelle Albert thinks I left for Europe because I loved her too much. I have not heard from her or have not written either. I had forgotten all about her until the other night when I talked to a drunken French soldier who had eyes exactly like hers. So much like hers that it gave me a terrific start and I could not remember for some time whose eyes they resembled.

Regards to Eleanore, I know she thinks that I am an embuscade, to use that dreadful word, but I am learning a great deal over here, much more than I have written to you.

Tolstoi is absolutely right.

> Love to all again,
> as ever,
> W. Slater Brown

P.S.—I have written this letter with a quill pen which I made, a very fine pen too.

Thought of a fine poem last night which for its simplicity of diction, its freedom from classical rhyme, its feeling for social equality is unrivaled in litterature, it is:

The moon is very democratic
It sits in pools so people can look at it.

17

MR. ANDERSON TELLS
SOME LIES

CUMMINGS SENT HIS declaration of love to Marie Louise in the middle of June, and on July 8, she finally replied. Her style is slightly breathless. Her emotion is open, honest, and experienced. "My darling," she wrote (in French). "I have received your letter, which brought me, as always, great happiness; yes, my darling, it is truly a great pleasure for me to hear from you, as your letters are beautiful; and since I feel that I love you more every day, I think that now you will believe me." She wrote that she, too, remembered their glorious day on the Marne. She remembered what she had done for him and rebuked him mildly for having failed to pay for the favor. But never mind. When he came back to Paris, they would make love without inhibition. "I await your return with impatience." Wednesday past was the Fourth of July, and she had watched the Americans parade in Paris. It seemed that she saw him in every face, and by the end of the day, she was overwhelmed with sadness. Above all—write to me, she said. "Au revoir mon petit poète."

Cummings's June love letter to Marie Louise survives because he drafted it twice in his notebook before tearing out the pages he sent to her. The rest of the notebook he filled with sketches of soldiers, French villagers, and the French countryside. His mind was overflowing and he yearned to paint. Somehow Cézanne had achieved texture through color, and Cummings saw Cézanne's colors everywhere. If the moon was a "starshell over the Celtic grass," the French sun was "Cézanne orange."

By the time he reached the back of his notebook, he had received Marie Louise's reply. He was elated, and he wrote again full of his love for her. "My absolute darling, I cannot say, I cannot express, the pleasure and the happiness which your letter has brought to me." "How the war is treacherous, cruel, and evil! Especially, because it keeps us apart."

Cummings was growing more and more desperate for leave, awaiting his turn for the seven-day *permission* that would allow him to see Paris once more. He knew that he would have to serve for at least two months before the chance of a regular *permission*. But there were also extraordinary grants of leave. There was a drawing of lots for the Fourth of July, offering forty-eight hours' freedom to go to Paris for the parade and celebration. Ten of the forty-six Americans attached to the unit at that date would be allowed to go. But Cummings was refused entry even to the drawing, as was Brown. Mr. Phillips claimed that leave was controlled out of respect for seniority of service—which Cummings did not believe, since an equally recent arrival to the unit had been included in the draw. He challenged Mr. Phillips, who changed his tune and accused Cummings of a slack attitude, "lacking in sticktuitiveness and enthusiasm." This was truly unfair (Cummings said in a letter to his mother), since he had lived up to all of his responsibilities, stepped up to "goat" for another driver, and kept going even in spite of a severe case of diarrhea attributable to the poor food hygiene, which had sent two of the other ambulance drivers to hospital.

But at last, in spite of the pettiness of Mr. Phillips and his successor, Mr. Anderson, Cummings met Marie Louise once more, on the fourteenth of July, exactly a month to the day after he had first left her. We can conjecture the circumstances. It is surely not a coincidence that July 14 is Bastille Day, and that American soldiers, who had only just begun to arrive in France in June, paraded through the streets of

Paris on both the fourth and the fourteenth of July. We know of the lottery for July 4. There must have been a second drawing for forty-eight hours' leave for Bastille Day, and this time Cummings must have been permitted to enter and drew lucky. With leave on such short notice, he would have gambled on finding Marie Louise on the spot. He was lucky again. She wrote later how happy a day it had been, to spend the fourteenth together. We know nothing further, except that they parted as much in love as before.

Two days later, Cummings wrote again. But weeks went by, and this time there was no response.

At the front, Cummings felt detached from death and the war around him. He tried to sketch out what it would mean to capture the war in art. He felt somehow that shells were satiric, whereas the rapid fire of the machine guns was ironic. In moonlight they would bubble over an earth that was the color and consistency of oatmeal porridge. It bothered him that his own sense of detachment was so unflinchingly echoed by the detached world around him. He painted tiny pen portraits of the destruction wreaked by the war: "the tree which used to grow against a wall—flattened—now absurd—embraces nothing." He marveled that the very same river could flow through France and into Germany, "an uncaring coolness." He clung to his love for Marie Louise, not only for her sake but also because to him she embodied everything about beauty and tragic nobility that would seem to give some romanticized meaning to war and death. He was at work on a poem about her, written in French. She was his Cleopatra, with snowy complexion, poised at the moment when the snake was pressed to her breast. Her languid eyes drink death.

But still he heard nothing, and so he wrote to Mimi. He wrote a long letter, full of news and memories. He disguised his angst in chattering: I've lost my favorite pipe—a beautiful pipe gifted to me by an old friend in America. But it doesn't matter. I've heard nothing from Marie Louise, though I wrote on the sixteenth of July, and I've been fretting. I think she is bored of me, although I hope not. Nevertheless, if it's true, I can make no complaint. She has been always kind, and I know well that I am often too cruel. No more of that. We swam today, in a lake hidden among the walls of an old quarry, where the water was perfect and we dived from 5 meters up, and I remembered our outing—the four of us, when we went swimming all together. Oh, how we were happy!

As he nattered on about their day at the Marne, he joked, with no sense of foreboding, about his own outsize shirt. Oblivious to the omen, he wrote that the ill-fitting shirt he had worn on that day, with its broad stripes, had made him think, suddenly, that he was in prison. On he chattered, about the weather and the mosquitos. Pardon me, he said. I am boring you with this long and stupid letter. But do write me if Marie Louise is angry. I beg you.

The letter was returned to him, with a large, intemperate pencil scrawl. "Monsieur, we do not know this woman and I ask you to give me some peace." There was a second scrawl in the margin: "You could at least bother to seal your letters."

Cummings's morale faltered. His French comrades were ribbing him about Marie Louise, preying on his own earlier doubts. She was a prostitute, and it was crashingly naïve to suppose that she loved him. He was a damn fool and he had been played. The rest of July and the whole of August passed with no word.

Indeed, by this time, Marie Louise could not have known whether a letter to the front would reach him. He could be injured, or dead, or transferred. When she finally wrote, on the very last day of August, she sent the letter to 104 Irving Street. It was a short letter, but full of love. Just after the fourteenth of July, she had fallen ill, and had been since then in the hospital. Mimi was away in the countryside, and there had been no one to buy her writing paper or to post her letters. She hoped he was not angry, and that he would come soon on leave. Tell me, she wrote, that you still think of your Marie Louise. She sent her new address: 23 Rue Henri Monnier.

The envelope shows that, from Irving Street, her letter was forwarded to 11 Charles Street, New York. That is Cummings's address from 1918, after his return from the war. It must have been a long time before Cummings saw this letter. He heard something, though, from a letter or letters that are lost. Marie Louise was a sensible woman.

Perhaps she wrote simultaneously to Irving Street and to the front, reaching Cummings there in spite of the lapse of time. But whatever she said, Cummings now had doubt in his heart. He wrote again to her. He must have offered her money, as a gentleman did to close his account with a mistress—convinced by his friends that this was all he had been to her. All that we know of his letter is from her anguished response, written in the same gushing and breathless style as before.

> *Paris 7 September 17*
>
> *My darling,*
> *I have indeed received your letter. It gave me some pain; you say that all of this has changed you, and if I've understood correctly you tell me also that it is not nice to think that we were playing you for fools. Why would you have such an opinion of me? and why also listen to the ideas of men who <u>themselves</u> think of nothing other than to play others for fools and drum doubt into the spirit of others; why? You know well, my darling, that one never learns anything from louts— permit me to so designate them. These men take women for—I really don't know what, in the end. You know me, and only your opinion matters to me; but you, if you listen to them, there will be no end to it, you will always doubt and never be easy in your mind; believe me I know all of this; sadly there is no shortage of mean-spirited men. My darling, you will write to me often and beautiful little letters like before; and this doubt, and these trivial second thoughts which you have, will end by dissolving; and then you will come on leave and we will talk properly the two of us, and you will see I haven't changed in the slightest. I love you as before. Thank you for what you say about money, but I want none for the present; only when you come on leave, because I would not want you to believe that I write only for that.*
> > *Awaiting my darling your news*
> > *I finish by saying I love you I love you*
> > *Your girl, Marie Louise*

Perhaps if Cummings had obtained his seven-day *permission* for Paris, all would have righted itself when all was understood. But Mr. Anderson withheld the *permission*, although it was now overdue. And Marie Louise was not the only one writing letters on the seventh of September. On that very same day, the censors picked up a new packet of correspondence written by Brown.

The letter to Charlie was particularly damning. When it was first published, forty years later, by Cummings's early biographer Charles Norman, Brown was indignant. He felt sure that the letters had been enhanced by the French authorities in order to incriminate him. But these letters had not seen the light of day for forty years; even Brown himself had not seen them for four decades. What sixty-year-old man would not be surprised to reencounter the correspondence of his twenty-year-old self?

At the center of everything lies this mystery: why were Cummings and Brown arrested, and was Brown framed?

Brown was vehement. "Unless I can see the originals of my letters in my own handwriting I won't be persuaded that some of the letters—particularly the one [to Charlie], were written by me. They seem to contain all sorts of interpolations expressing pro-German and anti-French opinions which neither Cummings nor I held." However, they also contain telltale signs of the journalist from Columbia. When Brown talks of men shooting their officers in the back as they surge over the top, he refers to "Bernard Shaw's advice on the matter." He means an antiwar pamphlet written by George Bernard Shaw in 1914, in which Shaw wrote, "No doubt the heroic remedy for this tragic misunderstanding is that both armies should shoot their officers and go home to gather in their harvests in the villages and make a revolution in the towns; and though this is not at present a practicable solution, it must be frankly mentioned, because it or something like it is always a possibility in a defeated conscript army if its commanders push it beyond human endurance. . . ." It was the *New York Times* who had republished Shaw's views in America, shortly before Brown came to be a student of journalism in New York, at Columbia University. The reference makes sense.

The letter to Charlie says that the men would shoot their officers as they charged "over the hill," which, as Brown later complained, is a ridiculous phrase, implausibly substituted for "over the top." The most likely explanation is simply error in the transcription of Brown's difficult handwriting. Other errors—like Dr. Lower for Dr. Lomer in another letter—are obviously mistakes in transcription. If a cursive *m* is written in a pointy and loose manner, it is easily read as a *w*. Brown was right about one thing: the American authorities never saw his own, handwritten letters. They were supplied with typed transcripts made by the French. Brown's "over the top" must have been a scrawl, and the French guessed "hill" for the illegible word.

The missing piece of the puzzle is surely alcohol. "At the café," Brown wrote, in another one of his letters, "one can buy beer that tastes as if it had been brewed in the stomach of a horse." A better solution was to drink the white wine. And when Brown drank, he drank a lot. "I have been drinking so much white wine at a little café in town that I feel as if I had been through many campaigns."

What was a lot of wine in Brown's world? Well, back at home in New York in 1918, he wrote to Cummings about one evening's perambulations. He started at a restaurant where he drank the best part of two quarts of wine—two and a half modern bottles—until the room swayed. He left, but forgot his hat, and returned for the hat and a last drink for the road. On his way home, he bought a quart of Chianti and had a glass of that in his lodgings, and then he went back out to a bar to chase it with India Pale Ale. From the bar, he crossed to a Romanian restaurant, where he settled in for four cognacs, "because a girl was looking at me." He rounded the evening off with a last beer back at the restaurant where he'd started.

Brown's drinking brought him some luck and some mishaps. When he first came round to view his prospective New York lodgings, he was so drunk ("it being about 8:30 P.M.") that he began to regale the landlady with the full story of his time in France, leading to many exclamations of "O My God" and an offer to lower the rent by a dollar a week. He found less indulgence from Gaston Lachaise, the French sculptor living in New York who was known to Cummings as the stepfather of his friend Edward Nagle and whose modernist style had already served Cummings as inspiration and bridge between

New York and the artistic world of Europe. Lachaise was an important man: famous, controversial, and at the heart of several New York artistic circles. One day, he took Brown out for lunch and asked him if he believed in reincarnation. Brown was two bottles of wine in, and averred that after death they would all rot and turn into witch hazel. He had no notion why he specified witch hazel, but he proceeded nonetheless to defend it vociferously. He wrote later to Cummings that he had no idea what Lachaise had said, having been too drunk to make sense of a word, but he was quite sure that he himself had defended the witch hazel hypothesis with vigor and at length.

After the witch-hazel incident, Lachaise began to avoid him.

During this time in New York, Brown regularly wrote his letters to Cummings when he was drunk. "I'm pretty tight, Cummings, I swear I can't write well." Cummings himself factored this in when reading Brown's missives. Of course, the French censors didn't. But odds are that Brown was far from sober when he penned the letters that landed him and Cummings in prison.

Brown never wanted to admit that the letters lay at the heart of it. "It was not those dumb, jejune letters of mine that got us into trouble. It was the fact that C. and I knew all about the violent mutinies in the French Army a few months before Cummings and I reached the front." The French authorities were deeply concerned that enthusiasm for the war might wane in the United States if it was widely known how demoralized the French Army were. "We two," claimed Brown, "were loaded with dynamite." And that may be true—as far as it goes. But the French were not mind readers, and they only knew what Brown and Cummings knew because of the letters Brown wrote. It all comes back to the letters, in the end.

However, it was only Brown whom the French police came for. Mr. Anderson saw his chance to get rid of the pair. He roped in Cummings on the grounds that whatever Brown had done, Cummings was surely up to his neck in the same. It was a truly unpleasant act of betrayal of an innocent man under his command.

Cummings had no idea even that he was under arrest. Some official-looking men arrived at the ambulance quarters. Cummings was told to collect his things and come. He witnessed them bundling Brown into one car; he himself was bundled into another. On the drive, his driver's hat flew off in a gust of wind. The driver stopped the car and Cummings moved to collect the hat; the guard pulled his revolver. Only then did Cummings grasp the way things stood.

He was taken back to Noyon, into a civic edifice that looked to him like a feudal dungeon. He was full of adrenaline and exhaustion, demoralized by months of cleaning mud at the front, and alienated from the Americans in his ambulance unit. He was still desperate for his *permission* to get to Paris, but also convinced that he had been taken for a chump by his girl. He was oddly thrilled to find himself under arrest, just to shake the tedium and to feel as though something at least might happen. It was a day for impulsiveness, and it would change his life forever.

PART V

LA FERTÉ-MACÉ

September 21, 1917–December 19, 1917

—

18

AT NOYON ONCE MORE

September 21, 1917

AT NOYON, CUMMINGS was kept separate from Brown. He was fed a good lunch. He rested, waited, under guard in and around the Hôtel de Ville and its complex of associated buildings. Then, abruptly, in midafternoon he was collected for interrogation and escorted toward an upper-floor room. As he walked up, Brown walked out—announcing in high spirits as they crossed, "I think we're going to prison all right." Cummings was searched and his pockets emptied, and he was beckoned into a room to face a panel of three men. The second of them sported a magnificent mustache and a not-unfriendly attitude, while the third was almost warmly amused. The first and primary interrogator, however, was Monsieur le Ministre de Sûreté de Noyon, at the apex of the forces of local law and order, and it can be fairly surmised that he still felt the sting of the recent German occupation and the consequent need to lord his recovered power over the district.

Le Ministre de Sûreté began his attacks by querying the origins of Cummings's name. He was convinced that Cummings's ancestry must be Irish, and therefore that he could be suspected of harboring sympathies for the Irish nationalists who themselves were believed to be looking to Germany for support. Cummings averred that the surname was Scottish and that the name Estlin had been given him in honor of his English godfather. "Monsieur, quite evidently disappointed, told the mustache in French to write down that I denied my Irish parentage; which the mustache did." Le Ministre then plowed through further subjects he deemed relevant and suspicious: Cummings's religious background, his education, his time in Paris, and his trouble with Mr. Anderson at the front.

He also pressed Cummings hard over a letter he and Brown and a third American belonging to the ambulance unit had attempted to send to the Undersecretary of State in French Aviation, asking if they could transfer to train and fly with the French Air Force, L'Escadrille Lafayette. Bored stiff with the mud and eager to find some new opportunity to feel valuable and valued, these three had—at the suggestion of a French friend at SSU XXI—gone straight to the top to offer their services. The Frenchman's advice to write to such an august minister in government may have seemed natural enough to the Americans, drawing on their own experience of the Norton-Harjes setup. The Norton-Harjes service had an oddly flat organizational structure between the powerful and influential men who ran the whole outfit and the rank and file: after all, Cummings had been interviewed by Eliot Norton in New York, chewed out by Harjes himself in Paris, and had met *the* Norton of Norton-Harjes, Richard Norton, at the front. Moreover, both Cummings and Brown came from families who knew American senators. Writing to the Undersecretary of State in Aviation did not seem outrageous to them; but it did to the French authorities who arrested them, who claimed that it was "contrary to all military law" to attempt to make such a contact.

It has often been claimed that the letter sent by these three Americans who sought to fly with the Escadrille also expressed an unwillingness to go as far as actually dropping bombs on the Germans. Richard Norton, when he came to investigate the case, offered this explanation in a letter to the Reverend. As the Reverend rather likeably scrawled in the margins of that Norton letter: nonsense. Norton's facts were demonstrably fudged: he thought, for starters, that the letter had been addressed to the Minister for War when Cummings is quite clear that it was addressed to the Undersecretary of State for Aviation. Norton's version is thirdhand at best and it clearly repeats what had been passed on to the American authorities by the French. The French must have registered their objections to the letter together with the scandalous refusal to commit to actually bombing Germans, and Norton assumed they meant "in the letter." Actually, as Cummings's own account makes clear, the notion of a refusal to bomb the Germans arose only during the French interrogation of Brown.

"'Your friend' said Monsieur in English, 'is here a short while ago. I ask him if he is up in the aeroplane flying over Germans will he drop the bombs on Germans and he say no, he will not drop any bombs on Germans.'" Cummings described himself as befuddled and stumped by these words, being "at the time innocent of third-degree methods"—which is to say that, once he had got his head around the French tactics of interrogation, he concluded that it was entrapment. He assumed that Le Ministre was simply lying about Brown's interrogation. More likely, since the French were scrupulous about generating the sort of paperwork that vindicated their actions at the same time that they were unreasonable in their methods for obtaining it, they probably did elicit some dubious pronouncement from Brown. Brown was far more impulsive in his speech than Cummings. He was also from a pacifist background and might easily have said something that the panel was able to contort or misuse for their own records: perhaps, for example, that he preferred the idea of aerial reconnaissance to bombing raids.

Cummings insisted passionately on his own patriotism and that of Brown. His excellent spoken French and his expressions of preference for French company over that of his fellow Americans had charmed two-thirds of his interrogating panel, when he saw the danger of leaving Brown to face imprisonment without him. Without hesitation, he took the plunge and handed deliberately to Le Ministre the ammunition needed to order his internment: his refusal to espouse any hatred of the Germans. Le Ministre—triumph now in hand—conversed briefly with his colleagues on the panel and announced Cummings's fate: indefinite detention on account of his friend.

Brown subsequently embraced the glamorous notion that they were both arrested and detained as spies. The truth was more prosaic. They were not identified as spies but rather designated as undesirables. The official order of detention for Brown and Cummings cites in prime of place Brown's letters, containing "troublesome estimates of the state of mind of the French servicemen, discouraging reflections upon the fate that is in store for the American troops, and alarmist resolutions capable of endangering the Allied cause." The document continues: "The commanding officer of the accused, Mr. Anderson, to whom Brown has been described as a Germanophile by an American volunteer, is of the opinion that the accused is an undesirable in the war zone, that he should not be left free to circulate in France, and that his immediate return to America would be dangerous." Cummings was accused of being "an intimate friend of Brown," and although it was specified that his personal correspondence was innocent, he was regarded as under the influence of Brown in terms of his ideas and his conduct. Moreover, "Mr. Anderson is of the opinion that he, like Brown, is an undesirable in the war zone. . . ." They were, therefore, to be removed as speedily as possible to a district safely distant from the war and detained pending further consideration of the case.

So much effort expended over the incarceration of two such insignificant individuals can only be comprehensible against the background of the French obsession with both army and civilian morale. The French—and equally, for that matter, the Germans—took it as axiomatic that victory in the war would depend ultimately upon morale. Received wisdom held that a lack of proper spirit among the troops had caused the French defeat in the Franco-Prussian war in 1870. Warfare had changed since then. Yet insistence on the importance of morale became all the more attractive as a means of denying the new realities of artillery firepower and clinging to the belief that victory came out of—and therefore also proved—the moral superiority of a nation.

Combatant governments monitored morale amongst their own soldiers and civilians and speculated about the morale of the enemy. Large questions of military strategy could be predicated on assessments of the mood of the opposition. At the time that Cummings faced interrogation at Noyon, the British were in the midst of an offensive push farther north along the line—a long engagement known as the Battle of Passchendaele or the Third Battle of Ypres—which they fought from July to November of 1917. British casualties mounted for two months after tactical gains ran dry because British strategic command, under General Haig, was utterly persuaded that German morale was on the point of breaking any day. Brown's letters home, seized by the French censors, refer to this belief that the war was at a military stalemate and that the only factor in victory would be the relative appetite of each side for continuing to the most bitter of ends.

The French had always taken active measures to manage the public perception of war. Even though the cost of the fighting was felt throughout France, the French authorities still made efforts to reduce its visibility. When the wounded were brought from the field to the larger-capacity hospitals in Paris, the trains were normally scheduled at night for immediate triage in large, covered depots, followed by nighttime transportation from the depot to the receiving hospital. The mutinies in 1917 raised fears of a crisis in army morale, even further compounded by worries about the fortitude of civilian spirit in the face of workers' strikes in spring of 1917 in Paris and elsewhere in France. The response of the French authorities was to tighten their stranglehold on information and communication. Indeed, their unwillingness to be forthright about their situation even with their allies led the British general Haig to assume more desperate circumstances in France than were actually the case.

Since war correspondents and reporters had, from the outset, been forbidden from visiting the French front, the letters of ambulance drivers or other American volunteers, often reprinted in local newspapers, had become a primary source of news in America. It is in such a context that Brown's acerbic letters were perceived as "capable of endangering the Allied cause." Cummings and Brown got the worst of the mood of France twice over, at a time when national authorities feared a collapse in the French determination to persevere and local authorities at Noyon were still smarting from German occupation of the town. Cummings sensed in passing these reverberations of Noyon's occupation and recent liberation. Even in a state of such personal turbulence, he was incredibly sensitive to atmosphere. When he and his guard descended from the interrogation room, they were driven to the square in front of the Hôtel de Ville. "A military band was executing itself to the stolid delight of some handfuls of ragged civils. My new captor paused a moment; perhaps his patriotic soul was stirred." Cummings is sarcastic and also acute. When the town had been recovered in March, French soldiers paraded in the square for the benefit of a small crowd of civilian onlookers. Six months later, the sight of French rather than German soldiers on maneuver was still deeply symbolic.

From the square at the Hôtel de Ville, Cummings was taken down an outdoor corridor to his first prison cell—the cell that was "fine" and where the prison door closed as an earthquake, and where he was to spend that night and the next. His new lodging was equipped with a pile of straw and a latrine pail, and Cummings had his own bedding with him, brought together with his other effects from the ambulance camp. Cummings named the latrine pail Ça Pue ("It Stinks"), but he appreciated its presence after his first meal of an extremely dubious cabbage-and-bean soup.

We begin to see a change in Cummings's writing. Cummings's earliest work conjures outdoor spaces. His Harvard paganism summoned a world of satyrs, nymphs, and woodland glades. It was the pagan realm of Pan, the bringer of spring and "the great goat-footed God of all out-doors." Now, in France, the focus shifts to rooms, their inhabitants, the light as it comes in, and the views looking out. In "the tasteless minute efficient room" of a Montmartre prostitute, the light of twilight marches through as the speaker smells and hears and tastes the contrast between the small room and the "huggering" flesh of the woman and the gushing, floating exuberance beyond, outside. That poem captures all the immediacy of Cummings's experience of

Paris, but it is also worth remembering that it was written later, from memory, in 1918. In other words, it was written after three months' incarceration had taught him the power of enclosed spaces: his cell at Noyon or the prison cell en route to La Ferté-Macé or the cells of solitary confinement at that prison; or, above all, the large, columned room at La Ferté where he and Brown and at least forty other men slept and lived and that he immortalized in the title of his own account of his imprisonment, *The Enormous Room.*

At Noyon, this obsession with the inhabitants of rooms and with their spaces and their windows already begins to crystallize. Cummings was fascinated by the traces of those who had inhabited the cell before him. His immediate predecessor had left a deposit in Ça Pue. But the traces went back through many cycles of incumbents, who had etched their personalities onto the walls around him in pencil drawings and little notes. The cell had hosted both German and French prisoners. Some of their drawings were mordant and some light-hearted; some sentimental, like the German who had drawn and labeled his boat from home; some were militaristic and patriotic or else poked fun at the war. One left a farewell to his wife, and another recorded the six-year sentence he had received for desertion. Cummings had no pencil, and so he added his own contribution as best he could, burning and using the charred ends from his supply of matches.

His prison window here was not a window properly speaking, but a long, thin grate that extended over the cell door and to the edge of the narrow four-foot wall. Through the grate, the dusk seeped in, and a hint of leaves was visible, and later the moon. Cummings had been given a small piece of chocolate prior to the cabbage soup. He broke off a smaller chunk and left it on the sill of the grate, where it was eventually discovered by "a little silhouette." This creature returned later, when Cummings had settled in for the night. "Then I lay down, and heard (but could not see) the silhouette eat something or somebody . . . and saw, but could not hear, the incense of Ça Pue mount gingerly upon the taking air of twilight."

In *The Enormous Room,* Cummings leaves this air of mystery

around his omnivorous, silhouetted companion. In a letter to Thayer, however, he writes about the rat whom he fed with chocolate while other rats swarmed Brown's blankets. Brown told him about the blankets later. On that first night in Noyon, Cummings and Brown did not exchange any conversation. Cummings only knew of Brown's presence in the prison in the early evening, when he heard the whistling of *Petrushka*, one of the avant-garde ballets which he and Brown had seen together in Paris—"a smooth whistle, cool like a peeled willow-branch" through the gloom. He returned the whistle, and then so did Brown, and so on for half an hour. It was an efficient signal. No one else, prisoner or guard, in a municipal town in the middle of the war zone was remotely likely to know the tune, and so each knew that it could only have been the other who whistled back.

During Cummings's interrogation, he had insisted that—whatever view the French officials chose to take—his own view of Brown's innocence must be put on record. Behind Cummings's loyalty; behind his desperation to escape the tedium of the ambulance unit; behind the recklessness that surged out of the fear that Marie Louise had never truly loved him, there is a deeper passion to protect Brown. Brown activated the protectiveness Cummings had always felt, even as a young child, toward any human or animal either younger or more vulnerable than himself. Brown was younger than Cummings: he was only twenty when he signed up for ambulance service and, for all his appearance of vivacity, he had a kind of helplessness in the face of life swirling around him. Part of what drew Brown to Cummings was Cummings's strange way of looking after the world. "I liked Cummings from the very beginning...," Brown said later. "When I met him on the boat he was seeing things in an entirely different way than I saw them. I remember one of the things that he said to me that impressed me. He remarked that he had seen a cook once being 'cruel to a cabbage.' It was an attitude toward the world—animism, I suppose. He had a strong animistic streak. He'd never kill anything."

Brown speaks casually. Cummings was not an animist in any full sense. He did not believe that cabbages were sentient or suffered at the hands of chefs. And Brown was only half right about Cummings's ability to kill. Cummings could only kill to protect, but for that he could and had killed his dog, Rex. Brown neither perceived nor understood that alpha and effective side of his friend.

Cruelty over a cabbage is equal parts overwhelming kindness and sardonic dryness. It was the kindness that dominated Cummings's feelings for Brown. Cummings whistled for Brown—*Petrushka* again—on his second night in the cell at Noyon. There was no answer. Brown had been sent ahead, but only by a day. On the next morning, Cummings himself was summoned from his cell to begin his own journey to the *camp de triage* at La Ferté-Macé.

19

LIFE UNDER *LES PLANTONS*

September 23, 1917

WHEN THE GUARDS pulled Cummings from his cell, they restored to him his baggage and belongings, although the two gendarmes who were now in charge of his person kept hold also of his money. Cummings was fortunate in that he was equipped with belongings including a bedroll, blankets, and a very heavy, full-length fur coat, all of which promised a modicum of future comfort and warmth. But somehow he had to carry these, starting with the walk from the cell at Noyon to the rail station. Staggering under the weight of his bags and weakened from lack of food, he at last managed to pay a passing child to carry the smaller of the two packs from the middle of town to the rail station. He secured the boy's services at the suggestion of one of his guards, who had made this suggestion only to taunt him, knowing that he had been stripped of all the cash he was carrying but not knowing that the search had missed a couple of pennies in a hidden inner pocket. The guard's taunt was the first of many acts of sadism that Cummings would encounter—casual sadism from some and a deep and twisted malice from others. It also signified the beginning of the psychology of cat and mouse by means of which prisoners survived, wherein the tiniest acts of outwitting their captors offered those precious slivers of selfhood and control of their own destiny that enabled them—though not all of them—to cling to sanity.

On the train from Noyon, Cummings met another prisoner. Like all of those whom he met at this time, Cummings assigned him a nickname: "the divine man." On the train journey, the divine man cheerfully shared, unasked, his own lunch of sausage and wine when Cummings had only *pain de guerre* ("war bread," deliberately made stale). One of the gendarmes spent the train journey covetously eyeing up a waterproof oilskin blanket belonging to this divine man. Foreseeing the inevitable and yet desperate to forestall it, Cummings tried to distract both guards by sketching them, one after the other. It worked for the duration of the journey, but as they got off the train, the guard began again on the subject of the blanket. The divine man did not protest; there was no point. He handed it over.

The divine man told Cummings that he was on his way to prison as a deserter, sentenced to three years of solitary to be followed by seven years of hard labor, because he had returned to his unit one day late from his *permission* in Paris. In counterpoint to the sadism and abuse of power that Cummings would experience throughout the months in prison, there was also the ridiculous: the risible nature of arbitrary authority. Cummings recalled this unfortunate fellow prisoner giving voice to the sheer foolishness of it all, as he told Cummings what he had said to the officer who declared him a deserter. "I said to him,It is funny. It is funny I should have come back,of my own free will,to my company. I should have thought that being a deserter I would have preferred to remain in Paris."

The first leg of the train journey went as far as Creil, the same town through which Cummings had passed three months earlier on the journey out from Paris to Noyon. There he was instructed to descend and was taken to another local prison where he was held overnight, passing a cell with a barred window through which countless hands reached begging for cigarettes as he passed; he gave what he had, and sorrowed afterward that he shortchanged the strange hands by four cigarettes missed in a different pocket. After a few hours' sleep, he was wakened in darkness and hustled back to the train station, where two new gendarmes took him into their custody for the train to Paris, whence they would change again for Briouze, in northwest France in the region of Normandy. Cummings asked where they were going and one of the gendarmes replied that they were headed to Macé, but Cummings heard "Marseille," famous as the port city on the south coast of France, and so he concluded that he must be traveling for deportation back to America.

In fact, he was on his way to a *camp de triage*, a sort of holding prison for detainees while further (leisurely) consideration was made of their cases. The *camp de triage* was a long way from the front, which indeed was the point. All those held there had been deemed too dangerous to remain free in France or to be allowed anywhere near the zone of military operations, and their relegation out of the war zone was implemented with uncompromising determination. By modern road direct from Noyon, Cummings would have come 230 miles. Eight of those miles were still ahead of him when they arrived at Briouze, and the last train from Briouze to their final destination, La Ferté-Macé, was canceled. His guards decided that they would walk, partly for fear of staying overnight at Briouze lest the villagers mount a rescue attempt merely out of solidarity for any prisoner passing through—so hated were all gendarmes, who were widely perceived as shirkers. The guards did Cummings the courtesy at least of allowing him to deposit the heavier of his two bags at the station, to be sent on later, and permitting a stop first for a drink of wine on condition that Cummings disguise his status as their prisoner.

It was a long road in a black night, at one point touching a cold stream and then, before the outskirts of La Ferté-Macé, passing a wooden crucifix of the sort that mark the entry to so many towns and villages in Catholic France. For Cummings, raised in Protestant New England, these ubiquitous crucifixes—some in wood and some in stone—wove themselves inextricably into the alien landscape of the war. Although there are several crucifixes within a 10-mile radius of La Ferté-Macé, the exact crucifix that Cummings describes does not now appear to stand. But Normandy was decimated in the Allied

Liberation of World War II and much was lost across the landscape, so it is easy to suppose that such a crucifix once stood as he says. In any case, the crucifixes of France held a deep fascination for him. In *The Enormous Room*, this wooden guardian of his road stands "clumsy with pain" so that Cummings can hear "the angular actual language of his martyred body." Elsewhere in his notes Cummings describes another crucifix: "rounding the road,behold that black butterfly,Jesus Christ,pinned upon sunset / surrounding,insidious poisoning leaves / tree 119 years old."

At last, they reached a building on the edge of the town of La Ferté-Macé. It had once been a seminary. Now it is a school, partially rebuilt and remodeled. During the Great War, when it served as a detention center, it was an interconnected complex consisting of a central building and two wings, all of it imposing, but in a style more heavy and functional than magnificent.

In the dark, Cummings could make out only gray, hulking stone. It was by now the very depth of the night, and after the briefest of interviews with the authorities at La Ferté, he was allocated a straw mattress, shown into a completely dark room, and told simply to lay out his mattress and go to sleep. He did not know where he was or what kind of room he was in until the next morning, when he woke to "the enormous room" itself: a cavern filled with mattresses and men, about forty of them, including, to his complete delight, Brown.

Brown was in a state of hilarity, triumphant in the grand (though misplaced) notion that he and Cummings and everyone around them had been identified as spies. He was thrilled to introduce Cummings to these new surroundings of which he, having left Noyon earlier and made better time, had thirty-six hours' prior knowledge. Brown was still crowing over his own arrival and his elegantly maddening deflation of the prison director, who had greeted him with a thundering denunciation of his character as one which was disgusting from every possible moral or patriotic angle, to which lengthy tirade Brown had simply replied that he did not understand French—saying so in French and thus leaving the director swinging between the one possibility that his entire peroration had been wasted on a prisoner who understood no French and the other, that he was made the fool by his prisoner's phlegmatic nonchalance.

It was Brown who finally explained to Cummings that he was not at Marseille, but in Macé, or rather, La Ferté-Macé. Brown buzzed here and there, introducing Cummings by ones and twos to his fellow prisoners. The men incarcerated at the *camp de triage* were mostly aliens. Its multinational, multilingual environment encompassed a large number of prisoners from Holland and Belgium as well as men from Mexico, Russia, Turkey, Denmark, Germany, Poland, Romania, Austria, the West Indies, and from the Romani people, and more, and there were also women and children, in quarters separate from the men.

The room in which Cummings awoke—the enormous room— was the room reserved as quarters for the single men, in the left wing of the complex as viewed from the street and on the very top floor of four. (Married men, if they had been arrested together with their wives, were held separately, on the floor just below, where some contact with wives and children was permitted.) The enormous room was open to a high, vaulted ceiling—Cummings judged it at twenty-five or thirty feet—and the only unboarded windows looked out over the back of the complex away from the town, across a stretch of uninspiring fields and toward a generic, dense and darkish woodland that Cummings found thoroughly unstimulating. The room itself was vast, and two rows of pillars ran down the middle.

Cummings had moved from the hands of the *gendarmerie* into the realm of the prison guards, *les plantons*. It was, he felt, essential to the regime of *les plantons* that their prisoners should be severed from all ordinary existence.

The blocking of all windows on three sides had an obvious significance:les hommes [the men] were not supposed to see anything which went on in the world without;les hommes might,however,- look their fill on a little washing-shed,on a corner of what seemed to be another wing of the building,and on a bleak lifeless abject landscape of scrubby woods beyond—which constituted the

view from the ten windows on the right. The authorities had mis-
calculated a little in one respect:a merest fraction of the barbed-
wire pen which began at the corner of the above-mentioned
building was visible from these windows,which windows(I was
told)were consequently thronged by fighting men at the time of
the girls' promenade.

There were around a hundred women at La Ferté. Some were
wives of men who had been arrested, and some of those women had
come together with their children. Most, however, were prostitutes.
Prostitution was only illegal within the actual war zone. But, as Cummings pointed out, the front moved rapidly at first when the Allies
retreated through Belgium and northern France. A prostitute could
be pursuing a perfectly legal activity one day and find herself sum-
marily rounded up the next.

The first serious historian of the sexual experiences of the Great
War, Magnus Hirschfeld, wrote of a view prevalent in the literature
of the time—especially on the German side—that deprivation of sex
would lead the soldiers to a higher, more refined, and more noble eroticism through yearning for the absent. This requisite military abstinence was widely referred to as "the steel bath of the nerves," and it
constituted an expectation hardly borne out by experience among
any set of troops on either side.

The primary outlet for male desire in the Great War was prostitution, and prostitutes are truly the forgotten women of the war.
Economic disruption—husbands gone, factories closed, children
to support—forced many women into sex work; even so, demand
exceeded supply. The financial side of prostitution could also extend
beyond sex itself. As has always been the case with the economy
of army camp followers, prostitutes and pimps played a role in the
shadow economy of procurement. Dos once availed himself of the
procurement services of a local pimp: not for sex, but for alcohol.
The great flu epidemic was sweeping through his unit when it was
stationed in England at an army camp near Winchester. To be dispatched to the hospital with flu was reckoned to be a death sentence.

So when Dos came down with it, he turned to the local pimp, who sourced him a bottle of rum, and he drank it out. He said: "I always thought that bottle saved my life."

The pimp who sold rum to Dos at Winchester was pimping prostitutes who worked from a sandpit. As that thought suggests, sex with prostitutes was far from glamorous. The better regulated it was, the safer it was. But the regulations were not pleasant. Brothels at the highest level of hygiene could be policed with the requirement that the customer, on the way in and again on the way out, should dose himself with Protargol—a silver solution injected up the urethra. All army authorities were concerned about the prevalence of venereal disease. There were high-level policy disputes concerning whether soldiers ought to be punished for contracting a venereal disease or only if they attempted to conceal it: did the former policy succeed in frightening soldiers off sex with prostitutes altogether, or was the latter a more realistic means of ensuring that soldiers would at least seek treatment and not spread disease any further? Soldiers were subjected to regular checks, referred to not so fondly as the "tail parade" or the "hydrant and hose parade." The German Army was especially concerned, as they anticipated a kind of proto–biological warfare. In the Franco-Prussian War in 1870, French magazines (in the words of Hirschfeld) "had plainly called on all the French whores to perform what it considered a task of the highest patriotism—to infect with venereal disease whole masses of the German invaders. It was constantly feared [by the Germans] that this method would again be used and it was ever being fed by rumors from the occupied territories of France or Belgium."

There was more than one venereal disease to fear, but one to dread. Syphilis is a terrible disease. In its primary stage, there are open lesions on the genitals or in the mouth. In its final stage, tertiary syphilis is a chameleon that can look like a dozen other illnesses. As late as the 1960s, doctors in medical training were still reminded to "think syphilis" in any case that awoke suspicion or defied diagnosis. At La Ferté, several inmates began to exhibit signs of primary syphilis, including mouth lesions, which Cummings found to be an unappealing thought, considering that all had shared the same communal water bucket and dipper to drink from. After the syphilis appeared, those prisoners were at least segregated and given separate utensils.

Apart from such exceptional circumstances as these, the men confined to the enormous room slept, woke, ate, and exercised together. The prison complex included offices for the prison officials, quarters for all the prisoners, cells for solitary confinement, a shower room, a kitchen, a refectory, and a laundry. Barbed wire topped the external walls, which descried two large open-air courtyards behind the main complex, one reserved for outdoor exercise (*promenade*) for the male prisoners and one for the female prisoners and children.

The day began at 5:30 a.m., with foul, cold coffee made with reused coffee grinds and served from a vast bucket into each prisoner's tin cup. The prisoners were responsible for cleaning and sweeping their own quarters and had to empty, daily, the buckets that stood in the enormous room and served as their toilets. When the door was unlocked to allow the coffee in, a crew chosen on a rota basis were allowed out in order to carry the buckets full of urine and excrement down to the sewers outside. Afterward, there was morning *promenade* in the courtyard. The men's courtyard included a sentry box, an iron bar suspended 7 feet high as an apparatus for exercise, a shed that housed the water wagon, and some apple trees. The only seating was made of iron, "a barbarously cold seat for any unfortunate who could not remain on his feet the entire time."

After *promenade*, there was soup for lunch. Each man was given his own spoon, which he brought with him from the enormous room down to the refectory in the main building on the ground floor. Like the enormous room, the refectory was large and pillared, but the ceiling here was oppressively low and flat. On the way in, the prisoners collected their piece of bread and then sat at long tables amongst the pillars where *la soupe* was dished out. Cummings described the broth as the color of urine and the bread, he said, "smelled rather much like an old attic in which kites and other toys gradually are forgotten in a gentle darkness." After lunch, there was afternoon *promenade* in the courtyard, soup for dinner, and lights-out at 8:00 p.m. The worst of all, on a biweekly basis, were the showers: freezing-cold water forced on the prisoners and "such was the terror they inspired that it was necessary for the planton to hunt under paillases [the straw mattresses] for people who would have preferred death itself."

La Ferté was not technically a prison, as the second-in-command, the Surveillant, was particularly keen to remind them: "You are not prisoners. Oh, no. No indeed. I should say not. Prisoners are not treated like this. You are lucky." That there were worse prisons in France is not to be doubted; but equally, it cannot be doubted that the status of not-prisoner is pure semantics when men are under lock and key or armed guard at every moment night and day, starved, and abused, and when the only two not-prisoners who attempted escape during Cummings's time at La Ferté incurred thereby a life sentence to hard labor. The one respite from this confinement was volunteering to "catch water," and Cummings and Brown sought out this chore as often as possible. Catching water involved wheeling a water wagon out to an old pump not 50 yards from the prison, where water was pumped into the barrel of the water wagon and returned to the kitchen to furnish the day's needed water supply. Catching water occurred, naturally, under armed guard—but it was a chance to exist, however briefly, outside of the walls of La Ferté. What is more, it was rewarded by the Cook with a drink of almost decent, sugared coffee. Cummings liked the Cook. The reason he gave is that the Cook liked him and Brown, and he was pleased to return the compliment. The Cook was German, and perhaps it satisfied Cummings also to make a point of avoiding partisanship. In the multinational world of La Ferté, every prisoner was a prisoner first and foremost.

The *plantons* who guarded this world were, at least in Cummings's eyes, abhorrent. What made the *plantons* unbearable was not per se an active avoidance on their part of service at the Front. They were *réformés*: that is, men who had been invalided out of front-line service and remanded to duty as prison guards on account of wounds or psychological trauma. But these men turned their own feelings of guilt and anger and shame into a cruelty that communicated clearly to the male prisoners that their lives were held on undeserved sufferance and to the female prisoners that they were fair sport for any *planton*'s pleasure. Cummings said that only once in the time he was there did he see a *planton* punished for the routine harassment and sexual assaults on the women—and only then because the *planton* had turned on the officer who caught him in flagrante. The prisoners could resist the *plantons* in their own small way by shouting "shirker," but this was a surefire way to end up in solitary.

Humor was a weapon, and here Cummings excelled. He had a sharply satiric streak. "He'd pretend he was a politician or something," said Brown, "and a flood of clichés and twisted phrases would pour out for fifteen minutes without a stop." In La Ferté, Cummings turned his mimetic attention especially to the odious *plantons* and to the Surveillant. "All the prisoners would gather around to hear these and roar with laughter at his imitation of the *Surveillant* giving a lecture on being clean and washing one's face and shaving every morning."

And so Cummings settled in to the people and the spaces of his prison life. Most of his time would pass in the enormous room itself, where daytime life occurred in the interstices of the straw mattresses that were laid out around three-quarters of the perimeter—that is, all the walls excepting the one with the door. The prisoners either paced the room—although it grew increasingly crowded with beds as numbers swelled to over sixty men—or they sat around on one another's mattresses conversing. They sang songs, held spitting contests at which Cummings excelled (not so much in distance as in accuracy), played cards, and played dominoes from a set that Brown had cut out of cardboard. Some of the prisoners were inclined to fight, but Cummings and Brown had a knack for staying out of trouble. They commanded a certain level of respect amongst their fellow prisoners. Their company was cultivated, and they were trusted. They were, for example, above suspicion of thieving, and when one of the other prisoners in a rage cut open and riffled all of the straw mattresses in a hunt for a stolen piece of property, he exempted Cummings and Brown amongst only a few who could be deemed obviously innocent.

Meanwhile, the women lived a parallel imprisonment in their own spaces and with their own courtyard for *promenade*. Communication was effected mostly through illicit notes, exchanged when the two sexes either chanced or could contrive to pass each other in corridors. These limited interactions provided one of the chief sources of hope and laughter, and also the torment of frustrated desire.

On October 14, exactly three weeks into his imprisonment, Cummings turned twenty-three years old. On November 13, Brown celebrated his twenty-first, with cocoa made on a fellow prisoner's stove.

Cummings was destined to stay at La Ferté for three months minus four days before he was set free. Brown was destined to be sent on to the terrifying hellhole that was the prison of Précigné before he, too, was released later in 1918. But of course neither of them knew this, and not knowing was an indissoluble fact of prison life.

20

TIME STANDS STILL

IN PRISON, time stood still. "It is like a vast grey box in which are laid helter-skelter a great many toys, each of which is itself completely significant apart from the always unchanging temporal dimension which merely contains it along with the rest. I make this point clear for the benefit of any of my readers who have not had the distinguished privilege of being in jail." To speculate about release was to risk insanity.

Cummings fought hard to stay sane. The loss of any sense of time was not merely a literary conceit. He could not remember when he met with a new panel of interrogators—a commission charged with hearing his case and putting forward a recommendation either for permanent detention or for release. In *The Enormous Room*, he dates the commission to late November, but external documents prove that it met on October 17. The three commissioners came to La Ferté to hear cases. Neither Cummings nor Brown was informed of the outcome of their hearing. So they waited.

He discharged his anger into his notebooks. One of the La Ferté notebooks opens to a spread of notes on the child, religion, art, life, and death. At the top is written:

Man is the inconsiderable excrement
Life of ages

His notes on religion suggest that religion gives scope to the "intellectual expression of revenge" in the shape of hell. Ditto the intellectual expression of envy. Religion therefore grows from the idea of punishment.

He rejected the intellect and embraced feeling. Fear is intellectual. Anger is intellectual. Any real community of spirit has to be built on shared feeling; shared discourse does not facilitate peace but in fact prevents it. He penned a note/query to self: "Since War is purely Thoughtful, no 2 nations speaking same language (= directing ideas) can make allies (?)." Or to put it another way, through an interchange with a Mexican national also imprisoned at La Ferté: "When we asked him once what he thought about the war,he replied 'I t'ink lotta bullshit' which,upon copious reflection,I decided absolutely expressed my own point of view." In one of the few letters that escaped the prison censors at La Ferté, Cummings wrote to Scofield Thayer: "How intellectual is war: a millimeter turn of a round-screw, x jumps high in the midst of his merriment over y's uncouth hop." It was his sarcastic way of referring to the technological advancements that allowed the turn of a screw to bring the "uncouth hop" of death as mud and men are blasted into the air.

The idea of war as a crime of thought against feeling made its way into his published poetry. His first solo collection of poems, *Tulips & Chimneys* (1922 ms), was divided into two sections, the first of which is the "Tulips," and the second, the "Chimneys" of the volume's title. The "Chimneys" section contains only sonnets, one of which begins:

> when my sensational moments are no more
> unjoyously bullied of vilest mind
> and sweet uncaring earth by thoughtful war
> heaped wholly with high wilt of human rind—

Cummings expects his reader to disentangle a kind of root meaning in his language. "Sensational" does not mean outrageously melo-dramatic, but instead something like "based on the senses," and "thoughtful" is not "considerate," as in a thoughtful gesture, but rather "full of thoughts or thinking." Cummings innovates a neo-literalism that brings forcefulness to the poem and underpins its indictment of militarism. He—or the poem's speaker—speaks of his sensing self as "bullied" by the thinking self, "vilest mind," while the "sweet uncaring earth" finds itself piled up with the human detritus of "thoughtful war." Cummings regarded this sonnet, even decades later, as a poem at the center of his own poetic pacifism.

The publisher of *Tulips & Chimneys*, Thomas Seltzer, had already been burned by the censors for his publication of the work of D. H. Lawrence and other controversial authors, and his personal editorial taste combined with the professional caution engendered by recent attacks on his press left him not wholly sympathetic to Cummings's project. In the end he refused 86 of the 152 poems which Cummings wished to include. The sonnet "when my sensational moments are no more" was among the discards—possibly Seltzer recognized the pacifistic undertones in the poem and objected to its politics, though he did not give his reasons individually for each rejected poem and Cummings was forced to accept the result whatever the reasoning. Seltzer also refused the ampersand of the volume's title, and published it in 1923 as *Tulips and Chimneys*. Cummings published the rejected poems in later collections of poetry, but it was not until 1976 that *Tulips & Chimneys* was available as one volume, ordered and presented as Cummings had intended.

Oddly enough, Seltzer allowed the very next poem of *Chimneys* to stand, even though it ranks among the most daring and disturbing of the original hundred and fifty-two. This sonnet was a direct product of Cummings's time in France: drafts appear in two of the French notebooks. The finished version reads:

god gloats upon Her stunning flesh.   Upon
the reachings of Her green body among
unseen things,things obscene (Whose fingers young

the caving ages curiously con)

—but the lunge of Her hunger softly flung
over the gasping shores
                                    leaves his smile wan,
and his blood stopped hears in the frail anon

the shovings and the lovings of Her tongue.

god Is The Sea.   All terrors of his being
quake before this its hideous Work most old
Whose battening gesture prophecies a freeing

of ghostly chaos
                        in this dangerous night
through moaned space god worships God—
                                                (behold!
where chaste stars writhe captured in brightening fright)

The poem is built on the eroticisms of pagan Harvard. The Sea as god
calls up the old cosmogonies, where earth, sea, sky, sun, winds and so
on appear as gods or goddesses, and where these deified forces also
take lovers amongst one another and bear divine offspring. In Greek
mythologies, for example, the goddess Gaea, who is Earth, takes the
god Ouranos, who is sky, as her lover. The "chaste stars" of the nighttime that "writhe captured in brightening fright" inherit the fate of
the chaste nymphs of the pagan sexuality of pursuit, so often depicted
in paintings or sculptures in the later European artistic tradition at
that precise moment of their capture, torso twisted in fright as they
try in vain to pull themselves from the grasp of their captors.

But if it is a lowercase god whom we first meet, gloating upon the flesh of the ocean, the uppercase treatment of "The Sea" brings in the capitalization that is so strongly associated with the God of monotheistic tradition. And it is not until the ninth line that the Sea is named. Until then, imagination searches for this green body, this stunning flesh that moves amongst obscenities and provokes the lust of god himself. The jolt of the poem and its iconoclastic eroticism arise from these suspended uncertainties.

Cummings began the poem inspired by his own transatlantic crossing, but his earliest drafted lines are insipid and a little false. His drafts evolved slowly and the final version moved further from his earliest notes than was his usual habit. The crossing brought home to him the beauty and the vastness of the ocean, but his real confrontation with the power of the sea came as he himself changed through war and prison. His dangerous night is infused not merely with the expanse of ocean to every distance, but also with the nights of shells exploding like stars and the nights locked within dank prison walls. Dislocated from the sea about which he writes and locked where time stands still, he reaches for the unreachable and ponders eternity.

The majesty of the sea has the appeal of the grand. Cummings needed legitimately grand topics, because prison tended otherwise toward the grandiose or the paranoid. In one of his notebooks, he scrawled incoherently surrounding the rhymed phrase "life in prison / leads to circumcision." Picking up on the theme of hell as punishment in religion, the rest of that page offers partially scored-through lines that dip into an Oedipal world of fear of father, desire for mother, and punishment of the child.

The best defense against paranoia was a sense of humor, together with a sense of proportion engendered by small victories—like the literary victory of reusing the phrase "je vous prie de me ficher la paix!" (I beg you to give me some peace). This excellent piece of colloquial French is borrowed from the grumpy note, "we do not know this woman," written impatiently across the top of his angst-ridden letter to Mimi, in which he had begged her to say if Marie Louise was angry. He found a place for the idiom in a La Ferté notebook in a French poem suing for peace from all that is distant, pale, or of nothingness.

Another small victory arose in the affair of the jam bucket. One afternoon, the prisoners ran out of water from their shared water bucket. Perishing with thirst, they had the idea of tying a rope to a small empty pail, previously a jam jar, so that they might lower it out of the window, past the lone guard, and down to one of the sympathetic female prisoners in the courtyard below who could fill it at a water pump on the way to the washing shed and then return it to them. They concocted the rope by looping together all that was long and thin from their own clothing: belt, necktie, shoestring, scarf, handkerchief. When the guard was at the far end of his patrol, they began lowering the jam jar, and it had only just reached their helper at the bottom when the sergeant of the guards unexpectedly rounded the corner. He swelled in outrage, shouted to recall his underling from the edge of the patrol, and ordered him to fire at the window.

> The planton took aim, falling fearlessly on one knee, and closing both eyes. I confess that my blood stood on tip-toe; but what was death to the loss of the jam-bucket, let alone everyone's apparel which everyone had so generously lent? We kept on hauling silently. Out of the corner of my eye I beheld the planton—now on both knees, musket held to his shoulder by his left arm and pointing unflinchingly at us one and all—hunting with his right arm and hand in his belt for cartridges! A few seconds after this fleeting glimpse of heroic devotion had penetrated my considerably heightened sensitivity—UP suddenly came the bucket and over backwards we all went together on the floor of The Enormous Room. And as we fell I heard a cry like the cry of a boiler announcing noon—
> "Too late!"

The near escape left the jam-jar conspirators shaking with hysterical laughter. "I believe no one(curiously enough)got punished for this atrocious misdemeanor—except the planton; who was punished for not shooting us, although God knows he had done his very best."

This was the stuff of mental survival, along with friendships, the silly songs that the prisoners made up and sang together, and little acts of kindness like the slightly larger than stipulated chunk of bread that the cook tried to pass to Cummings and Brown at mealtime because he liked them both.

Reaching for small victories also entailed a new credo.

I do not believe in war because war does not believe in youth & I am youth.
I believe in faeries in woodpiles . . .

These passing thoughts were not the credo of a lifetime. (He soon crossed them out.) But by next year, 1918, he was writing poetry that turned to fairies and fairyland as a fantastical protection against war and death.

In prison, he had notebooks and a pencil, but how really could he keep track of ideas in a place like this? He created a color palette, which he described in *The Enormous Room* as "a study of colour itself." He cut slits into a page of a notebook, and through the slits he threaded every scrap of colored paper he could find. He pasted in colored stamps. He threaded short lengths of yarn through two slits and tied them off. He numbered each square, and from this he could also mix his palette and plan his paintings. He aimed at the modern effect of emotion through color. A little man, seated, with a pipe, would be painted in colors 2/13—a blend of green-yellow and yellow-orange—and in 13/30—yellow-orange blended with baby pink. He and Brown also gathered up the fallen autumn leaves, and he pressed into the notebook the colors of the cherry trees, poplar, oak, and fern, and a section of lush, stippled poplar bark—beautiful mementos of the onset of autumn, all now a century later bleached brown.

He passed some of his time trying to learn bits of other languages, especially Spanish, from his fellow inmates. He continued both to sketch and to compose poetry. He drew the other prisoners and also such views as he had available: vistas as "seen from the Enormous Room" and "seen from *le cour*" (where they took their *promenades*). He also worked on female nudes and on erotic postures. He was particularly fascinated by the balanced posture of the 69, which offered from a compositional perspective the possibility of enmeshing the two torsos, each head buried in the other's hips, arms wrapped around each other's back, and the bodies thus completely contiguous from head to haunch.

On December 10, Cummings wrote to his father. He had now been in prison for just over eleven weeks. He commended "the generosity of 'le gouvernement français' which has seen fit to endow my friend William and myself with all the leisure which could possibly be desired for aesthetic study." His missive is simultaneously sarcastic and soft-pedaling of the hardships of prison in order to spare his parents' anxiety. "Our life here is *A 1*. Never have I so appreciated leisure. I continually write notes on painting, poetry, and sculpture, as well as music; and the Muse Herself has not been unkind. My days, spent in delightful discussions with my good friend, whose tastes so happily coincide with my own, remind me of the mental peregrinations of your favorite Socrates, insofar as they have already illumined many dark crannies in the greatest of all sciences—Art." The letter was confiscated and retained by the prison censors, and ended up in a French civic archive.

Cummings also wrote to Scofield Thayer about the pleasures of devoting himself to art at La Ferté. In the letter to Thayer, he concentrates on his artistic communion with Brown, whereas in *The Enormous Room*, he emphasizes the sharing of artistic purpose also with other prisoners, who—precisely because of their lack of much or any education (some were illiterate)—possessed the ingenuous and direct appreciation of art that Cummings associated with childhood and valorized throughout his life. Some scholars automatically assume that the letter represents the authentic version and that the sense of shared delight in art presented in *The Enormous Room* is a fictionalized construct. But the letter is not an absolute record: it is a product of the dynamics of Cummings's friendship with Thayer, and Thayer was a snob. Even Cummings's own relatively genteel background seemed vulgar to the blue-blooded Thayer, who made some rather vicious observations in his private notes about Cummings as a "Yahoo" bearing "the odour of a urinal." These are not insults that Thayer voiced aloud to his friend, but Cummings surely knew of Thayer's snobbery. The letter to Thayer is as self-consciously fashioned as Cummings's later account of his imprisonment, and neither has a more inherent claim to authenticity.

Cummings's populism has always been a part of his poetic appeal. It sets him apart from the other Anglo-American high modernists, like T. S. Eliot, who pitched for an elite readership. It is true that Cummings sometimes assumes literary knowledge among his readers, especially knowledge of the classical world. But the aim is not exclusionary. In large part, he learned to gauge his audience through sharing poems and ideas with his Harvard literary circle, all of whom were steeped in classical knowledge. As a result, he may at times have overestimated his readers' familiarity with certain themes. But this was, at least, not just male coterie writing: Cummings's sister, Elizabeth, read some Greek, and his letters to her are full of classical allusions.

On the other hand, Cummings's populism was not a pandering to the conventional or the accepted. On the contrary, he positively delighted in shock value. One of his early scandals came from the poem "Buffalo Bill 's": "Jesus // he was a handsome man." The poem was written before France as an immediate response to the death of Buffalo Bill (William F. Cody) on January 10, 1917. It was published in 1920 in *The Dial*, the literary magazine owned by Thayer and James Sibley Watson. Watson's own mother objected to her son printing a poem that took the Lord's name in vain. Cummings's attitude was: "We are due to wake up some (Stoopid)^{n}th power people."

In an era of censorship, these decisions were not taken lightly. Cummings had ways of working around the censors, like printing the word "fuck" in the letters of the Greek alphabet or switching to French for "otherwise scented merde" (shit). It was a point of integrity to print swearwords somehow. Many war writers felt this way, because swearing was the language of soldiers. Dos talked about learning to swear in the army and was upset that his printer forced him to "bowdlerize" his soldier's dialogue for *One Man's Initiation: 1917*. Those who wrote about the war felt that they owed an honest expression of the world of soldiers, and honesty meant not censoring the language in which soldiers expressed themselves any more than the views they expressed.

Although the censors focused on transgressive language, no "Jesus" or "fuck" comes close to "god gloats" and its transgressive portrayal of God in a lascivious sexual union with the Sea. The eroticism of "god gloats" is blatant: the erotic thrill of that lunging Hunger, the gasping, the stopped blood. It is not just sexual union, but sex down and dirty: "the shovings and the lovings of Her tongue"; "through moaned space god worships God." At La Ferté, Cummings wrote about "Life—chaos, feeling, *kinēsis* [Greek, "movement"], vibration" as opposed to "Death—cosmos, thinking, *stasis* [Greek, "a standing still"], solidity." The sea, always in motion, capable of releasing a chaos into the far reaches of the dangerous night, is freedom, life, and art. It is not thinking war or the solidity of prison walls. Cummings is a war poet not only because he wrote about the war but also because his aesthetic of chaos and art was shaped while he encountered the meaninglessness of war and the inner death of confinement.

Time stood still, but the season changed. It was late autumn, heading now toward midwinter. In one of Cummings's most famous poems, he describes spring as "like a perhaps hand." Much more often, however, he associated hands and fingers with autumn. At La Ferté, he wrote notes on "the soft-hard fingers of the roof-loving rain [...] . Fingers, hands, fingers whom a soul dwelt in, touched by the hard-softness of blood touching fingers made of horns [...] and all loveless things, clinging, caught, catching loveful hands which have held the world. Hands of the Autumn. hands hands."

In *The Enormous Room*, he wrote:

Rain did,from time to time,not fall:from time to time a sort of unhealthy almost-light leaked from the large uncrisp corpse of the sky,returning for a moment to our view the ruined landscape. From time to time the eye,travelling carefully with a certain disagreeable suddenly fear no longer distances of air coldish and sweet,stopped upon the incredible nearness of the desolate without motion autumn. Awkward and solemn clearness,making louder the unnecessary cries,the hoarse laughter,of the invisible harlots in their muddy yard,pointing a cool actual finger at the silly and ferocious group of manshaped beings huddled in the mud under four or five little trees,came strangely in my own mind pleasantly to suggest the ludicrous and hideous and beautiful antics of the insane. [...] Once I was sitting alone on the long beam of silent iron and suddenly had the gradual complete unique experience of death. ...

It became amazingly cold.

21

TYRANNY

IN OVERALL CHARGE at La Ferté was a tyrant whom Cummings named Apollyon, in reference to *Pilgrim's Progress*, where the "foul fiend" Apollyon—a monstrous hybrid of fish, dragon, bear, and lion— opposes the hero Christian in the Valley of Humiliation, demanding obedience, before Christian defeats him in bloody single combat.

The regime of this new Apollyon of La Ferté was an expression of his sadism. He ruled, Cummings said, through fear. Pillars of his regime of fear were the punishments meted out to prisoners. For lesser offenses, it was *pain sec*—dry bread. A prisoner on *pain sec* received two portions of entirely dry and hard bread per day, and nothing else save what his fellow prisoners, skimping on their own meals of soup and slightly less stale bread, could pass him. *Pain sec* was the usual punishment for male prisoners attempting to speak to or make any kind of signal toward one of the women incarcerated at La Ferté.

Those caught in more serious offenses, including the offense of attempting to pass letters to the women, were confined in solitary (or sometimes together in a group) in *cabinot*. The cells that comprised *cabinot* had no windows: no light entered. They had no bed or proper floor, so that the incumbent of the cell was left in midwinter mud or even in standing water. In *cabinot*, as on *pain sec*, the prisoner had nothing to eat but bread and whatever could be sneaked in by the other prisoners, in common decency, through the crack under the door.

Cummings was never confined in *cabinot*, but he saw inside the cells both as they were when prisoners were confined to them and as they were when the inspectors came round: an exemplary cell presented for inspection, dried, cleaned, and supplied with an iron bedframe, mattress, blankets, and quilt.

Apollyon visited his sadism even more upon the women than upon the men. The women were placed in *cabinot* more readily and longer for their offenses than the male prisoners. Cummings wrote that it freed him forever from the prejudiced notion of women as "the weaker sex." A woman named Lena was confined to *cabinot* for sixteen days. Cummings wrote in *The Enormous Room* that he could barely conjure the cold and the damp of the prison in any way that could somehow convey to his reader what was done to Lena: "to indicate—it is no more than indicating—the significance of the torture perpetrated under the Directeur's direction in the case of the girl Lena." The enormous room itself, Cummings explains, was heated by a wood stove, whose lung-tickling smoke rendered the air "next to unbreathable, but tolerated for the simple reason that it stood between ourselves and death." Nonetheless, the cold at night was "desolating," even in that main room and with his comparatively luxurious bedding and fur coat to serve as blanket. Most of the men and women at La Ferté, even the old women and the young children, had less than him. The policy for *cabinot* was one thin blanket only. When Lena was sent to *cabinot* for sixteen days, allowed out only once a day for thirty minutes, Cummings watched her skin turn gradually green. He watched her double up from her cough, "creasing her body as you crease a piece of paper with your thumb-nail, preparatory to tearing it in two."

Lena was Belgian. "Energy rather than vitality." "She never smiled." She was part of a gang of four: Celina, Lena, Lily, and Renée. Celina too was Belgian and about eighteen or nineteen. She was beautiful, and had somehow retained her health and her sexual allure. Although Cummings does not say so in *The Enormous Room*, Celina and Brown were involved. Once Brown and two other prisoners feigned illness, skipped the *promenade*, and managed to pick the lock into the women's quarters to enjoy an afternoon's liaison. Brown left Celina a gold cross that belonged to him—a souvenir of his childhood choir practice—and later, when Brown was moved on to Précigné, Celina trafficked a letter to him via another prisoner on the same prison journey. Lily was German and looked ancient, but was only eighteen. She was dying of tuberculosis. Renée was about twenty-five years old and had no teeth. "Renée was in fact dead. In looking at her for the first time, I realized that there may be something stylish about death."

This gang of four were united in Cummings's memory in one of the most terrible sights he witnessed during those three months at La Ferté. Celina, Lena, Lily, and Renée were all confined to *cabinot*, and the four of them, Lily especially, sang and shouted in defiance into the night. To keep out the noise, the guards stuffed straw round all the cracks in and under the door. Then they lit the straw. Lily and Renée were already unconscious by the time Celina managed to shout to the guards and secure their release. Cummings stumbled upon this scene as the corridor was full of smoke and Lily and Renée were being carried out, limp as rag dolls and to all appearances dead. "I will never forget what I saw."

Celina was punished for her heroism with another day in *cabinot*: a full twenty-four hours with no food at all.

Among his fellow inmates, Cummings saw generosity and nobility. But these qualities were not untainted. Some of the inmates were bullied by others. "It struck me at the time," Cummings mused, "as intensely interesting that,in the case of a certain type of human being,the more cruel are the miseries inflicted upon him the more cruel does he become toward any one who is so unfortunate as to be weaker or more miserable than himself. Or perhaps I should say that nearly every human being,given sufficiently miserable circumstances,will from time to time react to those very circumstances(whereby his own personality is mutilated)through a deliberate mutilation on his own part of a weaker or already more mutilated personality. I daresay that this is perfectly obvious. I do not pretend to have made a discovery. On the contrary,I merely state what interested me peculiarly in the course of my sojourn at La Ferté:I mention that I was extremely moved to find that,however busy sixty men may be kept suffering in common,there is always one man or two or three who can always find time to make certain of their comrades enjoying a little extra suffering."

The prisoner whom Cummings admired most was Jean, a black man who had things particularly bad, since in addition to the conditions of the prison, Jean had to contend with the racism of the guards and of many of his fellow prisoners. Jean was even more vulnerable than the other inmates. When he arrived, he had entrusted all his money—sixty francs to sustain him at the commissary where additional supplies could be purchased—to one of the *plantons* for deposit. The *planton* pocketed the money and denied everything, and Jean had no redress. "Of all the fine people in La Ferté,Monsieur Jean ("le noir" as he was entitled by his enemies)swaggers in my memory as the finest."

These memories—of Jean and Apollyon and the gang of four and of many others—materialize in *The Enormous Room* in a style as dry as bone. Literary critics have referred to this book both as a novel and as a memoir, but it is best just to call it an account. Cummings never sought to define it by genre. However, he regarded it in all meaningful senses as true, and he said that, insofar as it would have any appeal to the public, it would appeal as a document. When writing, he worked closely from his own notes as well as from his memory, which he cross-checked with the memory of Brown, who described the result as remarkably accurate. Many of its specifics are independently verifiable. As with all autobiographical writing, we have to assume, of course, that some material—like conversation—is shaped as it filters through memory. But what we have is far more valuable than any stenographer's transcript could have been: we have access to the internal as well as external realities of Cummings's world. The deliberate wryness and humor of the writing in *The Enormous Room* is the solution Cummings found in order to speak of nearly unspeakable things. Imprisonment was not an adventure. It was a terror.

Although the opportunity to purchase some food at the commissary mitigated the privations of imprisonment for Cummings and
Brown, this mitigation must be kept in context. Cummings's letters
to his parents aim to spare their feelings (and also to say nothing
about the conditions at La Ferté that would trigger censorship).
Cummings claimed in a letter to his father that supplies were ample:
"delicacies such as butter, cheese, eggs (which we scramble over a
bougie every morning) confiture and chocolate." All that he lacked
was a decent-tasting brand of tobacco. This was far from the truth.
Cummings and Brown stayed alive, but little more. Without exact
recipes for bread, potato, and broth, it is impossible to count the cal-
ories, but it was manifestly a severe calorie deficit. Such a starvation
diet could not be simply remedied by the morsel of meat that was
added to *la soupe* three times a week or by the provisions available at
the commissary.

Apart from the incident in *cabinot*, when the noxious smoke of
the hay fires set by the guards nearly consummated an act of cold-
blooded murder, it was not the policy of the authorities—even of
Apollyon—to kill off the prisoners deliberately. Ergo, when Cummings had several days of severe diarrhea—a potentially life-
threatening sickness for a body that is cold, weak, and starved—his
official diet was supplemented with milk. But Cummings's health
was precarious and Brown's even more so. By early December,
Brown had scurvy. His body creaked. The medical term is "crep-
itus," and the sound indicates that the joints have disintegrated
to the point of creaking when the body moves. It is a symptom of
scurvy that—to take an early medical description of the progression of the disease—would manifest at stage two (of four stages).
(In stage three, the body rots and smells of dying flesh; in stage
four, the skin is covered with black spots, and death—if the scurvy
remains untreated—is imminent.)

Brown was already, therefore, severely ill when, on the recommendation of the commission that had come to hear cases on October 17,
he was dispatched in mid-December to the prison at Précigné.

Précigné housed about four hundred prisoners. It was surrounded by barbed wire and searchlights. There was no food here beyond bread, potatoes, and beans. The potatoes were frozen and caused gastric bloating. The beans were laced with pebbles—a farmer's strategy for making up the weight. To be safe, it was necessary to eat the beans one at a time. But hunger often overrode self-preservation, and many men—Brown included—took urgent mouthfuls and cracked their teeth. There were many deaths from malnutrition and pneumonia. Others died from the fighting, which was pervasive and which the guards did nothing to prevent. One of the more aggressive inmates threatened Brown, who only survived because another prisoner threw the aggressor down a flight of stairs and then followed to pummel him when he was down. There was desperation at Précigné. Most reckoned that they had no chance of release until the war ended, and no one could know when that would be or who would survive to see it.

The months at La Ferté brought Cummings face-to-face with arbitrary and sadistic authority. Another of Apollyon's favorite tricks was to burst shouting out of his office exactly when the women and girls were carrying their latrine buckets down the stairs. "And I saw once a little girl eleven years old scream in terror and drop her pail of slops,spilling most of it on her feet;and seize it in a clutch of frail child's fingers,and stagger,sobbing and shaking,past the Fiend—one hand held over her contorted face to shield her from the Awful Thing of Things—to the head of the stairs;where she collapsed,and was half-carried half-dragged by one of the older ones to the floor below while another older one picked up her pail and lugged this and her own hurriedly downward." As soon as the girls disappeared Apollyon started screeching about filthy whores. The pain Cummings felt at his own inability to protect spilled into an absolute emotion of rage: "never in my life before had I wanted to kill to thoroughly extinguish and to entirely murder."

But Cummings knew that he was confronting more than just prison authority. He was also facing his own demons, including his anger and rebellion against his father. He analyzed the logic of his own inner life.

i obey masochistic,

(1) the symbol of Suppression — a policeman creates in me and makes me conscious of my own suppression = aggressive

(2) the object of his suppressions [...] coincides with mine therefore he becomes my FATHER
> (law + order
> cleanliness
> money
> respectability
> accuracy

I transfer to any / a / this policeman my hatred of / uprising against my father

Cummings was locked in an emotional battle in which a part of him still sided with the upright, uptight principles of his father. Part of him still believed that his life belonged to his family; that it was "our" adventure and not his own life; that when he drank or desired a woman or spent his time with his louche friends, he betrayed the noble self—the eagle—that his father wanted for a son. From this psychological perspective, prison brought liberation. The Reverend represented everything endorsed and approved by society: law and order, money, respectability. But a society that could behave with such institutional brutality was not a society worth bowing to. By embracing the very absurdity of his own imprisonment, Cummings finally found a way to reject the expectations of a society gone mad and to trust his own rebellious voice.

Meanwhile, and unbeknownst to Cummings, the Reverend was doing his utmost to secure his son's release.

He learned of the arrest on October 17 when he was cabled by Richard Norton, the Norton of the Norton-Harjes Ambulance Corps in which Cummings and Brown had been serving. A flurry of telegrams followed. Within days, the Reverend had the notion of launching a cause célèbre. He cabled to Norton on October 21 to say that he was perfectly prepared to mount a stink in Washington, with every hope of rousing the force of public indignation. He pronounced confidently to Norton: "France cannot afford to alienate American sympathy by disregarding rights of Citizens or dealing harshly with youths who volunteered to help her." Norton consistently promised progress and counseled patience.

A month later, on November 20, 1917, the American embassy at Paris informed the State Department in Washington that Cummings had already been released—and was dead. He was lost at sea aboard the torpedoed American vessel *Antilles*. But at the same time that official news of his son's death reached the Reverend at 104 Irving Street, Norton cabled to say that Cummings would be released within the next few days. There was hope, then, of a mistake. The Reverend cabled urgently to Norton demanding to know if his son were dead or alive. Four days later, on November 24, both the American State Department and 104 Irving Street were authoritatively informed that the man lost on the *Antilles* was H. H., not E. E., Cummings.

It is a hard piece of fortune to go down in history for the relief felt that it was you and not another who died. No man should be collateral damage in another man's story. I have been able to find out very little about H. H. Cummings. His was one of sixty-seven lives lost when the *Antilles* sank in a submarine attack. He was from Philadelphia: he was the only Philadelphian to die on the transport. He must be the same man who appears in the register of births for Philadelphia City, Pennsylvania, as Harold H. Cummings, born May 16, 1894, to Wm. P. Cummings and Clara E. Cummings. That makes him six months (minus two days) older than E. E. Cummings, and twenty-three when he died. There is nothing more to know about who he was or who he might have been had he not died on the ocean when the *Antilles* went down.

While American officialdom was wrong about the death of E. E. Cummings on board the *Antilles*, Norton was also wrong to think that Cummings would be released in a matter of mere days. The Reverend champed at the bit. He felt that he owed his son a debt for saving his own and his sister's life on Silver Lake on that day when Cummings pushed Rex under and kept himself and Elizabeth safe for rescue. The Reverend had even kept the box seats to which Cummings and Elizabeth clung as a kind of memento, preserved for the purpose of exuding their silent sermon on the subject of gratitude for life's blessings. "I keep them to remind me," he used to say, "whenever things seem to me to be bad." In the Reverend's world, a man's debts and obligations had to be honored. And he would honor his debt to his son now, by freeing his son from this French prison.

The weeks of inconsistent and contradictory reports finally prompted the Reverend's last missive in the Cummings/Brown case file. On December 8, in a spirit at once humble and peremptory, he addressed himself directly to the president of the United States, Woodrow Wilson himself. "Dear Mr. President," wrote Reverend Edward Cummings. "It seems criminal to ask for a single moment of your time." But at the end of his tether, the Reverend was prepared to do just that. And as unlikely as it seems, the letter was a needed spur. Although there is no reason to suppose that it ever impinged upon the consciousness of President Woodrow Wilson, it was processed by the president's own personal secretary, and the State Department soon communicated with the embassy in Paris in a sharper and more urgent tone: "Department cannot understand reasons for failure of Embassy to follow up matter promptly. Cable reply."

Cummings's release was put in motion.

He was interrogated by Apollyon himself about his intentions and desires. He said that he desired to be relocated to Oloron Sainte-Marie, to work there on his painting. It was a superb choice. Oloron Sainte-Marie is a stunning town, located in the Pyrenees near the border with Spain. The settlement dates back to the Roman era and the houses entwine themselves into the steep banks of two rivers flowing down from the mountains. A self-taught painter such as Cummings could flourish there in further months or years of self-study, and at this point in his life Cummings saw himself as a painter even before a poet.

The final release order came through from the French government. And so, on December 19, 1917, he walked free.

PART VI

FREEDOM

22

BERTHE

If you think, Marie Louise, that I have forgotten the days and
nights that we spent together . . .

CUMMINGS HAD TO forgo his dreams of the Pyrenees: he was summoned by telegram to Paris. It was a long trip, and he traveled second-
class until he was found out on a third-class ticket. He was well past
caring for authority or its rules and regulations. When he arrived in
the city, he was angry and disjointed, but he had purpose.

Paris was cold and deserted. It was late. He headed for the Boulevard des Italiens and then wandered until he found a hotel, where he
gained admittance from the night watchmen. He was desperate for a
wash: he was infested with fleas.

The next morning, Thursday, the twentieth of December, was
overcast and several degrees below freezing. It was, to be exact, 28
degrees Fahrenheit (or −2.8 Celsius). There was snow on the ground.
Cummings was lucky to have his fur coat. He presented himself, as
instructed, at the American embassy, where he encountered an official by the name of John C. Wiley. Mr. Wiley was second secretary

of the American embassy, and Cummings quickly sized him up as Brown's best chance.

It was only now that Cummings learned of the efforts that had been put into his case, and into Brown's. He got the short version. Three months' worth of telegrams, memos, and missives, involving his family and Brown's family, the director of the Norton-Harjes ambulance service, the US State Department, the American embassy in Paris, the US Army, US senators, lawyers, and more were boiled down to Wiley's explanation that (as Cummings passed on to Brown) "my family had, it seemed, cabled, etc. also your Aunt."

Cummings put Brown's case to Mr. Wiley. Meanwhile, Wiley persuaded Cummings to put his health first and prevailed upon him to sail immediately, on the *Espagne*, departing for America in just two days' time.

Paris was, as Cummings wrote in a letter for Brown at Précigné, "fearfully cold," and some of their favorite haunts were closed for the winter. In spite of the weather, Cummings set out to spend the rest of the day walking, as he and Brown had done in May. His nerves were jangled. The city was alive; everything was hurrying and cold and alive. In one of his tiniest notebooks, hardly larger than a cigarette paper, he jotted his rattled notes. He overheard a middle-aged man, ranting about those who shirked the draft. "I have a daughter & I am proud of her but if I found my daughter going with a young man of military age, physically fit, who was evading his duty, I'd take that girl, much as I love her, & lock her up in one of the rooms of the house. And throw the key IN THE RIVER." From the embassy, Cummings walked down to the Seine, crossed over to Île de la Cité, and basked once more in the grandeur of Notre-Dame de Paris. He scribbled incoherencies about Paris in snow, and walked long into the night.

Friday, the twenty-first of December, was more bitter yet. The thermometer fell to 25 degrees Fahrenheit. Cummings spent the morning racing around Paris, exhausting his last funds on taxis as he bounced from here to there in search of an identity photograph, a new passport, and a ticket for the next day's sailing. Once his departure was secure, he turned his thoughts to his last afternoon and evening in Paris. He set out to find Marie Louise.

Cummings had repented of his summer's loss of faith. He wanted to set things right and he wanted to be with her again. He tried the major boulevards. He started at the Place de l'Opéra and hunted along the Boulevard des Italiens, then he turned onto the Boulevard Poissonnière and followed it as it became the Boulevard de Bonne-Nouvelle and then the Boulevard Saint-Martin, all the way to the Place de la République. When he couldn't find her walking the street, he turned around, walked halfway back, and headed toward South Pigalle.

The new address that Marie Louise had sent to him was 23 Rue Henri Monnier, running parallel to the Rue des Martyrs, where Mimi used to live. The Rue Henri Monnier slopes very gently uphill toward Montmartre, phalanxed by buildings of six or seven stories on either side. Only from the very top of the street is it possible, looking out at an angle, to see the brilliant domes of Sacré-Coeur flashing into the gap and rendering the white stone façades of the street suddenly yellowed by contrast. This narrow street benefitted from prewar prosperity. Number 23, where Marie Louise had taken her room, was a smooth and solid building, seven stories in height, with large, rectangular windows and delicate railings. Either side of Number 23, buildings in the same style are incised with the names of their architects and their stonemasons and the date 1907. Cummings rang. He found only a doorman.

However desperate and guilty he felt, he had to accept that she was gone. He pulled out his tiny notebook and began to draft a letter. He rehearsed briefly the history of his imprisonment. He had already written much of this in a letter sent from La Ferté, but there had been no reply, and he had no way of knowing if she had ever received it. And so he explained again that he had been arrested on account of some of Brown's letters; that he had been in prison for eleven weeks, finally acquitted, and sent to the American embassy in Paris. He promised her that he had searched everywhere, and pleaded with her to understand that he was going home so quickly only because of his damaged health. He told her again that he loved her. "If you think,

Marie Louise, that I have forgotten the days and nights that we spent together, then you are mistaken. I do not forget; perhaps, though, it is you who has forgotten all: I would not know." He told her that by the time she read the letter, he would be pining already for Paris, and most of all, he would be worrying about her. He knew she had been ill, and again he pleaded with her to understand that he had had no *permission* to come to her. He wrote that he kept the photograph that she had given him, and treasured it along with his memories of her and their time together.

He promised her that he would return. Paris, he said, had stolen his heart. Meanwhile, he would be happy—so happy—to have news of her. He left her with Scofield Thayer's address in New York, in hopes that she would write.

Then he turned his back on the Rue Henri Monnier and walked down the Rue du Faubourg-Montmartre, the long street linking the subversive Quartier Pigalle to the boulevards of central Paris. By now it was evening, on the day before the winter solstice, nearly the shortest day of the year. An interval of clear sky had brought the thermometer further down to 23 degrees Fahrenheit, or −5 Celsius. The wind was picking up too. With a wind-chill factor, the effective temperature was more like 7 to 12 degrees Fahrenheit, or −11 to −14 degrees Celsius. It took him half an hour to find the North African couscous joint that he and Brown had favored over the summer. Only Berthe recognized him—a young waitress whom he had known back in May.

She invited him home. He managed first to nab a horse and carriage back to his hotel in order to collect his things and pay his bill. Then— still jangled, exhausted, and overwhelmed—he lost the address she had just given him, but found her place somehow. He piled into her room with all his goods, including packages of socks and sweets sent by his family during his imprisonment. These care packages had progressed no further than the embassy, where Cummings found them on the previous day. He now hoped to forward them to his still imprisoned friends, but couldn't think how. Berthe came to the rescue. She did up two packages and promised to send them on: socks to a friend at La Ferté-Macé and sweets to Brown at Précigné.

Berthe was no casual pickup. There was a genuine tenderness. Back in May, he had written a poem about her, in French, conceived through the terms of his Cubist experimentation. She was, in the language of the poem, stubborn but weary, with flesh that was green like a gourd, chewing a yellow rose between blue teeth, with red skin, heavy lips, and a mouth on fire. For her part, she cared enough about him to remember him when six months had passed, and to recognize him, changed as he was by the front and by his time in La Ferté-Macé. They smoked a cigarette, drank Champagne, "and talked gradually of the war France death my prison, all pleasant things."

At last, as he wrote to Brown, switching delicately to the French: "J'ai perdu quelque chose." (I've lost something.)

Then it occurred to him, perhaps, that a gentleman does not bandy a lady's name, and he went back, crossed out "Berthe," and substituted "B—" as a token to chivalry. At the same time, he made no effort to disguise her identity. In fact, he urged Brown to write to her if that package of sweets ever arrived, as she was so kindhearted and would awfully much like to know.

For Cummings, it was the revolution. "My thumb smashes the world—."

He wrote twice about that night with Berthe, in work that was somewhere between notes and poetry. He could not push the night far enough away from himself to turn it into art, and he did not really try. He left the two pieces unpublished. As autobiography, however, they capture the watershed in his world. "23years lying with thee in the bed in the little street off the Faubourg Montmartre."

At the age of twenty-three, sex brought completeness and relief. It was magnificent: "frot of furied eyes on brain!heart knotted with A suddenly nakedness—." Sex also brought sudden and utter newness: "Her Nudity seats Itself sharply beside. New person." It released Cummings into a flood of erotic poetry, sketches, and paintings. There are hundreds and hundreds of erotic pencil or ink sketches in the Cummings archives now held at Harvard University. They are drawn in a variety of styles. Some are naturalistic, some primitivist, and some Cubist. Some are stylized in a 1920s flapper manner that updates the pen and ink of Aubrey Beardsley. Some fly across the page as if they were figures from Chagall. They display a wide variety of positions: missionary, various seated postures, various front-to-back positions, men fingering women, women fingering themselves, men performing oral sex on women, the occasional 69, and some rather less realistically achievable Cubist positions. Many of them clearly show women in orgasm.

In the sketches, Cummings explores his fascination with how two bodies fit together. Sometimes they come together through impossible contortions, almost magnetized into each other across their distorted proportions and twisted postures. Other times, he obsesses over anatomical accuracy, drawing entry from behind again and again to work out the correct angle.

In the poetry about Berthe, Cummings draws on the Decadent language of exquisite pain that shaped the literary world of pagan Harvard. Berthe has echoes of the Decadent femme fatale, whose enticements awake a torturous desire: "I watched her Flesh graciously destroy its cruel posture." The sensuous agony she inspires even has a slight hint of kink:

> ".then is to be noticed . . . plural darkness spanked with
> singular light over
> the pink
> bed

But the literary inheritance of Decadent desires is now mingled with practical experience. For the first time, Cummings fully encountered the dual physicality of sex. There is the triumphant eroticism of rhythm and union.

> O with whom I lay
> Whose flesh is stallions
> Then I knew my youth trampled with thy hooves of
> nakedness

But there is also the fumbling awkwardness of whose limbs go where and the slightly risible aspect of sex when it is judged from the outside. There are bits of sex which are not that sexy. "To Undress—laughably mechanical." Decades of poetry written by Cummings about sex has its germ in that night with Berthe, his last night in France, and its blend of the literary, the erotic, and the realistic.

And so he sailed on the *Espagne*, on the twenty-second of December, leaving Paris behind. Brown was still incarcerated at Précigné. The other Harvard volunteers were also still in Europe. Dos Passos saw in the New Year from ambulance service with the American Red Cross in Italy. Dos spent New Year's Eve, 1917, writing letters to old friends: "in an hour or so the seventeenth abortion of an abortive century will have passed into the musty storehouse of history where all the bales of stupidity and greed and misery are finally bundled away—for the edification of that golden future that is always behind the curve of time—The water's boiling over—a cup o'tay to you!"

On New Year's Day, 1918, the *Espagne* docked on the other side of the Atlantic and Cummings was back home in New York. He never heard from Marie Louise, and he never saw her again.

23

THE GOOD OFFICES OF
MR. WILEY

CUMMINGS NOW HAD two matters on his mind. Brown was still imprisoned in France, and he himself was now liable for US military service.

Cummings's health was very poor. He was malnourished and underweight; he had a skin infection, a leg ulcer, and a cough. His hearing was temporarily affected, and he bore damage to his face and hands. But Brown was in a far more dangerous situation.

In spite of Cummings's desire to link their fates, the case of Cummings and the case of Brown were quite distinct. In terms of family, it was three months before Brown's father involved himself actively in the case, and then only the once. Persistent action was taken instead by the family of Brown's deceased mother, who had been the youngest of five sisters. One of those sisters had married a man by the name of Spaulding Bartlett, and it was with this Bartlett family that Brown lived for a year when he attended the Cambridge High and Latin School. Bartlett now took the lead in efforts to free Brown, seconded by one of the other sisters, Hope Slater. As an intermediary, Bartlett sought the assistance of a prominent Boston lawyer, Sherman L. Whipple.

Whipple first contacted the US State Department on November 12, 1917. The situation, he said, was "intolerable," and—like the Reverend—he, too, had the idea of launching a cause célèbre. There is a hint of a threat in his expostulations about the danger to the war effort if American parents should come to believe that their sons would be sent abroad into the mercy of blundering French authorities. The combined efforts of Whipple and of the Reverend's friends and connections prompted the State Department to press the American embassy in Paris for fuller information. But meanwhile, sympathy for Cummings's plight was rising and sympathy for the plight of Brown already falling. Richard Norton, director of the ambulance service, wired to the Reverend that he had finally seen all the documents and that there was "absolutely nothing against your boy who I understand after certain formalities will be in a few days his own master." In a longer letter, he added that Brown and Cummings were reported to have kept themselves "dirty and unkempt" during their period of service in SSU XXI, and that in a "life under canvas . . . you will realize that this is a real sin and may well get on people's nerves." However, he laid the main blame at the feet of Brown, "whom I judge to be a bumptious ass." Having seen Brown's letters, he adds that Brown "propounds very unbaked philosophical doctrines and quotes idiotic poetry." Even so, Norton regarded Brown's imprisonment as overzealous and unnecessary, and he continued to press Brown's case with the American embassy in Paris. But clearly he also regarded Brown as a not entirely worthy cause.

In what was already a mess of telegrams, letters, internal memos, reports, and telephone calls, the main official line was crystallizing. Cummings was innocent. He had been suspected only because of his friendship with Brown, and upon further examination it had been determined that such suspicions were unfounded. The American authorities knew that Cummings had been cleared by the French Examining Board on October 17, and that this board had recommended his release, subject to the ratification of the French Ministry of the Interior. For the latter part of November and the beginning of December, the efforts of the American embassy in Paris and the State

Department at home were directed almost exclusively toward locating Cummings and securing his promised freedom.

While Cummings's plight was treated as a priority, it took two weeks for the State Department to reply to Whipple. The task of writing was assigned to a junior official, Third Assistant Secretary of State, and the letter itself was temporizing. It informed Whipple that the Examining Board of October 17 had recommended the release of Cummings and the detention of Brown. When the Department had complete information from Paris, they would give the case their full consideration. Meanwhile, if Whipple cared to submit any further information concerning Brown's background, they would be pleased to receive it.

On the tenth of December, Whipple wrote again to the State Department, taking them up on their invitation to supply background on Brown and enclosing for this purpose an account of Brown's family, education, and character provided by Spaulding Bartlett. Bartlett vouched for his nephew: "He is a young man of much more than average intelligence and a poetic temperament, and has expressed many times youthful sentiments of a socialistic nature, which, in my judgment, are due to the effervescence of youth rather than conviction, and, judging from what I know of the boy myself, and of his antecedents, he will be the last person in the world to injure anybody." Bartlett and Whipple still felt that the cards fell on their side. American public opinion would not stand for the detention of American volunteers in France. Whipple returned to the hinted threat of his first communication: the circumstances "might easily develop serious complications," and he urged the State Department to think not only of Brown's liberty but also of some reparation for what he described as a grave injustice.

Whipple's and Bartlett's conviction that they occupied an unambiguous moral high ground was about to come crashing down, with the forwarding Stateside of Colonel Parker's original report into the arrest. Col. Frank Parker was stationed with the American military effort in France, and he had assembled a report as long ago as October 26. This early report appears to have been solicited by the American embassy, presumably in response to notification from the French authorities of the detention of two American citizens, but before the involvement of any of the American officials who came subsequently to have a real connection to the case. The report sat in a desk in Paris for nearly two months. By the time of Cummings's release and appearance in Paris on December 20, the embassy had been at the receiving end of several sharp prods from the US State Department, and the American ambassador, William G. Sharp, was feeling defensive. On the hunt for proof of his energetic handling of the case and command of the relevant facts, he lit upon the old report by Parker, and, following Cummings's release, forwarded it to the State Department by the next diplomatic pouch.

Not knowing that Colonel Parker's report was en route, Whipple wrote again to the State Department on the twenty-seventh of December: his most bullish letter yet. He castigated both them and the American embassy for their lethargy and opined that "if the State Department is so helpless, then a resolution from Congress will bring France to its senses." He had every intention of enlisting a family connection, Senator Lodge, to raise the Brown case on the congressional floor. To this purpose, on January 2, Brown's father bestirred himself for his one and only direct intervention in the case: a letter to Senator Lodge. The letter is written with an emotional coldness that itself must elicit today more human sympathy for his son than any other among the hundreds of documents in the Cummings/Brown file. The elder Dr. Brown's references to the "suspense" over Brown's situation, which is "greatly disturbing his relatives and friends," conveys as stiff and formal an impression as the uptight threat implied in his reference to "disquieting rumors" circulated by his son's friends and the chance that news of the arrest would "get into the public press with unpleasant notoriety to us all."

But just as the champions of Brown's case prepared to escalate to the Senate floor and the press—the ax fell. Colonel Parker's report, which included Brown's censored letters, arrived at the State Department, and sympathy for Brown evaporated.

While all previous replies to Whipple had been undertaken by the

third assistant secretary, the matter was now bumped up the hierar-
chy to the second assistant, who wrote on January 14, enclosing copies
of Brown's letters and informing Whipple firmly that "their character
is not such as would warrant the Department, under present conditions, to take the case up with the French Government." Neither did
the State Department feel that Brown's presence in the United States
was in fact a desirable outcome. In January of 1918, America was a
smaller world than it is today, and Washington was capable of actively
opposing the return of even just one man possessed of a journalistic
background, firsthand experience of the war, and worryingly subversive opinions. And, finally, the Department strongly disadvised having the matter raised on the congressional floor, firing as a warning
shot the suggestion that raising the case would only draw attention to
Brown's "improper statements." An almost identical letter was sent to
Senator Lodge, over the signature of the Secretary of State himself.

Bartlett and Whipple folded their cards immediately. Bartlett admitted to Whipple that the letters were "a little worse than I
expected." But he had made a promise to Brown's mother when
Brown was baptized that he would look after the boy if there were ever
need, and there must be some way at least to allow Brown to send and
receive letters. All thought of agitating for his release was dropped.
In fact, said Bartlett now: "The experience will be good for him. . . ."
Bartlett only wanted to be in contact. To this end, he thought that he
might pursue a suggestion made to him by Cummings and contact
Mr. Wiley directly at the American embassy in Paris.

If it had not been for Cummings and Mr. Wiley, Brown would
clearly have remained in prison until the end of the war and could
have died there. The State Department had reached their official
decision. Not only did they not feel motivated to pressure the French
on Brown's behalf, they actively preferred that he remain in French
custody rather than return to America to stir up trouble with his
seditious and socialistic ideas. Bartlett had thrown in the towel. But
unbeknownst to the State Department or to Bartlett or Whipple,
Cummings and Wiley had already set the key pieces in motion.

When Cummings reported to the American embassy on the

morning of Thursday, December 20, while he allowed Wiley to persuade him to sail for America on the *Espagne*, he put his own efforts into persuading Wiley not to forget his friend. He promised that Brown had meant no harm, that he was remorseful, that he was conducting himself stoically in the knowledge that he had brought this confinement upon himself. He got his point across. Two weeks later, the embassy in Paris took action and pleaded for Brown's release with the French Foreign Office. The line taken by Cummings formed the basis of the case that the Americans put to the French. There is an internal memo that records the details of the meeting between the lawyer serving as counselor for the American embassy and the representative of the French Foreign Office, and it shows clearly that Cummings's testimony was decisive. The counselor argued that "it had been learned from Mr. Cummings who had been held for a certain time with Brown as a possible sympathizer, that Brown was in no way complaining of his lot and was only sorry that he had been so foolish." The counselor emphasized Brown's youth and suggested that the worrying appearance of "serious socialism" was more likely "idle sophism." Perhaps Brown had endured punishment enough.

Just as Cummings was sensible enough to listen when Wiley urged him to have a care for his health and to sail immediately on the *Espagne*, likewise he was perceptive enough to see that Wiley was the key to Brown's freedom. After their December meeting, Cummings immediately dispatched a postcard to Brown at Précigné, advising him to appeal personally to Mr. Wiley. He followed with a long letter, reiterating his advice. And similarly, as soon as he arrived back in the United States, he had advised both Spaulding Bartlett and also Hope Slater to contact Mr. Wiley directly with their appeals.

Born in 1893, John Cooper Wiley was barely older than Cummings and Brown. He had been appointed as a clerk at the American embassy in Paris in 1915 at the age of twenty-one and promoted to secretary in the following year. When the jumble of documents in the Cummings/Brown file are all properly sifted, it is his energy and competence that stands out, and it is no surprise that ahead of him lay a highly successful career in the service of the US government.

He was posted throughout Europe as well as to Moscow in the 1930s, after which he rose to the position of US ambassador to Colombia, then Portugal, and then Iran. He returned briefly to Washington and conducted negotiations with the Soviet Union before ending his career in the early 1950s as the US ambassador to Panama. He led an honorable life. He and his wife, the painter and sculptor Irena Baruch, helped many refugees in the years leading up to the Second World War, during which they found themselves at the heart of crisis, posted to Vienna in 1938 at the Anschluss, when Austria was annexed by Germany, and then to the Baltic States in 1940 when they were invaded by Russia. Wiley was the kind of man who could see the need for haste when others could not, as in Vienna in 1938 when he cabled the State Department in America to press the urgency of his fears for the safety of Sigmund Freud.

Being of the younger generation himself, it is possible that Wiley had a little more perspective on Brown's peccadillos. Cummings wrote to Brown at Précigné that Mr. Wiley "is much puzzled as to your fiendishness, which seems to him I think too half-baked to be dangerous. Your poem on the moon he read with apparent gusto." Such empathy was notably lacking among the older men involved in the case. Richard Norton, director of the ambulance service, thought Brown an ass. The Reverend blamed him for landing Cummings in clink. And even Bartlett had decided that the imprisonment might be a usefully chastening experience for his nephew. Only Brown's aunt, Hope Slater, seemed to entertain the possibility that Brown might actually have been struggling with his experience on the front. She, too, wrote to Mr. Wiley at Cummings's urging: "No doubt he has been very foolish but he is young and has been tremendously moved by what he has seen and heard."

Right from the start, Wiley was the only one at the American embassy to provide useful information and updates to anyone outside it. Richard Norton, for example, had talked initially with the first sec-retary to the embassy, Mr. Frazier, and had been fobbed off with the story that the embassy had no information and would let him know when they did. It was not until Norton happened upon Mr. Wiley that he got the facts of the case. From late November onward, Wiley telephoned regularly to the French authorities to press for progress.

Ambassador Sharp wrote to Washington on the twenty-third of January and proclaimed: "I decided after a talk with Cummings to make informal representations to the French Government having in view the release of Brown." Considering that Sharp was still under the impression that Cummings had come from La Ferté-Macé via a stint at Précigné (which Sharp alternately misspelled as Presigny or Pressigny), his conversation with Cummings was hardly a discussion in depth—if indeed they spoke at all. Sharp's trumpeting of his own considered decision has every appearance of a blustering chief taking credit not only for the energy but also for the discernment of his twenty-four-year-old junior official—incidentally, the only official in the entire case to manage the correct spelling of Précigné. Sharp's "decision" to press for the release of Brown was almost certainly made by Mr. Wiley.

Cummings and Wiley were both dogged. In addition to pressing Brown, Bartlett, and Hope Slater to contact Wiley, Cummings also wrote as soon as he was home to Dos—still in Europe—pleading with him to send cigarettes and food to Brown. Dos (not his finest hour) found himself too preoccupied with troubles of his own to bother. Wiley became the primary node for the exchange of news from the New Year onward, and he continued, with the assistance of the counselor to the American embassy, to press the French to act on their promises to release Brown.

Meanwhile, Brown himself was beginning to feel a certain panic. In his January desperation, he even appealed by letter to his second cousin, Samuel Slater. Considering that Slater had made the news on the morning of Brown's arrival in Paris for the unlawful detention he had suffered at the hands of his housekeepers and for the Wild West cowboy outfit in which he had then greeted reporters, Brown must have regarded the appeal to Slater as a last resort. It elicited a predictably peculiar response. Slater wrote to the American consulate, forwarding Brown's letter with the eccentric caveat: "if he that is W. Slater Brown who signs the enclosed letter is a true signature...."

Slater even showed up at the American embassy in person on the nineteenth of January. His intervention led precisely nowhere; it is lucky for Brown that wheels were already in motion.

On the seventh of February, 1918, Brown was finally released from Précigné and sent in French custody to Bordeaux for the sailing on the eleventh of the *Niagara*. At Bordeaux, he remained for four further days in the custody of the French police. The American consul general at Bordeaux wrote to the American embassy with the details of Brown's embarkation by letter rather than by telegram, since it was forbidden to send an open telegram naming the time of a sailing. The French police, for their part, sent the Americans a bill. Three months of imprisonment for Cummings and more than four months' imprisonment for Brown ended in a diplomatic spat over the charge of 14 francs, 10 centimes levied by the French Caserne de Passage for Brown's custodial board. The final document in the Cummings/Brown file is a terse note from the embassy to the American consul at Bordeaux, suggesting that "inasmuch as Brown was arrested, interned, and subsequently transported to Bordeaux by the French Government, it would appear proper that any expenses attached to his subsistence up to the time of his actual release from French jurisdiction should be borne by the French authorities. You will kindly make informal representations in this sense. . . ."

Brown never realized how instrumental Mr. Wiley had been in securing his release, nor that Wiley's resolve to fight for Brown's freedom had been so fortified by the conversation with Cummings on December 20, nor that it was Cummings's tactically savvy line about Brown's foolishness, stoicism, and repentance that served as the embassy's formula in their further representations to the French. Cummings thought that the intervention of the Reverend had been the key to both his and Brown's freedom. Brown, on the other hand, grumpily resented the Reverend's attitude toward him. He weighed in on the subject late in life to correct a circulating misapprehension: "The author . . . writes that old Mr Cummings or rather Dr. C., got me out of the slammer in Précigné. Cummings' father did nothing to get me out. He blamed me for getting his son into the trouble. It was my Uncle Paul Bartlett, God bless him! who sprung me with the help of some friends in Washington. . . ." Neither Cummings nor Brown ever realized the truth: together with the aid and perseverance of John C. Wiley, it was Cummings himself who saved his friend.

24

CAMP DEVENS

July 23, 1918–January 17, 1919

Greeting: Having submitted yourself to a local board composed of your neighbors for the purpose of determining the
place and time in which you can best serve the United States
in the present emergency, you are hereby notified that you
have now been selected for immediate military service.

—ORDER OF INDUCTION INTO
MILITARY SERVICE OF THE UNITED STATES

WHEN BROWN MADE it back to the States, and as soon as he had sufficiently recovered, he moved in with Cummings in his rooms in New
York. Brown was spared the threat of army service on account of the
damage to his teeth—most of which he had lost from scurvy. When
his number arose, he was called up pending a medical; after a week,
he was handed $37.66 for his time and a discharge on dental grounds.
Cummings, on the other hand, was not immune to conscription.
When he first returned to America, his health was judged too poor,
but he was recalled for a further medical examination in late spring

and notified on May 4, 1918, that he had been passed fit for service. There was a heavy mood of expectation on young men. Harvard had even put forward special arrangements that permitted an expedited final exam for men entering the service. One of Cummings's younger friends, who was still at university, had availed himself of the shortened procedure and dropped by 104 Irving Street to borrow Cummings's old college gown for the purpose.

Cummings's draft number was 1849a, and the Reverend had heard from a friend that the call-up had only reached as far as 1300, so he advised his son that his number was unlikely to arise before autumn or later. In fact, the draft board moved much faster than the Reverend anticipated. A letter was posted to Cummings on the sixteenth of July ordering him to report at City Hall, Cambridge, Massachusetts, at 10:00 a.m. on the twenty-third. As usual, the family was at Joy Farm for the summer. Cummings was fortunate not to miss the call-up and find himself accidentally AWOL: the letter was forwarded to New Hampshire and arrived in the nick of time on the twenty-first.

And so while Brown settled into a life of freedom in New York, Cummings returned to a life under orders. He was posted for training at Camp Devens, Massachusetts. He was no more fond of military discipline now than he had been on the front under Mr. Anderson. Order was anathema. "Orderly," he wrote, was the very adverb to define the officer, and hence the "gruesome noun 'orderlies,'" the enlisted men at the officer's beck and call. But he stuck with life as an enlisted soldier. His father could not understand why he made no effort to join the officer class. Cummings explained to his sister, Elizabeth, that he had absolutely no intention of commanding men if that meant ordering them to die.

In late life, Cummings came to reflect a great deal more upon his youth, and at one point he set about typing up the notes scrawled in his notebooks from France and from the months at Camp Devens. As he plunged into the Camp Devens notebooks, he plunged with them into a temporary, but deep, turbulence: "into me,as I perceive these hieroglyphics,is coming once again whatever it was that drove me almost crazy."

At Camp Devens, the unthinking patriotism, the bloodlust, and the attempts of those in command to impose mental and emotional conformity reinflicted the traumas of France. Cummings wrote regularly to his father during this period, and truly tried to make him understand; failing that, to accept. He relayed to the Reverend the boasts of brutality that permeated the army atmosphere. One Lieutenant Snow, recently returned from the front, addressed the whole of Cummings's unit, Third Company. This Lieutenant Snow felt that bullets were an unimpressive way to kill and bragged how many Huns were, instead, slit by the American troops from ear to ear. The lieutenant added another proud story: An American corporal was escorting German prisoners and had been expected to report with nine, but showed up only with eight. " 'Where's the 9th?' The corporal says 'Well lieutenant I have <u>discipline</u> in my company, Lieutenant, and one of these Bosches wouldn't walk at attention, so I <u>stuck</u> him.' The Lieutenant reports this and the next day the corporal was promoted to a Sergeant."

The Reverend retorted that the army discipline would be good for Cummings's physique. This was too much. In a long letter, Cummings explained once again his feelings about the army. He voiced back to his father that still-hovering question: if he hated military discipline so much, why not become more his own master by joining the officer corps? "My answer: because I am he who would drink beer and eat shit, if he saw somebody else doing it, especially if that somebody were compelled to do it." He asterisked an elucidation of this comment: the Greek for this attitude was *poiētēs*, i.e., poet. (He wrote the word out in Greek letters.) His point was that poetry emerges out of the fullest empathy for one's fellow human creatures. Continuing the classical themes with an allusion to the ancient Greek poet Pindar, he softened with elegant flourishes a blunt request to his *"pater patrum,"* father of fathers, to shut up. "In other words, to cease Pindaric pleasantries, I commend you, pater patrum, to the worship of the cute and fastidious billikin of Silence, who sits on cushions of thistledown in the humorous throne-room of Imagination." Behind the showy rhetoric lies a heartfelt plea to his father to find the imagination that would allow him, if not to understand Cummings's life and values, then at least to refrain from criticism.

The traumas that were reinflicted at Camp Devens stayed with Cummings; army sergeants would come to haunt his nightmares. The steadfastness and clarity of purpose with which he stood up to his father belie the inner turmoil of these months in the US Army. The fact that for weeks that summer the camp was under quarantine for measles—meaning no weekend passes—cannot have helped the craziness that was coming into him.

Some of his writing spiraled so far into his crazed confusion that it is impossible now to see what he was driving at. He kept returning to a composition he called "The Fly Trap." He writes about it as "structure within structure," with squares and triangles and cracks. The notes are highly peculiar and it is not clear where he is telling the story and where he is trying to describe the story he wants to tell. The crack in the structure of the story seems to morph into a crack that attracts flies—more and more flies—who become stuck in the crack. There are notes about the flies, dead and mashed, and about a Fly Man and about putrid hunks of meat. The whole experiment is disturbed and disordered.

The disjointed, recursive state of the "Fly Trap" notes and prose suggest that even Cummings could not put his finger on what he was driving at. The work swirls in the muddiness of unprocessed experiences, and while it is obvious that it carries the emotional charge of the war, it is only guesswork what memories are impaled at the points of these sharp but arbitrary stabs at writing. It could be observed, for example, that Picardy in August, when Cummings was at the front, inclines to fountains of particularly energetic flies and that Dos Passos also experimented with the imagery of the flies in his war writing. In Dos's fictionalized account of ambulance service in 1917, when the main character, Martin, is posted out to the front, he meets a more war-weary character who talks about "the oceans of lies" that made the war possible. " 'Why, lies are like a sticky juice overspreading the world, a living, growing flypaper to catch and gum the wings of every human soul. . . . And the little helpless buzzings of honest, liberal, kindly people, aren't they like the thin little noise flies make when they're caught?'"

Since Dos and Cummings constantly exchanged letters, conversation, and ideas, it is possible that Dos's flypaper gives some insight into the ideas and feelings at stake in Cummings's story of putridity and flies and flycatchers, which never arrived at a sanity sufficient to communicate its meaning. Cummings was hunting for ways to disintegrate literary form and ended up, this time, only with uncommunicative distress. In other cases, however, there are gems amid the Camp Devens madness. As he tried to sift what he had been through, he arrived at some of the most startling and honest poetry he would ever write.

In a broken sonnet about sex between a soldier and a prostitute, he conjures the scene of an intense but damaging sexual connection, in a moment that distills the realities of the violence men do to women in times of war, and why.

> first she like a piece of ill-oiled
> machinery does a few naked tricks
>
> next into unwhiteness,clumsily
> lustful,plunges—covering the soiled
> pillows with her violent hair
> (eagerly then the huge greedily
> Bed swallows easily our antics,
> like smooth deep sweet ooze where
> two guns lie,smile,grunting.)
>
> "C'est la guerre"i probably suppose,
> c'est la guerre busily hunting
> for the valve which will stop this.
> as i push aside roughly her nose
>
> Hearing the large mouth mutter kiss pleece

The very smallness of the violence—the roughness as the soldier pushes her nose aside for the kiss—shows the brutality of sex with a prostitute who has notionally consented, but who is physically unready: "ill-oiled." The soldier is brutal because he has himself been brutalized. As the rhythm of the sex takes over, in the pounding of "eágerly thén the húge greédily / Béd," the soldier is mentally reabsorbed by the war. He seems to sink not into the welcoming bed but into the mud of the trenches, into the troublingly eroticized "deep sweet ooze." Sex and the act of killing have blurred into each other. The soldier cannot see his body or the body of the woman he is with except to imagine them stretched out as long, grunting guns. The woman with her "violent hair" is not the escape he needs. As the sex pounds, he wants to "stop this," to stop *la guerre*, but all he can do is to shove her nose aside for the demanded kiss.

Everything from France swirled around Cummings's mind during these miserable months at Camp Devens: sex, prostitution, thoughts of venereal disease, Marie Louise, the poplars. In the war zone and in Paris, sex and the army and venereal disease were all of a piece. This trinity was no less operative in America. Dos wrote that the army camp to which he himself was posted in Pennsylvania was known locally as Syphilis Valley. Cummings meanwhile observed the ludicrous nature of attempts to confront VD at Camp Devens. Nothing, he said, was accomplished by designating two latrine seats as "crabs only" and "venereal only"—except that the available seats in the latrine were effectively reduced by two, since no man would ever consent to mark himself by using the crabs or venereal seats. One of Cummings's most satirical war poems comments on "yon clean upstanding well dressed boy" who is fêted off to war, "with trumpets clap and syphilis."

His iconic statement about the Camp Devens experience was not published until much later, in 1931 in his collection *W [ViVa]*, when he finally channeled his anger into one of his most searing indictments of brutality inflicted in the name of patriotism. In "i sing of Olaf glad and big," Cummings immortalized a conscientious objector whom he had known at Camp Devens. The power of "i sing of Olaf" lies in the straightforward quality of Cummings's anger, as he recounts the imagined treatment of Olaf, rolled through freezing water, beaten with fists and boots and shit-covered toilet brushes, and then anally tortured with heated bayonets, before the army concludes that his pacifism is irremediable and throws him in prison to meet his death. The story is fictionalized, but the man remembered in this poem as "more brave than me:more blond than you" did in fact die while incarcerated for his pacifism at the military prison at Fort Leavenworth. "i sing of Olaf glad and big" carries a protest in its meter as well as its subject. "i sing of . . ." immediately signals the famous opening of Virgil's epic *Aeneid*, "I sing of arms and the man . . . ," but Cummings rejects both the hexameter meter of classical epic and the pentameter meter of many English epic poems in favor of tetrameter, a four-beat line associated with the Romantic poets and their celebration of individualism and emotional liberty. Cummings offers an epic hero in a Romantic mold—the man who is true to his own conscience, even to death.

Meanwhile, in more lyrical moments at Camp Devens, he was still composing poetry in French about French twilights and revisiting the phrases and words he associated with Marie Louise. He wrote poems about her as well as poems imagined in her voice, including one in which she speaks to a lover, "o mon amour," who knows her completely in the nakedness of a night in June.

Cummings spent a lot of his time digesting the implications of the artistic world to which he had been exposed in Paris as well as assimilating the irruption of a new literary extravagance: James Joyce's *Ulysses*. From 1918, *Ulysses* began to appear as a serial in the magazine *The Little Review*, and Cummings recognized an incipient masterpiece. His notes give an invaluable insight into his immediate and personal response, articulated before *Ulysses* became a work incapable of being approached without preconception. Cummings was spot-on. "Ulysses consists in the provocation by the trivial of the futile, the instigation of the actual by the real."

Cummings sought to incorporate his response to *Ulysses* into his ongoing search for an aesthetics of art that would unify painting, sculpture, dance, literature, and music. He compared *Ulysses* to *Petrushka* and commented on Joyce's "plastic" language (in the sense of sculpture as the "plastic" art). These unifying theories of art were still dominated by the obsession with Cézanne. Alluding to the common view that Cézanne's painting had a sculptural quality, he wrote: "To comprehend Cézanne's sculpture is to know that Cézanne is the first sculptor." The Greeks may have sought "marble equivalents of man and woman." But "Cézanne demonstrated that a given degree of depth demands a certain colour. Reverse (what is usually called) this plastic statement and you have the musical <u>truth which is</u> Colour. Colour with its appeal absolutely to the individual."

Cummings's artistic theories, like much else arising during his time at Camp Devens, have elements of madness. But they also have that mad energy that arises from a total commitment to the artistic life.

> Life is normal.
>
> Art is vital. Art is indeed that superfluous crisp minute inexcusable impulse which substitutes the actual syntheses of premeditated vitality for a probable comedy of cellular agglomeration, amoeboid improvisations, corpuscular statistics, or mess.

He covered the back of the page with erotica.

Against the backdrop of his attempts to synthesize the artistic worlds of Paris and America, 1917 and 1918, his own voice acquired a unique edge. His emerging corpus of love poetry evinces a fascination with death. He feels death's pull. The idea of an exquisite, aestheticized self-annihilation holds a perverse attraction rooted in his early love of Decadent poetry. At the same time, he feels a repulsion for "death's big rotten particular kiss."

Cummings's lyric embrace of the beloved may seem innocuous, but it is infused with his own struggles against the thought of his beloved's mortality. There is disbelieving recognition: "it is funny,you will be dead some day." The poetry yearns for a force strong enough to protect his beloved from her own death. He concocted an elaborate

fantasy in one of the poems he was working on at Camp Devens: "my
love is building a building / around you." His building is "a discrete /
tower of magic." And

> when Farmer Death(whom fairies hate)shall

> crumble the mouth-flower fleet
> He'll not my tower,
>   laborious,casual

> where the surrounded smile
>   hangs

>   breathless

Cummings uses this whimsical frame of fairies and towers of magic
in order to disguise his own fantasy: the fantasy that love can protect
the beloved. He leaves out his key verb: "when Farmer Death . . . shall
/ crumble the mouth-flower fleet / He'll not [crumble] my tower."
By skipping the second "crumble," he avoids the straightforward
statement. And by avoiding the straightforward statement, he avoids
the recognition of its obvious untruth: no love nor tower can keep
Farmer Death from any beloved. Cummings works hard to avert self-
knowledge and protect his fantasy.

These struggles with the inevitable physical death of the beloved
are one of the consequences of graduating beyond an adolescent imagination. In his early writing, Cummings prized an idealized beloved
who was barely even corporeal. In one of his Harvard prose short stories, he writes of a faun intoxicated by a woman whom he glimpses
as a not-quite-being in a forest pool, where she is "a whiteness in the
water." When he finally sees her in the flesh and then in the spirit, she
is "a great loneliness." She shimmers merely as an idea of the unat-
tainable. Now, however, Cummings was moving toward an appreciation of female sexuality in all its full and intense physicality—toward

images like that of a woman whose "sex squeaked like a billiard-cue / chalking itself."

Thus the love poetry rooted in the Camp Devens madness is stranger than it first appears. Cummings's fearlessness in facing both the cruel and the tender sides of human experience brought him to the simplicity of writing what is true.

All this time Cummings kept up a correspondence with Brown, though Brown—who wrote volubly, albeit not always in sobriety— had to pester for replies. One recurrent subject was the welfare of Bessie, a stray dog whom they had taken in. "Something terrible has happened," Brown announced in a letter of December 5. He had just discovered that Bessie was pregnant. He did not know what size of dog had fathered the pups and he worried that the pregnancy would endanger Bessie's life. In the next letter, he announced with relief the safe arrival of five puppies.

Brown waited eagerly for Cummings's release from the US military. His own loyalty to Cummings manifests itself in his efforts to keep Cummings's spirits up with news of the New York scene, offers to send cigarettes or anything else he might desire, and predictions of Cummings's imminent emancipation. That longed-for release was delayed well beyond the armistice of November 11, 1918. In January 1919, after a confrontation with his commanding officer that left Cummings shaking with anger, he finally obtained his discharge, and returned to New York, to chase a life as a painter and poet.

25

ELAINE

IN FEBRUARY 1919, Cummings and Brown moved to a cold, underfurnished, top-floor studio on West Fourteenth Street, New York, near to the corner with Fifth Avenue. They moved in with no gas and no coal. The next morning, in urgent search of heat, Cummings walked seven blocks down Fifth Avenue toward the heart of Greenwich Village and called on Elaine, who lived in one of the upmarket, luxury apartments of Washington Square. There he begged some coal off Elaine's maid. Elaine herself breezed into the West Fourteenth rooms shortly afterward, inspected the new digs, "and left,threatening innumerable luxuries for us,same to arrive in some hours." Elaine wanders with this apparently casual tone into Cummings's letter to his mother about the move. He did not tell his mother that Elaine was now his lover.

It used to be assumed that Scofield Thayer was gay, and that he and Elaine had agreed upon a lavender marriage. It was an assumption made while Thayer's life was largely shrouded in mystery as a result of the tight control exercised over his papers by his estate. It is only in the last few years that a new biography of Thayer has uncovered a much darker story. Thayer was, at least primarily, heterosexual, and he was completely caught up in the pagan sexuality of the chase. Elaine was the desired. Both men and women thought of her as a truly extraordinary beauty: there could be no more worthy object of pursuit. But once caught, she was worthless. Barely days after the wedding, Thayer wrote in his own notes that the allure had vanished. "From a 'spright' to a perfectly *banal* girl." It was "an intoxication *suddenly* removed."

Elaine and Scofield Thayer took their honeymoon in grand style—money no object—in Southern California, at Santa Barbara and at its luxury suburb Montecito, home to the super-rich. On honeymoon, Thayer destroyed her, and then he blamed her for being destroyed. At the Potter Hotel in Santa Barbara, he wrote: "E.O.'s cry at the Potter was not only the cry of the broken virgin, it was also the cry of the lost soul when, driven backwards, without the strength of backbone to withstand the Devil's push—when it feels the earth give way and only air beneath it."

Thayer was full of exultation and disgust. In a short note to self, simultaneously dispassionate and sadistic, he recorded Elaine's nausea when he told her that he intended an open marriage. A few months later, as a test of power, he pressured her into cutting short her beautiful hair. She did it. She was devastated, and Thayer triumphant in his victory. The woman who was the epitome of loveliness and grace in the eyes of her circle of friends had become, in the eyes of her husband, "limp," "like a dry + oil-wrung shark on her face." "Later I turned her over as I had one time turned over the bodies of dead snakes, white beneath."

Thayer's cruelty was not entirely under his own control. While he embraced that damaged sexual culture in which lusting satyrs chased shrinking nymphs, this sexuality of the chase gave a cultural shape, in his case, to a deeper biological instability. He was already in the early stages of psychosis, possibly paranoid schizophrenia. At this stage, however, Thayer's illness was not apparent to his friends or connections, and so his attitude landed on Elaine without warning or explanation. At the same time that her company was such a privilege and treat to Brown, who had to work himself up to phoning her with a three-ale head start, she was effectively renounced by Thayer. He deposited her in the Washington Square flat while he took separate lodgings for himself. He still made occasional use of her sexual availability, when it suited him.

Thayer's illness may complicate the question of his moral culpability, but Elaine's attempts to excuse him only betray the depth of the damage done to her. Elaine told Cummings that she never ceased to love and respect Thayer. "One thing I know," she said to Cummings. "I owe him everything, he taught me the lesson of my life gave me the shaking-up of my life." These are the words of a woman who has suffered, desperately trying to rationalize the damage done to her. She speaks as someone unable to bear the thought of her pain having no purpose, and so she consoled herself with that hollow line: it made me who I am.

Elaine was only sixteen when she first met Thayer; twenty when they married. She was an orphan. Both her parents were dead; her mother had died just a year before she and Thayer met. Her complete isolation and vulnerability shows in her most intimate moments, again recounted in Thayer's sadistic notes. After sex at Washington Square, he wrote how he left her with her "face the colour of yellowish toilet-paper," crying. To others, outside the marriage, the damage was also visible. Brown saw the effect of Thayer's presence without understanding what he saw. In the midst of a mélange of news reported to Cummings, he wrote: "Monday Elaine and her sister and a minister from Worcester and Scofield celebrated. And now Elaine has to talk in a funny little wobbly voice. I don't know why."

Cummings was not the first man Elaine turned to. She had had at least one lover already, after Thayer's unilateral decision about their marriage. Cummings and Elaine began spending time together soon after his return from France, even before he was drafted and sent to Camp Devens. The exact point at which their friendship became an affair is uncertain, but it was she who made that move.

Meanwhile, Cummings's father would not let go the past. Cummings had barely regained American soil when his father dreamed up the idea of suing the French government for damages, to wit, of a million dollars. The project was outrageous and pompous, and Cummings would have none of it. The Reverend's outrage at the whole

French affair only swelled as the months passed, but he couldn't proceed without his son's cooperation: he needed a full, written account of the arrest and imprisonment. The Reverend badgered, and again and again Cummings refused.

His father's insufferable side was on full display, but Cummings could not simply brush it off. The Reverend had regarded his efforts to secure Cummings's release as the squaring of an old debt: a debt he owed his son for saving his own and his sister's life on that day when they nearly drowned on Silver Lake. Now Cummings felt that he was indebted to his father in turn for having, as he put it, "boosted not only me but B out of hell." He accepted financial support from his father as a personal advance against his account of the imprisonment, but still he procrastinated. As early as March 1918, the Reverend was pressing and pestering, reminding him of the "masterpiece for which I contracted"—or, that is to say, "the manuscript which you contracted to produce as rapidly as circumstances would permit. My experience with myself is that 'Circumstances' cover a multitude of sins, especially so far as manuscript is concerned." (Indeed, the Reverend had cause to harbor suspicions about his own versions of "circumstances." He had never changed from the man who left academia because he could not produce research: for years he harbored plans to publish his collected sermons, but he never did.)

Camp Devens, for all its miseries, had at least provided respite from the Reverend's badgering. Now Greenwich Village was Cummings's refuge, but one that had to be protected by excuses—and perhaps, as Brown said, by the odd fib. Life in Greenwich Village was good. Cummings and his friends were daring and cavalier, and there was an atmosphere of success in the offing. Cummings focused on his painting, and he spent a lot of his time with Gaston Lachaise (the French sculptor who had been so unimpressed with Brown's inebriated thoughts on reincarnation) and with Lachaise's highstrung stepson Edward Nagle, who also sought to establish himself on the art scene.

From March 28 to April 14, 1919, two of Cummings's oils were exhibited at the Third Annual Exhibition of the Society of Independent Artists at the Waldorf Astoria, whose ethos of openness was embodied in a fierce declaration on the title page of their catalogue: No Jury No Prizes. Cummings entered two further oils for the fourth exhibition in 1920 and one for the fifth in 1921. His paintings were all assertive Cubist abstracts, which he titled: *Noise; Sound; Noise Number 5; Sound Number 5;* and *Noise Number 10.* He arrived at these relatively straightforward titles after he toyed with and discarded more sardonic tags, such as *Soft Shell Crab Defending Its Young.* Nagle, on the other hand, favored flamboyancy and entered two paintings for the Independent in 1920—one called *The Flying Dutchman* and the other bearing the blistering title *She Wears a Body Upon Her Dress.* However, when measuring his canvases, he picked up his yardstick from the wrong end. When the frames arrived, they did not fit his paintings, and he exhibited under his pre-advertised titles two paintings selected at random because they were the right size to match the frames.

Even Lachaise sometimes mistook the figurative substructure of Cummings's abstract paintings, and the cavalier attitude to titles taken in Cummings's artistic circle warns against approaching his paintings with their titles for a guide. The "Sound" and "Noise" series titles certainly meant something to Cummings, but their primary significance was probably synesthetic. Poetry has shape; paint has sound. Cummings's *Sound 1919,* which is now held at the Metropolitan Museum of Art in New York, is often described as a guitar on the basis of two horizontal bars that can be construed as a guitar fret, extending from the left edge to the center of the canvas, and a wavy white line that encircles the lower part of the image and might suggest the outline of a guitar. But if the painting were not titled "Sound," it would not suggest a guitar any more than a soft-shell crab or any other figure from rejected titles or subtitles.

It is also possible to see a head, Picasso-like and with an almond-orange eye, perched on a red platform atop a tall pillar, rising from the depth of the canvas toward the viewer, who looks from above and down. The viewer's angle down is tipped forward by about 15 degrees, so that the side of the pillar is visible, rosy-pink, as it stretches down toward a vanishing point. The painting from this perspective is a study in height; the challenge, to make the red platform as high as possible solely based on the juxtapositions of shape and color. "A given degree of depth demands a certain colour" was his summary of the brilliance of Cézanne. Every element of *Sound 1919* adds to its height, with the colors cool at the ground level and heating up as they rise towards the bird's eye viewer. A reverse twisted cone—an inverted whirlpool or tornado shape—swirls into the platform's pillar. That inverted cone is itself bisected by the two horizontal lines extending from the edge to the center of the canvas, and the division increases the height of the cone, which in turn elevates the platform the cone feeds into. The wavy white line that trails down along the right and lower edges of the image creates almost a river of height. "Sound" perceived as a guitar is flat and two-dimensional. Cummings was obsessed with the three-dimensional capacities of paint and canvas, and "Sound" perceived as a head posed on a platform reveals the magnificence of his absorption of Cézanne's ideas about depth and color. The lift upward and toward the viewer created by the platform relies on such an exact shade of tomato red that the canvas has to be viewed in person: no reproduction can capture the glorious height that Cummings achieved. More than guitar or crab, the 1919 canvas evokes the mood of the circus that Cummings so loved as a child, and recollects obliquely the endless sketches he made as an adult of tightrope walkers and other high-balance acts—sketches that also often place the viewer at an angle from above taking a squirming joy in the vertigo.

A few days after the 1919 exhibition, the Brown-Cummings household was joined by a kitten, rescued by Brown from a graveyard. The kitten had a gashed neck, weakness in its hind legs, and a strong tail that reminded Cummings of the upright Lombardy poplars of France. It had to be fed from a bottle. The rescue operation also necessitated keeping the kitten warm overnight. Cummings explained to his sister: "The main thing is to 'cook' the cat,every night,hot or cold, about 4. A.M. over a gas-stove. After all what is sleep?as Ovid said." As 1919 drew to a close, Cummings and Brown welcomed the most glorious of New Years. They raided a lot full of discarded trees, unsold

for Christmas, and filled their studio apartment with five of them—
or what they called a forest—and with the heady scent of sweet fir.

Cummings remained under pressure to spend summers with his
family at Joy Farm, but he enlisted the company of his friends to buffer
the proliferation of quarrels between himself and his father. During
the summer of 1920, both Nagle and Brown joined Cummings in
New Hampshire for the family sojourn. By now, Cummings and his
father were quarrelling frequently and over many topics, including
politics and the general direction of Cummings's life. Cummings
liked to bring up, sympathetically, the recent activities of the Bolshe-
viks and the Socialists—not because he shared their political ideas,
but because he sympathized with them as underdogs and because it
needled his father. Meanwhile, the Reverend needled his son back
with the suggestion of cures for his supposed aimlessness: in particular, he had the happy thought that Cummings could serve as his own
subordinate, working as secretary for the Reverend's activities with
the World Peace Foundation. (Since Cummings refused, Nagle wondered if he at least might score a job out of the quarrelling, and wrote
to the Reverend in September inquiring whether he, Nagle, might
suit the part instead.)

There was much going on in Cummings's life that the Reverend
knew nothing about. For a start, he did not know that his son was now
a father and himself a grandfather. In spring of 1919, Elaine had fallen
pregnant. Thayer and Cummings favored abortion, which Thayer
certainly had the wherewithal to arrange, but Elaine did not want to
risk the procedure and so she kept the pregnancy. Her daughter was
born on the twentieth of December. Elaine named her Nancy. The
day after she was born, Thayer sent Cummings a card inscribed "for
value received"—a sardonic acknowledgment of the true paternity of
the child who was officially recorded as Thayer's.

Elaine's affair with Cummings took place with Thayer's knowledge: indeed, with his active connivance. Thayer and Cummings
remained as close in their friendship as ever. It was a genuine and deep
tie with complicated undercurrents. Thayer co-owned *The Dial*, the
most prestigious modernist literary magazine in New York, and his

stalwart backing of Cummings's poetry was a decisive factor in Cummings's career. Cummings's own development as a poet was guided by Thayer's aesthetic priorities: intensity, vitality, and the nobility of art. *The Dial* published some of Cummings's pen-and-ink drawings as well as his poetry, and it was a highly emotional and important event for Cummings whenever Thayer would come to look through his work and select the art he wished to publish. The experience of putting his work in front of Thayer's careful attention and incisive scrutiny became a part of Cummings's own burgeoning adult relationship with himself as poet and painter.

Yet Cummings felt that Thayer withheld full support for the visual art. In late life, Cummings looked back on this rather bitterly. A part of him always believed that he should have been a painter. Ironically, the only major collection of Cummings's art in any museum today comes about as Thayer's doing. Thayer bequeathed his entire private art collection to the Metropolitan Museum in New York, including the seventy-four pieces by Cummings he had acquired from his friend.

Thayer's collection of Cummings's artwork included many drawings of Thayer himself; Cummings sketched and painted dozens more. The portraits are an insight into truths about Thayer that Cummings sensed but struggled to acknowledge. Cummings insisted that Thayer was the very definition of chivalry. But when he drew Thayer, he drew something cruel in the eyes, as well as perhaps some sadness. In one portrait done in three-quarters profile, the starkly narrowed eye has stubby, dark eyelashes that are exactly even above and below the eye and conjure—well in advance of Stanley Kubrick's vision—something remarkably similar in effect to the crazed eyes of *A Clockwork Orange*. Some of the portraits of Thayer are traditional and some Cubist, but all of them show tense contradictions. The Cubist portraits exaggerate the youthfulness of Thayer's bow-shaped mouth while they introduce a senility in the proliferating and sagging planes of the face. In *Scofield Thayer—The Afternoon of a Faun*, Cummings nods to Thayer's lecherous sexuality. The single raised eyebrow—which is characteristic of the Thayer portraits—is so high and pointed that it becomes the faun's goat-horn.

Cummings had allowed himself to glimpse the darker side of his friend years ago in his moment of shock over Thayer's crude reaction to "Epithalamion," but that insight was swiftly pressed into a discarded memory. Now Cummings felt that Thayer's readiness to give Nancy legal legitimacy was noble. He was too grateful, too adamant in his misplaced loyalty, and too much in awe of his powerful friend to trust any contradictory instincts. Even so, he harbored a lurking sense of some brutality in Thayer's treatment of Elaine, and his own later notes refer to Thayer as brutal and abusive toward her. For Elaine, however, Thayer's predatory aggression had become normalized, and her defense of Thayer pushed Cummings's instincts even further away from his own understanding.

When Elaine and Cummings were together, they sparkled. "Those of us who weren't in love with Cummings," said Dos, "were in love with Elaine." But during her pregnancy and after the birth of Nancy, Elaine became closer to the husband who had treated her so badly and pulled away from her lover. Elaine was a vulnerable woman who disliked her own vulnerability and put up a hard exterior. Her life was made easy, in one sense, by wealth, and she had practicality and social *nous*. She used her beauty, but she also suffered from being too much adored and too little seen for who she was. Like Marie Louise, she had been damaged by men. But where Marie Louise was conscious of her pain, Elaine was in denial. She developed a cold side. Afterward, when it had all gone wrong, Cummings blamed himself for never having truly known her—blinded to her as a person, he said, by intoxication with her beauty and sex appeal.

As Elaine kept her distance, Cummings's life was in a strange place when—realizing that his father could not be fobbed off forever—he finally sat down to write the account of his imprisonment in France. He did so on the strict condition that it would not be used in any lawsuit. He and Brown stayed on in New Hampshire after the rest of the family left Joy Farm that summer of 1920. They moved from the house down to the cabin on the shore of Silver Lake. Here Cummings worked like mad every day, typing ten or twelve hours from the morning until long after Brown had gone to bed. Brown fished, relaxed, and made the most of the lake. Cummings did some of the cooking, including an omelet of his own invention based largely around molasses. "We both ate it though Cummings admitted that it was not a success." In a few months Cummings had finished the manuscript.

Two years later, the release of *The Enormous Room* was nearly derailed by the last-minute realization at the publishing house that they were on their way toward legal trouble with the censors for having included one of Jean's outbursts: "My father is dead! Shit! Oh, well. The war is over, Good." The publishing staff sat in the office and inked out the word "shit" by hand in every printed copy. When it was finally out, the book divided readers and critics. Some regarded it as a flop, but it was greatly admired by others, including Ernest Hemingway, Robert Graves, Gertrude Stein, and T. E. Lawrence.

Meanwhile, Cummings handed the manuscript over to his father, and turned to Dos. Dos understood where Cummings was coming from these days. When Cummings was resisting pressure at Camp Devens to put in for the officer route, Dos more than sympathized; indeed, he had felt himself to be in the same boat during his posting in Allentown. He moaned in a letter to Cummings—written for their amusement in French with some *franglais*—about an interfering aunt of his who knew people. He wrote: "I understand perfectly well how it is that you do not want to allow yourself to be made a corporal. There are limits to submission." His own aunt was a terrible one for pulling strings and he had been living in fear that any day now he'd wake up a general.

These two simpatico friends decided to return to Europe together. They left before *The Enormous Room* appeared; in fact, before the Reverend had even secured a publisher. They sailed out in April of 1921 and together they toured Spain—Salamanca, Seville, Toledo, Madrid—before Cummings traveled to Paris. Brown returned to Paris as well, in July, in the capacity of Thayer's personal assistant— paying no attention to the fact that he had been told, when expelled from France in 1918, that he was not welcome back. He and Cummings took rooms at the same hotel. To these rooms, said Cummings, Brown would rush with his piles of dictation from Thayer, "where he types it on whichever of our respective typewriters happens to work

244 THE BEAUTY OF LIVING

at the moment. And one always does(work)." However, Brown was heading off the rails and into his three decades of alcoholism. Cummings wrote around the same time to Nagle (making reference to the psychoanalyst, L. Pierce Clark, with whom Nagle had sought treatment): "For Christ's sake,don't tell me that Clark has sent the devil of destruction out of you into Brown—who smashes windows and chairs regularly nowadays,selecting only those over 60 fr. in value and peculiarly sturdy."

There was another point to this encampment of friends in Paris. Paris had some of the most liberal divorce laws in America or Europe, and Elaine and Thayer had come there in order to end their marriage quickly and cleanly. They obtained their initial decree almost immediately upon arrival, on July 28, 1921, and their final decree on the tenth of October.

It was a good time for Cummings with Elaine and Nancy in Paris. However, neither Elaine nor Cummings ever really worked out what they wanted from each other. Eventually, in March of 1924, they would marry. It was short-lived. Just as Thayer had tired of Elaine as soon as he possessed her, Elaine lost interest in Cummings and fell in love with another man only months after she married him. Cummings was far from blameless in the breakup, but Elaine was also passing on the damage of what had been done to her, and Cummings was a destroyed man when she left.

Thayer still held out some hope for his own health. He knew that something was wrong. He had already tried analysis back in America and now he was fixated on the ambition of undergoing analysis with Sigmund Freud himself. He even moved to Vienna for the purpose. But Thayer was torn between seeking help and nurturing his paranoid grandiosity. When he turned to Freud, half of him desperately sought salvation, while half of him was determined to resist—to prove himself the great mind that even Freud could not crack.

In any case, there was not much that Freud could do. Psychotherapy was evolving to treat psychological neurosis; Thayer's psychosis was almost certainly biological. As his mental condition deteriorated, it was Cummings he wanted by his side. Cummings's ability to rebel at the most profound level—without madness—held a fascination for men who teetered closer to that brink, and his capacity for absolute individuality was an anchor in their desperation. Many, many years later, when Ezra Pound was incarcerated in the mental hospital of St. Elizabeth's in lieu of facing trial on the charge of treason, it was a photograph of Cummings that sat on his mantelpiece.

By 1926, Thayer's mental health had deteriorated completely. He was declared legally insane in 1931, and remained thereafter in the care of private nurses.

Cummings spent the next two and a half years in postwar Paris. Poems from this era show a lonely side to the postwar city. He writes of a woman, sitting alone in a café in the "Fields Elysian"—a literal translation into English of the Champs-Élysées, restoring the latent meaning in the name: the classical field of the dead. Another poem, abandoned before publication, speaks of the isolation of a crippled black veteran as the children stare and the music of "la(proudly) marseillaise" turns cruel.

Once, Cummings and Dos and Gilbert Seldes, another of their Harvard friends, were out for a large evening. On the way from café to nightclub and bursting with wine, Cummings nipped into a dark alley near the Place Saint-Michel to relieve himself. He had not spotted the presence of the French *gendarmerie,* and he was set upon by the agents of the law and arrested for public indecency. Dos and Seldes chased the *gendarmes* to the police station, where Dos was twice ejected trying to rescue his friend. "Cummings finally emerged, somewhat shaken," Dos wrote, "because he remembered La Ferté all too well." Cummings still faced charges, and so Seldes turned to a French friend of theirs, another writer, who knew the right people; as a professional courtesy, writer to writer, he saw to it that the charges were dropped. Cummings made light of it all. But in truth, Dos had seen a glimpse of memories that Cummings carried with him, whether he spoke of them or no.

Many people assumed that Cummings had put La Ferté-Macé behind him. But that is not the whole story. There were little habits that remained. One of his old Harvard friends remembered watching

Cummings light his cigarette by picking up a live coal out of the fireplace grate with his fingertips, as he had learned to do in prison when out of matches. Apart from his notebooks, Cummings kept little to remind him of his imprisonment—except a few trinkets, which he kept safely until the very end of his life. Three small, broken, and dirty shards of ceramic, in three shades of blue. A pencil, used right to the very end; only the flat grip remained, bearing an advertisement for Chocolat Menier. And a daisy, dry stem broken off from the tiny, colorless, dried flower head. More inward traces remained as well. There is a haunted look in his eyes in photographs from 1919 onward that defies reproduction, since the photos are old and faded and most of the negatives are gone. But it is plain to see in the originals. And there are other hints, here and there, that his time at La Ferté still haunted him. It lingered, unspoken, behind his life and his poems. Spring, for Cummings, always felt like freedom. In the dying of the year, "there is a general feeling of autumn, of less leaves and more policemen."

In 1927, Cummings sat down to try to explain how he felt about the war. He came up with the following:

ARMISTICE

On the 11th of November we celebrate the anniversary of the armistice.

This word armistice means more to some of us than to others.

To those who did not participate in the war itself,either as soldiers or as the mothers and lovers of soldiers,"armistice" means merely a wild outbreak of joy at the cessation of hostilities. It suggests streets jammed with dizzy crowds,air scintillating with confetti and streamers,horns and cries and hysteria and shouting.

To others, "armistice" means their own lives or the lives of those whom they most loved.

In the nine years which have elapsed since the armistice,many things have been said about our so-called "great" war:it was an international crime,a blot on the scutcheon of civilization;it revealed at once the noblest and the most ignoble characteristics of mankind;it constituted the darkest moment in human history. These and a thousand other sentiments have been echoed and reechoed by innumerable orators.

Briefly:this war was like other wars.

We know that today. Some of us knew it even before this war began. Others learned it during the course of the war. Still others did not find out until after the fighting had ceased that what they had taken for reality was illusion. Sooner or later,however,nearly all of us came to realise that the signing of the armistice put an end to another blunder on the part of humanity.

Does anything remain to be said about war?

Yes.

One thing has not yet been said;or,if it has been said,apparently noone has heard it -war is not what war seems.

Actually,war is neither beautiful nor horrible. It is much less than beautiful and much more than horrible--it is a fake.

War is a fake in the sense that a panacea is a fake. Nor does war merely resemble a panacea;war actually is a kind of panacea. It is that colossal fake of fakes in which whole nations indulge,secretly hoping that it will give them a beauty or a courage which they inherently fail to possess.

The only importance of war lies in the fact that it appeals,not to individuals,but to nations. So long as a few individuals here and there permit themselves to be tricked into sampling this or that cure-all,the world goes on very much as before;but when millions of people simultaneously delude themselves into believing that they will be reborn through the same magic formula--then we are deluged by that gigantic nonexistence which is called war.

Like all wars,the war whose conclusion we are now once again celebrating was a fake and a nonexistence.

Our so-called "great" war was actually not great at all. To call it great is completely to miss the meaning of greatness. It is to confuse two perfectly distinct qualities:bigness and deepness. It is not to realise that,while a truly great thing may be (and sometimes is) a big thing,it must always be a deep thing.

We have heard of the "art" of war. Let us therefore turn to Art Itself:in Michaelangelo's painting of the Sistine Chapel ceiling,bigness and deepness combine. But Michaelangelo's ceiling is truly great,not because it is big--it is great because,beyond the fact of its bigness,it is deep. By "deep" we mean that it does not merely astonish or overwhelm or destroy the spectator. We mean that it leads the spectator into itself and escorts him through all its intricacies,in such a manner that when he finally emerges he is more alive than when he entered.

The "great" war did not make people more alive. It made them less alive or else it killed them.

It was not,like the Sistine ceiling,big and deep. It was merely extraordinarily big.

Because it involved more men and more weapons than any other war,it was bigger than any other war. But it was not deeper than any other war. It was not deep at all--because no war ever has been,or ever will be,deep.

Only a very few persons,such as have not simply suffered but have understood their suffering,are able to realise that war is without any fundamental deepness. But such is the truth. What is terrible about war is precisely that war is trivial and unreal. What is ghastly about war is,that war calls upon most human beings to sacrifice their happiness in exchange for the most temporary of illusions.

And yet most of us will part with anything more readily than with our illusions.

Rather than admit frankly that we have been tricked by war,most of us will prefer to cling to the essentially cowardly notion that there is something profound and lofty in war. But should we not,at any cost,be honest with ourselves? How comes it that--only nine years after the biggest war in human history--we have almost forgotten that this war existed? And do not you and I find ourselves wondering when the next "war to end war" will occur? Why,then,should we persist in attributing something fundamental or glorious to the most trivial of all tricks,the most pernicious of all panaceas--the fatal fake of war?

An answer to this question immediately suggests itself. You know the answer and I know it. We have been brought up from earliest childhood to confound the shallow ugliness of war with the deep beauty of death.

But this does not mean that war is beautiful.

Quite the contrary.

This merely suggests that our education has been woefully at fault. Instead of encouraging us to think,our teachers have compelled us to believe. They have taught us the worship of ideas,whereby we have neglected the reality of our minds and forgotten the wisdom of our hearts. When you and I consult these hearts and minds of ours,what do we learn? That there actually exists a deeper beauty even than the beauty of death-- the beauty of living.

It is high time the human race as a whole stopped admiring death and began to try to live.

It is high time we,as individuals,realised that to live is deeper and more beautiful and more difficult than to die.

Men will be the fools of glory,peoples will exterminate peoples and civilization will tremble to its very foundations so long as death is glorified at the expense of living. But when living comes into its own--when not to die,but to live,becomes the most heroic deed of which anyone is humanly capable-- war will cease.

26

THE PORCUPINE HUNT

July 1956

CUMMINGS IS AT Joy Farm with his third wife, Marion Morehouse, pondering the misdeeds of an orange-brown feral cat. Summer came late that year—it seemed to Cummings that the flowers were opening at least a month later than usual. The cat was after the chipmunks. " 'I think what happens' (say to M) 'is that the cat comes to a place,takes all the prey it can,& then goes off & waits until the remaining prey forgets all about it--then it returns & cleans up. That's how it took all 3 of our chipmunks.' 'isn't that dreadful!' she exclaims."

It was cat versus chipmunks. The intention was to save the chipmunks by shooting the cat. But Cummings couldn't bring himself to do it. He had a .22 pistol, and he shot in the direction of the cat twice—first with a dead cartridge; second time, "missed by a mile." Why, he fretted, did he sympathize with the chipmunks? Why with one creature more than the other? He mused in his notes that it was, after all, exactly what they had asked him all those years ago. And he had replied: it wasn't that he hated the Germans, but that he loved the French. The cat wasn't to blame. It was only hunting the chipmunks because it had been cast off by some human being; and, anyway, it's feline nature to kill chipmunks, even if the chipmunks were his darlings.

"'if there weren't so many flies' M says sadly 'I could have gone out & sat for an hour or two & waited for the cat.'"

"'yes' I hear myself reply 'all things work together for evil in this case.'"

Cummings did not understand why he would adjudicate between some creatures and not others. Killing a "loathsome" spider to save a sphinx moth was easy. Shooting a raccoon to protect the swallows was his decision. He buried the raccoon. He fretted later that it had been female, and therefore probably pregnant. And he was panged with guilt when a second raccoon lurked around the grave, missing— Cummings thought—its mate.

Then, there was the porcupine vendetta.

Only that year, his beloved Porter apple tree had begun to recover from years of porcupine decimation. For any other tree, it might have been different. The Porter was a native Massachusetts variety, prized for its flavor and its beautiful yellow-green fruit. More than that, it represented the history of his family at Joy Farm. He worried that it was a sign of growing old: to take the side of vegetation over animal life. He must be "merely 'vegetating'" in his dotage. His mother had loved the porcupines. And yet, he couldn't abandon the tree to its fate.

He inspected the damage on the tree; he staked out the house. He woke at night and prowled out on restless 4 a.m. patrols for the porcupine. One night, he hunted it into the pitch-dark hemlocks.

through shoulderhigh brakes I(crazily slipping over unseen boulders)chased a never quite visible something into deeper & deepest dark:to finally enter(crouching)a tentlike hollowness, made by the groundward lowest limbs of a group of tall & inter-twisted hemlocks. Here I paused; gazing helplessly around me at whatever my flashlight revealed;& thinking "he's got away!" But suddenly,from somewhere overhead,came a familiar sound--the teeth-chattering of an angry-or-frightened porcupine. He had climbed one of the hemlocks . . . yes;after many efforts,I could just distinguish his mostly black body with its white here & there quills against the black summer sky with its white here & there stars. Now I can't make him out--but once again comes the chattering . . . why? If only he kept quiet, I'd never have begun to guess where to look for him. "You strange clownlike being" I think to myself "now I must murder you!"

Having, with enormous difficulty, propped my searchlight in such a way that it caught the creature on his high limb, I kneeled; sighted: & fired. Nothing happened--then, far away in dark space, I felt a letting-go . . . & slowly down was tumbling something big, striking the ground perhaps a yard in front of me. Picking up my light in one hand, & with my reloaded rifle in the other, I inspected my victim: no, he was not dead; but terribly wounded, unable even to move. Lying on his belly, hugely & wholly breathing, panting, gasping, he tried & tried & tried to live. Stepping close, I fired into his skull pointblank--at which, out of the alive but hitherto expressionless eye(which may or may not have seen myself)leaped a lurch of amazement . . . & he(collapsing)shut together slowly.

The porcupine invasion continued. As the summer went on, Cummings grew angry: angry at being made a multimurderer of porcupines. Angry at what they drove him to do. He was, as he saw it, a predator for the sake of saving the tree from predators. If only they would confine themselves to eating the fruit. "So far as I'm concerned, porcupines could eat apples forever," if they would simply leave the precious tree alone. He grumbled about the state of the world and about the limits of his own poetic renown. He channeled his feelings into epigrammatic observations on motherhood and fatherhood. The mother is the equivalent of nature, benevolent in itself. The father is protection against nature's malevolence. He thought again about war, and he thought more about growing old.

He made breakfast, one morning, for himself and for Marion, when a mouse came some few feet away to nibble at a tray of poison. The mouse was soon sick with it: "sickness & oldage are brothers--

a poisoned mouse behaves(& looks)like an old man." Cummings
thought of the mouse, the newly "palsied caricature," as it had been
perhaps moments before, "a dashing little immaculate beast" of "acrobatic beauty(flickering in*&-out of my upstairs nightworld)," and he
felt ashamed.

> Me up at does
>
> out of the floor
> quietly Stare
>
> a poisoned mouse
>
> still who alive
>
> is asking What
> have i done that
>
> You wouldn't have

Is it a war poem? Unlike many of the poets of the Great War, Cummings survived. He had a long life ahead of him. But forty years later,
we still see the traces of La Ferté-Macé even in such a poem as this
that does not, on the face of it, have anything to do with the war.

The poem is an accusation. It is all the more powerful because the
compassion in the poem is all for the mouse, and the "Me" of the poem
is the accused. Capitalized, and on trial: "Me up at does." The dying
mouse, "still who alive," voices the most human of questions: "What
have i done that You wouldn't have?" That meal call, that "ferocious
and uncouth miracle," that "beautiful manifestation of the sinister
alchemy of hunger": does the meal call not turn us all into animals,
when we are starving? And the mouse is so small and powerless. All
of Cummings's outrage at brutality, at injustice, at the mindless institutional abuse of the innocent, is poured into this simple poem. And

his own guilt as well. He did not hate the cat, and he could not kill it. He hated the porcupines for making him a killer. The buzz from the 4 a.m. hunts, the dark hemlock pressing down, the tension, the chattering: the excitement of murder might be the worst of all.

There is a way in which Cummings remained a war poet until the end of his life. His sympathy with the smallest of creatures, and the beauty that he saw in the world, come out of the destruction that he saw during the war. As he wrote in a note from 1917: "sunsets do not hate."

—"just up to the white" say to myself again & again(while not quite awake):all the mystery of life being(as i now feel) between the darkness of a pencil & the tone of a paper;"you don't need to seek anywhere else,everything which God intends for you is findable within these from-darkness-to-lightness gradations--are they not,after all,infinite?"

—E. E. CUMMINGS

Author's Afterword

—

I HAVE NOT invented any dialogue. All dialogue, along with all other quotations, is attributed to its source in the endnotes that follow. Some dialogue has been translated from the French, and all translations from French are my own. At a few points, I represent a stream of thought as a blend of paraphrase and quotation, and this also is indicated in the endnotes.

Wherever I discuss Cummings's emotional state, I draw on letters, notes, or other archival evidence. I never speculate.

I have drawn at points on Cummings's poetry and on his account of his imprisonment, *The Enormous Room,* but I have only treated Cummings's writing as autobiographical where, on a case-by-case basis, I felt confident that such an approach was justified.

I capitalize E. E. Cummings (not e. e. cummings), as does almost everyone who works on or writes about Cummings today. Although Cummings sometimes typed his own name without capitals for rhetorical effect, he never intended for e. e. cummings to become an authorized moniker (see Friedman 1992; Friedman 1996). When he refers to himself in the lowercase, he means to be witty. For example, in a letter to his agent, when flattered by her desire to buy one of his paintings, he refers to himself with appealing self-deprecation as that "nonillustrious artist demioccasionally semiknown as smalls smalls kew-mangs." (Letter to his agent, Betty Kray, quoted in the "News, Notes, & Correspondence" section of *Spring* 19, 2012 [2013].)

Quotes from Cummings retain his punctuation and spacing, of which he was so protective. Very occasional correction of evident misspellings are always noted in the endnotes.

Acknowledgments

—

I ACKNOWLEDGE WITH deep gratitude the financial assistance provided by the award of a Joan Nordell Fellowship (Houghton Library, Harvard) and a Harry Ransom Center Research Fellowship in the Humanities, supported by the Frederic D. Weinstein Memorial Fellowship; these two fellowships made possible my archival research in Cummings's papers. The research environment at both libraries is magnificent, and I wish to thank the incredibly kind and helpful library staff, both at the Houghton Library and at the Harry Ransom Center, for all their support and assistance.

I owe a considerable practical and intellectual debt to previous biographers of Cummings—especially Charles Norman and Richard S. Kennedy. I indicate in the notes where I draw on them directly, but I owe additionally a broader debt to their efforts in first structuring the story of Cummings's life. Among the community of current Cummings scholars, I would especially like to thank Mike Webster. I also owe a great debt to Jim Dempsey's excellent biography of Scofield Thayer, which helped me tremendously in writing about Thayer and about the breakdown of the marriage between Thayer and Elaine.

I cannot sufficiently thank my agent, Georgina Capel, and everyone at Georgina Capel Associates, and likewise my editor at W. W. Norton, Jill Bialosky, who gave me the chance to write this book. I am enormously grateful to Jill and to the whole team at Norton, especially Drew Elizabeth Weitman, for seeing the book through. I also thank Robin Lane Fox for his help and for believing in me as a writer.

My greatest debt, as always and ever, is to my husband, Jonathan Thorpe. Finally, for their love and support, I wish to thank my parents, mother-in-law, sister, and brother-in-law, and Fleur de Wit, Emily Craig, James Maclaine, and Robbie Smith.

A Note on Previous
Biographies of Cummings

 ‒

WE DO NOT normally think of Cummings as a war poet, nor has his relationship with Marie Louise received anything like the attention accorded to his later relationships. In *The Beauty of Living*, my argument is that Cummings is indeed a war poet, and that we must understand this period of his life if we wish to understand his ideas about love, justice, injustice, humanity, and brutality. I also aim to restore Marie Louise to her rightful place in Cummings's story. She was his first love, and she was clearly a remarkable woman. She has been pushed to the margins because she was a sex worker, and that is wrong. It is an injustice to her, and it is also an injustice to the hundreds of thousands of women who worked as prostitutes during the Great War: at one point the number of women working as prostitutes in Paris alone was estimated at 75,000.

Commemoration of the role of women in the Great War has for a long time sought to recollect and acknowledge the heroism of nurses. I do not doubt for a second the courage and grit that it took to serve as a nurse during the war, but our remembrance should not be confined only to the nurses. Prostitution was as central to the female experience of war as nursing, and the lives of sex workers are as valuable as the lives of nurses.

Marie Louise was Cummings's Cleopatra, and as he said of Cleopatra in one of his most sensual poems:

> Cleopatra had a
> body
> it was
>
> thick slim warm moist
> built like an organ
> and it
> loved

Or, to return to the cliché that Cummings surpasses: Cleopatra was once flesh and blood. And so was Marie Louise. She was a real person, who loved Cummings and was loved by him. All I aim to do is to capture some of the humanity of a woman who once lived and breathed and loved.

My own academic work on Cummings and my time in the archives with Cummings's papers leaves me in no doubt that previous biographers have understated the depth of the love affair between Cummings and Marie Louise. Sawyer-Lauçanno (2006) calls her Cummings's "girlfriend," in scare quotes, as if he cannot quite imagine her counting as a legitimate girlfriend, presumably because she was also a prostitute. Cheever (2014) gives Marie Louise fewer than two paragraphs' discussion and leaves her name out of the index. Kennedy's somewhat fuller account (1980, reprint 1994) remains better than subsequent accounts, but even he underestimates the depth of feeling, underplays the extent of their correspondence, and seems to imply a certain surprise that Cummings and Brown treated Marie Louise and Mimi "like ladies."

Moreover, the attitude that puts "girlfriend" in scare quotes and relegates Marie Louise to the margins is not confined to work on Cummings. The main biographical source on William Slater Brown is a long article by his nephew James Lincoln Collier. Concerning their month in Paris, Collier writes that Cummings and Brown attended performances of *Petrushka* and *Parade*, took in the local painting scene, and "established relationships with some little Parisian tarts." As much as I am grateful for Collier's work, which was especially invaluable for my chapter "Across," I find that attitude indefensible.

My disagreements with previous biographers do not lessen my gratitude for their work or my debt to them. I am especially indebted to the work of Charles Norman and Richard S. Kennedy. Norman (1958, reprint 1972) collected primary documents, conducted interviews, and solicited letters from friends of Cummings—the kind of research that can only be done for a biography while friends and family are still alive. I was lucky to be able to consult Charles Norman's papers, as well as Cummings's papers, at the Harry Ransom Center at the University of Texas at Austin. Kennedy's biography was the first scholarly account of Cummings's life, and his scholarship has not been supplanted by either of the more recent biographies. I am particularly conscious of my deep debt to Kennedy's basic framework of facts. I have always tried to verify what I repeat, but I have not faced anything like the monumental task that faced Kennedy—the task of organizing the narrative of a life essentially from scratch—precisely because such work is only done once, and in this case by him.

In some cases, I have indicated minor disagreements with previous biographers in the notes. There are certain other major differences of interpretation.

As much as *The Beauty of Living* is a story about war and imprisonment and Marie Louise, it is also a story about fathers and sons. Cummings, Dos Passos, and Brown all, in different ways, struggled with their relationships to their fathers.

I take the Reverend's apparent success in life rather less at face value than others who have written about him. The hints of defensiveness about his departure from academia that surface throughout the later years reveal an aspect of his father that even Cummings never fully allowed himself to see. Moreover, the magnificent impressiveness, to the family, of Cummings's father's appointment as minister is also undercut by his role as *assistant* minister to the Rev. Edward Everett Hale. Hale was quite the nineteenth-century patriarch. He was also author of "The Man Without a Country"—a fervently patriotic short story that will still be familiar to many American readers from their own schooldays. (I read it in mine.) The Reverend was clearly made to feel his subordinate status. A casual note from Hale to

Reverend Cummings in 1902, planning the day's work, begins "Semble ["it seems" (in French)] that tomorrow is a Holiday! Most days are, to my disgust. . . ."

The Reverend's nine years as assistant to Hale, from 1900 to 1909, are the formative years of Cummings's childhood, from the age of six to the age of fifteen. Most biographers find in Cummings a straightforward inferiority complex in the face of a capable, successful father. However, I see that as only one layer of Cummings's experience. I believe that he also imbibed some of his father's own struggles with denied and deeply buried feelings of failure.

As, perhaps, the flip side of the coin, I also lay more emphasis than previous biographers on Cummings's own effective and capable character. In the drowning incident on Silver Lake, the coincidence of Cummings's family motoring out for sunset on the lake and discovering Cummings and Elizabeth has been allowed to obscure the fact that Cummings's cool-headedness and his decisions about how to ration their collective energies had already secured their safety: their shouts for help had been heard by campers on the shore. Likewise, amid the vicissitudes of Brown's fortunes, it has not been grasped that it was Cummings's representations at the American embassy in Paris in December 1917, in conjunction with the efforts of the admirable John C. Wiley, that made the difference.

Cummings could be naïve. Certainly, at Noyon, he had no grasp of the seriousness of laying himself open to imprisonment by the French authorities. But he was not callow or imprudent or a babe in the woods. His naïveté was the recklessness of a decisive and effective personality. In making the case for Cummings's effectiveness and realism as a person, I hope I might contribute in whatever small way to the case for war poems such as "first she like a piece of ill-oiled," which is nearly peerless for its quiet brutality and realism about what men do to women in times of war, and why they do it.

Finally, one last note about other biographies and archival material. I have not copied archival references from anyone else. Where I give archival references together with reference to, e.g., Kennedy, I have consulted the material in the archives but acknowledge also its previous use by others. The exceptions to this rule are a letter from Cummings to Thayer held in the archives at Yale, where I have not worked—this letter was shared with me by James Dempsey and used with his permission—and one letter from Cummings to Dos Passos, shared with me by Michael Webster and used with his permission.

Glossary of Minor Characters

~

Carpenter, (Joseph) Estlin (1844–1927). English godfather to E. E. Cummings, after befriending Cummings's father during the latter's stay in England as a sociological researcher. Carpenter was a prominent Unitarian minister and theological scholar. He spent the latter part of his career at Manchester College—now Harris Manchester College—within the University of Oxford and served as principal of the college from 1906 to 1915.

Cowley, Malcolm (1898–1989). Born and raised in Pennsylvania, Cowley was a freshman at Harvard when Cummings was in his master's year. He suspended his studies at Harvard in order to serve in the Camion Corps (driving munitions trucks) with the American Field Service (AFS). He is best known as the author of *Exile's Return* (1934), which became a definitive account of the "lost generation" of Americans in Paris and New York in the 1920s.

Damon, S. Foster (1893–1971). S. (Samuel) Foster Damon was a member of *The Harvard Monthly* circle and a close friend of Cummings during their time together at the university. Damon majored in music and promoted amongst his peers a love of Debussy and of the poems of William Blake. Although in later life Damon continued to publish poetry and to compose music, he was better known as an academic. After a brief stint teaching at Harvard, he moved in 1927 to spend the rest of his career at Brown University. He became one of the twentieth century's most significant and expert Blake scholars. In 1935, he published a biography of Amy Lowell. He also liked square dancing and Punch & Judy shows.

Hale, Edward Everett (1822–1909). Reverend Cummings's predecessor and boss at South Congregational Church. Born and raised in Boston and educated at Harvard, Hale served at South Congregational for forty-three years. He was a prolific writer, best known for his patriotic short story, still famous throughout American schools: "The Man Without a Country," which details the pain of a traitor whose punishment was never to hear another word spoken of America nor to receive a scrap of news of the development of the nation. Six years before his death, Hale was elected to serve as chaplain to the US Senate.

Hillyer, Robert Silliman (1895–1961). Part of the circle of *The Harvard Monthly* along with Cummings and Dos Passos, Hillyer was two years behind Cummings at Harvard and served in the Great War as an ambulance driver with the American Field Service (AFS). Hillyer spent his life as an academic, poet, and novelist, and won a Pulitzer Prize for his 1933 volume, *Collected Verse*. He was a traditionalist: an "ancient" rather than a "modern." He was one of the most outspoken opponents of the award of the Library of Congress's prestigious Bollingen Prize in 1949 to Ezra Pound. This award had been keenly desired by Pound's supporters, who hoped that such rehabilitation in the public eye would be a crucial step toward securing his release from St. Elizabeth's mental hospital, where Pound was detained on grounds of insanity in lieu of standing trial for treason. Hillyer argued publicly that it was scandalous to solicit and exploit such a literary award in service of the rehabilitation of an anti-Semite and a traitor.

Lachaise, Gaston (1882–1935). A French sculptor born in Paris. While still in Paris, Lachaise met Isabel Nagle, an American woman abroad (married and with a son, Edward). They returned together to the United States, settling in Boston in 1906 before moving to New York in 1912; they married in 1917 after she was finally able to obtain a divorce from her first husband. Lachaise's work appeared in the famous 1913 Armory Show. Cummings's friendship with Edward

Nagle, son of Isabel Nagle and stepson of Lachaise, brought the great sculptor into Cummings's circle.

Lowell, Amy (1874–1925). Belonging to one of the most prominent families of Boston and Brookline—a family established in Massachusetts since 1639—Lowell turned seriously to poetry in 1902 and was first published in 1910. She was directly involved in the formulation of Imagism and was the primary conduit of Imagism into America. The narcissistic Ezra Pound resented her power within the Imagist movement and began to refer to Imagism dismissively as "Amygism." Lowell was a champion of free verse and an overwhelmingly grand and formidable personality, with a gender-transgressive penchant for cigars. From 1912 onward, her life partner was the actress Ada Dwyer Russell. They shared a home in what was then often called "a Boston marriage" (a term in use for a two-female household, whether lesbian or platonic), and some of Lowell's poetry exhibits a clear lesbian eroticism. Cummings called her "the American Sappho" and the fact that some of her poetry is copied into his Harvard notes along with that of Keats and Tennyson is testament to her impact on him. She won a posthumous Pulitzer Prize in 1925 for the volume of poetry *What's O'Clock*, and was the subject of a biography written by S. Foster Damon in 1935.

Nagle, Edward Pierce (1893–1963). As the stepson of Gaston Lachaise, Nagle served as a link between Lachaise and Cummings's artistic circle. Nagle struggled with uneasiness about his own creative ambitions. He entered psychoanalysis in the early 1920s, from which he appeared to benefit greatly: Cummings observed that the analysis seemed to set him free to paint. Around this time, Cummings drew a satiric sketch of Nagle, titled *Edud Nahgult chez lui: a prêt. Freudian glimpse*. In this sketch, Nagle appears in a frenzy of painting, with a huge pile of scrunched up sheets labeled "15 minutes work," a painting captioned "ma mère" (my mother) hung on the wall, and a painting of "ma maîtresse" (my mistress) under way on the easel.

Norton, Richard (Dick) (1872–1918). In the view of John Dos Passos, Norton was "a Harvard man of the old nineteenth-century school, snob if you like, but solid granite underneath." An energetic person and a notable archaeologist, Norton spent eight years in Rome as director of the American School of Classical Studies (1899–1907) and subsequently led an archaeological dig in Cyrene (Libya). Over the course of September and October 1914, he founded the Anglo-American Volunteer Motor-Ambulance Corps, which merged at the beginning of 1916 with the Morgan-Harjes Section, thereby forming the combined Norton-Harjes Ambulance Corps, which Cummings later joined. Norton kept himself heavily involved at all levels in the day-to-day running of the ambulance corps, in which context he was a sharp-tongued taskmaster but effective. His father was Charles Eliot Norton (of Norton's Woods); his brother was Eliot Norton, who remained stateside and played a role in the recruitment of volunteer drivers. Norton wore a monocle and a full toothbrush mustache with pomaded twists at the ends, and he died in August 1918 of meningitis.

SOURCES: *Oxford Dictionary of National Biography* (Carpenter). *Dictionary of American Biography* (Hale, Hillyer, Lachaise, Lowell). *American National Biography* (Cowley, Lachaise, Lowell). For Damon: Monteiro 1974; Mitchell 1993. Nagle: birth/death dates from art auction information; psychoanalysis: Cohen 1983: 594; sketch: *HRC* Norman Papers 12.20. Norton: information from Hansen 1996/2011 and Carver (ed.) 2014; quote from Dos Passos at Hansen 1996/2011: v and 21.

Recommendations for Further Reading

—

The Enormous Room (1922), Cummings's own account of his imprisonment in La Ferté-Macé, is drily hilarious and irreplaceable. For another perspective on Cummings's generation, mostly in the decade following the war, the classic account is Malcolm Cowley's memoir of his own life and his recollections of his friends: *Exile's Return: A Literary Odyssey of the 1920s* (1934; expanded edition 1951). John Dos Passos's memoir is also highly readable and full of personality (his own and the personalities of Cummings, Fitzgerald, Hemingway, and others): *The Best Times: An Informal Memoir* (1966). Finally, the life of Scofield Thayer is much more comprehensible now that we have James Dempsey's biography, *The Tortured Life of Scofield Thayer* (2014).

Notes on the Text

—

ABBREVIATIONS

CP	Cummings, *Complete Poems: 1904–1962* (2016)
ER	Cummings, *The Enormous Room* (1978 [1922])
HL	Houghton Library, Harvard University
HRC	Harry Ransom Center, University of Texas at Austin
nonlectures	Cummings, *i: six nonlectures* (= Cummings 1967)
Qualey	*HL, E. E. Cummings letters to Elizabeth Cummings Qualey,* MS Am 1765.1: "When I was a little girl," by Elizabeth Cummings Qualey
Spring	*Spring: The Journal of the E. E. Cummings Society*

ARCHIVAL PAPERS

HL manuscripts with call numbers beginning 1823 are from E. E. Cummings Papers, 1870–1969 (MS Am 1823–1823.10). Manuscripts with call numbers beginning 1892 are from E. E. Cummings Additional Papers, 1870–1969 (MS Am 1892–1892.11). Other subcollections from the Cummings papers are given long-form references in the notes.

HRC call numbers, unless otherwise specified, refer to "Cummings, E. E. (Edward Estlin) (1894–1962). Collection, 1902–1968."

HRC Norman Papers refers to the Charles Norman Collection, 1909–1972.

Online archive of *The Boston Globe* = from 1872 to 1922, the *Boston Daily Globe*.

NOTE ON THE TITLE

"The Beauty of Living" and the opening epigraph are taken from Cummings's essay "Armistice," *HL,* MS Am 1892.6 (9).

PROLOGUE: "ONLY MY DOOR CLOSING"

1   "it was with a genuine ...": *ER*, 16.
1   Details of the cell: *ER*, 16–17. "I am sorry for you ...": *ER*, 15.
1   Letters going missing: *ER*, 62, 152, 221. "ferocious and uncouth miracle ...": *ER*, 66.
2   Date of sail for *La Touraine* and the accident that detached Cummings and Brown: Norman 1972 [1958], 69–70; Kennedy 1994, 137–39; Collier 1997, 139; see also Chapter 10: "Across."
2   "What did you do in Paris? ...": *ER*, 12.
3   Letter to his mother dated July 7, 1917, Cummings 1972, 28.
3   "Do you hate the Germans? ...": *ER*, 14.

Further notes on the prologue:

Doubt has been expressed by other Cummings scholars about letters going missing from La Ferté-Macé. Cummings makes the claim about missing letters in *The Enormous Room*, where he writes about a letter that *did* reach his family, posted by a fellow prisoner who had managed to finagle a brief foray from the prison into town: "And I wonder to this day that the only letter of mine which ever reached America and my doting family should have been posted by this highly entertaining personage en ville ..." (*ER*, 152).

Gill 2007, 106, objects that three letters to the family and one letter to Scofield Thayer are known to have got through. Subtracting the one sent from the village, that leaves two to the family and one to Thayer—that is, three in total from prison. It does seem, therefore, that Cummings exaggerated the isolation at La Ferté. On the other hand, three known letters does not make an impressive total considering that Cummings was allowed to write one letter and one postcard from prison each week (as he explains to Thayer: Cummings 2007, 104), which means he could have written up to eleven letters and eleven postcards. Even if Cummings exaggerated the extent of the interference with communication, it would be a mistake to dismiss entirely his claim that letters went astray.

CHAPTER 1. BEYOND THE RIVER

7   Snowballs: *nonlectures*, 31.
8   Lowell, "Mary Winslow," in Lowell 2003, 28.
8   Size of Boston according to the World Almanac from 1901 (reporting 1900 census data).
8   Motorcars: *Qualey*, 169–70; *nonlectures*, 8; images and further information: https://www.american-automobiles.com/Orient-Buckboard.html.
9   Cummings's sketches: *HL*, MS Am 1892.8 (1). Ticket to Estlin's Great Animal Arena: *HL*, MS Am 1823.7 (5).

10 Paradox of chaos and order: *HL*, MS Am 1823.7 (9).

10 Starting school late: *Qualey*, 48.

10 Secret hiding place: *Qualey*, 25. Kite-flying: *Qualey*, 23–24; Norman 1972 [1958], 17. Furnace and fires: *Qualey*, 26. Speaking tubes: *Qualey*, 28.

11 Elizabeth's date of birth: Sawyer-Lauçanno 2006, 13.

11 Bicycle rides: *Qualey*, 44–45.

11 Norton's Woods "semiwilderness" and nickname, lilacs, and chased by coachman: *nonlectures*, 32–34.

11 Report card: *HRC*, 10.6.

12 Joy Farm: Kennedy 1994, 26; Sawyer-Lauçanno 2006, 10–11.

12 Compass and matches: *Qualey*, 153. Lost neighbors: *Qualey*, 163–64.

12 Dynamite: *Qualey*, 120–21.

13 Neighborhood gang and codes: *Qualey*, 29–31 (quote at 29).

13 Derby-hat incident: *Qualey*, 41–42.

13 Whooping cough: *Qualey*, 20–21; Norman 1972 [1958], 21; Sawyer-Lauçanno 2006, 23–24.

13 Cold baths and showers: *Qualey*, 14, 123–24 ("ice cold" are her words); in prison: *ER*, 55–56, 65.

14 May flowers: listed at *HL*, MS Am 1892.7 (284), Folder 1 of 8. (Cummings describes the blossom from June 4, but noting "season at least 1 month late.")

14 White pine stumps: *Qualey*, 160. Floorboards: *Qualey*, 115.

14 Blueberries: *HL*, MS Am 1823.9 (16).

14 Haymakers' mixture: *Qualey*, 147.

15 Fireplace and beams: *Qualey*, 115–16.

15 Description of father: *Qualey*, 17; voice: *Qualey*, 61. Brown's view: *HL*, MS Am 1892.2 (102), letters from Brown to Marion Morehouse, dated January 16, 1966, and May 17, 1966. "always afraid": Sawyer-Lauçanno 2006, 19.

Further notes on Chapter 1:

Haymakers' mixture: Elizabeth only says "vinegar," but the Internet verdict is that Haymakers' mixture (or switchel) is made specifically with apple-cider vinegar; honey or maple syrup can stand in for the molasses. The drink is currently undergoing a limited hipster revival. Personally, I found today's version a bit watery and underwhelming, though it does leave a distinct aftertaste of vinegar on the tongue—sort of like a sweetened and watered-down juice with a built-in mouthwash. The shopkeeper who sold us the switchel tried really, really hard to cut us a bulk price for the cases of switchel stuck in his basement.

CHAPTER 2. THE REVEREND

16 Place of birth and childhood: Kennedy 1966, 439.

16 Fluffy: *Qualey*, 88.

16 The Reverend's academic studies and teaching: Norman 1972 [1958], 14–15;
    Kennedy 1966: 439–40; cf. Kennedy 1994, 13.

16 Child's *Ballads* and rose garden: see *nonlectures*, 24–25; Rosenblitt 2016,
    104–6.

18 *Boston Globe*: I refer respectively to articles of February 26, 1900; February 7,
    1905; March 27, 1911; June 17, 1907; January 19, 1920; and September 9, 1913 (the
    summerhouse).

18 Failure to research and Harvard career: Kennedy 1976, 267.

18 Second choice: Webster 2015, 76; exact relation to T. S. Eliot: Eliot 1887.

18 Cummings's paternal grandfather: Sawyer-Lauçanno 2006, 10; *nonlectures*,
    12.

18 Mask of Zeus: *HL*, 1892.7 (234). (Cummings's note qualifies the date of 1900
    with a question mark.) This is not a free-standing bust, but a large plaster
    mask that hangs on a wall. Cummings refers to it as "hung" at the stairs, and
    the fact that it is a mask, not a bust, is confirmed by a photograph published
    with "Silver Lake Revisited" (Michael Webster, photos by Gillian Huang-
    Tiller and Ken Tiller) on the Cummings' Society blog (www.eecsocietyblog
    .org).

18 Oil painting of Hale: *Boston Globe*, December 3, 1915.

19 "whose sense...": Brown to Morehouse, May 17, 1966: *HL*, MS Am 1892.2
    (102).

19 Liberalization of Sundays: "Advocate of Sunday Play," *Boston Globe*, March
    27, 1911.

19 Turtle: *HL*, MS Am 1892.8 (1): Box 109.

19 "dear Father": *HL*, MS Am 1892.8 (1). "Dad": *HL*, MS Am 1823.9 (16).

19 Jealousy: Kennedy 1994, 48; Sawyer-Lauçanno 2006, 30–31.

19 Crying: Kennedy 1994, 29; Sawyer-Lauçanno 2006, 21; "tears and nose-
    bleeds": *nonlectures*, 30. Last year of junior school: Kennedy 1994, 30; teased
    for height: Kennedy 1994, 39.

20 Falling from trees: *HL*, MS Am 1892.7 (254).

20 Uncle George was his mother's brother: *nonlectures*, 26. Uncle George and
    gore: *nonlectures*, 27–28; boxing: Sawyer-Lauçanno 2006, 30; encouragement
    of poetry and *The Rhymester*: Kennedy 1994, 44. *The Rhymester* = Tom Hood,
    The Rhymester or the Rules of Rhyme: A Guide to English Versification, New
    York 1882.

20 The Reverend's cruel comments to Rebecca: Kennedy 1994, 102–3; Sawyer-
    Lauçanno 2006, 30, 37. Rebecca's age at marriage: Kennedy 1994, 18. Images
    of Rebecca: Kennedy 1994, 16; *HL*, MS Am 1823.8 (46) and 1823.10 (45). Five
    foot four: Kennedy 1994, 15.

21 "The History of a Grizzly": *HRC*, 3.3.

21 Cows: Cummings, quoted by Sawyer-Lauçanno 2006, 24 (but without com-
    ment on the significance of gender); I rely here on Sawyer-Lauçanno and have
    not myself seen this passage in the archives.

CHAPTER 3. THE LAST SUMMER OF CHILDHOOD

23 "Can you . . .": *HRC,* 2.2. "A Father to his Son": *HRC,* 3.5 (and partially quoted by Kennedy 1994, 49).

24 Taussigs: *nonlectures,* 25. "surrounded": *nonlectures,* 8. Debate over Harvard's relationship to Boston: "Pres. Lowell and Rev Edward Cummings Discuss Relation of University to the City": *Boston Globe,* October 18, 1910.

25 Pagan poets: Malcolm Cowley, in an obituary of Cummings published September 9, 1962, in the *Herald Tribune: HL,* E. E. Cummings Miscellaneous Papers: MS Am 1769. Rossetti and necktie: *nonlectures,* 25, 29–30.

25 Harvard entrance modernization: Eliot 1890, 2–3. Cummings's entrance examination: *HRC,* 8.11 and *HL,* 1823.8 (33). Admission details: *HRC,* 8.1. Most took five: Kennedy 1994, 39; Sawyer-Lauçanno 2006, 40.

26 Rex: *Qualey,* 78–99, and *HRC* Norman Papers, 10.14, letter from Elizabeth to Norman, August 27, 1971. Silver Lake facts: http://silverlakemadison.com/lakefacts.aspx [accessed September 12, 2016]. Details of the boat and the accident: *Qualey,* 92–99 and *HRC* Norman Papers, 11.5 (Cummings explaining that it was a canvas boat, not a canoe properly speaking). For the drowning incident in general, see also Norman 1972 [1958], 26–27; Kennedy 1994, 49–50; Sawyer-Lauçanno 2006, 41–42; and Cheever 2014, 24–26. Kennedy dates the incident one year earlier, to the summer before Cummings's last year of school. However, Elizabeth's account first describes the plan to build a house at Silver Lake as a plan conceived during the summer that she was nine, and then moves to "the next summer": she was ten in the summer of 1911. Poem: *HRC,* 6.2; Rex's body and burial: *Qualey,* 99 and *HRC,* 6.2; dreaming about Rex: *HL,* MS Am 1892.7 (206). No fear of swimming is clear from an anecdote told to Charles Norman by one of Cummings's Harvard friends and recorded in one of Norman's interview notebooks: "1914 or 15 can of paint kicked off motorboat -- C delighted, stripped, dove in & fetched it": *HRC* Norman Papers, 12.4.

29 College adviser: *HRC,* 8.1.

29 Financial information and athletic information: *HRC,* 10.5; height from a New Hampshire driver's license issued 1951: *HRC,* 8.11. Room and board: *HRC,* 8.11 and 10.5.

CHAPTER 4. TEMPTATIONS

33 Exhortation to self: *HRC,* 6.8.

35 "guilt-fear": *HL,* MS Am 1892.7 (196); cf. Kennedy 1994, 426.

35 Sex-education debate: "Guarding the Race," *Boston Globe,* February 16, 1914.

36 "am almost 62 . . .": *HL,* MS Am 1892.7 (234); "defacatory" corrected to "defecatory."

36 Marlowe's Ovid: Cummings to Norman: Norman 1972 [1958], 30.

36 Cummings's gift to Miller: newspaper clipping held in *HRC*, 11.3. Quote on Miller from exhortation to self: *HRC*, 6.8. Cummings does not name Miller, but clearly he is the friend referred to; cf. Sawyer-Lauçanno 2006, 47. Much of the other information on Miller is from Kennedy 1994, 53–56. Cummings, Miller, and sexuality; falling out of touch when Miller moved on: Sawyer-Lauçanno 2006, 48, 56. Catullus, etc.: *nonlectures*, 50–51; Norman 1972 [1958], 39. Miller's doctorate ("a genial lover of good things . . ."): *HL*, MS Am 1892.7 (90).

38 "Not God, madam . . ." anecdote: Kennedy 1994, 63.

38 Harvard course notes, see *HRC* collection, especially 9.5, 9.6, 10.1, 10.2; see 10.1 for the specific point that European literatures were never isolated from each other and the point about fairy tales. Study of Italian and Dante: see R. S. Kennedy's notes (*HRC*, 8.11) and Kennedy 1994, 60–61.

40 Three weeks' absence: *HRC*, 2.1. Freshman year report card: *HRC*, 10.6; professor's notes on the grades: *HRC*, 10.5; with R. S. Kennedy's notes at *HRC*, 8.11. Petition: *HL*, MS Am 1892 (467). The petition related to English 2, which is also the course for which he penned the note of apology relating to his three-week absence, so it is not implausible to connect the two; however, there is no direct proof of connection.

40 Dyslexia: for the issues and methodologies of diagnosing dyslexia in writers from the past, see Siegel 1988; Miner and Siegel 1992; and Siegel 2013. I have raised the possibility of dyslexia in Rosenblitt 2016, xxii. Linda Siegel and I hope to say something together in the future about the possibility that Cummings was dyslexic. These particular examples of spelling mistakes are taken from *HL*, MS Am 1892.5 (741); *HL*, MS Am 1892.6 (114); *HL*, MS Am 1892.6 (124); *HRC*, 3.2; and *HRC*, 6.1, but similar examples are littered throughout his papers. "I can rarely read . . .": Cummings 1972, 249. Drawing upside-down: Norman 1972 [1958], 20. Struggles with analytical prose: Kennedy 1994, 53, 209, 440–41. These struggles may partly explain Cummings's low output in terms of literary criticism, in spite of a tremendous interest in theory and criticism evidenced in his personal notes. Most of the little criticism and theory that Cummings did publish has been collected in *A Miscellany Revised*, ed. George J. Firmage (1965). Cummings's lack of critical-theory output is also discussed by Fallon 2002 and Rosenblitt 2016: 198–206, esp. 199.

CHAPTER 5. A WORLD OF AESTHETES

42 *Cambridge Review*: Kennedy 1994, 41. For the five poems: *CP*, 897–901.

42 *Advocate*'s recruitment of Cummings and his preference for the *Monthly*:

Kennedy 1994, 77–78. Election to *Monthly*: HL, MS Am 1892 (861), letter Thayer to Cummings dated May 16, 1913. *Monthly* headed paper: *HRC*, 7.9.

42 Aesthete and "rather moony": Robert Lehan to Charles Norman, *HRC* Norman Papers, 11.12. Hazel-brown eyes: *HRC* Norman Papers, 6.11; listed as brown on his driver's license: *HRC*, 8.11.

43 Dos, signed "me": *HRC*, 7.5. Cheering effect of Dos's visits and (in Cummings's estimate, at least) rambunctious children: *HL*, MS Am 1892.7 (234).

43 Dos's background and his father: Dos Passos 1966, 1–40; further details: Davis 1962, 5–7; Carr 1984, 15–16. Carr explains that, during childhood, Dos had met John R., but infrequently and only as his "guardian." "I came to know him . . .": Dos Passos 1966, 4. "I don't remember . . .": Dos Passos 1966, 16. "As much as any eighteenth-century Etonian . . .": Dos Passos 1966, 15–16.

44 "Alas, intimations of immortality . . .": Robert Lehan to Charles Norman, undated: *HRC* Norman Papers, 11.12.

45 "mental masturbation": Brown to Cummings, letter of June 13, 1943, *HL*, MS Am 1823 (150).

45 Malcolm Cowley on reading poems, quoted in Norman 1972 [1958], 46.

45 "We kept saying . . .": S. Foster Damon to Charles Norman, in Norman 1972 [1958], 36–37.

45 "seemed more important . . .": Dos Passos 1966, 23.

46 Moderns and ancients: Hillyer to Norman, quoted in Norman 1972 [1958], 36.

46 The Armory Show Catalogue = Association of American Painters and Sculptors. *Catalogue of International Exhibition of Modern Art*. New York: Vreeland Advertising Press, 1913.

46 Duchamp, *Nude Descending a Staircase, No. 2*: now in the Philadelphia Museum of Art, accession number 1950–134–59. The online museum catalogue regards time-lapse photography as one of the inspirations for the painting.

47 Eberle's *White Slave* (reference to child prostitution): *HRC*, 3.2 for Cummings's reference and Casteras 1986 on Eberle and on the sculpture. "the specialized eye of society," quoted by Casteras 1986, 33. Controversy divided between subject matter and disbelief at the achievement of a female sculptor: Casteras 1986, 34.

47 Lowell and Stein: see "The New Art" in Cummings 1965, 8–11.

48 Grumpy letter: *HRC*, 8.5.

48 Damon on the streetcar and the photographs: Norman 1972 [1958], 35. Norman on eye color: letter from Norman to Cummings, July 16, 1952, *HL*, MS Am 1823 (945).

48 Sketch of doe and "good but poor": letter from Hillyer to Norman, February 24, 1958, *HRC* Norman Papers, 11.10; Norman 1972 [1958], 33.

49 Keats period: Cohen 1983, 593. Keats's "Lamia": *HRC*, 6.9.

50 Man versus poet: *HRC*, 2.7, draft dated August 1912.

50 "Sapphics": published in *The Harvard Monthly*, January 1916; *CP*, 923.

Further notes on Chapter 5:

Cummings saw the Armory Show in Boston, not New York (Kennedy 1994, 78), and only the European artists were included in the Boston version of the show; the American artists were dropped in order to fit into a smaller exhibition space. It is an interesting question, therefore, why Cummings singled out the work of the American sculptor Eberle when he saw the show in Boston, where her work did not appear. How, indeed, did he even know of it? I believe Michael Webster (personal communication) has the solution: Eberle's sculpture was featured on the cover of the May 1913 volume of *The Survey* (vol. 30, no. 5). *The Survey* is a magazine that—Webster suggests—is quite likely to have appealed to the Reverend, and the Cummings family may well have been regular subscribers.

CHAPTER 6. REBELLION STIRS

51 Sneaking up in his socks: letter from Anne Barton to Charles Norman, *HRC* Norman Papers, 10.8.

51 Cummings's room was 29 Thayer Hall, first floor in the British sense or second floor in the American sense: *HRC* Norman Papers, 10.6.

51 Old Howard as "the Temple of Titillation": Cummings to Thayer, from the researches of Jim Dempsey and used with his permission, Dial/Scofield Thayer Papers, Yale Collection of American Literature, Beinecke Rare Book and Manuscript Library, Yale University, YCAL MSS 34 Box 30 Folder 783.

51 Historian on the Old Howard: "Old Days of the Howard Athenaeum," *Boston Globe*, November 22, 1916. For the repertoire of the Howard Athenaeum, see regular notices in the *Boston Globe* archives.

52 Watch and Ward Society: Miller 2010; Kemeny 2018. "a regret that has lingered...": Norman 1972 [1958], 35. Cummings's shame: letter from Anne Barton to Charles Norman, *HRC* Norman Papers, 10.8; Kennedy 1966, 446.

52 Updates on World Series (October 2, 1917) and election (November 6, 1917), *Boston Globe*.

52 "greeted by...": *nonlectures*, 48.

52 Secret marriage: "Banker's Bride," *Boston Globe*, March 19, 1901.

52 "It was a Saturday night..." Hillyer to Charles Norman, February 24, 1958, *HRC* Norman Papers, 11.10; Norman 1972 [1958], 33.

53 President of abstinence league: "Temperance at Harvard," *Boston Globe*, March 24, 1883. Cambridge teetotal: Kennedy 1994, 9. Tea with rum: Hillyer to Charles Norman, February 24, 1958, *HRC* Norman Papers, 11.10. Beer and wine: *HRC* Norman Papers, 6.18; 11.7; Norman 1972 [1958], 35, 38.

53 All details of Massachusetts and the penal code on drunkenness from "Dealing with Drunks," *Boston Globe*, February 26, 1900.

54 Young criminals and prison conditions: "Save the Boys," *Boston Globe*, February 7, 1905.

54 Hairpins: *HL,* MS Am 1892.7 (242); letter from Anne Barton to Charles Norman, *HRC* Norman Papers, 10.8.

54 Car incident: *HRC* Norman Papers, 10.8; Malcolm Cowley, obituary for Cummings, "Books—September 9, 1962," *Herald Tribune, HL,* E. E. Cummings Miscellaneous Papers: MS Am 1769; Norman 1972 [1958], 34–35; Kennedy 1994, 89–90, 103; Sawyer-Lauçanno 2006, 69–70; Cheever 2014, 26–27, 28.

55 "Bobby Hillyer...": letter from Cummings to Thayer, 1916, from the researches of Jim Dempsey and used with his permission, Dial/Scofield Thayer Papers, Yale Collection of American Literature, Beinecke Rare Book and Manuscript Library, Yale University, YCAL MSS 34 Box 30 Folder 783; Cummings's "here" corrected to "hear." Cummings wrote "Masfieldically," which presumably is a reference to the poet John Masefield; thus corrected to "Masefieldically."

55 Thayer Hall cheaper: Hillyer to Charles Norman, March 7, 1958, *HRC* Norman Papers, 11.10.

55 Expenditure: *HRC,* 9.5.

55 Date of graduation: Norman 1972 [1958], 41. Note that he was class speaker and not valedictorian, as Cheever 2014, xi, wrongly suggests. Selection process: Kennedy 1994, 84. There are various versions of this essay, including *HRC,* 5.6; Cummings 1965, 5–11, republished from *The Harvard Advocate,* June 1915. Satie's "truly extraordinary sense of humour...": Cummings 1965, 7; quotes concerning Lowell, 8–9.

56 Poems copied out: *HRC,* 6.8, 6.9, 8.11 (the last for Lowell's "Bullion," "The Bungler," "The Letter," and "Grotesque"). He may have copied out the Lowell and Evans in connection with thinking through this essay, since he also quotes Evans.

56 Audience numbers inferred from the number of degrees given, Norman 1972 [1958], 41.

56 Damon: "One aged lady...," quoted in Norman 1972 [1958], 43–44.

CHAPTER 7. PAGAN HARVARD

58 "But look beneath the surface..." from "ESSAYS UPON COLLEGIATE INHUMANITIES BY ONE OF THEM": *HL,* MS Am 1892.6 (31); "Hygene" corrected to "Hygiene."

58 "Here we behold..." from "Veritas": *HL,* MS Am 1892.6 (117).

59 Relaxed organization of master's: letter from F. N. Robinson to Cummings, February 5, 1916, *HRC,* 8.1.

59 "Dialogue of the Dead," titled by Cummings as "Manuscript Found in a Bottle" and dated May 2, 1916, *HRC,* 2.6.

59 Courses with Briggs: Cummings's full course schedule outlined by R. S. Kennedy in a document generously left with *HRC,* 8.11, to aid future researchers.

59 Damon suffering from Briggs's exemplification of a poetic horror: Norman 1972 [1958], 36.

59 "felt at liberty . . .": letter from Hillyer to Charles Norman, February 24, 1958, *HRC*, 11.10.

60 Harvard major: Kennedy 1976, 269, 281–82. The Reverend's preference: Kennedy 1966, 446.

60 "I believe that the most ultra-modern . . .": from "The Greek Spirit," *HL*, MS Am 1892.6 (47); published in full in Rosenblitt 2016, 304.

61 "In my revulsion . . .": Dos Passos 1966, 134.

61 Aristophanes of today: Dos Passos 1966, 84–85. See also Cummings's comments on burlesque and satyr plays: "Burlesque, I Love It!" (Cummings in *Stage*, March 1936), Cummings 1965, 292.

61 Lowell as the American Sappho, in "Manuscript Found in a Bottle": *HRC*, 2.6.

61 Helen of Troy: see *CP*, 967; also R. S. Mitchell's "Helen" in *Eight Harvard Poets* (Cummings et al. 1917).

61 "pagans, in the sense that they invoked . . .": from Cowley's obituary for Cummings, published September 9, 1962, in the *Herald Tribune* and titled "A Farewell to the Last Harvard 'Dandy,'" *HL*, E. E. Cummings Miscellaneous Papers: MS Am 1769. As a point of comparison for the influence of classical paganism on lives and sexualities and concerning the ramifications of a classicizing cultural background for another, very different war poet, see Paul Delany, *The Neo-Pagans: Friendship and Love in the Rupert Brooke Circle* (1987).

61 "Not the loud lusting . . .": *HRC*, 2.2; see also Rosenblitt 2016, 63–109; Rosenblitt 2016c; Rosenblitt 2016d.

61 "the great goat-footed God . . . ," "the little God Pan," and "the first smoke o' Spring": *HRC*, 6.8.

62 "Saturnalia": from Cummings et al., *Eight Harvard Poets*.

62 "Pan by noon and Bacchus by night": from Swinburne's *Atalanta in Calydon* (1865).

62 "exceeding pleasure . . .": from "Laus Veneris" (*Poems and Ballads*, 1866).

62 "libidinous laureate": John Morley, quoted in McGann 2004, 208.

63 "The god pursuing, the maiden hid": from Swinburne's *Atalanta in Calydon* (1865).

63 "run along . . ." and "I had a hard time . . .": letter from Cummings to Thayer, 1916, from the researches of Jim Dempsey and used with his permission, Dial/Scofield Thayer Papers, Yale Collection of American Literature, Beinecke Rare Book and Manuscript Library, Yale University, YCAL MSS 34 Box 30 Folder 783; cf. Webster 2011.

63 "My soul like an old dog . . .": *HRC*, 10.3.

63 On Cummings's stylistic breakthroughs in 1916–1917: see Kennedy 1979. Generally on Cummings's studies: Kennedy 1976; on Cummings's Harvard circle of friends: Kennedy 1977.

63 Imagism as promotional strategy: Rainey 1998, 10–41.

64 "of evident invisibles": *CP*, 81.

65 Damon's role in exposing Cummings to Imagism: Kennedy 1994, 78–79.

65 Debussy: dates are those of first public performance, from the catalogue of works in Dietschy 1990. Debussy's nostalgia and sensual richness: see letter from Mallarmé to Debussy, December 23, 1894, in Debussy 2005, 229–30. Fuller discussion, see Rosenblitt 2016, 72–77. For modernism and Swinburne and demythologizing the "clean break" from the past: see Laity 1989, 1996, and 2004. Cummings on Debussy: *HRC*, 3.2.

66 Metrical notes: *HRC*, 1.6.

67 Draft of "of evident invisibles": *HL*, MS Am 1823.5 (259).

CHAPTER 8. DORIS AND ELAINE

68 "my loveliest playmate": *nonlectures*, 25. Poems about Betty: *HRC*, 3.2, 3.5, 6.1.

68 Doris Bryan: letters, *HL*, MS Am 1892 (113) and 1892.7 (190); all quotes from her are from these letters. On Doris, see also Kennedy 1994, 87–88.

72 Cummings's letter to Thayer: Dempsey 2011; Dempsey 2014, 16. Thayer's response: *HL*, MS Am 1892 (861), dated May 13, 1913.

72 Thayer's stay in Oxford and entanglement with Vivien Haigh-Wood: Dempsey 2014, 19–23, 26–28.

73 Doris on Thayer: letter to Cummings, October 7: *HL*, MS Am 1892 (113).

73 Details of Thayer's life: see Dempsey 2014, including "dabbler," 21; "Longfellow," 26, 67; "heightened," Farrar on Thayer, 25; age gap between Thayer and Elaine, 35.

73 Cummings meeting Elaine late March: *HL*, MS Am 1892 (545); Kennedy 1994, 111; incorrect in Sawyer-Lauçanno 2006, 86. On errors in Sawyer-Lauçanno, see further: Webster 2004.

73 Cummings's first response to Elaine: "exquisite" and "worship from afar" are his words: *HL*, MS Am 1892.7 (211). On Elaine, Thayer, and Cummings, see also Cohen 2003.

73 Chicago: Dempsey 2014, 30–34.

73 "Epithalamion": *CP*, 3–7. Cummings presenting the poem to Thayer and his discomfort at Thayer's response: Kennedy 1994, 111–13; Sawyer-Lauçanno 2006, 88. Drawings: *HL*, MS Am 1892.8 (1). Cf. Kidder 1979, 267–68, who also identifies the stained-glass aesthetic and the similarity between the Thayer and Christ portraits.

Further notes on Chapter 8:
Regarding Thayer's month in Chicago: British readers of a 1990s vintage might see this, as I do, as Thayer's "Common People" episode (Pulp, *Different Class*).

CHAPTER 9. HARVARD IN NEW YORK

76 "we were one . . .": Dos Passos 1966, 24.
76 The Reverend scandalized: Kennedy 1994, 113.
76 Perry's advice: letter from Perry to Cummings, July 16, 1915: *HL*, MS Am 1892 (674).
76 Brush-off from the *Evening Post*: *HRC*, 7.9.
77 Lowell's visit to the Poetry Society and quote on Whitman and *vers libre*: Norman 1972 [1958], 47–48. Lowell's letter of reference: *HRC*, 11.3; *HL*, MS Am 1823 (782) (Lowell to Cummings, letter of June 13, 1916); *HRC*, 6.18; Norman 1972 [1958], 65–66; Kennedy 1994, 113. Bet with Thayer: Dempsey 2014, 67, 154.
77 hellfire Christian: *nonlectures*, 12.
78 Cummings's notes on hating and fearing his grandfather, including "I'll see you there . . . ," quoted by Sawyer-Lauçanno 2006, 10.
78 Stop on the Railroad: *HL*, MS Am 1892.7 (18) and MS Am 1892.7 (90) ("the child who was I . . ." from the latter).
78 The Reverend striving to leave his father's tyranny behind: I agree with Sawyer-Lauçanno 2006, 10, that the purchase of Joy Farm likely represented an attempt on the Reverend's part to carve a life for his immediate family away from his own father.
78 The Reverend and civil rights: *Boston Globe*, February 26, 1904. Cummings's school: mentioned there and also *nonlectures*, 8, 30.
78 The Reverend charming pain away: *Qualey*, 16; playing in snow: *Qualey*, 39; "children and not grass": *Qualey*, 29; Norman 1972 [1958], 18; Sawyer-Lauçanno 2006, 16.
79 Forgery: *HL*, MS Am 1892.7 (18); *nonlectures*, 11.
79 Christmas fight: *HL*, MS Am 1892.7 (202).
80 Collier & Son: Norman 1972 [1958], 64–65; Kennedy 1994, 129, 131.
80 Furniture: Cummings to the Reverend, January 4, 1917, and January 26, 1917, *HL*, MS Am 1823.1 (152).
80 Nagle: Dos Passos 1966, 23–24.
81 End of the *Monthly*: Cowley's obituary for Cummings, September 9, 1962, in the *Herald Tribune*: *HL*, E. E. Cummings Miscellaneous Papers: MS Am 1769. See also letter from J. Donald Adams to Charles Norman, March 3, 1958: *HRC* Norman Papers, 11.14.
81 Dos and Mitchell in lead: Norman 1972 [1958], 50.
81 Guarantee of costs: letter from Dos to Norman, September 29, 1957: *HRC* Norman Papers, 11.7; Norman 1972 [1958], 59.
81 William Norris's destruction of copies: Norman 1972 [1958], 53–54. The book is available in an ULAN Press reproduction, but some poems in this reproduction are missing altogether and others are missing lines. The Project Gutenberg edition (available online at www.gutenberg.org) is superior.

81 The eight poets are: E. E. Cummings, S. Foster Damon, J. R. Dos Passos, Robert Hillyer, R. S. Mitchell, William A. Norris, Dudley Poore, and Cuthbert Wright.

81 Dudley Poore: from "The Philosopher's Garden" (*Eight Harvard Poets*). Poore as best verse: Dos Passos 1966, 49.

82 "Frail azures...": from Cummings's "This is the garden: colors come and go" (*Eight Harvard Poets*), republished as "this is the garden:colours come and go," (*CP*, 156, with typesetting more under Cummings's control).

82 Dos, Wright, and Cummings's typography: Norman 1972 [1958], 55–58.

82 "dimly": Dos Passos 1966, 23.

82 Dirth of acrobats in the Old Howard; shows from the trenches; plotlines; news: *Boston Globe*, "News, Notes and Gossip about Plays and Players," February 4, 1917. Patriotic songs, e.g., *Boston Globe* March 27 and April 24, 1917.

83 "'What will you do ...'": Damon to Cummings, February 6, 1917: *HL*, MS Am 1823 (307).

83 Considering service before declaration of war: Shaw 1979.

83 Worries about the six-year sign-on: the Reverend to Cummings, April 16, 1917: *HL*, MS Am 1823 (296).

83 "It will mean everything...": letter from Cummings to the Reverend, postmarked April 18, 1917: *HL*, MS Am 1823.1 (152).

83 World Peace Foundation: Kennedy 1966, 444.

83 Report of sermons, *Boston Globe*, "SOUNDS CALL TO THE MINUTEMEN OF TODAY," April 16, 1917.

84 "I was all for...": Dos Passos 1966, 25; cf. Dos to Norman, *HRC* Norman Papers, 11.7.

84 Sailing on the *Touraine*, including list of volunteers and list of items to pack: *HL*, MS Am 1823.8 (35).

84 "Being neither warrior...": *nonlectures*, 52.

84 Approach to *The Seven Arts*: letter of November 13, 1916: *HRC* 8.5.

CHAPTER 10. ACROSS

87 Sailing of the *Touraine* and details of the ship: *HL*, MS Am 1823.7 (18).

87 "Looking back...": *HL*, MS Am 1823.7 (17). Kennedy 1994, 138, quotes this same phrase, with "real" (for "reel") and "unpunctual" (for "unpuncturable"), citing MS Am 1823.7 (18)—a call number for a folder with some loose notes, poems, and drawings, including typed versions of earlier notes. According to my own archival notes, 1823.7 (18) reads "reel" and "unpunctuable" (the second obviously a typing error). The handwritten original in 1823.7 (17) (a Paris notebook) unquestionably reads "reel" and "unpuncturable."

87 Thayer and intensity: *HL*, MS Am 1892.7 (90); see also Webster 2015, 77.

88 Valedictory telegram: *HL*, MS Am 1823 (296); Kennedy 1994, 137.

88 Seasickness and "The 'boat' . . .": letter to his parents, May 4, 1917, Cummings 1972, 18–19. *La Touraine* was built in 1890 and her maiden voyage was in June 1891: Bonsor 1978, 657.

89 History of U-boat warfare: Kennedy 2014, especially 337–42. U-boat success in April 1917: the Germans sunk 870,000 tons of shipping; see Winton 1983, 48 (and figures for subsequent months, Winton 1983, 78).

89 "Should the blond captain . . .": Cummings to his parents, May 4, Cummings 1972, 18.

89 Eleven-day crossing: Cummings's letters (see Cummings 1972, 22–24) show that he arrived at Bordeaux on the morning of May 8.

90 "a wholly possible boy": Cummings to his parents, May 4, Cummings 1972, 18.

90 Samuel Slater: Collier 1997, 133.

90 "Slater the Traitor": Neil Heath, "Samuel Slater: American Hero or British Traitor," September 22, 2011, BBC News, https://www.bbc.co.uk/news/uk -england-derbyshire-15002318; "Samuel Slater—Hero or Traitor?" Belper News January 6, 2005, https://www.bbc.co.uk/news/uk-england-derbyshire -15002318.

90 Brown's mother's death and the smash: Collier 1997, 135–36. James Lincoln Collier was one of Brown's nephews. He delved as a researcher into his own family history and I am much indebted to his work. Collier is comparatively more exculpating of the family's treatment of Ruth; cruelty and social snob-bery is what I take to be implicit in his account.

91 Brown's names: Collier 1997, 130, and evidence across the *HRC* and *HL* archi-val papers.

91 Rebellion: Collier 1997, 136. Some secondary sources write that Brown lived in Boston while he attended the Cambridge High and Latin School, and other sources write that he lived in Cambridge. Cambridge is correct. Brown stayed with his uncle S. Bartlett, who later wrote to provide details of Brown's back-ground in connection with his detention in France. Bartlett says clearly that Brown "was one year a member of my family when I lived in Cambridge, and attended the Cambridge Latin School" and that Reverend Cummings was "a next door neighbor": letter of December 7, 1917, from S. Bartlett to Sherman L. Whipple, *HRC* Norman Papers, 12.19.

91 Cousin as a friend of Elizabeth: letter from Cummings to his parents, May 4, 1917, Cummings 1972, 18–19; Pritchard 1990, 132.

91 "out of New England": Collier 1997, 133.

91 "phony": Collier 1997, 136–37; Pritchard 1990, 131, clearly puts the move from the Columbia School of Journalism to Columbia itself before Brown's ambu-lance service.

92 Brown drinking a gin fizz or something of that kind ("some sort of plebeian drink like a gin fizz, a regular collegiate drink at the time"): Brown to Wickes, quoted in Collier 1997, 128; see also Pritchard 1990, 130.

92 Brown and Cummings's shared sardonic take on the world: see also Collier 1997, 129.

92 "I envy you...": letter of condolence from Charles Simmons to Louisa Alger, September 12, 1962: *HL*, E. E. Cummings Miscellaneous Papers: MS Am 1769, "Clippings and printed matter."

92 "Cummings's only fault": Richard Norton to the American ambassador, November 22, 1917, *HRC* Norman Papers, 11.14; "under whose influence," official report of arrest (see Chapter 18: "At Noyon Once More") and report by Col. Frank Parker, October 26, 1917: *HRC* Norman Papers, 11.5.

92 Brown's voice: Collier 1997, 136.

93 "afraid of people...": Brown to Cummings, December 5, 1918, *HL*, MS Am 1892 (110).

93 "danger-zone": Cummings to his parents, May 5, Cummings 1972, 20.

93 shuttered in iron: Dos Passos 2003 [1920], 4. Dos Passos's short narrative, *One Man's Initiation: 1917*, is a fictional account drawing on his own experience. I take it that details about the crossing and the atmosphere in Bordeaux and Paris reflect Dos Passos's actual experience and observation. In his memoir, Dos Passos says that he took the character of Martin Howe out of a previous unfinished novel and, in *One Man's Initiation*, "put him through everything I had seen and heard that summer": Dos Passos 1966, 70–71.

93 slept on the deck in their clothes: Cummings to his parents, May 7, Cummings 1972, 22.

93 Lights, "danger-time," and other details of arrival: Cummings to his mother, May 11, Cummings 1972, 23–24.

93 First impressions of Bordeaux: *HL*, MS Am 1823.7 (11).

93 Dos Passos's own crossing to Bordeaux: Dos Passos 1966, 48. Fictionalized version and "mellow houses": Dos Passos 2003 [1920], 8.

94 Mix-up about stations and arrival in Paris: Cummings to his mother, May 11, Cummings 1972, 24.

Further notes on Chapter 10:
The Reverend's rhyme—"... I envy your chance of breaking a lance for freedom in France..."—is not unlike Swinburne's lines, in "To Victor Hugo":

Who said "Let there be freedom," and there was
Freedom; and as a lance
The fiery eyes of France
Touched the world's sleep [...]

Had the Reverend, like Cummings, also been reading Swinburne? It is hard to imagine Swinburne's sadomasochistic fantasies, his femmes fatales, and his celebration of "deviant" sexualities being much to the Reverend's taste.

CHAPTER 11. MARIE LOUISE LALLEMAND

95 Dates for arrival in Montmartre: *HRC* Norman Papers, 11.3; Cummings 1972, 22–24.

95 Brown to Marion Morehouse, letter of May 3, 1965, *HL*, MS Am 1892.2 (102).

95 "L'Affaire Slater": Pritchard 1990, 132–33.

96 Enlistment details: *HL*, MS Am 1823.8 (35). Passage to France at discounted price of a little over $78: Sawyer-Lauçanno 2006, 106.

96 Airplanes and dirigibles: letter to his parents [May 1917], Cummings 1972, 26.

96 "We were astonished . . .": Dos Passos 1966, 50.

97 "The less they find . . .": prefatory statement of the Armory Show catalogue, by Frederick James Gregg. Cummings at the Armory Show: see above, Chapter 5. Damon and Debussy: see above, Chapters 6 and 7. *Des Imagistes*: Kennedy 1994, 79. *Blast*: *HRC*, catalogue for Cummings's personal library.

98 Picasso and Olga; information and quotation from Cocteau on *Parade* ("to them we opposed Satie . . ."; "I asked him . . ."): Cocteau 1951 (quotes translated from the French).

98 "flex your cheekbones" (in reference to the part which Massine himself danced in the original), from an interview with Gary Chryst (including footage) from the revival of *Parade* undertaken by the Joffrey Ballet: "Joffrey: Mavericks of American Dance" (American Masters Series), PBS, 12/28/12; http://www.pbs.org/wnet/americanmasters/joffrey-film-excerpt-the -parade-revival/2398/.

98 Surrealism: Wickes 1969, 194.

98 ". . . each individual is an adult": Cocteau 1951 (quote translated from the French).

99 Cummings threatening to fight at *Parade*: Wickes 1969, 70–71.

99 Invention of Dada in 1916; manifesto written in 1918: see Cowley 1994 [1951], 138–47.

99 "The ballet would do for our time . . .": Dos Passos 1966, 147.

99 Political nature of *Parade*: see also interview with Claude Samuel and Jean Cocteau (YouTube), https://www.youtube.com/watch?v=WATQDqjAOUc, accessed October 6, 2019.

99 Brown at *Petrushka* after inoculations: Pritchard 1990, 134.

100 "The immediate thing . . .": Dos Passos 1966, 49. Delay in acquiring uniform, letters to his mother or mother and father, May 11, 1917, [undated, May 1917], June 4, 1917, Cummings 1972, 24–27. Cummings not wearing uniform: letter to his parents [May 1917], Cummings 1972, 25.

100 Prostitution in *Goodbye to All That*: Graves 2000 [1957], 67, 79 (Le Havre), 103–4 (queue of 150 men for 3 women; making excuse of fear of VD), 150–51 (the Red Lamp and the Blue Lamp: "Whether, in this careful maintenance . . ."), 153, 195, 247.

101 Sultana Cherqui: letter to his parents [May 1917], Cummings 1972, 25; to Brown, December 28, 1917: *HL*, MS Am 1892.1 (15). Name of the restaurant as Oasis: Kennedy 1994, 140. In the letter to his parents, Cummings says that it was off the Rue Montmartre, which is the continuation of the Rue Faubourg-Montmartre but farther south, heading down past the grand boulevards towards the Seine. To Brown, Cummings says Rue Faubourg-Montmartre, which suggests that the earlier reference is a shorthand.

102 Address for Mimi inferred from Cummings's poem: *HL*, MS Am 1823.7 (7). Address for Marie Louise: *HL*, MS Am 1892.7 (81).

102 Assignation: *HL*, MS Am 1892.7 (81).

102 Many of the descriptions of Mimi and Marie Louise are from Cummings's published, unpublished, and draft poetry or poetic notes. The poems give artistic shape to his observations, but they can be relied upon as true accounts. His compositional practice at this point in his life involved a search for realism and the exquisitely observed detail. "*à la voix fragile*": *CP*, 61. Singer: *HL*, MS Am 1823.7 (7). Cummings says "*devant la guerre chanteuse*" (a singer in the face of the war), but it seems probable that he meant *avant* la guerre (not *devant*): that is, a singer before the war broke out. A different draft of the poem, including Jewish mother and Spanish father: *HL*, MS Am 1892.7 (78). Sketches of Mimi and Marie Louise: *HL*, MS Am 1823.7 (16). Brown slept with Mimi: Sawyer-Lauçanno 2006, 111.

103 Marie Louise and Musset's "Lucie": letter from Cummings to Dos, 1918: *HL*, MS Am 1892.13 (111), with thanks to Michael Webster for bringing this letter to my attention.

103 Sketch, titled *L'Agonie*, signed "Edouard C.": *HL*, MS Am 1823.7 (11).

103 Cummings's early poems about prostitution, e.g., *HRC*, 6.1. Liz, Mame, Fran: *CP*, 237, 238, 241. Generally, on Cummings's poems about prostitutes, see also Yablon 1998; Fallon 2012 [2013]; Huang-Tiller 2012 [2013]. Marie Louise: *CP*, 61.

104 Letter to Elizabeth, May 3, 1922, Cummings 1972, 85–86.

104 Dos Passos character dialogue on Parisian prostitutes: Dos Passos 2003 [1920], 9.

105 *Putain* and "queenly legs"; "Marie / Vierge / Priez / Pour / Nous": *CP*, 61. *Reine, pucelle*: *HL*, MS Am 1823.7 (10). Cleopatra: *HL*, MS Am 1892.7 (78) and 1823.7 (7).

105 Drawings of the day at Nogent-sur-Marne: *HL*, MS Am 1823.7 (16); her list here of the names of the four of them is also how we know that she called him Edouart.

105 Sex: Kennedy suggests that Cummings held back at least partly from anxiety about venereal disease: Kennedy 1994, 142. Payment and the implication that he had not returned the favor sexually: letter from Marie Louise to Cummings, July 8: *HL*, MS Am 1823 (831).

106 Cummings loved her kindness: her kindness is a refrain in all his letters to her.

Further notes on Chapter 11:

The urban topography of prostitution: Paris is divided into its arrondisse-ments, which are divisions of the city numbered in a spiral pattern from the center outward. Montmartre, with its nightclubs and demimonde nightlife, occupies the 18th arrondissement, and the Quartier Pigalle can be found on its southern edge—that is, farther in toward the center of Paris, overlapping the meeting of the 18th and the 9th arrondissements. The 10th arrondissement, immediately to the east of the 9th, includes the major rail stations, the Gare du Nord and Gare de l'Est, and registered statistically the highest level of prostitution during the war (Corbin 1990, 335). The Place de la République, where Cummings and Marie Louise met up for a rendezvous (possibly their first), marks the corner of the 3rd, 10th, and 11th arrondissements. Marie Louise's first address, Rue Dupetit-Thouars, is near the Place de la République just inside the 3rd arrondissement.

CHAPTER 12. "A TWILIGHT SMELLING OF VERGIL"

107 "The only Vice . . . ," together with thoughts on artistic media, kerosene, and "ego"; "the solemnity of mass . . ." (Cummings, "sollemnity"): all *HL*, MS Am 1823.7 (17).

108 Sketches throughout his French notebooks; those described here are particu-larly from *HL*, MS Am 1823.7 (20).

108 Attitude toward Eliot: Cummings 1965, 25–29 ("T. S. Eliot," reprinted from *The Dial*, June 1920); significant notes on Eliot and Pound from *HL*, MS Am 1892.7 (70) in folders 6–8; Webster 2015; Rosenblitt 2016, 206–44.

108 "I bought . . .": *HL*, MS Am 1892.7 (78).

109 Cummings to his parents on walking and buying books and prints, letter [May 1917], Cummings 1972, 25.

109 Cézanne propping fruit: Danchev 2013, 361.

109 Ancient art: see *HL*, MS Am 1823.7 (17), 1823.7 (18), and further discussion in Cohen 1987 and Rosenblitt 2016: 198–206.

109 "*art is The Verb Cold": *HL*, MS Am 1823.7 (17).

110 Cummings on Picasso: *HRC* Norman Papers, 11.5; Norman 1972 [1958], 188.

110 Cowley on Antheil: letter to Charles Norman, *HRC* Norman Papers, 11.4.

110 Cowley on *The Waste Land*: Cowley 1994 [1951], 112 ("At heart . . ."); 113 ("we felt the poet . . ."); 114 ("When *The Waste Land* appeared . . ."); cf. Norman 1972 [1958], 150–51. Webster 2015, 84, points out that Cummings may have intervened to soften "betrayal" in Norman's book.

111 Book with pages of differing shapes: *HL*, MS Am 1823.7 (17). On Cummings's visual approach to poetry, see Babcock 1963; Webster 1995. Funerary urn, or possibly (Webster suggests) an ironic representation of a traditional loving cup: Webster 2002, 13.

111 Word lists: *HL*, MS Am 1823.7 (17).

112 Solon; cardinal like Caesar: *HL*, MS Am 1823.7 (17).

112 Dante and Cummings: see Metcalf 1970.

112 Virgil representing a failed imperialism for Pound: Comber 1998, 54, *n*.113, where Comber cites this line from the *Homage to Sextus Propertius* (1919) and connects it with a comment in Pound's letters about "the infinite and ineffable imbecility of the British Empire."

112 Virgil and Dos Passos: Dos Passos 1966, 150.

112 Eliot on Virgil: Eliot 1957, 124, 131.

113 "through the tasteless minute efficient room": *CP*, 1000; ms on Camp Devens notepaper, *HL*, MS Am 1892.5 (704). I have also written about this poem in Rosenblitt 2014; Rosenblitt 2016, 113–32.

114 "striding the rising...": *HL*, MS Am 1823.7 (18) ("of the evening" is written superscript, as an addition; I have incorporated it into the text).

115 Conversation with Marie Louise: *HL*, MS Am 1823.7 (16). What is marked in direct quotes is translated exactly from the French. What is not in quotes is faithfully translated from Cummings's words, but the flow of the words has been slightly adjusted, since the original text is heavily scored through, twice-drafted, and difficult to reconstruct.

CHAPTER 13. SIN

117 "Cummings reacted so violently...": letter of October 7, 1971 from Brown to Norman, *HRC* Norman Papers, 10.1.

117 Carpenter to Cummings: *HL*, MS Am 1892 (131). Carpenter to Rev. Edward Cummings, May 23, 1917: *HL*, MS Am 1823.3 (61a). Address book: *HL*, MS Am 1823.7 (6).

119 Letter, the Reverend to Cummings, dated June 28, 1917: *HRC*, 7.5. "ours has been correspondingly intensified and exaggerated": ms "our," corrected to "ours."

121 Mock letter from the Reverend: *HL*, MS Am 1823.7 (17). Exactly quoted text in quotation marks; the rest paraphrased and condensed using much of Cummings's own wording and phrases.

122 Early draft of poem: *HL*, MS Am 1823.7 (9); reworked later in connection with Elaine (cf. Kennedy 1994, 196), but the connection to the earlier draft remains. It was posthumously published as "chérie / the very,picturesque,last Day": *CP*, 1015.

Further notes on Chapter 13:
The mock letter cannot be dated precisely. It is written into a notebook that otherwise contains poems and notes of observations on Paris, a few notes from places Cummings saw near the front, and also notes from La Ferté-Macé. Gener-

ally speaking, Cummings does not appear to have added anything to his French notebooks after his return from France. However, this letter speaks of Cummings's refusal to heed the call of his country. Kennedy 1994, 161, therefore dates it to January 1918, after Cummings had been back in the United States for a few weeks, and he connects the writing of the mock letter to the Reverend's advice that he should enlist for officer training. Cummings refused to do so, maintaining instead his intention to return to his life in New York and await the draft. Kennedy's date is possible—maybe even probable. But it is also not impossible that the letter was written in France in 1917 and that it refers to friction over Cummings's intentions previously, in the spring of that year, as he debated his own course of action while it became clear that the United States was on the verge of a declaration of war and that military service would be expected of the young men of Cummings's generation. Either way, it remains true that the emotional focus of the letter is on the Harvard and prewar estrangement and the Christmas fight of 1916.

CHAPTER 14. CALLED FOR SERVICE

127 Other volunteers moved on; uniform delays: Cummings to his mother, [May] and June 4, 1917, Cummings 1972, 25–27.

127 Description of uniform and missing belt/puttees: letter to his mother, August 2, 1917, Cummings 1972, 33.

127 "Mr. Harjes himself . . .": quoted by Pritchard 1990, 134.

128 Assuming a return: draft letter from Cummings to Marie Louise: *HL*, MS Am 1823.7 (16); goodbye to Mimi closely paraphrased from the letter.

128 Luggage: *HL*, MS Am 1892.1 (15); *HRC* Norman Papers, 6.18, 11.3, 12.19.

128 Population today of around 15,000: en.noyon-tourisme.com, accessed July 9, 2018.

129 Schlieffen Plan and deletion of Schlieffen's caveats: Prior 2014, 204.

129 Development and history of the western front: Prior 2014.

129 Information about Noyon under occupation primarily derived from a public *exposition photographique* at Noyon, visited August 2016. Forbidding of contact with army: de Schaepdrijver 2014, 255; men already gone to war from occupied France: de Schaepdrijver 2014, 246.

130 Verdun offensive and Somme offensive, with casualty figures: Prior 2014, 212–16; Haig and Lloyd George: Prior 2014, 217–20; see also Neiberg 2014, 117–18.

130 Hindenburg Line: Prior 2014, 217–18; Neiberg 2014, 113–15.

130 Sketches: *HL*, MS Am 1823.7 (14).

131 Selection at Noyon: draft letter from Cummings to Marie Louise: *HL*, MS Am 1823.7 (16).

131 Date (June 15): Vernier 1979; Norman 1972 [1958], 82; *HRC* Norman Papers, 11.5 (copy of report by Colonel Parker). Kennedy 1994, 144, gives the date June 13 (without any note for his evidence).

CHAPTER 15. AT THE FRONT

132 "While (at the hating touch . . .": *nonlectures,* 53.

132 Dated sketch: *HL,* MS Am 1823.7 (16).

132 Number of cars and men: letter to his mother, July 7, 1917, Cummings 1972, 29; *ER,* 3–4.

133 Locations: letter to his mother, August 2, 1917, Cummings 1972, 33.

133 1,000 square miles; scorched earth: Neiberg 2014, 114.

133 Poem to Thayer: *HL,* MS Am 1823.7 (14).

134 "cruelly,love": *CP,* 19; part of the thematically linked sub section, "Songs," in *Tulips & Chimneys* (1922 ms). Several of the "Songs" are drafted in one of the French notebooks: *HL,* MS Am 1823.7 (17). See also my discussion of "Songs" in Rosenblitt 2016, 133–65.

135 Letter, Cummings to Marie Louise (translated from the French): *HL,* MS Am 1823.7 (19).

136 Three-day rotation: letter to his mother, July 2, 1917, Cummings 1972, 27–28. Daily hours: letter to his mother, August 9, 1917, Cummings 1972, 36.

136 Nearly walking into no-man's-land: Wickes 1969, 73 and 1969b, 32.

136 Cummings on the shells: letter to Marie Louise, *HL,* MS Am 1823.7 (19); letter to his father, July 20, 1917, Cummings 1972, 31.

136 Wilfred Owen: quoted in Stallworthy 2013, 153.

137 "the bigness of cannon": *CP,* 60; draft, *HL,* MS Am 1892.5 (533), where it is hand-written and signed (in very tiny writing): "EE Xmas '18" on Camp Devens note-paper. On the poem, see also Osborne 1965 (though I read the poem differently).

137 Beauty of shelling: Martin 2007, 49 and *n*25.

138 "shell-song": Cummings to his mother, August 2, 1917, Cummings 1972, 32.

138 "There was a daily exchange . . .": Graves 2000 [1957], 143. According to Fus-sell (2013 [1975], 224), the mechanics of the guns make this story an impossi-bility. But even if Graves's account does not stand up as fact, it still reflects his cultural world.

138 Gas attack: the Reverend to Cummings [marked "Not Sent"], August 30, 1917, *HL,* MS Am 1823 (296).

138 Wounded; shells; sound of war: *HL,* MS Am 1823.7 (19).

138 Jussy and letter to Thayer: Cummings 2007; to his mother, August 2, 1917, Cummings 1972, 32.

138 Sketches: *HL,* MS Am 1823.7 (10) and (14).

138 "fun to see . . .": Graves 2000 [1957], 91.

139 "poplars are,": *HL,* MS Am 1823.7 (17).

139 Orchids: *HL,* MS Am 1823.7 (7). Thoughts on alternative flower troping of the war inspired partly by Kozak and Hickman 2014. On traditional flower trop-ing of the Great War, see Fussell 2013 [1975], 266–77.

139 "along the justexisting road to Roupy": *CP,* 999. Casualty figures from village monuments at Roupy and Ham.

140 "As for the Germans . . ." = "*Quant aux allemands . . .*": letter from Cummings

to his mother, August 9, 1917, Cummings 1972, 34. Rebecca's French novels: letter from Marion Morehouse to Charles Norman, July 27, 1949, *HRC* Norman Papers, 10.11.

141 AFS advertisement: *HRC*, digital collection titled "Posters from the First World War, 1914–1918" at https://hrc.contentdm.oclc.org/digital/collection/p15878coll26.

141 "gentlemen drivers": I repeat the point made by Hansen 1996/2011 with his book title, *Gentlemen Volunteers: The Story of the American Ambulance Drivers in the First World War*; cf. Cowley 1994 [1951], 37.

141 The challenges of ambulance driving are collated from the firsthand accounts of Dos Passos 2003 [1920] and 1966; letters in Cummings 1972, 27–36; and Carver (ed.) 2014.

142 "One fine thing…" and "tight-fisted…": Cummings to his mother, letter of July 2, 1917, Cummings 1972, 27–8.

142 Route map: *HL*, MS Am 1823.7 (11).

142 Road accident on the bridge: Cummings to his mother, August 2, 1917, Cummings 1972, 31–32.

143 "slouch of silver": *HL*, MS Am 1823.7 (10); for the road to Roupy, see also *HL*, MS Am 1892.7 (123).

143 Shelling in the rear area and accuracy of shells: Prior 2014, especially 207–8; Carver (ed.) 2014, 42.

143 "Dissecting the sensations…": Dos Passos 1966, 55 [Dos's own ellipses].

144 Fixed belief that the right location and strategy was the answer: Prior 2014, especially 219; Neiberg 2014, especially 118.

144 Nivelle offensive: Neiberg 2014, 115–23; Prior 2014, 219–20.

145 Mutiny: Neiberg 2014, 121–24; Smith 2014, 202–4; Prior 2014, 220.

145 "typical": e.g., letter to his mother, August 2, 1917, Cummings 1972, 32; bunking with the French: *ER*, 5.

145 "So Cummings and I…": Quoted in Wickes 1969b, 32; Wickes 1969, 72–73; cf. *ER*, 217.

145 "Making the Trenches 'Comfy'": *Wipers Times* (as the *B.E.F. Times*), "A Plea from the Trenches," 92.

146 "my sweet old etcetera": *CP*, 292. On "my sweet old etcetera," see also Dayton 2010.

147 "300 in this hospital…": *HL*, MS Am 1823.7 (10); Cummings later reworked a version of this monologue and included it in *The Enormous Room*: see *ER*, 146–47.

147 American army VD figures: Hirschfeld 2006, 108.

148 Graffiti in Paris: Brown to Cummings, June 13, 1943, *HL*, MS Am 1823 (150).

148 "Water Closet": *HL*, MS Am 1823.7 (17).

148 Censorship of *All Quiet on the Western Front*: Wagener 2009, 104–5.

148 Latrine rumors: Dos Passos 1966, 51–52. Dos on the garden and latrine: Dos Passos 1966, 42–43.

149 Mr. Phillips's departure, rumor: letter to his mother, July 7, 1917, Cummings 1972, 30; joined army: letter to his mother, August 9, 1917, Cummings 1972, 36.

149 Car taken away from Cummings and Brown: letter to his mother, August 2, 1917, Cummings 1972, 31–32.

149 "Liberty, Equality, Fraternity, or Death": *HL*, MS Am 1823.7 (7).

149 "The Woman -- / has a face . . .": *HL*, MS Am 1892.7 (78). Cummings has typed "Behind her she hels," which must be a mistake for "held."

150 balloon man: "in Just-" (*CP*, 29).

150 Balloon-woman in Paris: *HL*, MS Am 1823.7 (17). ("Baloon" is Cummings's spelling.)

150 "when the big <u>ship</u> Death . . .": *HL*, MS Am 1823.7 (7); see also *HL*, MS Am 1892.7 (78).

150 "propaganda of sunset" and color scheme: *HL*, MS Am 1823.7 (17) and *HL*, MS Am 1892.7 (78). "Separture" may be a typographical error for "departure," or he may have thought that "separture" was French for "separation."

151 Vaginas on doorknobs / Holocaust: *HL*, MS Am 1892.7 (234); cf. Fussell 2013 [1975], 343.

151 Letter, William Slater Brown to Charles Francis Phillips ["Charlie"], dated September 4, 1917: HRC Norman Papers, 11.5; Norman 1972 [1958], 85–87.

Further notes on Chapter 16:

"my sweet old etcetera" represents a second phase of publishing about the war. It appeared in his 1926 collection, *is 5*, among a set of poems that collectively display a more hard-bitten, cynical, and angry attitude to the Great War taken in more distant retrospect. In one poem, a man rehearsing his memories of gas and shrapnel spells out explicitly how "everyone / that's been there knows," unlike "a god damned lot of / people" who "don't want // to / no." Another poem condemns the politicization of the Tomb of the Unknown Soldier in France, artistically and hypocritically arranged "(so as not to hurt the perspective of the(hei /-nous thought) otherwise immaculately tabulated vicinity)." In the monologue of "'next to of course god america i," the speaker gushes:

> why talk of beauty what could be more beaut-
> iful than these heroic happy dead
> who rushed like lions to the roaring slaughter
> they did not stop to think they died instead

As Cummings looked back in the mid-1920s with less lyricism and more sarcasm, it was the pointlessness of death that he remembered.

"everyone / that's been there knows," from "lis" (*CP*, 288). "(so as not to hurt . . ." from "opening of the chambers close" (*CP*, 283). The poem puns on the French *paix* / "Pay," and the French pun makes it clear that this is specifically the French Tomb of the Unknown Soldier: see note 2, the editor's (i.e., Michael Webster's) note, to Sychterz 2007. " 'next to of course god america i": *CP*, 284.

CHAPTER 17. MR. ANDERSON TELLS SOME LIES

154 Marie Louise to Cummings: *HL*, MS Am 1823 (831). (Here and below, I have added some punctuation to Marie Louise's style. Her almost complete avoidance of punctuation does not detract from her clarity in French, but it would in English.)

154 Notebook with letters to Marie Louise, sketches, color chart, and leaves: *HL*, MS Am 1823.7 (19).

155 Moon and sun: *HL*, MS Am 1892.7 (78).

155 No leave: *ER*, 5, 13; lottery for July 4: letter to his mother, July 7, 1917, Cummings 1972, 28–30.

155 Sole attestation of meeting on the fourteenth of July: letter of Marie Louise to Cummings, August 31, 1917, *HL*, MS Am 1823 (831).

155 Arrival of American soldiers in June: Kennedy 1982, 169.

156 Notes on death: *HL*, MS Am 1892.7 (78). Exact text of notes on shells and machine guns: "machine guns / obus=satire (mitrailleuses)= / irony bubbling / (moonlight)earth colour & consis / tency of a porridge of / oatmeal." On satire, irony, and the Great War, see further Fussell 2013 [1975], 3–38.

156 Flattened tree and uncaring river: *HL*, MS Am 1823.7 (7).

156 Draft of poem with Marie Louise as Cleopatra: *HL*, MS Am 1892.7 (78):

> l'amie de Mimi, d'une mine toujours neigeuse,
> ressemble un peu à Cléopatra, en ce moment
> quand son sein a trouvé le serpent
> et ses prunelles sont larges de la Mort ennuyeuse

(the friend of Mimi, her complexion always snowy, a little resembles Cleopatra, in that moment when her breast found the snake and her eyes are large with troubling Death)

See also with minor variants (notably, "et de la Mort boivent ses prunelles parasseuses"): *HL*, MS Am 1823.7 (7).

156 Cummings to Mimi: *HL*, MS Am 1823.1 (409), closely paraphrased from the French, with many of Cummings's own words (translated).

157 Marie Louise to Cummings: *HL*, MS Am 1823 (831). Rue Henri Monnier, as it was then, is now Rue Henry Monnier.

159 Brown's letters picked up on September 7: *HRC* Norman Papers, 11.5.

159 Brown's indignant reply to Norman ("Unless I can see..."): Norman 1972 [1958], 88; see also relevant correspondence at *HL*, MS Am 1823 (150); *HRC* Norman Papers, 10.1.

159 George Bernard Shaw on the war = Shaw 1914, 12.

159 Brown on "over the hill" and other points about the letters: letter to Cummings, August 22, 1959, *HL*, MS Am 1823 (150); see also Norman 1972 [1958], 88; *HRC* Norman Papers, 10.1.

160 Beer and white wine: letters from Brown to Lewis G. Levenson and Dr. Lomer, published in Norman 1972 [1958], 84, 87; also *HRC* Norman Papers, 11.5.

160 An evening's drinking, rent, Lachaise, and "pretty tight": *HL*, MS Am 1892 (110).

161 Cummings's reference to Brown's inebriated letters: *HL*, MS Am 1823.7 (24).

161 Not the jejune letters: letter from Brown to his nephew, dated July 6, 1988; reproduced by Friedman and Forrest 1992, 90. See also *HRC* Norman Papers, 11.3, where Brown admits that it was reference to the mutinies *in the letters* that got him and Cummings into trouble, and not just the fact that they had such knowledge.

161 Roped in by Mr. Anderson: see text and notes on Chapter 18: "At Noyon Once More."

161 Arrest: *ER*, 3–8. Prominent in Cummings's account is "t-d," or one of the men who came to arrest him in "tin derby" hats. Cummings explains why the ambulance men thought of these as tin derby hats in a letter to Elizabeth Kaiser-Braem, March 9, 1954, Cummings 1972, 227.

162 feudal dungeon: *ER*, 8.

Further notes on Chapter 17:

Brown was confronted with a French translation of his letters when he was interrogated. One of Brown's later theories (*HL*, MS Am 1823 (150), letter to Cummings, August 22, 1959; cf. Pritchard 1990, 147) was that the transcripts of his letters supplied to the American authorities had been retranslated back into English from these French translations of the originals. (This also enabled him to believe that they had been enhanced, so as to egg up the inflammatory content.)

It is not disputed that the American authorities relied on typescripts, in English, which had been supplied by the French. Nor is it disputed that at some point Brown's letters were translated into French for the purposes of the French authorities handling the case. Therefore, either (1) as Brown believed, his letters were translated into French, then retranslated into English in order to supply copies to the Americans; or, (2) Brown's English originals were typed up in English by the French authorities and then translated for their own purposes into French, while the original English typescripts remained available and were supplied to the Americans. The latter seems a more natural way of proceeding, whereas the former seems highly elaborate. Faced with (badly) handwritten letters as evidence, one naturally gives them to a secretary to type up, and then passes the typescripts to a translator if one wishes to have handy a French translation.

Moreover, I do not think that Brown's theory is convincing from the textual perspective. It is true that the letters contain certain Francophonisms, like "shooting of the officers" in the sentence "It is said that the Americans are already considering shooting of the officers whom they do not like." However, Cummings and Brown clearly picked up a somewhat French style, either as an affectation or as an unconscious absorption of their environment, and I find it perfectly plausible that Brown (particularly when inebriated) would come up with a phrase like "shooting of the officers." (Or, alternatively, such a small interpolation could be an error of transcription.) I find it less plausible that a French retranslation would use "whom" so correctly, or that it could reconstruct the ditty about the moon, which—though hardly a literary tour-de-force—nonetheless clearly reflects the wit of a native speaker.

Brown also thought that the French had been more concerned about other letters, not included in the dossier supplied to the American authorities, which made more explicit mention of the mutinies (Pritchard 1990, 135, 148). Perhaps; although, as can be seen from the effect of the dossier on the opinion of the American authorities involved in Brown's case (see Chapter 23: "The Good Offices of Mr. Wiley"), these seized letters were quite shocking enough to account for the French reaction.

CHAPTER 18. AT NOYON ONCE MORE

165 All details of the interrogation: *ER*, 9–16. "I think we're going to prison . . .": *ER*, 10.

166 "Monsieur, quite evidently disappointed . . .": *ER*, 11.

166 Meeting Norton at the Front: Cummings to his mother, August 9, 1917, Cummings 1972, 36.

166 Norton for "contrary to all military law" and refusal to bomb Germans: Norman 1972 [1958], 79–80. Cummings on the letter, including " 'Your friend' . . . ": *ER*, 13.

168 Spies: *ER*, 46.

168 Detention documents: unearthed and published (in translation only) by Vernier 1979. Translations credited by Vernier to Willis Buck. As Vernier points out (1979, 346), the documents highlight unequivocally the central role of Mr. Anderson.

168 Victory believed to depend on morale: Watson 2014, 174, including the points about denial of the realities of industrial warfare and beliefs about moral superiority. Belief about French defeat in the Franco-Prussian War: Prior 2014, 210. Morale and the Passchendaele offensive: Neiberg 2014, 125; Prior 2014, 222. Nighttime transport: Carver 2014, 56–57, 64. Coincidence of mutiny and strikes: Neiberg 2014, 123; on the strikes, see also Becker 1985, 205–16. Haig

believed the situation to be worse than it was: Neiberg 2014, 124. The significance of the letters of ambulance men: Hansen 1996/2011, 85–87.

170 "A military band...": ER, 16. German occupation and photograph of the liberation: from an *exposition photographique* at Noyon, seen August 2016.

170 "The great goat-footed God...": HRC, 6.8. Nature: Gill 1998, 106–23, writes about the disconnect from nature expressed in ER, but interprets it as a literary conceit; his approach ignores questions of larger change in Cummings's writing.

171 All details of the cell: ER, 16–21.

171 "a little silhouette": ER, 18; "Then I lay down...": ER, 21. Letter to Thayer: Cummings 2007, 103. Whistling: ER, 18.

172 Insistence on record of his own view of Brown's innocence: ER, 14.

172 Brown's age: HRC Norman Papers, 10.1.

172 "I liked Cummings...": Brown to Fitzgerald, quoted in Collier 1997, 139.

173 Brown gone on the second night: ER, 20.

CHAPTER 19. LIFE UNDER *LES PLANTONS*

174 Walk to the train station at Noyon: ER, 22–23.

175 "divine man": ER, 23–25 (quote at 24).

175 Journey to La Ferté: ER, 21–43 (Marseille at 35). Distance from Noyon to La Ferté-Macé: AA Route Planner.

176 Possibility of rescue: ER, 37.

177 "clumsy with pain"; "the angular actual language...": ER, 38. "rounding the road...": HL, MS Am 1892.7 (78). Other scholars have doubted that Cummings saw a cross on this particular journey (e.g., Gill 2007, 114), but I see no particular reason for such doubt. In general on the imagery of the crucifixion in the Great War, but taking a rather harsh view of Cummings's passage in ER, see Fussell 2013 [1975], 126–29, 174.

177 Brown and the director: ER, 61.

177 Thirty or forty men: ER, 50; Cummings 2007, 104. Gill 2002, 168–72, establishes that the enormous room was in the wing. Generally for the building and its history, I draw on my own visit and also on Cummings's account in *The Enormous Room* and on Gill 1998; Gill 2002; Huang-Tiller 2007; Webster and Persenaire 2007.

178 "The blocking...": ER, 51–52.

179 One hundred women: Cummings 2007, 104; cf. ER, 75.

179 Movement of the front: ER, 60.

179 Higher eroticism: Hirschfeld 2006, 71–73 ("steel bath" at 71).

179 Economic conditions and sex work: Hirschfeld 2006, 160; demand exceeded supply: Hirschfeld 2006, 102.

179 Prostitutes as procurers: Hirschfeld 2006, 34; Dos at Winchester: Dos Passos 1966, 74.

180 Protargol at brothels: Hirschfeld 2006, 150. On the US Army and its attitudes toward Protargol and other methods of prophylaxis, see Byers 2012, 264–69.

180 Policy disputes: Hirschfeld 2006, 97–102; "tail parade": Hirschfeld 2006, 96; "hydrant and hose": Hirschfeld 2006, 100.

180 "had plainly called . . .": Hirschfeld 2006, 93.

180 Inmates with syphilis: *ER*, 146–47.

181 Description of prison environment: *ER*, 50–51 (enormous room), 57 (*le cour*, including "a barbarously cold seat . . ."), 67–68 (refectory; "smelled rather much . . ." at 68).

181 La Ferté daily routine: *ER*, 63–65; cf. letter to his mother, October 1, 1917, Cummings 1972, 37–38.

182 Shower: *ER*, 55–56, 65 (quote at 65).

182 "You are not prisoners . . .": *ER*, 83; escape: *ER*, 91–93. To be exact: it was reported to the prisoners that the escapees had been recaptured and sentenced to a lifetime of hard labor, but since Cummings did not know this except by report, he leaves open the possibility that the announcement was made *pour encourager les autres*.

182 Catching water: *ER*, 57, 62, 108, 112, 157–59.

182 Liking the cook: *ER*, 111, cf. 104, 108.

183 Sexual assaults on the female prisoners: *ER*, 59, 111, 162.

183 Shouting "shirker": *ER*, 59, 62, 89.

183 "He'd pretend . . .": Brown to Fitzgerald, quoted by Collier 1997, 139.

183 "All the prisoners . . .": Brown quoted by Wickes 1969, 75.

183 Sixty men: *ER*, 152, 177.

183 Songs: *ER*, 84–85, 96, 104–5, 112, 184, 200, 202, 223; spitting: *ER*, 89; cards: *ER*, 80, 89, 95–97, 101, 152; dominoes: *ER*, 132, 202.

183 Riffling of mattresses: *ER*, 97–99.

184 Illicit notes: *ER*, 52, 59, 62, 89, 94, 102, 111, 113.

184 Brown's twenty-first birthday: *HRC* Norman Papers, 10.1 (birthdate, age), 10.16 (cocoa on birthday); Norman 1972 [1958], 88; Kennedy 1994, 152; cf. *ER*, 135.

Further notes on Chapter 19:

I have credited above the individual points of information taken from Magnus Hirschfeld's *Sexual History of the World War*; beyond individual points, my understanding of and writing about the nature of sexual experience, including prostitution, in the Great War owes a great debt to Hirschfeld's work. Magnus Hirschfeld was an extraordinarily progressive Jewish German sexologist who campaigned during the first decades of the twentieth century for pacifism, feminism, legalization of abortion, and gay and transgender rights. For his biography and thought, see Mancini 2010.

CHAPTER 20. TIME STANDS STILL

185 Timelessness ("It is like a vast grey box..."): *ER*, 82; fear of insanity more explicitly at 87–88.

185 Date of commission: see Gill 2007, 106; *HRC* Norman Papers, 11.5 (Colonel Parker's report); cf. 12.17, Sharp to Lansing; 11.6, Anderson to the Reverend; 11.13, Breckinridge Long to Whipple. Commission in *ER*, 215–21.

186 "Man is ..."; religion; fear and anger intellectual: *HL*, MS Am 1823.7 (9).

186 "Since War is purely Thoughtful": *HL*, MS Am 1823.7 (17) ("directing" is my best reading of a semi-illegible word).

186 "When we asked him ...": *ER*, 132.

186 "How intellectual is war ...": Cummings 2007 (letter to Thayer from La Ferté-Macé); cf. comments of Gill 2007, 109–10.

186 "when my sensational moments are no more": *CP*, 152. Later comments on poetic pacifism and *CP*, 152: *HL*, MS Am 1892.7 (234).

187 Publication history of *Tulips & Chimneys*: see the introduction by Kennedy and the afterword by Firmage in Cummings 1976. There was a flawed 1937 edition of *Tulips & Chimneys*, which attempted to return to authorial plans but contained errors: see Ordeman and Firmage 2000, 161. See also discussion in Rosenblitt 2016, 10–12. For more detail on Seltzer, see Sawyer-Lauçanno 2006, 225–26.

188 "god gloats upon Her stunning flesh. Upon": *CP*, 153; drafts: *HL*, MS Am 1823.7 (11); *HL*, MS Am 1823.7 (17).

189 "life in prison ...": *HL*, MS Am 1823.7 (9).

189 Reuse of "je vous prie ...": *HL*, MS Am 1823.7 (15).

190 Bucket: *ER*, 177–80; quote at 180. Larger chunk of bread: *ER*, 67, cf. 110.

191 "I do not believe ...": *HL*, MS Am 1823.7 (11). (Cummings writes, "I do not believe in w"; it must be a personal abbreviation for "war.") Later use of fairies: see discussion of "my love is building a building" (*CP*, 177) in Chapter 24: "Camp Devens."

191 Notebook with color palette: *HL*, MS Am 1823.7 (19); *ER*, 224.

191 Spanish-language notes: *HL*, MS Am 1823.7 (8); *ER*, 132–33.

191 Sketches in many of the notebooks; specifically vistas from prison in *HL*, MS Am 1823.7 (8) and the 69 position in *HL*, MS Am 1823.7 (8) and 1823.7 (15).

192 Letter to the Reverend, December 10, 1917, discovered and published by Vernier 1979. Gill points out the difference between the Thayer letter and *ER*: see Gill 2007, 111, 119 ("actual experiences" contrasted to *The Enormous Room* clearly privileges the letter). Thayer's snobbery and attitude toward Cummings's background: Dempsey 2014, 65–67; 186 (quotes at 66–67).

193 "Buffalo Bill 's / defunct": *CP*, 98. See Kidder 1976 for the composition of the poem, including 373–74 for the controversy anticipated with the *Dial* publication. "We are due ...": quoted by Kidder 1976: 373–74.

193 "Fuck" in Greek letters: "if Hate's a game and Love's a fuck" (*CP*, 466). Cummings also used Greek letters to spell out "fucking" in "the waddling" (*CP*, 106); see Gerber 1988, 198; Hadas 1998. "otherwise scented merde" from "take it from me kiddo": *CP*, 242. Essential article on Cummings and censorship: Gerber 1988. Dos and swearing: Dos Passos 1966, 50, 85–86 (on publishing *One Man's Initiation: 1917*).

194 Notes on Life / Death: *HL*, MS Am 1823.7 (9) (*kinēsis* and *stasis* written out in the Greek alphabet); cf. *HL*, MS Am 1823.7 (15), where Cummings has written "chaos" and "cosmos" in Greek on the back of a map of France.

194 "Spring is like a perhaps hand": *CP*, 210. "the soft-hard fingers...": *HL*, MS Am 1823.7 (9). "Rain did...": *ER*, 224–25.

Further notes on "god gloats..." (*CP*, 153):

"Con" here means "to get to know; to study or learn, *esp.* by repetition (mental or vocal)" (*Oxford English Dictionary*). As the Sea bashes again and again upon time, She carves time just as She carves the cliffs and the seascape, and the ages learn intimately, erotically, to know the Sea—shaped by Her as if time itself yawns open like the caves opened by millennia of erosion where water works on rock at the sea edge.

The form of "god gloats..." is based on the Petrarchan sonnet, which is a form whose aesthetic depends upon the "Petrarchan turn," which shifts tone, mood, or focus between the first eight lines and the last six. Cummings exploits that form here. Only at the point of the Petrarchan turn does he openly refer to the sea, illuminating the poem up to that point by now naming, for the first time, the Sea as god's lover.

CHAPTER 21. TYRANNY

196 Apollyon: from *ER*, especially 107–28.

196 *pain sec*: *ER*, 112–13.

196 *cabinot*: *ER*, 61–62, 113–14.

197 Harsher treatment of women: *ER*, 120. Women as "the weaker sex": *ER* 120–21. Lena in *cabinot*: *ER*, 120–23.

197 Celina, Lena, Lily, and Renée: *ER*, 117–19. Celina and Brown: Pritchard 1990, 137.

198 Near death of the gang of four: *ER*, 123–25.

198 "It struck me...": *ER*, 191–92.

199 "Of all the fine people...": *ER*, 198; theft of money: *ER*, 199–200.

199 Document: Cummings 1972, 88. Brown's view of *The Enormous Room*: Pritchard 1990, 136; Wickes 1969, 75; and Wickes 1969b, 33.

200 "delicacies such as butter...": letter to the Reverend: published in Vernier 1979.

200 Diarrhea and milk: letter to Thayer, Cummings 2007. Cf. Gill 2007, 115 on the point that Cummings was more ill than he generally revealed.

200 Brown's scurvy and the creaking: *ER*, 230. Progression of scurvy: Pimentel 2003, 330; Fain 2005, 125–26; Brown would be at stage 3 by the time he gained his freedom.

200 Brown's mid-December dispatch, number of prisoners, and diet: Brown to Norman: *HRC*, 10.16. Frozen potatoes and pebbles: Collier 1997, 140. Conditions, fighting, and deaths of prisoners at Précigné: Pritchard 1990, 137–38; Collier 1997, 140–41.

201 Apollyon bursting upon the women: *ER*, 114–17; "And I saw once...": *ER*, 115; "never in my life before...": *ER*, 117.

202 "i obey masochistic...": *HL*, MS Am 1823.7 (25).

202 For the Cummings/Brown file, I rely on the documents collected by Charles Norman and held at the Harry Ransom Center among Norman's papers. Telegram Norton to the Reverend: *HRC* Norman Papers, 11.14. Cable to Norton proposing cause célèbre: *HRC* Norman Papers, 11.5, 11.6. Lost on the *Antilles*: *HRC* Norman Papers, 12.17. Norton on Cummings's anticipated release, cable of November 21: *HRC* Norman Papers, 11.14. The Reverend to Norton asking if his son lived: *HRC* Norman Papers, 11.5, 11.6. H. H. Cummings lost on the *Antilles*: *HRC* Norman Papers, 12.17, 12.10.

203 H. H. Cummings from Philadelphia: *Philadelphia in the World War*, 34.

204 "I keep them to remind me...": *Qualey*, 99; Norman 1972 [1958], 27. Securing Cummings's release as payment of debt: Kennedy 1994, 152–53.

204 Letter to the president in *HRC* Norman Papers, 11.6, and also reproduced in the preface to *The Enormous Room* (*ER*, xxiii). Processed by the president's secretary, J. P. Tumulty: Norman 1972 [1958], 96. "Department cannot understand": cipher telegram of December 15: *HRC* Norman Papers, 11.12. Norman is probably right to understand this as an urgency finally stirred by the Reverend's letter to the president.

204 Oloron Sainte-Marie: letter from Cummings to Brown, December 28, 1917, *HL*, MS Am 1892.1 (15); Vernier 1979, 346; *ER*, 234–35. Cummings was self-taught as a painter because of the Reverend's attitude toward artistic training: see Kidder 1975, 120.

Further notes on Chapter 21:

Cummings's fellow prisoner Jean raises the question of Cummings and race. (On Cummings, Jean, and race, see also Mott 1995.) Cummings was far more aware of and interested in a multiracial world than many white writers of the early twentieth century. Whereas many writers whitewashed the Great War, Cummings repeatedly acknowledges the presence of African American, Afro-Carribean, and Algerian men, and he saw that the isolation of postwar life for veterans was compounded for black veterans by racial exclusion. However, later in life (long after the narrative of this book), Cummings was heavily and publicly censured for a poem that used a racial slur. He thought that he could use such language to comment on race and on American society, but he was wrong. His poem participates in the racism that he thought he was commenting upon. It is an artistic failure, and one for which there is ethical culpability: he misjudged his language and his art because he was not as much in control of his own feelings about race as he believed himself to be.

CHAPTER 22. BERTHE

207 "If you think...": *HL*, MS Am 1892.7 (124) (translated from the French).

207 Dates for this chapter, including release, arrival in Paris, sailing on the *Espagne*, and arrival in New York: *HRC* Norman Papers, 11.13, 11.5; Kennedy 1994, 156–57, 159; *HL*, MS Am 1892.1 (15).

207 Summoned to Paris; third-class ticket: letter from Cummings to Brown, December 28, 1917, *HL*, MS Am 1892.1 (15); *ER*, 239.

207 Fleas: *ER*, 240.

207 Weather: Met Office historical data. Snow on the ground: postcard to Brown, December 22, 1917, *HL*, MS Am 1892.1 (15).

207 Fur coat: *HRC* Norman Papers, 11.3; Kennedy 1994, 156.

208 "My family had ... cabled ...": letter from Cummings to Brown, December 28, 1917, *HL*, MS Am 1892.1 (15).

208 Wiley persuading Cummings to depart: *HL*, MS Am 1892.1 (15) and 1892.7 (124).

208 Alive: *ER*, 241; Sawyer-Lauçanno 2006, 129.

208 Notebook: *HL*, MS Am 1892.7 (124).

208 Necessaries for sailing: letter from Cummings to Brown, December 28, 1917, *HL*, MS Am 1892.1 (15).

209 Hunt for Marie Louise: *HL*, MS Am 1892.7 (124).

209 Desperate and guilty: letter from Cummings to Brown, December 28, 1917, *HL*, MS Am 1892.1 (15).

209 Letter to Marie Louise, partly quoted/summarized in translation from the French: *HL*, MS Am 1892.7 (124).

210 *Fiacre* (horse and carriage) to hotel, care packages, night with Berthe: letter from Cummings to Brown, December 28, 1917, *HL*, MS Am 1892.1 (15).

211 Poem about Berthe (spelled Berte) from May: *HL*, MS Am 1823.7 (14); partly paraphrased/partly quoted in translation from the French. The original reads:

la femme tenace
qui s'appelle Berte,
à la chair tout verte
comme d'une gourde
d'une mine lasse
qui serve cous-cous
toujours en mangeant
une jaune rose
entre les dents bleus
la femme au peau rousse
à la bouche en feu
à les levres lourdes

211   "and talked gradually . . .": from "Perhaps it was Myself sits down in this chair. There were two chairs, in fact.": *CP*, 1005, and *HL*, MS Am 1823.7 (18).

211   "J'ai perdu . . ." and B—: letter from Cummings to Brown, December 28, 1917, *HL*, MS Am 1892.1 (15).

211   "My thumb smashes . . . ," details of the night, and further lines about sex from two poems about Berthe: "Perhaps it was Myself sits down in this chair. There were two chairs, in fact.": *CP*, 1005, and *HL*, MS Am 1823.7 (18). "The moon-lit snow is falling like strange candy into the big eyes of the": *CP*, 1004, and *HL*, MS Am 1823.7 (18), with earlier draft of the poem at *HL*, MS Am 1892.7 (124). I take the text of "The moon-lit snow . . ." from *HL*, MS Am 1823.7 (18), slightly correcting *CP*, 1004. Where the text appears to me to be written as prose and not lineated as poetry, I have not marked line breaks. The poems about Berthe lie somewhere in between autobiographical notes and poetic texts. It seems clear that the details of the encounter are directly autobiographical and that they recount how Cummings and Berthe actually spent that evening. For newness of the body in Cummings's erotic poetry, see also Fairley 1979, 210.

211   Erotic sketches: *HL*, MS Am 1892.8 (1).

213   Dos Passos on New Year's Eve: Dos Passos 1966, 62.

CHAPTER 23. THE GOOD OFFICES OF MR. WILEY

My conclusions about the Cummings/Brown case differ from those of Charles Norman, who collected the documentary evidence in the case. It has only been possible to come to independent conclusions thanks to Norman's original efforts in obtaining and preserving the documents and thanks to an opportunity to work with the Charles Norman Papers as a Harry Ransom Center Research Fellow in the Humanities in March–April 2016. I remain so grateful for that chance. I give citations here for the specific documents on which I draw, but my overall conclusions are based on the entirety of the case file, to be found in the Charles Norman Collection, 1909–1972. Most of the case file originated as government records from the US National Archives.

214 Health: *ER*, xxiii, 230, 240, 241; Cummings to Brown, December 28, 1917, *HL*, MS Am. 1892.1 (15); the Reverend to Cummings, May 10, 1918, *HL*, MS Am 1823 (296); Sawyer-Lauçanno 2006, 128.

214 Five sisters: Collier 1997, 134.

214 Whipple to the State Department, November 12, 1917: *HRC* Norman Papers, 12.19.

215 "nothing against your boy": telegram, Norton to the Reverend, filed November 20 and received November 21, 1917: *HRC* Norman Papers, 11.14, 11.6, 6.18. Letter, Norton to the Reverend: Norman 1972 [1958], 90–91. Norton pressing Brown's case: *HRC* Norman Papers, 11.14.

216 Letter from Breckinridge Long (Third Assistant Secretary of State) to Whipple, November 28, 1917: *HRC* Norman Papers, 11.13.

216 Whipple to the State Department, December 10, 1917: *HRC* Norman Papers, 12.19, with enclosure, Bartlett to Whipple, dated December 7, 1917; "grave injustice" quoted from Whipple's letter.

216 Col. Frank Parker's report: *HRC* Norman Papers, 11.5; forwarded by Sharp: *HRC* Norman Papers, 11.5 and 12.17.

217 Whipple on the twenty-seventh of December: *HRC* Norman Papers, 12.19.

217 Dr. Brown to Senator Lodge, January 2, 1918: *HRC* Norman Papers, 11.13.

218 Alvey A. Adee (Second Assistant Secretary of State) to Whipple, January 14, 2018: *HRC* Norman Papers, 11.13. Secretary of State Lansing to Senator Lodge, January 17, 1918: *HRC* Norman Papers, 11.13.

218 Bartlett to Whipple, January 21, 1918: *HRC* Norman Papers, 12.19.

219 Details about Wiley and Brown: Cummings to Brown, postcard of December 22 and letter of December 28, 2017, *HL*, MS Am 1892.1 (15).

219 Memo, January 4: *HRC* Norman Papers, 11.5.

219 Wiley's exact date of birth: September 26, 1893, confirmed from photos of his grave headstone at https://www.findagrave.com. Wiley's career from the information provided online by the Franklin D. Roosevelt Presidential Library & Museum, which houses Wiley's papers (the John Cooper Wiley Papers, 1898–1967) and http://diplomacy.state.gov/documents/organization/112183 .pdf (accessed 2016; now offline); similar information now posted at https:// history.state.gov/departmenthistory/people/wiley-john-cooper (accessed 2018, in beta version). See also Wiley 1962 (the memoirs of Irena Wiley).

220 Telegram regarding Freud: posted online by the Freud Museum, London.

220 "much puzzled…": Cummings to Brown, December 28, 2017, *HL*, MS Am 1892.1 (15).

220 Hope Slater to Wiley, written January (exact date obscured) and received February 8: *HRC* Norman Papers, 12.17.

220 Norton and Frazier: *HRC* Norman Papers, 11.14, 11.8; Norton and Wiley: *HRC* Norman Papers, 11.14.

221 Sharp to Lansing (Secretary of State), January 23, 1918: *HRC* Norman Papers, 12.17.

221 Cummings seeking help for Brown from Dos: Dos Passos 1966, 67.

221 Brown fearing that he would be in prison until the end of the war: letter to Samuel Slater, January 3, 1918: *HRC* Norman Papers, 11.3. Slater to the American consulate, January 13, 1918: *HRC* Norman Papers, 12.17; Slater at the embassy: *HRC* Norman Papers, 11.5.

222 Brown's release: *HRC* Norman Papers, 11.3, 12.17.

222 Bill: *HRC* Norman Papers, 11.5, 11.3, 11.1, 12.17. "inasmuch...": F. A. Starling, Second Secretary of the Embassy, to George A. Bucklin, American Consul, Bordeaux, March 22, 1918: *HRC* Norman Papers, 12.17.

222 Cummings crediting the Reverend: *nonlectures*, 9–10. Brown (and his wider family) crediting Bartlett: Pritchard 1990, 138; Friedman and Forrest 1992, 90 (including quote, "The author ... writes ..."); Collier 1997, 141.

Further notes on Chapter 23:

In their accounts of Cummings at the American embassy on December 20, Kennedy 1994, 156, and Sawyer-Lauçanno 2006, 129, refer only to Ambassador Sharp, but it is important to be clear about Cummings's meeting with Wiley. Wiley was instrumental in achieving Brown's freedom, and it was the conversation with Cummings that influenced Wiley to push further. Thus Cummings's key role in securing Brown's freedom is only apparent if we are accurate about the meeting on December 20 and its impact on Wiley. Whether Cummings ever met with Sharp is unclear. In Cummings's stream-of-consciousness account in *The Enormous Room*—an account that, though highly stylized, is extremely close in a sequence of details to the evidence of Cummings's letters—the only reference made is to a meeting at the embassy with "a young man, very young in fact" (*ER*, 240): obviously Wiley. Considering the exactitude of *The Enormous Room* at this point, I incline to think that Cummings never met Sharp at all and that Sharp simply appropriated the meeting with Wiley.

CHAPTER 24. CAMP DEVENS

224 Letter of draft: *HL*, MS Am 1823 (1336).

224 Scurvy: Norman 1972 [1958], 98–99, 123. Brown moved in with Cummings: Norman 1972 [1958], 123. Brown's discharge in a letter to Cummings: *HL*, MS Am 1892 (110).

224 Correspondence regarding the draft: *HL*, MS Am 1823 (296).

225 Shortened exams: letter from the Reverend to Cummings, May 6, 1918, *HL*, MS Am 1823 (296).

225 Draft summons: *HL*, MS Am 1823 (1336).

225 "Orderly": *HL*, MS Am 1892.7 (123).

225 Reverend on becoming an officer: Kennedy 1994, 161; *HL*, MS Am 1892.7 (90). Cummings to Elizabeth, letter of May 3, 1922, *HL*, Cummings, Edward Estlin, 1894–1962. 425 letters to Elizabeth (Cummings) Qualey, 1917–1962, MS Am 1765 (1–10); Cummings 1972, 83–87. See also Kennedy 1994, 172–78.

225 Crazy: *HL*, MS Am 1892.7 (196).

226 Lieutenant Snow: letter from Cummings to the Reverend, August 4, 1918: *HL*, MS Am 1823.1 (152).

226 "My answer . . ." and "In other words . . .": letter from Cummings to the Reverend, August 19, 1918, *HL*, MS Am 1823.1 (152). Greek *poiētēs*: Cummings has written *poiētos*, which I take to be a slip for *poiētēs*.

227 Nightmares: *HL*, MS Am 1892.7 (208).

227 Quarantine: *HL*, MS Am 1823.1 (152). Cummings's notes decades later refer to the "flu," and 1918 was the year of the Spanish influenza (flu) epidemic; Kennedy 1994, 174, refers to a flu quarantine. However, a letter of 1918 from Cummings to his father refers to measles. Although it is less widely remembered than the flu epidemic, the US Army did contend with a measles epidemic in its training camps in 1917–1918, which led to approximately 3,000 deaths: see Morens and Taubenberger 2015. The quarantine at Camp Devens may have been caused by both flu and measles.

227 The Fly Trap: *HL*, MS Am 1823.7 (24) and *HL*, MS Am 1892.7 (123).

227 "'Why, lies . . .'" Dos Passos 2003 [1920], 13.

228 "first she like a piece of ill-oiled": *CP*, 1002. Discussion, see also Rosenblitt 2016, 15–17.

229 Poplars, twilight, Marie Louise: see especially *HL*, MS Am 1823.7 (10), *HL*, MS Am 1892.7 (7), *HL*, MS Am 1892.7 (123), and *HL*, MS Am 1892.7 (242).

229 Syphilis Valley: Dos Passos 1966, 71.

229 Latrine: *HL*, MS Am 1892.7 (123).

229 "yon clean . . .": from "come,gaze with me upon this dome" (*CP*, 289).

229 "i sing of Olaf glad and big": *CP*, 362; see also Collins 1976 (especially on the meter and epic connotations); Kennedy 1994, 320–22. Cummings's notes toward California lectures, *HL*, MS Am 1892.7 (90), make it clear that "i sing of Olaf" commemorates a specific individual from the Camp Devens days.

230 Nakedness in June: from an abandoned poem, "Je suis la prostituée . . .": *HL*, MS Am 1892.7 (70).

230 Notes on *Ulysses* and Art: *HL*, MS Am 1892.7 (70).

231 "death's big rotten particular kiss" from "autumn is:that between there and here" (*CP*, 176).

231 "it is funny,you will be dead some day.": *CP*, 167.

232 "my love is building a building / around you": *CP*, 177; early draft at Camp

Devens: *HL*, MS Am 1892.7 (123). For Cummings's eroticized exquisite anni- hilations, see more fully Rosenblitt 2016. "a whiteness in the water" and "a great loneliness" from "The Young Faun," published in Rosenblitt 2016, 305–7. "sex squeaked like a billiard-cue / chalking itself": from "the mind is its own beautiful prisoner." (*CP*, 169).

233 Brown to Cummings: *HL*, MS Am 1892 (110), including pestering for replies (November 21 and 26, 1918), worries about Bessie (December 5, 1918), and news of her five puppies in the following letter.

233 Confrontation with the captain over discharge: letter to the Reverend, Janu- ary 13, 1919: *HL*, MS Am 1823.1 (152). Date of discharge: Kennedy 1994, 188.

Further notes on "first she like a piece of ill-oiled" (CP, 1002):

"first she like a piece of ill-oiled" is in the form of a broken sonnet. Cummings repeatedly pushed the sonnet form to the edge of aesthetic success. Here, the lines are uneven and reject regular syllable counts or regular rhythm, but they pulse more persistently as the sex begins to pound. The fourteen lines that signify the sonnet form are divided into stanzas of two, four, three, four, and one. That divi- sion is totally alien to sonnet structure. However, the peculiar rhyme scheme—*a b c a ; d c b d ; e f e g f g*—implies two quatrains and a concluding sestet: in other words, the conventional division of a Petrarchan sonnet. Through this mixture of the acceptance and rejection of form, Cummings's jarring poem transmits to the reader some of the disturbance of war. He summons the ambivalence of an experi- ence that is both utterly alienating and terrifyingly erotic.

On Cummings and sonnets: see Huang-Tiller 2001; Huang-Tiller 2005/2006; Huang-Tiller 2007b; Huang-Tiller 2012 [2013]; Sychterz 2007. For a study of the attraction and repulsion of meter and form in the war poets Owen and Sassoon, see the brilliant article by Martin 2007.

CHAPTER 25. ELAINE

234 Move to West Fourteenth: Cummings to his mother, February 9, 1919, Cum- mings 1972, 56–57.

234 Quotes from Thayer's notes and details of the honeymoon, all from Dempsey 2011 and Dempsey 2014, 42–43.

235 Dempsey 2014, xii and *passim*, argues that Thayer's mental illness was most likely paranoid schizophrenia; in any case, it was clearly some form of para- noid psychosis.

235 Brown's three-ale head start: letter to Cummings, December 15, 1918, *HL*, MS Am 1892 (110).

236 Elaine's profession of love for Thayer and "One thing I know . . .": quoted by Kennedy 1994, 260; Dempsey 2011 and Dempsey 2014, 35.

236 Elaine's age and death of parents: Dempsey 2014, 35–36; Kennedy 1994, 189–90; *HL*, MS Am 1892.10 (27). Kennedy has Elaine's date of birth as April 9, 1896; Cummings's notes have it as April 10, 1896. Dempsey corrects Kennedy's information about Thayer and Elaine's earliest meeting.

236 "face the colour . . ." and crying after sex: Dempsey 2014, 44.

236 "Monday Elaine and her sister . . .": Brown to Cummings, November 16, 1918, *HL*, MS Am 1892 (110).

236 Previous lover: Dempsey 2014, 52. Spending time with Elaine: Kennedy 1994, 193–94. Elaine who made the first move: Kennedy 1994, 194; see also *HL*, MS Am 1892.7 (198).

237 "boosted . . .": Cummings to Malcolm Cowley, quoted in Norman 1972 [1958], 118; cf. Cummings to Norman, letter of August 4, 1957, *HRC* 10.6: *The Enormous Room* was "written at my father's urgent request,because I felt that Brown & I owed him our lives."

237 "masterpiece for which I contracted . . .": letter from the Reverend to Cummings, March 19, 1918, *HL*, MS Am 1823 (296).

237 Unrealized plans for collected sermons: Kennedy 1966, 447.

237 Fibs: Brown to Fitzgerald, quoted in Collier 1997, 143. The Reverend, Cummings, the projected lawsuit, and the arguments it occasioned: recollected by Brown in letters to Marion Morehouse, *HL*, MS Am 1892.2 (102).

237 Exhibit: *Catalogue of the Third Annual Exhibition of the Society of Independent Artists (Incorporated)* (1919); see also the fourth (1920) and fifth (1921) exhibition catalogues and Cohen 1987, 38–40, 49–51.

238 Toying with and dropping other tags: Cohen 1987, 39.

238 Nagle's frames: Brown to Marion Morehouse, *HL*, MS Am 1892.2 (102). In this letter, Brown writes about Cummings's 1919 entries and then adds, ". . . Nagle also exhibited. His titles were 'She Wears Her Body on Her Clothes' and 'The Flying Watchman.' The titles had nothing to do with the paintings as Nagle had measured them for frames from the wrong end of the yardstick and when the frames arrived he had to find pictures that would fit them, having left framing them to the last moment." Nagle exhibited in both 1919 and 1920, and it is clear from double-checking the catalogues of the two exhibits that Brown has antedated the incident. It was, in fact, in 1920 that Nagle entered these titles, which Brown has remembered only approximately. According to the catalogue, they were *The Flying Dutchman* and *She Wears a Body Upon Her Dress*.

238 Lachaise misperceiving: Cohen 1987, 38.

238 *Sound 1919* identified as a guitar in Cohen 1987, 208–9 and in the recent Ashmolean museum exhibit "America's Cool Modernism" (exhibit plaque and catalogue, Bourguignon, Kroiz, and Mazow 2018).

239 "A given degree of depth": see Chapter 24: "Camp Devens."

239 Circus sketches: scattered in *HL*, MS Am 1892.8 (1).

239 Kitten: Cummings to his mother, April 24, 1919, and to Elizabeth, May 6, 1919, Cummings 1972, 58–59.

240 Christmas tree forest: Cummings to his mother, January 9, 1920, Cummings 1972, 68.

240 Sympathy with the underdog and needling the Reverend, not ideological commitment: Cohen 2010, 89.

240 Nagle to the Reverend: September 13, 1920, *HL*, MS Am 1823.3 (137).

240 Abortion: Kennedy 1994, 199; Sawyer-Lauçanno 2006, 155.

240 Nancy: see Kennedy 1994, 199–201; Webster 2005/2006.

240 "value received": *HL*, MS Am 1892.7 (196); cf. Kennedy 1994, 200, 424–25.

241 Thayer's aesthetic priorities: *HL*, MS Am 1892.7 (90).

241 Thayer selecting art: Kidder 1976b, 472; cf. preface to *CIOPW* (Cummings 1931).

241 Cummings's feeling that Thayer had withheld full support for the visual art: Sawyer-Lauçanno 2006, 455–56.

241 Thayer's collection and the Metropolitan Museum: Dempsey 2014, 1–6, 185–88.

241 Cummings's sketches of Thayer: see collection held by the Metropolitan Museum of Art (New York); Cohen 1987, 38, 41, 105; *HL*, MS Am 1892.8 (1). *Scofield Thayer—The Afternoon of a Faun*: Metropolitan Museum of Art, accession number 1984.433.89.

242 Brutality of Thayer: *HL*, MS Am 1892.7 (211); 1892.7 (198).

242 "Those of us . . .": Dos Passos 1966, 82.

242 Cummings blamed himself: *HL*, MS Am 1892.7 (198).

242 Elaine pulling away: Kennedy 1994, 199–201.

242 Details of writing *The Enormous Room*: Brown to Norman, October 7, 1971, *HRC* Norman Papers, 10.1, and Brown to Marion Morehouse, letters of December 30, 1965; January 16, 1966; February 20, 1966; and May 17, 1966, *HL*, MS Am 1892.2 (102).

243 "Shit": Norman 1972 [1958], 106; *HRC* Norman Papers, 6.18, 10.14, 11.1; cf/ *ER* 198–99.

243 Admiration for *ER*: *HRC* Norman Papers, 6.11 (T. E. Lawrence), 12.8 (Gertrude Stein); Graves 1972, 172; Samuelson 1984, 14 (Hemingway).

243 Dos to Cummings about being made officers: *HRC*, 7.5 (quote translated from the French).

243 Tour of Spain: *HRC* Norman Papers, 10.6 (postcard from Cummings to Norman, July 25, 1958); Kennedy 1976, 275. Publisher for *The Enormous Room*: Kennedy 1994, 213–15.

243 Brown sailed in July: letter from Brown to his mother, *HL*, MS Am 1823.3 (34).

243 Brown instructed not to return to France: Pritchard 1990, 141.

243 "where he types . . .": Cummings to his parents, July 23, 1921, Cummings 1972, 80.

244 "For Christ's sake . . .": Cummings 1972, 81.

244 Divorce dates: Dempsey 2014, 98, 100.

244 Analysis in America: Dempsey 2014, 97. I rely on Dempsey's interpretation of Thayer and Freud: Dempsey 2014, xii; 97–104. Thayer wanted Cummings by

his side: Dempsey 2011. See Dempsey 2014 for a full account of Thayer's mental health and deterioration.

245 Photo of Cummings in Pound's room: see photograph of Pound with Cummings's photo in the background, reproduced in Sawyer-Lauçanno 2006, second centerfold; discussed Webster 2012, 64; Sawyer-Lauçanno and Webster assign different dates to the photograph of Pound.

245 "Fields Elysian" from "inthe,exquisite;" (*CP*, 95). "la(proudly) / marseillaise": full text quoted in Rosenblitt 2016, 185–86; *HL*, MS Am 1892.7 (197).

245 "Cummings finally emerged...": Dos Passos 1966, 133. Episode of *le pisseur*: Dos Passos 1966, 133; Cummings to Brown, April 12, 1923, Cummings 1972, 100; *HRC* Norman Papers, 11.6; 11.7; 12.17; Norman 1972 [1958], 179–81.

246 Cigarette lit with coal: Philip Hillyer Smith, viva voce to Charles Norman: *HRC* Norman Papers, 12.4; Norman 1972 [1958], 102.

246 Ephemera from La Ferté-Macé: *HL*, MS Am 1823.8 (48).

246 Photographs: *HL*, MS Am 1823.8 (46).

246 "there is a general feeling...": *HL*, MS Am 1823.7 (25).

247 "Armistice": *HL*, MS Am 1892.6 (9); "ressemble" corrected to "resemble."

Further notes on Cummings, Elaine, sex, and sexuality:

The breakdown of Elaine and Cummings's marriage is beyond the scope of this book. It was a sad and damaging time for both. It was, to say the least, messy, and there was bad behavior on both sides. Part of the problem was sexual. Cummings could not find a way to position his own natural gentleness in a sexual culture that expected men to be sexually aggressive, even predatory. He internalized these standards, blamed himself for insufficient aggression, and became deeply self-loathing. Elaine had experienced an extreme level of predatory and abusive behavior from Thayer, and her marriage to Thayer normalized these standards for her. She brought these expectations to Cummings and found him lacking—insufficiently aggressive, and therefore insufficiently manly. She also told him that it would have been better if he had shown more masculinity by cheating on her with other women. The relationship between them and their sexual encounters have been misunderstood, and the facts mischaracterized, by Sawyer-Lauçanno. In the end, Elaine found some stability with the man she left Cummings for, Frank MacDermot.

CHAPTER 26. THE PORCUPINE HUNT

251 The feral cat, porcupines, etc. from *HL*, MS Am 1892.7 (234). Direct quotes are indicated; chipmunks as "darlings," "multimurderer," and "predator" are also Cummings's own words. Every detail here is found in Cummings's notes;

nothing is simply imagined. Marion Morehouse recounts the same events in a letter to Charles Norman, July 16, 1956, *HRC* Norman Papers, 10.11.

252 Information on the Porter apple variety: Powell 2014, 132–33.

254 "Me up at does": *CP*, 828.

254 Meal call: quotes from *ER*, 66 (see also Prologue, above).

255 "sunsets do not hate": *HL*, MS Am 1823.7 (17).

257 Closing epigraph: *HL*, MS Am 1892.7 (245).

A Note on Previous Biographies of Cummings

263 Number of prostitutes in Paris, around 5,000 licensed and around 70,000 estimated to be working as unlicensed prostitutes: Chamberlain and Weed 1926, 913.

264 Cleopatra: from "Cleopatra built": *CP*, 99.

264 Marie Louise in Sawyer-Lauçanno 2004, 110–12, 129; "girlfriend" in the caption to the image between 224 and 225. Marie Louise in Cheever 2014, 53–54. "like ladies": Kennedy 1994, 142; "tarts": Collier 1997, 139.

266 "Semble that tomorrow...": letter from Hale to Cummings, 1902, *HL*, MS Am 1892.4 (64).

Bibliography

~

Aldington, Richard, et al. 1914. *Des Imagistes: An Anthology*. London: Poetry Bookshop.

Association of American Painters and Sculptors. 1913. *Catalogue of International Exhibition of Modern Art*. New York: Vreeland Advertising Press.

Babcock, Mary David. 1963. "Cummings's Typography: An Ideogrammic Style." *Renascence: Essays on Value in Literature* 15: 115–23.

Becker, Jean-Jacques. 1985. *The Great War and the French People*. Translated by Arnold Pomerans. Leamington Spa: Berg.

Bonsor, N.R.P. 1978. *North Atlantic Seaway*. Volume 2. Jersey, Channel Islands: Brookside Publications.

Bourguignon, Katherine M., Lauren Kroiz, and Leo G. Mazow. 2018. *America's Cool Modernism: O'Keeffe to Hopper*. Oxford: Ashmolean Museum.

Byers, John Andrew. 2012. *The Sexual Economy of War: Regulation of Sexuality and the U.S. Army, 1898–1940*. PhD dissertation, Duke University.

Carr, Virginia Spencer. 1984. *Dos Passos: A Life*. Garden City, NY: Doubleday.

Carver, Douglass M., ed. 2014. *The Harvard Volunteers in World War I: One Hundred Years After*. CreateSpace Independent Publishing Platform = a reissue of M. A. DeWolfe Howe, ed. 1916. *The Harvard Volunteers in Europe: Personal Records of Experience in Military, Ambulance, and Hospital Service*. Cambridge, MA: Harvard University Press; London: Humphrey Milford; OUP.

Casteras, Susan P. 1986. "Abastenia St. Leger Eberle's 'White Slave.'" *Woman's Art Journal* 7: 32–36.

Chamberlain, Weston P., and Frank W. Weed. 1926. *The Medical Department of the United States Army in the World War*. Volume 6: Sanitation. Washington, DC: Government Printing Office.

Cheever, Susan. 2014. *E. E. Cummings: A Life*. New York: Pantheon.

Cocteau, Jean. 1951. Interview, by André Parinaud. Text: http://www.andre -parinaud.fr/Cocteau.html [accessed August 2, 2018]. Voice recording: "Jean Cocteau, Le Poète du Temps Perdu," Ina / Radio France: Harmonia Mundi, 2011.

Cohen, Milton A. 2010. *Beleaguered Poets and Leftist Critics: Stevens, Cummings, Frost, and Williams in the 1930s*. Tuscaloosa, AL: University of Alabama Press.

———. 2003. "'The Lily Maid of Astolat': Elaine Orr's Presence in E. E. Cummings' Poems and John Dos Passos' Prose." *Spring* 12: 139–49.

———. 1987. *PoetandPainter: The Aesthetics of E. E. Cummings's Early Work.* Detroit: Wayne State University Press.

———. 1983. "Cummings and Freud." *American Literature* 55: 591–610.

Collier, James Lincoln. 1997. "'B' [William Slater Brown]." *Spring* 6: 128–52.

Collins, Michael J. 1976. "Formal Allusion in Modern Poetry." *Concerning Poetry* 9: 5–12.

Comber, Michael. 1998. "A Book Made New: Reading Propertius Reading Pound. A Study in Reception." *Journal of Roman Studies* 88: 37–55.

Corbin, Alain. 1990. *Women for Hire: Prostitution and Sexuality in France after 1850.* Translated by Alan Sheridan. Cambridge, MA: Harvard University Press.

Cowley, Malcolm. 1994 [1951/1934]. *Exile's Return: A Literary Odyssey of the 1920s.* New York: Penguin.

Cummings, E. E. 2016. *Complete Poems 1904–1962: Revised, Corrected, and Expanded Edition Containing All the Published Poetry.* Edited by George J. Firmage. New York: Liveright.

———. 2007. "Letter to Scofield Thayer [undated, but probably late October, 1917]." *Spring* 16: 103–4.

———. 1983. *Etcetera: The Unpublished Poems of E. E. Cummings.* Edited by George James Firmage and Richard S. Kennedy. New York: Liveright.

———. 1978 [1922]. *The Enormous Room.* Edited by George James Firmage. Foreword by Richard S. Kennedy. New York: Liveright.

———. 1976. *Tulips & Chimneys: The Original 1922 Manuscript with the 34 Additional Poems from &.* Edited and with an afterword by George James Firmage. Introduction by Richard S. Kennedy. New York: Liveright.

———. 1972. *Selected Letters of E.E. Cummings.* Edited by F. W. Dupee and George Stade. London: André Deutsch.

———. 1967. *i: six nonlectures.* New York: Athenaeum. [First published Harvard University Press, 1953.]

———. 1965. *A Miscellany Revised.* Edited by George J. Firmage. New York: October House.

———. 1937. *Tulips & Chimneys. Archetype Edition of the Original MS 1922.* Mount Vernon: The Golden Eagle Press.

———. 1935. *No Thanks.* New York: Golden Eagle Press.

———. 1931. *CIOPW.* [*Charcoal Ink Oil Pencil & Watercolors.*] New York: Covici-Friede.

———. 1923. *Tulips and Chimneys.* New York: Thomas Seltzer.

Cummings, E. E., S. Foster Damon, J. R. Dos Passos, Robert Hillyer, R. S. Mitchell, William A. Norris, Dudley Poore, and Cuthbert Wright. 1917. *Eight Harvard Poets.* New York: Laurence J. Gomme.

Damon, S. Foster. 1969. *William Blake: His Philosophy and Symbols.* London: Dawsons of Pall Mall.

Danchev, Alex. 2013. *Cézanne: A Life.* London: Profile.

Davis, Robert Gorham. 1962. *John Dos Passos*. Minneapolis: University of Minnesota Press.

Dayton, Tim. 2010. "'Wristers Etcetera': Cummings, the Great War, and Discursive Struggle." *Spring* 17: 116–39.

Debussy, Claude. 2005. *Correspondance: 1872–1918*. Edited by François Lesure and Denis Herlin; notes by François Lesure, Denis Herlin, and Georges Liébert. Paris: Gallimard.

de Schaepdrijver, Sophie. 2014. "Populations under Occupation." In *The Cambridge History of the First World War*, vol. 3, edited by Jay Winter, 242–56. Cambridge: Cambridge University Press.

Delany, Paul. 1987. *The Neo-Pagans: Friendship and Love in the Rupert Brooke Circle*. London: Macmillan.

Dempsey, James. 2014. *The Tortured Life of Scofield Thayer*. Gainesville, FL: University Press of Florida.

———. 2011. "A Lost E. E. Cummings Poem Discovered." *The Awl*, unpaginated. [online magazine; article published May 25, 2011]. http://www.theawl.com/2011/05/a-lost-e-e-cummings-poem-discovered.

Dietschy, Marcel. 1990. *A Portrait of Claude Debussy*. Edited and translated from the French by William Ashbrook and Margaret G. Cobb. Oxford: Clarendon Press.

Dos Passos, John. 2003. *Novels 1920–1925. One Man's Initiation: 1917. Three Soldiers. Manhattan Transfer*. New York: The Library of America.

———. 1966. *The Best Times: An Informal Memoir*. London: André Deutsch.

Eliot, Charles W. 1890. "Address of Welcome." *Publications of the Modern Language Association* 5.1: 1–4.

Eliot, T. S. 1957. *On Poetry and Poets*. London: Faber & Faber.

———. 1969. *The Complete Poems and Plays*. London: Faber & Faber.

Eliot, Walter Graeme. 1887. *Eliot Family*. New York: Press of Livingston Middleditch.

Fain, Olivier. 2005. "Musculoskeletal Manifestations of Scurvy." *Joint Bone Spine* 72: 124–28.

Fairley, Irene R. 1979. "Cummings' Love Lyrics: Some Notes by a Female Linguist." *Journal of Modern Literature* 7: 205–18.

Fallon, April D. 2012 [2013]. "Love, Unlove, and Lust: Cummings' Use of the Surreal in His Love and Erotic Poetry." *Spring* 19: 75–85.

———. 2002. "E. E. Cummings, High Modernist: A Defense or 'Little Estlin, Our Nonhero, Modernist Faiteur.'" *Journal of Kentucky Studies* 19: 119–25.

Feibleman, James Kern. 1949. *Aesthetics: A Study of the Fine Arts in Theory and Practice*. New York: Duell, Sloan and Pearce.

Friedman, Norman. 2006. "Cummings, Oedipus, and Childhood: Problems of Anxiety and Intimacy." *Spring* 14–15: 46–68.

———. 1996. "'Not "e.e. cummings"' Revisited." *Spring* 5: 41–43.

———. 1992. "Not 'e.e. cummings.'" *Spring* 1: 114–21.

Friedman, Norman, and David V. Forrest. 1992. "William Slater Brown and *The Enormous Room.*" *Spring* 1: 87–91.

Fussell, Paul. 2013 [1975]. *The Great War and Modern Memory.* New edition. Oxford: Oxford University Press.

Garraty, John A., and Mark C. Carnes, eds., and the American Council of Learned Societies. 1999–. *American National Biography.* New York & Oxford: Oxford University Press.

Gerber, Philip L. 1988. "E. E. Cummings's Season of the Censor." *Contemporary Literature* 29: 177–200.

Gill, John M. 2007. "A Forgotten La Ferté-Macé Letter: E. E. Cummings to Scofield Thayer." *Spring* 16: 105–20.

———. 2002. "*The Enormous Room* Remembered." *Spring* 11: 159–82.

———. 1998. "*The Enormous Room* and 'The Windows of Nowhere': Reflections on Visiting La Ferté-Macé." *Spring* 7: 94–123.

Graves, Robert. 2000 [1957]. *Goodbye to All That.* London: Penguin.

———. 1972. "Review of *i: Six Nonlectures.*" In *E. E. Cummings: A Collection of Critical Essays.* Edited by N. Friedman, 172–76. Englewood Cliffs, NJ: Prentice-Hall. [Originally published 1954 in *The New Statesman* and *Nation.*]

Hadas, Rachel. 1998. "On E. E. Cummings' Poet Corner Induction, 26 October 1997." *Spring* 7: 11.

Hansen, Arlen J. 1996/2011. *Gentlemen Volunteers: The Story of the American Ambulance Drivers in the First World War.* New York: Arcade Publishing.

Hirschfeld, Magnus. 2006 [1941]. *The Sexual History of the World War.* Uncredited translation from the German. Honolulu, Hawaii: University Press of the Pacific.

Huang-Tiller, Gillian. 2012 [2013]. "A(r)more amoris: Modernist *Blason*, History, and the Body Politic of E. E. Cummings' Erotic Sonnetry in *&* [*AND*]." *Spring* 19: 110–29.

———. 2007. "*The Enormous Room* Seven Years after John M. Gill's Final Visit to La Ferté Macé." *Spring* 16: 95–98.

———. 2007b. "Reflecting *EIMI*: The Iconic Meta-Sonnet, Manhood, and Cultural Crisis in E. E. Cummings' *No Thanks.*" In *Words into Pictures: E. E. Cummings' Art Across Borders,* edited by Jiří Flajšar and Zénó Vernyik, 27–57. Newcastle: Cambridge Scholars Publishing.

———. 2005/2006. "The Modernist Sonnet and the Pre-Postmodern Consciousness: The Question of Meta-Genre in E. E. Cummings' *W* [*ViVa*] (1931)." *Spring* 14–15: 156–77.

———. 2001. "Modernism, Cummings' Meta-Sonnets, and Chimneys." *Spring* 10: 155–72.

Johnson, Allen, and the American Council of Learned Societies. 1995. *Dictionary of American Biography* [New ed.]. New York: Charles Scribner's Sons.

Kemeny, P. C. 2018. *The New England Watch and Ward Society.* Oxford: Oxford University Press.

Kennedy, David M. 1982. *Over Here: The First World War and American Society.* New York: Oxford University Press.

Kennedy, Paul. 2014. "The War at Sea." In *The Cambridge History of the First World War*, vol. 1, edited by Jay Winter, 321–48. Cambridge: Cambridge University Press.

Kennedy, Richard S. 1994. *Dreams in the Mirror: A Biography of E. E. Cummings.* 2nd ed. New York: Liveright.

———. 1979. "E.E. Cummings: The Emergent Styles, 1916." *Journal of Modern Literature* 7: 175–204.

———. 1977. "E.E. Cummings at Harvard: Verse, Friends, Rebellion." *Harvard Library Bulletin* 25: 253–91.

———. 1976. "E.E. Cummings at Harvard: Studies." *Harvard Library Bulletin* 24: 267–97.

———. 1966. "Edward Cummings, the Father of the Poet." *Bulletin of the New York Public Library* 70: 437–49.

Kidder, Rushworth M. 1979. "Cummings and Cubism: The Influence of the Visual Arts on Cummings's Early Poetry." *Journal of Modern Literature* 7: 255–91.

———. 1976. "'Buffalo Bill 's': An Early E. E. Cummings Manuscript." *Harvard Library Bulletin*, 24: 373–80.

———. 1976b. "'Author of Pictures': A Study of Cummings' Line Drawings in *The Dial.*" *Contemporary Literature* 17: 470–505.

———. 1975. "E. E. Cummings, Painter." *Harvard Library Bulletin* 23: 117–38.

Kozak, Lynn, and Miranda Hickman. 2014. "Poppies and Wild-Hyacinth: H. D.'s 'Hellenic' Responses to the First World War." *Viva voce: Classics and Classicists in the First World War.* Conference, University of Leeds, April 8–10, 2014.

Laity, Cassandra. 2004. "T. S. Eliot and A. C. Swinburne: Decadent Bodies, Modern Visualities, and Changing Modes of Perception." *Modernism/modernity* 11: 425–48.

———. 1996. *H. D. and the Victorian Fin de Siècle: Gender, Modernism, Decadence.* Cambridge: Cambridge University Press.

———. 1989. "H. D. and A. C. Swinburne: Decadence and Modernist Women's Writing." *Feminist Studies* 15: 461–84.

Lowell, Robert. 2003. *Collected Poems.* Edited by Frank Bidart and David Gewanter, with DeSales Harrison. London: Faber & Faber.

Mancini, Elena. 2010. *Magnus Hirschfeld and the Quest for Sexual Freedom: A History of the First International Sexual Freedom Movement.* New York: Palgrave Macmillan.

Martin, Meredith. 2007. "Therapeutic Measures: *The Hydra* and Wilfred Owen at Craiglockhart War Hospital." *Modernism/modernity* 14: 35–54.

Matthew, H.C.G., Brian Harrison, and Lawrence Goldman. 2004. *Oxford Dictionary of National Biography.* Oxford: Oxford University Press.

McGann, Jerome J. 2004. "Swinburne's Radical Artifice; or, The Comedian as A. C." *Modernism/modernity* 11: 205–18.

Metcalf, Allan A. 1970. "Dante and E. E. Cummings." *Comparative Literature Studies* 7: 374–86.

Miller, Neil. 2010. *Banned in Boston: The Watch and Ward Society's Crusade Against Books, Burlesque, and the Social Evil.* Boston: Beacon Press.

Miner, Marylou, and Linda S. Siegel. 1992. "William Butler Yeats: Dyslexic?" *Journal of Learning Disabilities* 25: 372–75.

Mitchell, Martha. 1993. "Damon, Samuel Foster." In *Encyclopedia Brunoniana,* edited by Martha Mitchell. Providence, RI: Brown University Library.

Monteiro, George. 1974. "S. Foster Damon." *The Journal of American Folklore* 87: 164–65.

Morens, David M., and Jeffery K. Taubenberger. 2015. "A Forgotten Epidemic That Changed Medicine: Measles in the US Army, 1917–18." *The Lancet: Infectious Diseases* 15: 852–61.

Mott, Christopher M. 1995. "The Cummings Line on Race." *Spring* 4: 71–75.

Neiberg, Michael S. 2014. "1917: Global War." In *The Cambridge History of the First World War,* vol. 1, edited by Jay Winter, 110–32. Cambridge: Cambridge University Press.

Norman, Charles. 1972. *E. E. Cummings: The Magic-Maker.* New York: Bobbs-Merrill. [First published 1958.]

Ordeman, John T., with George J. Firmage. 2000. "Cummings' Titles." *Spring* 9: 160–70.

Osborne, William R. 1965. "Cummings' 'The Bigness of Cannon' ('La Guerre,' I)." *Explicator* 24, no. 28.

"Pennsylvania, Philadelphia City Births, 1860–1906." Database with images, *FamilySearch* (https://familysearch.org/ark:/61903/1:1:VB1K-P8L: December 8, 2014), Harold H. Cummings, May 16, 1894; citing 312, Department of Records; FHL microfilm 1,289,334.

Philadelphia War History Committee. 1922. *Philadelphia in the World War, 1914–1919.* New York: Wynkoop Hallenbeck Crawford Co.

Pimentel, L. 2003. "Scurvy: Historical Review and Current Diagnostic Approach." *American Journal of Emergency Medicine* 21: 328–32.

Pound, Ezra. 1977. *Collected Early Poems of Ezra Pound.* Edited by M. J. King, with an Introduction by L. L. Martz. London: Faber & Faber.

Powell, Russell Steven. 2014. *Apples of New England: A User's Guide.* Woodstock, VT: The Countryman Press.

Prior, Robin. 2014. "The Western Front." In *The Cambridge History of the First World War,* vol. 1, edited by Jay Winter, 204–33. Cambridge: Cambridge University Press.

Pritchard, Stanford. 1990. "My Friend B." *The Kenyon Review* 12: 128–49.

Rainey, Lawrence. 1998. *Institutions of Modernism: Literary Elites and Public Culture.* New Haven: Yale University Press.

Rosenblitt, J. Alison. 2016. *E. E. Cummings' Modernism and the Classics: Each Imperishable Stanza.* Oxford: Oxford University Press.

———. 2016b. Review of James Dempsey, *The Tortured Life of Scofield Thayer*. (Gainesville, FL: University Press of Florida, 2014). In *Spring* 22: 245–48.

———. 2016c. "Fellows Find: The Goat-Footed Paganism of E. E. Cummings." Cultural Compass: The Harry Ransom Center (University of Texas at Austin) blog, http://blog.hrc.utexas.edu/2016/06/08/fellows-find-the-goat-footed -paganism-of-e-e-cummings/.

———. 2016d. "Pagan Poetry: The Faun, the Satyr, and the Chase." *The Worcester Review* 37: 103–9.

———. 2014. " 'a twilight smelling of Vergil': E. E. Cummings, Classics, and the Great War." *Greece & Rome* 61: 242–60.

———. 2013. "Pretentious Scansion, Fascist Aesthetics, and a Father-Complex for Joyce: E. E. Cummings on Sapphics and Ezra Pound." *Cambridge Classical Journal* 59: 178–98.

Samuelson, Arnold. 1984. *With Hemingway: A Year in Key West and Cuba*. New York: Random House.

Sawyer-Lauçanno, Christopher. 2006. *E. E. Cummings: A Biography*. London: Methuen.

Shaw, George Bernard. 1914. "Common Sense about the War." In *Current History of the European War*, vol. 1, no. 1: What Men of Letters Say. New York: New York Times Company, 11–60.

Shaw, Marte. 1979. "Documents from the Richard Norton Papers." *Journal of Modern Literature* 7: 341–44.

Siegel, Linda S. 2013. *Understanding Dyslexia and Other Learning Disabilities*. Vancouver, BC: Pacific Educational Press.

———. 1988. "Agatha Christie's Learning Disability." *Canadian Psychology / Psychologie Canadienne* 29: 213–16.

Smith, Leonard V. 2014. "Mutiny." In *The Cambridge History of the First World War*, vol. 2, edited by Jay Winter, 196–217. Cambridge: Cambridge University Press.

Society of Independent Artists. 1921. *Catalogue of the Fifth Annual Exhibition of the Society of Independent Artists (Incorporated)*. New York: The Society.

———. 1920. *Catalogue of the Fourth Annual Exhibition of the Society of Independent Artists (Incorporated)*. New York: The Society.

———. 1919. *Catalogue of the Third Annual Exhibition of the Society of Independent Artists (Incorporated)*. New York: Flying Stag Press.

Stallworthy, Jon. 2013 [Revised edition; first edition 1974]. *Wilfred Owen*. London: Pimlico.

Swinburne, Algernon Charles. 2004. *Major Poems and Selected Prose*. Edited by Jerome McGann and Charles L. Sligh. New Haven: Yale University Press.

———. 2000 [1866/1865]. *Poems and Ballads & Atalanta in Calydon*. Edited by Kenneth Haynes. London: Penguin.

Sychterz, Jeffrey S. 2007. "E. E. Cummings' Subversive Petrarchan Politics." *Spring* 16: 7–19.

Vernier, J. P. 1979. "E.E. Cummings at la Ferté-Macé." *Journal of Modern Literature* 7: 345–49.

Wagener, Hans. 2009. "All Quiet on the Western Front." In *Erich Maria Remarque's All Quiet on the Western Front*, edited by Harold Bloom, 81–106. New York: Bloom's Literary Criticism.

Watson, Alexander. 2014. "Morale." In *The Cambridge History of the First World War*, vol. 2, edited by Jay Winter, 174–95. Cambridge: Cambridge University Press.

Webster, Michael. 2015. "Cummings Rewrites Eliot." In *T. S. Eliot, France, and the Mind of Europe*, edited by Jayme Stayer, 75–91. Newcastle upon Tyne: Cambridge Scholars Publishing.

———. 2012. "Pound Teaching Cummings, Cummings Teaching Pound." In *Ezra Pound and Education*, edited by Steven and Michael Coyle, 47–66. Orono, ME: National Poetry Foundation.

———. 2011. "Learning to Be Modernist: Some Cummings Letters to Scofield Thayer." Unpublished talk, shared with the author.

———. 2005/2006. "A Memorial: Nancy T. Andrews, Daughter of E. E. Cummings." *Spring* 14–15: 260–68.

———. 2004. Rev. of C. Sawyer-Lauçanno, *E. E. Cummings: A Biography* (London: Methuen, 2006; first published, 2004). In *Spring* 13: 147–53.

———. 2002. "Poemgroups in *No Thanks*." *Spring* 11: 10–40.

———. 1995. *Reading Visual Poetry after Futurism: Marinetti, Apollinaire, Schwitters, Cummings*. New York: Peter Lang.

Webster, Michael, and Philip Persenaire. 2007. "Cummings' Plan of the Dêpot de Triage at La Ferté-Macé." *Spring* 16: 99–102.

Wickes, George. 1969. *Americans in Paris*. Garden City, NY: Doubleday.

———. 1969b. "E. E. Cummings at War." *Columbia University Forum* 12, no. 3: 31–33.

Wiley, Irena. 1962. *Around the Globe in 20 Years: An Artist at Large in the Diplomatic World*. New York: David McKay Company, Inc.

Winton, John. 1983. *Convoy: The Defence of Sea Trade 1890–1990*. London: Michael Joseph.

Wipers Times. 1918. *The Wipers Times: A Facsimile Reprint of the Trench Magazines:—The Wipers Times—The New Church Times—The Kemmel Times—The Somme Times—The B.E.F. Times*. London: Herbert Jenkins Limited.

World Almanac. 1901. *The World Almanac and Encyclopedia*. New York: Press Pub. Co. (The New York World).

Yablon, Alys Rho. 1998. " 'myself is sculptor of / your body's idiom': Representations of Women in Cummings' Love Poetry." *Spring* 7: 39–67.

Credits

~

ILLUSTRATIONS

1. *HL*, MS Am 1823.10 (45). (Photograph of the photograph taken by author.)
2. *HL*, MS Am 1823.8 (46). (Photograph of the photograph taken by author.)
3. *HL*, MS Am 1892.8 (1), Cummings Collection at Houghton Library, Harvard University by E. E. Cummings. Copyright by the Trustees for the E. E. Cummings Trust. Used by permission of Liveright Publishing Corporation. (Photograph by author.)
4. *HL*, MS Am 1892.11 (92). (Photograph of the photograph taken by author.)
5. *HL*, MS Am 1823.8 (46). (Photograph of the photograph taken by author.)
6. *HL*, MS Am 1892.11 (92). (Photograph of the photograph taken by author.)
7. *HL*, MS Am 1892.11 (92). (Photograph of the photograph taken by author.)
8. *HL*, MS Am 1892 (113). (Photograph of the photograph taken by author.)
9. Harry Ransom Center, the University of Texas at Austin, Digital Collection, "Posters from the First World War, 1914–1918."
10. Harry Ransom Center, the University of Texas at Austin, Digital Collection, "Posters from the First World War, 1914–1918."
11. Author's own collection. (Photograph by author.)
12. *HL*, MS Am 1823.7 (16). Cummings Collection at Houghton Library, Harvard University by E. E. Cummings. Copyright by the Trustees for the E. E. Cummings Trust. Used by permission of Liveright Publishing Corporation. (Photograph by author.)
13. *HL*, MS Am 1823.7 (16). Cummings Collection at Houghton Library, Harvard University by E. E. Cummings. Copyright by the Trustees for the E. E. Cummings Trust. Used by permission of Liveright Publishing Corporation. (Photograph by author.)
14. *HL*, MS Am 1823.7 (16). Cummings Collection at Houghton Library, Harvard University by E. E. Cummings. Copyright by the Trustees for the E. E. Cummings Trust. Used by permission of Liveright Publishing Corporation. (Photograph by author.)
15. *HL*, MS Am 1823.7 (16). Cummings Collection at Houghton Library, Harvard University by E. E. Cummings. Copyright by the Trustees for the E. E. Cummings Trust. Used by permission of Liveright Publishing Corporation. (Photograph by author.)
16. *HL*, MS Am 1823.7 (16). Cummings Collection at Houghton Library, Harvard University by E. E. Cummings. Copyright by the Trustees for the E. E. Cum-

mings Trust. Used by permission of Liveright Publishing Corporation. (Photograph by author.)

17. *HL*, MS Am 1823 (831). (Photograph by author.)
18. *HL*, MS Am 1823 (831). (Photograph by author.)
19. *HL*, MS Am 1892.11 (92). Reproduced by permission of Rachel Brown. (Photograph of the photograph taken by author.)
20. *HL*, MS Am 1823.7 (16). Cummings Collection at Houghton Library, Harvard University by E. E. Cummings. Copyright by the Trustees for the E. E. Cummings Trust. Used by permission of Liveright Publishing Corporation. (Photograph by author.)
21. *HL*, Ms AM 1823.7 (14). Cummings Collection at Houghton Library, Harvard University by E. E. Cummings. Copyright by the Trustees for the E. E. Cummings Trust. Used by permission of Liveright Publishing Corporation. (Photograph by author.)
22. *HL*, Ms AM 1823.7 (14). Cummings Collection at Houghton Library, Harvard University by E. E. Cummings. Copyright by the Trustees for the E. E. Cummings Trust. Used by permission of Liveright Publishing Corporation. (Photograph by author.)
23. *HL*, MS Am 1823.3 (61a). (Photograph by author.)
24. Author's own collection. (Photograph by author.)
25. *HL*, MS Am 1823.7 (19). Cummings Collection at Houghton Library, Harvard University by E. E. Cummings. Copyright by the Trustees for the E. E. Cummings Trust. Used by permission of Liveright Publishing Corporation. (Photograph by author.)
26. *HL*, MS Am 1892.11 (92). (Photograph of the photograph taken by author.)
27. *HL*, MS Am 1892.8 (1), Box 110. Cummings Collection at Houghton Library, Harvard University by E. E. Cummings. Copyright by the Trustees for the E. E. Cummings Trust. Used by permission of Liveright Publishing Corporation. (Photograph by author.)
28. *HL*, MS Am 1892.8 (1), Box 120. Cummings Collection at Houghton Library, Harvard University by E. E. Cummings. Copyright by the Trustees for the E. E. Cummings Trust. Used by permission of Liveright Publishing Corporation. (Photograph by author.)
29. *HL*, MS Am 1892.8 (1), Box 110. Cummings Collection at Houghton Library, Harvard University by E. E. Cummings. Copyright by the Trustees for the E. E. Cummings Trust. Used by permission of Liveright Publishing Corporation. (Photograph by author.)
30. *HL*, MS Am 1892.8 (1), Box 110. Cummings Collection at Houghton Library, Harvard University by E. E. Cummings. Copyright by the Trustees for the E. E. Cummings Trust. Used by permission of Liveright Publishing Corporation. (Photograph by author.)
31. *HL*, MS Am 1892.8 (1), Box 115. Cummings Collection at Houghton Library, Harvard University by E. E. Cummings. Copyright by the Trustees for the E. E. Cummings Trust. Used by permission of Liveright Publishing Corporation. (Photograph by author.)

TEXT

Index of Poems Cited

—

General Index

Aldington, Richard, 63

Anderson, Mr. (unit commander, SSU XXI), 92, 149, 155, 158–59, 161, 166, 225

Antheil, George, 110

Aphrodite (Venus), 74, 149

Apollinaire, Guillaume, 98–99

Aristophanes, 61

Armory Show (New York, 1913), 46–47, 60–61, 97, 282

Bacchus, 25, 62

Ballets Russes, 98–99

Bartlett, Spaulding, 214, 216, 218, 219, 220, 221, 223

Baruch, Irena, 220

Beardsley, Aubrey, 211–12

Berthe, 210–13

Blake, William, 44, 45

Boston, Mass., 8–9, 18, 24–25, 35, 37, 46, 51–54, 75, 76, 95, 97

Bordeaux, 93–94, 222

Briggs, Dean LeBaron Russell, 29, 49, 59–60

Brown, Frederick Augustus, 90, 91, 214, 217

Brown, William Slater, 90–94, 199, 208, 210, 211, 224–25, 233, 234, 235, 236, 237, 239–40, 242–44, 265, 266

  arrest, 1–4, 161–62, 165–68, 172–73

  at the front, 131, 132, 136, 142, 145, 149, 155

  imprisonment, 171, 177–78, 183–84, 191, 200–201, 210, 213

  letters, 1, 3, 151–53, 159–61, 166–67, 168, 169, 209, 217–18, 299–300

  in Paris, 95–100, 105, 109, 117, 127–28, 148, 243–44

  perspective on Cummings, 92, 145, 172–73, 183

  perspective on Cummings's family, 15, 19, 222–23

  release from prison, 185, 208, 214–23, 237

  romantic and sexual relationships, 102, 197–98

Bryan, Doris, 68–72, 73

burlesque, 51–52, 61, 75, 76, 82, 99

Cambridge, Mass., 7, 13–14, 21, 53, 56, 72–73, 89, 91

Cambridge (High and) Latin School, 7, 11, 20, 26, 91

Cambridge Review, The, 42

Camp Devens, Mass., 225–233, 237, 243

Carpenter, (Joseph) Estlin, 8, 117–18, 120, 166, 269

censorship, 3, 118, 120, 187, 192, 193–94, 200, 243. *See also* Great War, the, censorship and morale

Cézanne, Paul, 10, 46, 66, 97, 109, 112, 128, 155, 231, 239

Chagall, Marc, 212

chaos, 10

Charlemagne, 129

Chemin des Dames, 144

Child, Francis James, 16–17

Clark, L. Pierce, 244

Cleopatra, 105, 156, 264

Cocteau, Jean, 98–99

Cowley, Malcolm, 45, 61, 84, 110, 269

Creil, 128, 135, 175–76

Eberle, Abastenia St. Leger, 47, 282
Eight Harvard Poets, 81–82
Elaine. *See* Orr, Elaine
Eliot, Charles William, 18, 19
Eliot, George, 59
Eliot, Samuel Atkins, II, 18
Eliot, Thomas Stearns (T. S.), 18, 38, 39,
    72–73, 80, 108, 110, 112–13, 193
Evans, Donald, 56

faun, 65–67, 232, 241
Fluffy (cat), 16, 27
free verse, 66–67, 77
Freud, Sigmund, 189, 220, 244
Futurism, 55, 60, 75, 97, 98

Germaine, France, 133, 138
Graves, Robert, 100–101, 138, 243
Great War, the, 45, 61, 96, 118
    atrocities, 3, 152, 226
    censorship and morale, 3, 118, 120,
        168–70, 192, 200
    entry of US, 81, 82–84, 88, 145, 151,
        154–56
    Hindenburg Line, 130, 133, 144
    military history, 129–30, 144–45, 169
    mutiny and desertion, 131, 145, 151–52,
        161, 169, 171, 175
    propaganda, 83–84, 89, 145–46, 149,
        150–51
    racial diversity, 152, 245
    submarine warfare, 89, 93–94
    war atmosphere in Paris, 96, 99–100,
        108, 114, 127

Haigh-Wood, Vivienne, 72
Hale, Edward Everett, Rev., 17, 18–19,
    265–66, 270
Ham, France, 133, 140, 142
Harjes, Henry Herman, 127–28, 166
Harvard Advocate, The, 42, 81
Harvard Monthly, The, 42–45, 48–49, 50,
    53, 59, 62, 72, 81, 82
Harvard University, 7, 9, 18, 24–26,
    29–30, 51, 55–57, 66, 77, 88, 91, 97,
    121, 150, 211, 212, 225, 232

course system and educational style,
    16–17, 36–40, 45, 47, 49, 58–60
friendship circle from, 75, 76, 80, 92,
    97, 99, 193, 213, 245
H. D., 63
Hemingway, Ernest, 243
Hillyer, Robert, 44–46, 53, 55, 59–60, 81,
    84, 148, 270
Homer, 9, 60, 61

Imagism, 63–67, 97

Jean (fellow-prisoner at La Ferté-Macé),
    199, 243
Joyce, James, 63, 230–31
Joy Farm, New Hampshire, 11–15, 19, 26,
    27, 140, 225, 240, 242, 251–55
Jussy, France, 138, 142

Keats, John, 37, 38, 49, 56
Khokhlova, Olga, 98
Kittredge, George Lyman, 38

Lachaise, Gaston, 80–81, 160–161, 237,
    238, 270–71
La Ferté-Macé, France, 2, 171, 173, 176–
    204, 209, 210, 211, 221, 245–46, 276
Lallemand, Marie Louise, 2, 100, 101–6,
    115–16, 122, 127–28, 133–36, 138, 154–
    59, 162, 172, 189, 207, 209–10, 213,
    229–30, 242, 263–65, 292
La Touraine (ship), 2, 84, 87–93, 96, 118,
    127, 172
latrines, 148, 229
Lawrence, D. H., 80, 187
Lawrence, T. E. (Lawrence of Arabia),
    243
Longfellow, Henry Wadsworth, 73
Lowell, Abbott Lawrence, 24, 56
Lowell, Amy, 47, 56–57, 59, 61, 63, 77,
    269, 271
Lowell, Robert, 8

Marlowe, Christopher, 36
Marseille, France, 176, 178
Massine, Léonide, 98

THE RANCHER AND THE
RUNAWAY BRIDE

**Center Point
Large Print**

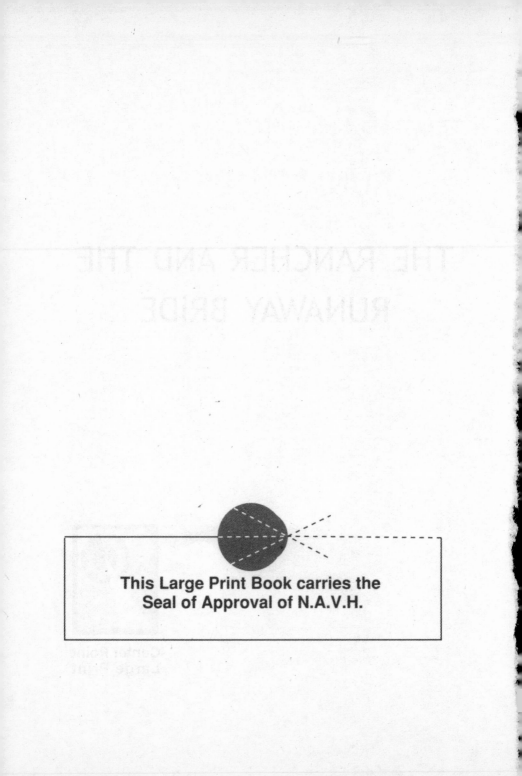

**This Large Print Book carries the
Seal of Approval of N.A.V.H.**

THE RANCHER AND THE RUNAWAY BRIDE

JOAN JOHNSTON

CENTER POINT PUBLISHING
THORNDIKE, MAINE

This Center Point Large Print edition
is published in the year 2006 by arrangement with
Harlequin Enterprises Ltd.

Copyright © 1993 by Joan Mertens Johnston.

The text of this Large Print edition is unabridged. In other
aspects, this book may vary from the original edition. Printed in
Thailand. Set in 16-point Times New Roman type.

ISBN 1-58547-705-2

Library of Congress Cataloging-in-Publication Data

Johnston, Joan, 1948-
    The rancher and the runaway bride / Joan Johnston.--Center Point large print ed.
        p. cm.
    ISBN 1-58547-705-2 (lib. bdg. : alk. paper)
        1. Large type books. 2. Ranchers--Fiction. 3. Brides--Fiction. I. Title.

PS3560.O3896R36 2006
813'.54--dc22

                                                                    2005021622

ACKNOWLEDGMENTS

I'm indebted to Ken Alstad's collection of *Savvy Sayin's* as a source of cowboy wit and wisdom. I would also like to thank the ladies of my critique group, Debbie St. Amand and Pam Mantovani, for their astute support and for reminding me, "A wishbone ain't no substitute for a backbone." Finally, I would like to thank my early-morning walking partner, Pam Rappaport, for her cheerful smile and sparkling conversation, and those mushing sled dogs, Beau and Max, for leading us on and protecting us from small children, ducks and little old lady joggers.

One

"May I kiss you good night, Tate?"

"Of course you can, Hank."

"Your brothers—"

"Forget about them! I'm a grown woman. I certainly don't need permission from Faron or Garth to give you a simple little good-night kiss." Tate Whitelaw stepped closer to the tall cowboy and slipped her arms around his neck. The bright light over the front door didn't quite reach to the corner of the railed porch where she was standing with Hank.

Hank took advantage of Tate's invitation, drawing her into his arms behind one of the massive fluted columns that graced the front of the house and aligning their bodies from breast to hip. She was uncomfortably aware of his arousal, since only two layers of denim—her jeans and his—separated their warm flesh. His mouth sought hers, and his tongue thrust inside. It was more than a simple good-night kiss, and Tate suddenly found herself wishing she hadn't been quite so encouraging.

"Hank—" she gasped, pulling her head back and trying to escape his ardor. "I don't think—"

Hank's arms tightened around her, and Tate found herself in a wrestling match. She struggled to get the heels of her hands to his shoulders to push him away. He gripped her short black hair with one hand and angled her face for his kiss.

"Hank! S-stop it!" she hissed.

Caught up in his lust, Hank was oblivious to Tate's urgently whispered entreaties. Tate had already decided it was time to take desperate action when the issue was taken out of her hands. Literally.

Tate knew someone had arrived on the scene when Hank gave a grunt of surprise as he was jerked away from her. Her brother Faron had a handful of Hank's Western shirt in his grasp and was holding the young man at arm's length.

"What the hell do you think you're doing with my sister?" Faron demanded.

Hank blinked owlishly. "Kissing her?"

"Who the hell gave you permission to kiss her?"

"I did!" Tate said through gritted teeth. Fisted hands on hips, chin up, she faced her brother defiantly. "Who gave *you* permission to interfere!"

"When I see my kid sister getting mauled—"

"I can take care of myself!"

Faron arched a brow, and Tate knew it was because she hadn't denied the fact she was being mauled. Hank had just been a little exuberant, that was all. She could have escaped her predicament without her brother's interference.

To Tate's horror, Garth shoved open the front screen door and asked, "What in blue blazes is going on out here?"

"I found this coyote forcing his attentions on Tate," Faron said.

Garth stepped onto the porch, and if the sheer size of

him didn't intimidate, the fierce scowl on his face surely would have. "That true?" Garth demanded of Hank.

Hank gulped. Perspiration dripped at his temple. The color left his face. "Well, sir . . ." He looked to Tate for rescue.

Tate watched Garth's lips flatten into a grim line as he exchanged a decisive look with Faron. Hank had been tried and convicted. All that was left was sentencing.

"Get your butt out of here," Garth said to Hank. "And don't come back."

Faron gave Hank a pretty good shove in the right direction, and Garth's boot finished the job. Hank stumbled down the porch steps to his pickup, dragged open the door, gunned the engine and departed in a swirl of gravel and choking dust.

There was a moment of awful silence while the dust settled. Tate fought the tears that threatened. She would *never* let her brothers know how humiliated she felt! But there was nothing wrong with giving them the lash of her tongue. She turned and stared first into Garth's stern, deep brown eyes, and then into Faron's more concerned gray-green ones.

"I hope you're both happy!" she snapped. "That's the fourth man in a month you've run off the ranch."

"Now, Tate," Faron began. "Any man who won't stand up to the two of us isn't worth having for a beau."

"Don't patronize me!" she raged. "I won't be placated like a baby with a rattle. I'm not three. I'm not even thirteen. I'm twenty-three. I'm a woman, and I have a woman's needs."

"You don't need to be manhandled," Garth said. "And I won't stand by and let it happen."

"Me neither," Faron said.

Tate hung her head. When she raised it again, her eyes were glistening with tears that blurred her vision. "I could have handled Hank myself," she said in a quiet voice. "You have to trust me to make my own decisions, my own mistakes."

"We don't want to see you hurt," Faron said, laying a hand on Tate's shoulder.

Tate stiffened. "And you think I wasn't hurt by what happened here tonight?"

Garth and Faron exchanged another look. Then Faron said, "Maybe your pride was pricked a little, but—"

"A *little!*" Tate jerked herself from Faron's grasp. "You're impossible! Both of you! You don't know the first thing about what I want or need. You can't imagine what it's like to have every step you take watched to make sure you don't fall down. Maybe it made sense when I was a baby, but I'm grown up now. I don't need you standing guard over me."

"Like you didn't need our help tonight?" Garth asked in a cold voice.

"I didn't!" Tate insisted.

Garth grabbed her chin and forced her face up to his. "You have no idea what a man's passions can lead him to do, little sister. I have no intention of letting you find out. Until the right man comes along—"

"There's no man who'll come within a hundred miles of this place now," Tate retorted bitterly. "My loving brothers have seen to that! You're going to keep me a virgin until I dry up and—"

Garth's fingers tightened painfully on her jaw, forcing her to silence. She saw the flash of fury in his dark eyes. A muscle flexed in his jaw. At last he said, "You'd better go to your room and think about what happened here tonight. We'll talk more about this tomorrow."

"You're not my father!" Tate spat. "I won't be sent to my room like a naughty child!"

"You'll go, or I'll take you there," Garth threatened.

"She can't go anywhere until you let go of her chin," Faron pointed out.

Garth shot a rueful look at his brother, then released Tate. "Good night, Tate," he said.

Tate had learned there were only two sides to Garth's arguments: his and the wrong one. Her stomach was churning. Her chest felt so tight it was hard to breathe, and her throat had a lump in it that made swallowing painful. Her eyes burned with tears that she would be *damned* if she'd shed!

She looked from Garth to Faron and back again. Garth's face was a granite mask of disapproval, while Faron's bore a look of sympathetic understanding. Tate knew they loved her. It was hard to fight their good intentions. Yet their love was smothering her. They would not let her *live!*

Her mother had died when she was born, and she had been raised by her father and her three brothers,

11

Garth, Faron and Jesse. Their father had died when Tate was eight. Jesse had left home then, and Garth and Faron had been responsible for her ever since. It was a responsibility they had taken very seriously. She had been kept cloistered at Hawk's Way, more closely guarded than a novice in a convent. If she went any-where off the ranch, one of her brothers came along.

When Tate was younger she'd had girlfriends to share her troubles with. As she got older, she discovered that the females she met were more interested in getting an introduction to her brothers than in being her friend. Eventually, she had simply stopped inviting them.

Tate hadn't even been allowed to go away to col-lege. Instead she had taken correspondence courses to get her degree in business. She had missed the social interaction with her peers, the experience of being out on her own, that would have prepared her to deal with the Hanks of the world.

However, Garth and Faron had taught her every job that had to be done on a ranch, from branding and cas-trating to vaccinating and breeding. She wasn't naive. No one could be raised on a ranch and remain totally innocent. She had seen the quarter horse stallions they raised at Hawk's Way mount mares. But she could not translate that violent act into what happened between a man and a woman in bed.

So far, she had found the fumbling kisses of her swains more annoying than anything else. Yet Tate had read enough to know there was more to the male-female relationship than she had experienced so far. If her brothers had their way, she would never unravel the mysteries of love.

She had come to the dire conclusion over the past few months that no man would ever pass muster with her brothers. If she continued living with them, she would die an old maid. They had given her no choice. In order to escape her brothers' overprotectiveness, she would have to leave Hawk's Way.

This latest incident was the final straw. But then, kicking a man when he's down is sometimes the only way to make him get up. Tate took one long, last look at each of her brothers. She would be gone from Hawk's Way before morning.

When the front door closed behind Tate, Faron settled a hip on the porch rail, and Garth leaned his shoulder against the doorjamb.

"She's too damn beautiful for her own good," Garth muttered.

"Hard to believe a woman can look so sexy in a man's T-shirt and a pair of jeans," Faron agreed with a shake of his head.

Garth's eyes were bleak. "What're we going to do about her?"

"Don't know that there's anything we can do except what we're already doing."

"I don't want to see her get hurt," Garth said.

Faron felt a tightness in his chest. "Yeah, I know. But she's all grown up, Garth. We're going to have to let go sometime."

Garth frowned. "Not yet."

"When?"

"I don't know. Just not yet."

The next morning, Garth and Faron met in the kitchen, as they always did, just before dawn. Charlie One Horse, the part-Indian codger who had been chief cook and bottle washer at Hawk's Way since their mother had died, had coffee perking and breakfast on the table. Only this morning there was something—someone—missing.

"Where's Tate?" Garth asked as he sat down at the head of the table.

"Ain't seen her," Charlie said.

Garth grimaced. "I suppose she's sulking in her room."

"You drink your coffee, and I'll go upstairs and check on her," Faron offered.

A moment later Faron came bounding into the kitchen. "She's not there! She's gone!"

Garth sprang up from his chair so fast it fell over backward. "What? Gone where?"

Faron grabbed Garth by the shoulders and said in a fierce voice, "She's not in her room. Her bed hasn't been slept in!"

Garth freed himself and took the stairs two at a time to see for himself. Sure enough, the antique brass double bed was made up with its nubby-weave spread. That alone was an ominous sign. Tate wasn't known for her neatness, and if she had made up the bed, she had done it to make a statement.

14

Garth headed for the closet, his heart in his throat. He heaved a sigh of relief when he saw Tate's few dresses still hanging there. Surely she wouldn't have left Hawk's Way for good without them.

Garth turned and found Faron standing in the doorway to Tate's room. "She probably spent the night sleeping out somewhere on the ranch. She'll turn up when she gets hungry."

"I'm going looking for her," Faron said.

Garth shoved a hand through his hair, making it stand on end. "Hell and the devil! I guess there'll be no peace around here until we find her. When I get hold of her, I'll—"

"When we find her, I'll do the talking," Faron said. "You've caused enough trouble."

"Me? This isn't my fault!"

"Like hell! You're the one who told her to go to her room and stay there."

"Looks like she didn't pay a whole helluva lot of attention to me, did she?" Garth retorted.

At that moment Charlie arrived, puffing from exertion, and said, "You two gonna go look for that girl, or stand here arguin'?"

Faron and Garth glared at each other for another moment before Faron turned and pressed his way past Charlie and down the stairs.

Charlie put a hand out to stop Garth. "Don't think you're gonna find her, boy. Knew this was bound to happen sooner or later."

"What do you mean, old man?"

15

"Knew you had too tight a rein on that little filly. Figured she had too much spirit to stay in them fences you set up to hold her in."

"It was for her own good!"

Charlie shook his head. "Did it as much for yourself as for her. Knowin' your ma like you did, it's no wonder you'd want to keep your sister close. Prob'ly fearful she'd take after your ma, steppin' out on your pa like she did and—"

"Leave Mother out of this. What she did has nothing to do with the way I've treated Tate."

Charlie tightened the beaded rawhide thong that held one of his long braids, but said nothing.

Garth scowled. "I can see there's no sense arguing with a stone wall. I'm going after Tate, and I'm going to bring her back. This time she'll stay put!"

Garth and Faron searched canyons and mesas, ridges and gullies on their northwest Texas ranch, but not a sign did they find of their sister on Hawk's Way.

It was Charlie One Horse who discovered that the old '51 Chevy pickup, the one with the rusty radiator and the skipping carburetor, was missing from the barn where it was stored.

Another check of Tate's room revealed that her underwear drawer was empty, that her brush and comb and toothpaste were gone, and that several of her favorite T-shirts and jeans had also been packed.

By sunset, the truth could not be denied. At the age of twenty-three, Tate Whitelaw had run away from home.

16

Two

Adam Philips normally didn't stop to pick up hitch-hikers. But there was no way he could drive past the woman sitting on the front fender of a '51 Chevy pickup, its hood raised and its radiator steaming, her thumb outstretched to bum a ride. He pulled his late-model truck up behind her and put on his Stetson as he stepped out into the heat of a south Texas midsummer afternoon.

She was wearing form-fitting jeans and an off-the-shoulder peasant blouse that exposed a lush female figure. But the heart-shaped face, with its huge hazel eyes and wide mouth framed by breeze-ruffled, short-cropped black hair, was innocence itself. He was stunned by her beauty and appalled at her youth. What was this female doing all alone on an isolated stretch of southwest Texas highway in an old rattletrap truck?

She beamed a trusting smile at him, and he felt his heart do a flipflop. She slipped off the rusty fender and lazily sauntered toward him. He felt his groin tighten with desire and scowled. She stopped in her tracks. About time she thought to be wary! Adam was all too conscious of the dangers a stranger presented to a young woman alone. Grim-lipped, he strode the short distance between the two vehicles.

Tate had been so relieved to see *someone* show up on the deserted rural route that the danger of the situation didn't immediately occur to her. She got only a

17

glimpse of wavy blond hair and striking blue eyes before her rescuer had slipped on a Stetson that put his face in shadow.

He was broad-shouldered and lean-hipped, with a stride that ate up the distance between the two trucks. It was a fair assumption, from his dusty boots, worn jeans and sweat-stained Western shirt, that he was a working cowboy. Tate saw no reason to suspect he meant her any harm.

But instead of a pleasant "May I help you?" the first words out of his mouth were, "What the hell do you think you're doing?"

Tate was alarmed by the animosity in the stranger's voice and frightened by the intensity of his stare. But his attitude was so similar to what she had recently gone through with her brothers that she lifted her chin and retorted, "Hitching a ride back to the nearest gas station. In case you hadn't noticed, my truck's broken down."

The scowl deepened but he said, "Get in my pickup."

Tate had only taken two steps when the tall cowboy grabbed her arm and pulled her up short.

"Aren't you going to ask anything about me? Don't you want to know who I am?"

By now Tate was more irritated than frightened. "A Good Samaritan with a bad temper!" she retorted. "Do I need to know more?"

Adam opened his mouth to make a retort, took one look at the mutinous expression on the young woman's face, and shut it again. Instead he dragged her unceremoniously to the passenger's side of his long-bed pickup, opened the door, shoved her inside, and slammed it closed after her.

"My bag! It's in the back end of the Chevy," Tate yelped.

Adam stalked back to the rattletrap Chevy, snagged the duffel bag from the rusted-out truck bed and slung it into the back of his pickup.

Woman was too damned trusting for her own good! he thought. Her acid tongue wouldn't have been much help to her if he had been the kind of villain who preyed on stranded women. Which he wasn't. Lucky for her!

Tate didn't consider herself at all lucky. She recognized the flat-lipped expression on her Good Samaritan's face. He might have rescued her, all right, but he wasn't happy about it. The deep crevices formed around his mouth by his frown and the webbed lines at the edges of his eyes had her guessing his age at thirty-five or thirty-six—the same as her eldest brother Garth. The last thing she needed was another keeper!

She sat back with her arms crossed and stared out the window as they drove past rolling prairie. She thought back to the night two weeks ago when she had decided to leave Hawk's Way.

Her escape from her brothers, while apparently sudden, hadn't been completely without direction. She had taken several ranch journals containing advertise-

19

ments from outfits all over Texas looking for expert help and headed south. However, Tate soon discovered that not one rancher was interested in hiring a woman, especially one without references, as either foreman or ranch manager.

To confound her problems, the ancient pickup she had taken from the barn was in worse shape than she had thought. It had left her stranded miles from the Lazy S—the last ranch on her list and her last hope for a job in ranch management.

"Do you know where the Lazy S is?" she asked.

Adam started at the sound of her voice. "I expect I could find it. Why?"

"I understand they're looking for a ranch manager. I intend to apply for the job."

"You're just a kid!"

The cowboy could have said nothing more likely to raise Tate's neck hairs. "For your information, I'm twenty-three and a fully grown woman!"

Adam couldn't argue with that. He had a pretty good view of the creamy rise of her breasts at the frilly gathered edge of her blouse. "What do you know about ranching?" he asked.

"I was raised on a ranch, Hawk's Way, and—" She stopped abruptly, realizing that she had revealed more than she had intended to this stranger. Tate hadn't used her own last name to apply for any jobs, knowing that if she did her brothers would be able to hunt her down and drag her back home. "I hope you'll keep that to yourself," she said.

20

Adam raised an inquiring brow that met such a gamine smile that his heart did that disturbing flipflop again.

"You see," Tate said, "the truth is, I've run away from home."

Adam snorted. "Aren't you a little old for that?"

Tate's lips curled ruefully. "I suppose so. But my brothers just wouldn't let me *live!* I mean, they watched every breath in and out of my body."

Adam found the thought rather intriguing himself.

"My brothers are a little overprotective, you see. I had to run away if I was ever going to meet the right man and fall in love and have children."

"Sounds like you could do that better at home than traipsing around the countryside," Adam observed.

"You don't know my older brothers! They want to wrap me in cotton batting and keep me safe. Safe, ha! What they mean is, they want to keep me a virgin forever."

Adam choked at this unbelievable revelation and coughed to clear his throat.

"It's true! They've chased away every single beau I've ever had. Which is only a waste of time and energy because, you know, a man who's born to drown can manage to drown in a desert."

Adam eyed her askance.

"I mean, if something is destined to happen, it'll happen no matter what."

Tate waited for Adam to say something, but when he remained silent, she continued, "My older brother,

Jesse, left home, too, when I was just eight. It was right after my father died. We haven't seen him for years and years. I don't plan to stay away for years, of course, but then, who knows how long it will take to find my Prince Charming. Not that I have to marry a prince of a man."

Tate grinned and shrugged. "But it would be nice, you know, to just once kiss a man goodnight, without having my brothers send him packing because he's not good enough for me."

Tate realized she was talking to fill the silence and forced herself to shut up.

Behind the young woman's bravado Adam saw the desperation that had sent her fleeing from the safe haven her brothers had provided for her. He felt sick inside. Was this the way his younger sister had felt? Had Melanie seen him as an oppressive tyrant, the same way this young woman perceived her brothers?

Tate held her breath as the stranger looked into her eyes. There was an awful sadness there she felt constrained to dispel. So she began talking again.

"I've been looking everywhere for a job," she said. "I must have been to fifteen different spreads in the past two weeks. But I haven't had so much as a nibble of interest.

"What I find so frustrating is the fact that most owners don't treat me seriously. I mean, I know I'm young, but there isn't anything I don't know about running a ranch."

"Do you know how to figure the amount of feed you

need for each head of stock?" Adam asked.

"Depends on whether you plan to keep the stock penned or let it graze," Tate said. "Now if it's penned—"

Adam interrupted with, "Give me some symptoms of colic."

"A horse might have colic if he won't eat, or if he starts pawing, or gets up and down a lot. Generally an animal that can't get comfortable has a problem."

"Can you keep books on a computer?"

Tate snorted inelegantly. "Boy can I ever! I got stuck with all the bookkeeping at Hawk's Way. So, if you were hiring at the Lazy S, would I get the job?"

"What will you do if you *don't* get the job?" Adam asked instead.

Tate shrugged, not realizing how revealing the gesture was of the fact she wasn't the least bit nonchalant about that distressing possibility. "I don't know. I only know I *won't* go back home."

"And if your brothers find you?"

Her chin took on a mulish tilt. "I'll just run away again."

Adam wondered if his sister was so forthright and disarmingly honest with the man who had picked her up the night she ran away from home. Had that stranger known all about the young woman he had raped and murdered and left lying in a ditch on the side of the road?

Adam's teeth clenched in determination. If he had anything to say about it, the innocent young woman in his pickup would not become another such statistic. And he, of all people, was in a perfect position to help her. Because he owned the Lazy S Ranch.

However, in the months since Adam had put his advertisement in the ranch journal, he had changed his mind about needing a foreman. He had decided to place his country medical practice on hold and put the Lazy S Ranch back in the black himself.

But if he told this young woman he had no job for her, where would she go? What would she do? And how would he feel if he sent her away and she ended up dead somewhere on the side of the road?

"Say, there's the Lazy S Ranch!" Tate pointed at a wrought-iron sign that bridged a dirt road off the main thoroughfare. To her surprise, the cowboy turned and drove across a cattle guard onto the Lazy S.

"I thought you were going to take me into town!" she said.

"I thought you wanted to interview for a job!" he retorted.

Tate eyed the cowboy. She was perplexed. Many western men were the strong, silent type, but the stranger who had picked her up was something more. Aloof. The more distant he was, the more intrigued she became. It was a surprise to find out he had been kind enough to take her directly to the Lazy S.

She could have kicked herself for telling him so much personal information without finding out anything about him—not even his name. When he dropped her off, she might never see him again. Tate suddenly realized she wanted to see him again. Very much.

As the cowboy stopped his pickup in front of an impressive adobe ranch house, she said, "I can't tell you how much I appreciate your giving me a ride here. I'd like to thank you, but I don't even know your name!"

Adam turned to look at her and felt a tightening in his gut as she smiled up at him. Well, it was now or never. "My name is Adam Philips," he said. "I own the Lazy S. Come on inside, and you can interview for that job."

Three

Tate was stunned when the mysterious cowboy revealed his identity, but buoyant with hope, as well. She scrambled out of the pickup after Adam, certain that he wouldn't have bothered bringing her here if he didn't intend to at least consider her for the job of ranch foreman.

"Follow me," he said, heading into the house.

Tate stopped only long enough to grab her duffel bag and sling it over her shoulder before scampering up the three steps after him.

Adam's living room was masculine through and through, filled with massive Spanish furniture of natural leather studded with brass. There was not another frill or a furbelow to soften the room. *No woman has lived here in a long time—if ever,* Tate decided.

She discovered that the adobe hacienda formed a U shape. The two wings enclosed a garden shaded by immense moss-laden live oaks and bright with blooming bougainvillea. A central tile fountain splashed with cascading water.

They finally arrived at Adam's office, which was located at the tip of one wing of the house. The thick adobe walls and the barrel-tile roof kept the inside of the house dark and cool, reminiscent of days gone by when everyone took an afternoon siesta.

Tate saw from the immaculate condition of the office that Adam must be an organized person. Everything had a place and everything was in its place. Tate felt her heart sink. She wasn't averse to order, she just refused to be bound by it. That had been one small rebellion she was capable of in the space in which her brothers confined her.

Instead of sitting on the leather chair in front of the desk, she seated herself on a corner of the antique oak desk itself. Adam refused to sit at all, instead pacing the room like a caged tiger.

"Before we go any further, I want to know your real name," he said.

Tate frowned. "I need a promise from you first that you won't contact my brothers."

Adam stopped pacing and stared at her.

Tate stared right back.

"All right," he said. "You've got it."

Tate took a deep breath and said, "My last name is Whitelaw."

Adam swore under his breath and began pacing again. The Whitelaws were known all over Texas for the excellent quarter horses they bred and trained. He had once met Garth Whitelaw at a quarter horse sale. And he was intimately acquainted with Jesse Whitelaw. Tate's brother Jesse, the one she hadn't seen in years, had recently married Honey Farrell—the woman Adam loved.

Honey's ranch, the Flying Diamond, bordered the Lazy S. Fortunately, with the strained relations between Adam and Jesse Whitelaw, Tate's brother wasn't likely to be visiting the Lazy S anytime soon.

27

Adam turned his attention to the young woman he had rescued from the side of the road. Her short black hair was windblown around her face, and her cheeks were flushed with excitement. She was gnawing worriedly on her lower lip—something he thought he might like to do himself.

Adam felt that telltale tightening in his groin. He tucked his thumbs into his jeans to keep from reaching out to touch her.

Tate crossed her legs and clutched her knee with laced fingers. She could feel the tension in Adam. A muscle worked in his jaw, and his expression was forbidding. A shiver ran down her spine. But it wasn't fear she felt, it was anticipation.

She was so nervous her voice cracked when she tried to speak. She cleared her throat and asked, "So, do I get the job?"

"I haven't made up my mind yet."

Tate was on her feet and at Adam's side in an instant. "I'd be good at it," she argued. "You wouldn't be sorry you hired me."

Adam had his doubts about that. His blood thrummed as he caught the faint scent of lilacs from her hair. He was already sorry he had stopped to pick her up. He couldn't be anywhere near her without feeling as randy as a teenager. That was a fine state of affairs when he had appointed himself her guardian in her brothers' stead. But he believed Tate when she had said she would just run away again if her brothers tried taking her home. Surely she would be better off here where he could keep a close eye on her.

He carefully stepped away from her and went around to sit behind his desk. Perhaps it would provide a more comfortable barrier between himself and the uncontrollable urges that struck him when he got within touching distance of this engaging runaway.

He steepled his fingers and said, "The job I have available isn't the same one that was advertised."

She braced her palms on the desk and leaned toward him. "Oh? Why not?"

Adam took one look at what her careless posture in the peasant blouse revealed and forced his gaze upward to her wide hazel eyes. "It's complicated."

"How?"

Why didn't she move? He had the irresistible urge to reach out and— He jumped up from behind his desk and started pacing again. "You'd have to know a little bit about what's happened on the Lazy S over the past couple of months."

Tate draped herself sideways across the chair in front of the desk, one leg swinging to release the tension, and said, "I'm listening."

"My previous ranch manager was a crook. He's in prison now, but besides stealing other people's cattle, he embezzled from me. He left my affairs in a mess. Originally, I'd intended to hire someone else to try to straighten things out. Lately I've decided to put my medical practice on hold—"

"Wait a minute!"

Tate sat up and her feet dropped to the floor,

depriving Adam of the delicious view he'd had of her derriere.

"Do you mean to tell me you're a doctor?" she asked incredulously.

He shrugged sheepishly. "Afraid so. Over the past few months I've been transferring my practice to another physician who's moved into the area, Dr. Susan Kowalski. Now I have time to supervise the work on the Lazy S myself. What I really need is someone I can trust to organize the paperwork and do the bookkeeping."

Adam pointed to the computer on a stand near his desk. "That thing and I don't get along. I can't pay much," Adam admitted, "but the job includes room and board." That would keep her from sleeping in her truck, which was about all Adam suspected she could afford right now.

Tate wrinkled her nose. She had cut her teeth on the computer at Hawk's Way, and what she didn't know about bookkeeping hadn't been discovered. But it was the kind of work she liked least of everything she'd done at Hawk's Way. Still, a job was a job. And this was the best offer she had gotten.

"All right. I accept."

Tate stood and held a hand out to Adam to shake on the deal.

When Adam touched her flesh he was appalled by the electricity that streaked between them. He had suspected his attraction for Tate, all the while warning himself not to get involved. His powerful, instanta-

30

neous reaction to her still caught him by surprise. He blamed it on the fact that it had been too damn long since he'd had a woman. There were plenty who would willingly satisfy his needs, women who knew the score.

He absolutely, positively, was not going to get involved with a twenty-three-year-old virgin. Especially not some virgin who wanted a husband and a family. For Adam Philips wouldn't give her one—and couldn't give her the other.

Tate was astonished by the jolt she received simply from the clasp of Adam's hand. She looked up into his blue eyes and saw a flash of desire quickly banked. She jerked her hand away, said, "I'm sure we're both going to enjoy this relationship," then flushed at the more intimate interpretation that could be put on her words.

Adam's lips curled in a cynical smile. She was a lamb, all right, and a wily old wolf like himself would be smart to keep his distance. He didn't intend to tell her brothers where she was. But he was betting that sooner or later word of her presence on the Lazy S would leak out, and they would find her. When they did, all hell was going to break loose.

Adam shook his head when he thought of what he was getting himself into. Tate Whitelaw was Trouble with a capital *T*.

"Where do I bunk in?" Tate asked.

Adam dragged his Stetson off and ruffled his blond hair where the sweat had matted it down. He

31

hadn't thought about where he would put her. His previous foreman had occupied a separate room at one end of the bunkhouse. That obviously wouldn't do for Tate.

"I suppose you'll have to stay here in the house," he said. "There's a guest bedroom in the other wing. Come along and I'll show you where it is."

He walked her back through the house, describing the layout of things as they went along. "My bedroom is next to the office. The living room, family room and kitchen are in the center of the house. The last bedroom down the hall on this other wing was set up for medical emergencies, and I haven't had time to refurnish it. The first bedroom on this wing will be your room."

Adam opened the door to a room that had a distinctively southwestern flavor. The furniture was antique Americana, with woven rugs on the floor, a rocker, a dry sink, a wardrobe and a large maple four-poster covered with a brightly patterned quilt. The room felt light and airy. That image was helped by the large sliding glass door that opened onto the courtyard.

Tate sat down on the bed and bounced a couple of times. "Feels plenty comfortable." She turned and smiled her thanks up at Adam.

The smile froze on her face.

His look was avid, his nostrils flared. She was suddenly aware of the softness of the bed. The fact that they were alone. And that she didn't know Adam Philips . . . from Adam.

However, the part of Tate that was alive to the danger of the situation was squelched by the part of her that was exhilarated to discover she could have such a profound effect on this man. Adam was quite unlike the men her brothers had so peremptorily ejected from Hawk's Way. In some way she could not explain, he was different. She knew instinctively that his kiss, his touch, would be unlike anything she had ever experienced.

Nor did she feel the same person when she was near him. With this man, she was different. She was no longer her brothers' little sister. She was a woman, with a woman's need to be loved by one special man.

Instead of scooting quickly off the bed, she stayed right where she was. She tried her feminine wings just a bit by languidly turning on her side and propping her head up with her hand. She pulled one leg up slightly, mimicking the sexy poses she had seen in some of her brothers' magazines—the ones they thought she knew nothing about.

Adam's reaction was everything she could have wished for. His whole body tautened. A vein in his temple throbbed. The muscles in his throat worked spasmodically. And something else happened. Something which, considering the level she was lying at, she couldn't help observing.

It was fascinating. She had never actually watched it happen to a man before. Mostly, the men she had dated were already in that condition before she had an opportunity to notice. The changing shape of Adam's

33

Levi's left no doubt that he was becoming undeniably, indisputably, absolutely, completely *aroused*.

She gasped, and her eyes sought out his face to see what he intended to do about it.

Nothing! Adam thought. *He was going to do absolutely nothing about the fact this hoyden in blue jeans had him harder than a rock in ten seconds flat!*

"If you're done testing your feminine wiles, I'd like to finish showing you the house," Adam said.

Humiliated by the sarcasm in his voice, Tate quickly scooted off the bed. She had no trouble recognizing his feelings now. Irritation. Frustration. She felt the same things herself. She had never imagined how powerful desire could be. It was a lesson she wouldn't forget.

She stood before him, chin high, unwilling to admit blame or shame or regret for what she had done. "I'm ready."

Then strip down and get into that bed.

Adam clenched his teeth to keep from saying what he was thinking. He didn't know when he had felt such unbridled lust for a woman. It wasn't decent. But he damn sure wasn't going to do anything about it!

"Come on," he growled. "Follow me."

Tate followed Adam back through the house to the kitchen, where they found a short, rotund Mexican woman with snapping black eyes and round, rosy cheeks. She was chopping onions at the counter. Tate was treated to a smile that revealed two rows of brilliant white teeth.

34

"Who have you brought to meet me, Señor Adam?" the woman asked.

"Maria, this is Tate Whitelaw. She's going to be my new bookkeeper. Tate will be staying in the guest bedroom. Tate, I'd like you to meet my housekeeper, Maria Fuentes."

"*Buenos días, Maria,*" Tate said.

"*¿Habla usted español?*" Maria asked.

"You've already heard all I know," Tate said with a self-deprecating grin.

Maria turned to Adam and said in Spanish, "She is very pretty, this one. And very young. Perhaps you would wish me to be her *dueña*."

Adam flushed and answered in Spanish, "I'm well aware of her age, Maria. She doesn't need a chaperon around me."

The Mexican woman arched a disbelieving brow. Again in Spanish she said, "You are a man, Señor Adam. And her eyes, they smile at you. It would be hard for any man to refuse such an invitation. No?"

"No!" Adam retorted. Then added in Spanish, "I mean, no I wouldn't take advantage of her. She has no idea what she's saying with her eyes."

Maria's disbelieving brow arched higher. "If you say so, Señor Adam."

Tate had been trying to follow the Spanish conversation, but the only words she recognized were "Maria," "chaperon," "Señor Adam" and "No." The look on Maria's face made it clear she disapproved of the fact Tate would be living in the house alone with

35

Adam. Well, she didn't need a chaperon any more than she needed a keeper. She could take care of herself.

Fortunately, it wasn't necessary for her to interrupt the conversation. A knock at the kitchen door did it for her. The door opened before anyone could answer it, and a young cowhand stuck his head inside. He had brown eyes and auburn hair and a face so tanned it looked like rawhide.

"Adam? You're needed in the barn to take a look at that mare, Break of Day. She's having some trouble foaling."

"Sure. I'll be there in a minute, Buck."

Instead of leaving, the cowhand stood where he was, his eyes glued on the vision in a peasant blouse and skin-tight jeans standing in Adam's kitchen. He stepped inside the door, slipped his hat off his head, and said, "Name's Buck, ma'am."

Tate smiled and held out her hand. "Tate Wh—atly."

The cowboy shook her hand and then stood there foolishly grinning at her.

Adam groaned inwardly. This was a complication he should have foreseen, but hadn't. Tate was bound to charm every cowhand on the place. He quickly crossed past her and put a hand on Buck's shoulder to urge him out the door. "Let's go."

"Can I come with you?" Tate asked.

Before Adam could say no, Buck spoke up.

"Why sure, ma'am," the cowboy said. "Be glad to have you along."

36

There wasn't much Adam could say except, "You can come. But stay out of the way."

"What kind of trouble is the mare having?" Adam asked as they crossed the short distance to the barn, Tate following on their heels.

"She's down and her breathing's labored," Buck said.

Tate saw as soon as they entered the stall that the mare was indeed in trouble. Her features were grim as she settled onto the straw beside the mare's head. "There now, pretty lady. I know it's hard. Just relax, you pretty lady, and everything will be all right."

Adam and Buck exchanged a look of surprise and approval at the calm, matter-of-fact way Tate had insinuated herself with the mare. The mare lifted her head and whickered in response to the sound of Tate's voice. Then she lay back down and a long, low groan escaped her.

Tate held the mare's head while Adam examined her. "It's twins."

"Why that's wonderful!" Tate exclaimed.

"One of them's turned wrong, blocking the birth canal." In fact, there was one hoof from each of the twins showing.

"Surely your vet can deliver them!"

Adam's features were somber as he answered, "He's out of town at his daughter's wedding." Adam couldn't imagine a way to save either foal, entangled as they were.

Tate's excitement vanished to be replaced with fore-

37

boding. She had encountered this problem once before, and the result had come close to being disastrous. Garth had managed to save the mare and both foals, but it had been a very near thing.

"I'll have to take one foal to save the other," Adam said in a flat voice.

"You mean, destroy it?" Tate asked. She couldn't bring herself to say "dismember it" though that was what Adam was suggesting.

"There's nothing else I can do." Adam turned to the cowboy and said, "Buck, see if you can find me some rope."

Tate stroked the mare's neck, trying to keep the animal calm. She looked up and saw the dread in Adam's eyes. It was never easy to make such decisions, yet they were a constant part of ranch life.

She was hesitant to interfere, but there was the tiniest chance the second foal could be saved. "My brother Garth went through this not too long ago. He was able to save both foals by—"

Buck arrived and interrupted with, "Here's the rope, Adam. Do you need my help?"

"I'm not sure. I'd appreciate it if you'd stay."

Buck propped a foot on the edge of the stall and leaned his arms across the top rail to watch as Adam knelt beside the mare and began to fashion a noose with the rope.

Adam paused and glanced over at Tate. She was gnawing on her lower lip again while she smoothed her hand over the mare's sleek neck.

Adam found himself saying, "If you know some-thing that can be done to save both foals, I'm willing to give it a try."

He watched Tate's whole face light up.

"Yes! Yes, I do." She quickly explained how Garth had repositioned the foals.

"I'm not sure I—"

"You can do it!" Tate encouraged. "I know you can!"

Her glowing look made him think he might be able to move mountains. As for saving two spindly foals . . . It was at least worth a try.

A half hour later, sweat had made damp patches under the arms and down the back of Adam's cham-bray shirt. He had paused in what he was doing long enough to tie a navy blue bandanna around his fore-head to keep the salty wetness out of his eyes. He worked quietly, efficiently, aware of the life-and-death nature of his task.

Adam knew a moment of hope when he finished. But now that the foals had been rearranged, the mare seemed too exhausted to push. He looked across the mare to Tate, feeling his failure in every inch of his body. "I'm sorry."

Tate didn't hear his apology. She took the mare's head onto her lap and began chanting and cooing to the exhausted animal—witchcraft for sure, Adam thought—until the mare amazingly, miraculously birthed the first of the foals.

Adam knew his grin had to be as silly as the one on

Tate's face, but he didn't care. Buck took care of cleaning up the first foal while Tate continued her incantations until the mare had delivered the second. Buck again took over drying off the foal while Tate remained at the mare's head, and Adam made sure the afterbirths were taken care of.

When Adam was finished, he crossed to a sink at one end of the barn and scrubbed himself clean. He dried his hands with a towel before rolling his sleeves down from above the elbow to the middle of his forearms.

Adam watched in admiration as Tate coaxed the mare onto her feet and introduced her to her offspring. The mare took a tentative lick of one, and then the other. In a matter of minutes both foals were nudging under her belly to find mother's milk.

Tate's eyes met Adam's across the stall. He opened his arms and she walked right into them. Her arms circled his waist, and she held him tightly as she gave vent to the tears she hadn't shed during the awful ordeal.

"Everything's fine, sweetheart. Thanks to you, everything's just fine," Adam said, stroking her short, silky hair. "Don't cry, sweetheart. You did just fine."

Adam wasn't sure how long they stood there. When he looked up to tell Buck he could go, he discovered the cowboy was already gone. Tate's sobs had subsided and he became aware for the first time of the lithe figure that was pressed so intimately against him.

Tate Whitelaw might be young, but she had the body

40

of a woman. He could feel the soft roundness of her breasts against his chest, and her feminine hips were fitted tight against his masculinity. His growing masculinity.

He tried shifting himself away, but her nose buried itself more deeply at his shoulder and she snuggled closer.

"Tate." He didn't recognize the voice as his own. He cleared his throat and tried again. "Tate."

"Hmm?"

If she didn't recognize the potential danger of the situation was he honor bound to point it out to her? She felt so good in his arms!

Before he could stop himself, his hands had tangled in her hair. He tugged and her head fell back. Her eyes were limpid pools of gold and green. Her face was flushed from crying. She had been gnawing on that lip again and it was swollen. He could see it needed soothing.

He lowered his head and caught her lower lip between his teeth, letting his tongue ride the length of it, testing the fullness of it.

Tate moaned and he was lost.

His tongue slipped into her mouth, tasting her, seeking solace for a desolation of spirit he had never admitted even to himself. Her whole body melted against him, and he was aware of an excruciatingly pleasurable heat in his groin where their bodies were fitted together. He spread his legs slightly and pulled her hard against him, then rubbed them together, creating a friction that turned molten coals to fire.

Tate was only aware of sensations. The softness of his lips. The slickness of his tongue. The heat and hardness of his body pressed tightly against hers. The surge of pleasure as his maleness sought out her femaleness. The urgency of his mouth as it found the smooth column of her neck and teased its way up to her ear, where his breath, hot and moist, made her shiver.

"Please, Adam," she gasped. "Please, don't stop."

Adam's head jerked up, and he stared at the woman in his arms. Good Lord in Heaven! What was he doing?

Adam had to reach behind him to free Tate's arms. He held her at arm's length, his hands gripping hers so tightly he saw her wince. He loosened his hold slightly, but didn't let go. If he did, he was liable to pull her back into his arms and finish what he had started.

Her eyes were lambent, her face rosy with the heat of passion. Her body was languid, boneless with desire, and it wouldn't take much to have her flat on her back beneath him.

Are you out of your mind? What's gotten into you? You're supposed to be protecting her from lechers, not seducing her yourself!

Tate could see Adam was distraught, but she hadn't the least notion why. "What's wrong?" she asked.

Her voice was still breathless and sounded sexy as hell! His body throbbed with need.

"I'll tell you what's wrong, *little girl!*" he retorted. "You may be hotter than a firecracker on the Fourth of July, but I'm not interested in initiating any virgins! Do you hear me? *Flat not interested!*"

"Could have fooled me!" Tate shot back.

Adam realized he was still holding her hands—was in fact rubbing his thumbs along her palms—and dropped them like hot potatoes. "You stay away from me, *little girl.* You're here for one reason, and one reason only—keeping books. You got that?"

"I got it, *big boy!*"

Adam started to reach for her but caught himself. He stalked over and let himself out of the stall. A moment later he was gone from the barn.

Tate curled her arms protectively around herself. What had happened to change things so quickly? One minute Adam had been making sweet, sweet love to her. The next he had become a raving lunatic. Oh, how it had stung when he called her *little girl!* She might be small in stature, but she was all grown up in every way that mattered.

Except for being a virgin.

Tate had to admit she was a babe in the woods when it came to sexual experience. But she recognized that what had just happened between her and Adam was something special. He had wanted her as much as she had wanted him. She couldn't be mistaken about that. But their attraction had been more than sexual. It was as though when she walked into his arms she had found a missing part of herself. And though Adam

43

might discount what had happened because she was so young, she wasn't going to let him get away with denying what had happened between them—to her or to himself.

She wasn't some *little girl* he could dismiss with a wave of his hand. Powerful forces were at work between them. Tate had to find a way to make Adam see her as a woman worthy of his love. But how best to accomplish that goal?

Because the physical attraction between them was so powerful, Tate decided she would start with that. She would put temptation in Adam's path and just see what happened.

Four

Adam watched Tate smiling up at the cowboys who surrounded her at the corral while she regaled them with another of her outrageous stories about life at Hawk's Way, as she had often done over the past three weeks. As usual, she was dressed in jeans, boots and a T-shirt with some equally outrageous slogan written on it.

Only this T-shirt had the neckline cut out so it slipped down to reveal one shoulder—and the obvious fact that she wasn't wearing a bra. Anyone with eyes in his head could see she was naked under the T-shirt. The three cowboys were sure as hell looking. The wind was blowing and the cotton clung to her, out-lining her generous breasts.

Adam told himself he wasn't going to make a fool out of himself by going over there and dragging her away from three sets of ogling male eyes. However, once his footsteps headed in that direction, he didn't seem to be able to stop them.

He arrived in time to hear her say, "My brothers taught me how to get even when some rabbit-shy horse bucks me off."

"How's that, Tate?" one of the cowboys asked.

"Why, I just make that horse walk back to the barn all by himself!" Tate said with a grin.

The cowboys guffawed, and Tate joined in. Adam caught his lip curling with laughter and straightened it back out.

"Don't you have some work to do?" he demanded of the three cowboys.

"Sure, Boss."

"Yeah, Boss."

"Just leaving, Boss."

They tipped their hats to Tate, but continued staring at her as they backed away.

Adam swore acidly, and they quickly turned tail and scattered in three different directions.

He directed a cool stare at Tate and said, "I thought I told you to stay away from my cowhands."

"I believe your exact words were, 'Finish your work before you go traipsing around the ranch,'" Tate replied in a drawl guaranteed to irritate her already irritated boss.

"Is your work done?"

"Had you been home for lunch, I'd have offered to show you the bookkeeping system I've set up. Everything's been logged in and all the current invoices have been paid. I have some suggestions for ways—"

He interrupted with, "What the hell are you doing out here half-dressed, carousing with the hired help?"

"*Carousing?* I was just *talking* to them!" Tate flashed back.

"I want you to leave those boys alone."

"Boys? They looked like grown men to me. Certainly old enough to make up their minds whether or not they want to spend time with me."

Adam grabbed the hat off his head and slapped it against his thigh. "Dammit, Tate. You're a babe in the

46

woods! You're playing with fire, and you're going to get burned! You can't run around here half naked and not expect—"

"Half naked?" she scoffed. "You've got to be kidding!"

"That T-shirt doesn't leave much to the imagination! I can see your nipples plain as day."

Tate looked down and realized for the first time that twin peaks were clearly visible beneath the T-shirt. She decided to brazen it out. "So what if you can? I assume you're familiar with the female anatomy. Besides, you're not my father or my brother. You have absolutely no right to tell me what to wear!"

Since the erotic feelings Adam was experiencing at the moment weren't the least fatherly or brotherly, he didn't argue with her. However, he had appointed himself her guardian in their stead. As such, he felt it his duty to point out to her the dangers of such provocative attire.

He explained in a reasonable voice, "When a man sees a woman looking like that, he just naturally gets ideas."

Tate looked sharply at Adam. "What kind of ideas?"

"The *wrong* kind," Adam said emphatically.

Tate smiled impishly and batted her lashes at him. "I thought you were 'flat not interested' in li'l ole me."

"Cut it out, Tate."

"Cut what out?"

"Stop batting those lashes at me, for one thing."

Tate pouted her lips like a child whose candy had

been taken away. "You mean it isn't working?"

It was working all right. Too damn well. She was just precocious enough to be charming. He was entranced despite his wish not to be. He felt his body begin to harden as she slid her gaze from his eyes, to his mouth, to his chest, and straight on down his body to his crotch. Which was putting on a pretty damn good show for her.

"You're asking for it," he said through clenched teeth.

She batted her eyelashes and said, "Am I going to get it?"

"That's it!"

The next thing Tate knew she had been hefted over Adam's shoulder like a sack of wheat, and he was striding toward the house.

"Let me down!" she cried. "Adam, this is uncomfortable."

"Serves you right! You haven't been the least worried about my comfort for the past three weeks."

"Where are you taking me? What are you planning to do with me?"

"Something I'm going to enjoy very much!"

Was Adam really going to make love to her? Would he be rough, or gentle? How was she supposed to act? Was there some sort of proper etiquette for the ravishing of virgins? Not that she had ever worried too much about what was proper. But she felt nervous, anxious about the encounter to come. Finally, Adam would have to acknowledge that greater forces were at

48

work between them than either of them could—or should—resist.

The air inside the adobe house hit her like a cooling zephyr. The dimness left her blind for an instant. Just as she was regaining her sight, they emerged once more into sunlight and she was blinded again. Several more strides and she felt herself being lowered from Adam's shoulder.

Tate barely had time to register the fact that they were in the courtyard when Adam shifted her crosswise in his arms. Grinning down into her face, he said "Maybe this will cool you off!" and unceremoniously dumped her into the pool of water that surrounded the fountain.

Tate came up spluttering. "Why you!" She blinked her eyes furiously, trying to clear the water from them.

"Why, Miss Tate, are you batting your eyelashes at me again? Guess I'll have to try another dunking."

He took one step toward her, and Tate retreated to the other side of the fountain. "I'll get you for this, you rogue! You roué!"

Adam laughed. It had been so long since he had done so, that the sound brought Maria to the kitchen window to see what Señor Adam found so funny. She shook her head and clucked when she saw the new bookkeeper standing dripping in the fountain. She grabbed a bath towel from the stack of laundry she was folding on the kitchen table and hurried outside with it.

She handed it to Adam and said in Spanish, "This is

49

no way to treat a young woman."

Adam's eyes crinkled at the corners with laughter. "It is when she's bent on seducing an older man."

Maria hissed in a breath and turned to eye the bedraggled creature in the pool. So that was the way the wind was blowing. Well, she was not one to stand in the way of any woman who could make Señor Adam laugh once more.

"Be sure you get the *señorita* dried off quickly. Otherwise she might catch a cold."

Maria left Adam standing with the towel in his hand and a smug grin on his face.

Once the housekeeper was gone, Adam turned back to Tate. And quickly lost his smirk. Because if the T-shirt had been revealing before, it was perfectly indecent now. He could easily see Tate's flesh through the soaked cotton. The cold water had caused her nipples to peak into tight buds.

His mouth felt dry. His voice was ragged as he said, "Here. Wrap yourself in this."

Only he didn't extend the towel to her. He held it so she would have to step out of the pool and into his arms. When he encircled her with the terry cloth she shivered and snuggled closer.

"I'm freezing!" she said.

He, on the other hand, was burning up. How did she do it to him? This time, however, he had only himself to blame. He felt her cold nose burrow into his shoulder as his chin nuzzled her damp hair. The water had released the lilac scent of her shampoo. He took a deep breath and realized he didn't want to let her go.

Adam vigorously rubbed the towel up and down Tate's back, hoping to dispel the intimacy of the moment.

"Mmm. That feels good," she murmured.

His body betrayed him again, responding with amazing rapidity to the throaty sound of her voice. He edged himself away from her, unwilling to admit his need to her. In fact, he felt the distinct necessity to deny it.

"I'm not going to make love to you, Tate."

She froze in his arms. Her head lifted from his shoulder, and he found himself looking into eyes that warmed him like brandy.

"Why not, Adam? Is it because I'm not attractive to you?"

"Lord, no! Of course you're a beautiful woman, but—" Adam groaned as he realized what he had just admitted.

"I am?"

What had those brothers of hers been telling her, Adam wondered, *to make her doubt herself like this?*

"Is it because I don't dress like a lady?"

His only objection to the clothes she wore was his reaction to her in them. "Contrary to what you might have heard, clothes *don't* make the man—or the woman."

"Then it must be the fact that I'm a virgin," she said.

Adam felt himself flushing. "Tate, you just don't go around talking about things like that."

51

"Not even with you?"

"*Especially* not with me!"

"Why not?"

They were back to that again. He turned her so he had an arm around her shoulder, and began ushering her across the courtyard to her bedroom. "I think it's time you got out of those wet clothes."

Tate's impish smile reappeared. "Would you like to help me?"

"Not on your life!" He opened the sliding glass door and gave her a nudge inside. "I'll meet you in the office in fifteen minutes and you can show me whatever bookkeeping wonders you've accomplished today." He turned and marched across the courtyard, fighting the urge to look back.

Once she was alone in her room, Tate let the towel drop. She stared at herself in the standing oval mirror in the corner and groaned. She looked like something the cat had dragged in! No wonder Adam hadn't been interested!

Tate sat down on a wooden chair to pull off her wet boots, then yanked her T-shirt off and struggled with the wet zipper of her jeans. She peeled her silk panties down and quickly began replacing her clothing with an identical wardrobe. All except the wet boots, for which she substituted a pair of beaded Indian moccasins Charlie One Horse had given her for Christmas.

While Tate dressed, she reviewed the events of the past three weeks since she had arrived at the Lazy S. Teasing Adam had begun as a way of making him admit the sexual attraction—and something more—that existed between them. But she had discovered that kidding some folks was like teasing a loaded polecat. The satisfaction was short-lived.

Tate hadn't been enjoying the game much these days, mainly because she had begun to suffer from the sexually charged situations as much as Adam. The problem was, on her side at least, her heart followed where her hormones lead.

She would give anything if Adam was as interested in her as Buck seemed to be. The lean-hipped cowboy had been asking her every day for a week if she would go out with him on Saturday night. Well, maybe she should. Maybe if Adam saw that somebody else found her worth pursuing, he would get the same idea.

Tate had a cheerful smile on her face by the time she joined Adam in his office. He already had the computer on and was perusing the statistics she had input there.

"So what do you think?" she asked, perching herself on the arm of the large swivel chair in which he was sitting.

"It looks good." Of course his office wasn't as neat as it had once been. There were half-filled coffee cups amidst the clutter on the desk, and a collection of magazines and a dirty T-shirt decorated the floor. A bridle and several other pieces of tack Tate was fixing were strewn around the room.

But he couldn't argue with what she had accomplished. Tate had set up a program to handle data on

53

each head of stock, providing a record that would be invaluable in making buying and selling decisions. "You didn't tell me you knew so much about computers."

Tate grinned and said, "You didn't ask." She leaned across him and began earnestly discussing other ideas she had regarding possible uses of the computer in his business.

He started automatically cleaning the debris from his desk.

"Don't worry about those," Tate said, taking a handful of pebbles from him. "Aren't they pretty? I found them down by the creek." She scattered them back onto the desk. "I play with them while I'm thinking, sort of like worry beads, you know?"

"Uh-huh."

Adam forced himself to concentrate on what she was saying, rather than the way her breast was pressed up against his arm. By the time she was done talking about the projects she had in mind, she had shifted position four times. He knew because she had managed to brush some part of his anatomy with some part of hers each time she moved.

Tate was totally oblivious to Adam's difficulty, because she was having her own problems concentrating on the matters at hand. She was busy planning how she could make Adam sit up and take notice of her by accepting Buck's invitation to go out tomorrow evening. She just had to make sure that Adam saw her leaving on the date with the auburn-haired cowboy.

54

Her thoughts must have conjured Buck, because he suddenly appeared at the door to Adam's office.

"Need you to take a look at that irrigation system to see whether you want it repaired or replaced," Buck said.

"I'll be right there," Adam replied.

Buck had already turned to leave when Tate realized she had the perfect opportunity to let Adam know she was going out with another man. "Oh, Buck."

Buck turned and the hat came off his head in the same motion. "Yes, ma'am?"

"I've decided to take you up on your offer to go dancing tomorrow night."

Buck's face split with an engaging grin. "Yes, ma'am! I'll pick you up at seven o'clock if that's all right, and we can have some dinner first."

The thunderous look on Adam's face was everything Tate could have wished for. "I'll see you at seven," she promised.

Buck slipped his hat back on his head and said, "You coming, Boss?"

"In a minute. I'll catch up to you."

Adam's fists landed on his hips as he turned to confront Tate. "What was that all about?"

"Buck asked me to go dancing at Knippa on Saturday night, and I thought it might be fun."

Adam couldn't very well forbid her going. As Tate had so pointedly noted, he wasn't related to her in the least. But he couldn't help having misgivings, either. There was no telling what Buck Magnesson's reaction would be if Tate subjected him to the same teasing sensuality that Adam had endured for the past three weeks. If Tate said "Please" Buck was damned likely to say "Thank you" and take what she offered.

Adam suddenly heard himself forbidding his sister Melanie from going out on a date with a boy he had thought a little wild. Heard himself telling Melanie that he knew better than she what was best for her. And remembered the awful consequences of his high-handedness. Adam didn't have to like the fact that Tate had decided to go out with Buck Magnesson. But if he didn't want to repeat the mistakes he had made with his younger sister, he had to put up with it.

"Have a good time with Buck tomorrow night," he said. Then he turned and walked out the door.

Tate frowned at Adam's back. That wasn't exactly the reaction she had been hoping for. Where was the jealousy? Where was the demand that she spend her time with him instead? Suddenly Tate wished she had thought things through a little more carefully. Agreeing to date Buck simply to make Adam realize what he was missing wasn't turning out at all as she had hoped.

She felt a little guilty that she had even considered using Buck to make Adam jealous. But since her plan had failed—quite miserably—she could at least enjoy the evening with Buck with a clear conscience.

Tate had gotten the broken water hose fixed on her '51 Chevy, and she used the pickup to drive the ninety miles east to San Antonio that afternoon to go shopping. She could have worn jeans to go dancing, but had decided that she owed it to Buck to show up for their date looking her best.

She found a pretty halter sundress that tied around the neck and had an almost nonexistent back. The bodice fit her like a glove and showed just a hint of décolletage. The bright yellow and white floral print contrasted with her dark hair and picked up the gold in her eyes. The mid-calf length skirt was gathered at the waist and flared at the hem. She whirled once in front of the mirror and saw that the dress was going to reveal a great deal of her legs if Buck was the kind of dancer who liked to twirl his partner a lot.

Buck's smile when she opened the door on Saturday night was well worth the effort spent shopping. She couldn't help feeling a stab of disappointment that Adam wasn't around to see her off. Apparently he had made plans of his own for the evening.

Tate found Buck surprisingly entertaining company. The cowboy had older brothers of his own, and Tate was quick to agree, "Nothing is harder to put up with than a good example!" He and Tate shared older brother horror stories that kept them both laughing through dinner.

The country and western band was in full swing when they crossed the threshold of the Grange Hall in Knippa. The room was fogged with cigarette smoke that battled with the overwhelming odor of sweat and cologne. The sawdusted dance floor was crowded, elbow to elbow, with men in cowboy hats partnered by ladies wearing flounced Western skirts and boots.

Just as they made their way to the dance floor, a two-step ended and the band began playing a waltz.

"Shall we?" Buck asked, making a dance frame with his arms.

"Absolutely!" Tate said, stepping into his embrace.

Tate got another welcome surprise when she and Buck began to waltz around the room. The lean cowboy was graceful on his feet. He led her into several intricate variations of the dance that left her breathless and feeling like a prima ballerina by the time the song ended.

"That was wonderful!" she exclaimed.

"Would you like something to drink?" Buck asked.

"Just a soda, please."

Buck found a seat for Tate at one of the small tables that surrounded the dance floor and forced his way through the crowd toward the bar.

Tate was tapping her foot to another two-step tune and enjoying watching the couples maneuver around the dance floor when she thought she saw someone she recognized. She followed the couple until they turned at the corner of the room.

Tate gasped aloud. It was Adam! He was dancing the two-step with a buxom redheaded woman.

As he passed by her table, Adam smiled and called out, "Hi, there! Having fun?"

Before she could answer, they had danced on past her, and she was left with the trill of the woman's laughter in her ears.

Tate felt sick. *Who was she?* The Redheaded Woman in Adam's arms was absolutely beautiful. No wonder Adam hadn't been interested in pursuing her when he was acquainted with such a gorgeous female.

"What's caught your eye?" Buck asked as he set a soda in front of Tate.

"Adam's here." She pointed him out. "See there. With that redhead."

To Tate's amazement, Buck scowled and swore under his breath.

"What's wrong?" she asked.

"Nothing I can do anything about."

"That's the sort of statement that's guaranteed to get a nosy female's attention," Tate said. "Out with it."

Buck grinned sheepishly and admitted, "All right. Here goes." He took a deep breath and said, "That woman dancing with Adam is my ex-wife."

"You're kidding!"

" 'Fraid not."

Tate watched Buck watching the Redheaded Woman. His feelings were painfully transparent. "You're still in love with her."

Buck grimaced. "Much good it'll do me."

"I assume Adam knows how you feel."

"He asked my permission before he took Velma out the first time."

"And you gave it to him?" Tate asked incredulously.

"She isn't my wife anymore. She can see whoever she pleases."

Tate snorted in disgust. "While you suffer in noble silence. Men!"

Tate had been so involved with talking to Buck that she hadn't realized the song was ending. She was less than pleased when Adam and Velma arrived at their table.

"Mind if we join you?" Adam asked.

Tate bit her lip to keep from saying something censorable. She slipped her arm through Buck's, put a gigantic smile on her face, and said, "Why sure! We'd love to have the company, wouldn't we, Buck?"

It was hard to say who was the more surprised by her performance, Buck or Adam. What she hadn't expected was the militant light that rose in Velma's green eyes when Tate claimed Buck's arm. Well, well, well. Maybe there was more here than met the eye.

Adam made introductions, then seated Velma and caught one of the few waitresses long enough to ask for two drinks.

"I didn't expect to see you here," Tate said to Adam.

"I enjoy dancing, and Velma's a great partner."

Tate could imagine what else Velma was great at. She had observed for herself that the redhead had a wonderful sense of rhythm.

Tate was aware of Buck sitting stiffly beside her, quieter than he had been at any time during the evening. How could Adam not be sensitive to the vibrations that arced across the table between the cowboy and his ex-wife?

In fact, Adam was imminently aware of how much

Buck Magnesson still loved his ex-wife. It was why he had brought Velma here this evening. Adam knew that with Velma in the room, Buck wasn't liable to spend much time thinking about Tate.

There was more than one way to skin a cat, Adam thought with satisfaction. He had known Tate would rebel against an ultimatum, so he hadn't protested her date with Buck. He had simply sought out a more subtle way to get what he wanted.

Bringing Velma to the dance seemed like the answer to his problem. He was pretty sure Velma was as much in love with Buck as the cowboy was with his ex-wife. He didn't mind playing Cupid, especially if it meant separating Tate from the virile young cowboy.

"How about trading partners?" Adam said, rising from his chair and reaching for Tate's hand.

Before Tate could protest, Buck said, "That sounds fine to me," took Velma by the hand and headed for the dance floor.

Tate wasn't sure what to make of Adam's ploy. She waited until they were half a dance floor away from the other couple before she said, "That was a pretty sneaky thing to do."

"I wanted to dance with you."

"Are you sure you aren't matchmaking?"

Adam smiled. "You could feel it, too?"

"I think he might still love her."

"I'm sure he does."

"Then why did you bring Velma here tonight?"

"I would think that's obvious."

61

"Not to me."

"I enjoy her company."

"Oh."

He grinned. "And I knew Buck would be here with you."

He sent her into a series of spins that prevented her from making any kind of retort. By the time she was in his arms again the song was over and he was ushering her back toward their table, where Buck and Velma were sitting across from each other arguing vociferously.

"Buck?" Tate didn't want to interrupt, but she wasn't sure whether she should leave him alone with Velma, either.

"Let's get out of here," Buck said, jumping up and turning his back on Velma. "Good night, Adam. I'll see you tomorrow."

As Buck hurried Tate away, she heard Velma say, "I'd like to go home now, Adam. If that's all right with you?"

Tate wasn't sure where Buck was taking her when he burned rubber on the asphalt parking lot. It was a safe guess from the dark look on his face that he had no romantic intentions toward her.

"Want to talk about it?" she asked at last.

Buck glanced quickly at her, then turned his eyes back to the road. "I don't want to bother you with my problems."

"I'm a good listener."

He sighed and said, "Velma and I were high school

sweethearts. We married as soon as we graduated. Pretty soon Velma began to think she had missed something. She had an affair."

Tate bit her lip to keep from saying something judgmental. She was glad she had when Buck continued.

"I found out about it and confronted her. She asked for a divorce, and I gave it to her."

"Why?"

"Pride. Foolish damn pride!"

"And you regret it now?"

"My life's been running kind of muddy without her."

"So why don't you do something about it?" Tate asked.

"It's no use. She says that I deserve better. She doesn't believe I can ever forgive or forget what she did."

"Can you?"

The cowboy's eyes were bleak in the light from the dash. "I think so."

"But you're not sure?"

A muscle worked in his jaw. "If I were, I'd have her back home and under me faster than chain lightning with a link snapped!"

Tate had thought they were driving without direction, yet she realized suddenly that they had arrived back at the front door of Adam's house. She saw Adam's truck parked there. So, he was home. And there was a light on in the living room.

She let herself out of the truck, but Buck met her on

the front porch. He put an arm around her waist and walked her away from the light.

"May I kiss you good night, Tate?"

Tate drew a breath and held it. This was so exactly like the scene she had played out the night she had left home that it was eerie. Only there were no brothers here to protect her from the big, bad wolf.

"Of course you can kiss me good night," she said at last.

Buck took his time, and Tate was aware of the sweetness of his kiss. And the reluctance in it. When he lifted his head their eyes met, and they smiled at each other.

"No go, huh?" he said.

Tate shook her head. "I like you an awful lot, Buck. I hope we can be friends."

"I'd like that," the cowboy said.

He leaned down and kissed her again. Both of them knew how much—and how little—it meant.

However, it was not so clear to the man watching them through a slit in the living room curtains.

Five

It had taken every ounce of willpower Adam possessed to keep from stalking out onto the front porch and putting his fist in Buck Magnesson's nose. It wasn't just the thought of his sister Melanie that kept him from doing it. There were things he couldn't offer Tate that Buck could.

But he wasn't a saint or a eunuch. If Tate persisted in tempting him, he wasn't noble enough to refuse her. He was determined to keep his hunger leashed at least until he was certain Tate knew what she *wouldn't* be getting if she got involved with him. She was too young to give up her dreams. And there was no way he could fulfill them.

Before Adam had time to examine his feelings further, the front door opened. Tate stepped inside to find him sitting in one of the large Mediterranean chairs before the blackened fireplace, nursing a half-empty glass of whiskey.

"Hello," she said. "I didn't expect to see you again tonight."

"I was waiting up for you."

Tate immediately bristled. "Look, I don't need a caretaker." She wanted a lover. But not just that. A man who loved her, as she was beginning to fear she loved him.

"Old habits die hard."

"What's that supposed to mean?"

65

"I used to wait up for my sister Melanie."

"You have a sister? Why haven't I met her?"

"She died ten years ago."

"I'm so sorry."

Adam had drunk just enough whiskey to want to tell her the rest of it. "Melanie ran away from home when she was seventeen. She was picked up by a stranger while hitchhiking. He raped her, and then he stabbed her to death."

"That must have been awful for you!" Tate wanted to put her arms around Adam to comfort him, but his body language posted obvious No Trespassing signs.

She used sitting on the couch as an excuse to cross closer to him, slipped off her boots and pulled her feet up under her. She folded her arms under her breasts to give herself the comfort he wouldn't accept.

Then another, more troubling thought occurred to her. "Is that why you picked me up on the road? Because of your sister?"

Adam nodded.

Tate felt as though she'd been physically struck. She hesitated and asked, "Is that why you offered me a job?"

"It seemed like a good idea at the time."

Tate swallowed over the lump that had grown in her throat. "So I'm just a charity case to you?"

Adam heard the pain in Tate's voice and realized he had handled this all wrong. If he didn't do some fast talking, he knew she would be gone by morning. "You can hardly blame me for offering help under the circumstances, can you? I couldn't take the chance that I might be responsible for another young woman's death!"

Tate wasn't so wrapped up in her own feelings that she failed to recognize the significance of what Adam had just said. "How can you blame yourself for your sister's death? What happened couldn't possibly be your fault!"

"Oh, no?" Adam's nostrils were pinched, his blue eyes like shards of ice. "Didn't you tell me that you left home because your brothers made your life miserable?"

"They only did what they did because they love me!" Tate protested.

"So that makes it all right for them to interfere in your life? To aggravate you enough to send you running in that old rattletrap truck?"

It was clear Adam was searching for answers that would release him from the guilt he suffered over what had happened to his sister. Tate found herself equally confounded by the issues he had raised. Was love a good enough excuse for the high-handed way Garth and Faron had acted? What if she had met the same fate as Adam's sister? Would they have blamed themselves for her death?

She knew they would have, just as Adam had blamed himself for Melanie's death all these years. She didn't know what to say to ease his pain. She only knew she had to do something.

Tate stood and crossed to Adam. She knelt on the

cool tile floor at his feet and laid a hand on his thigh. She felt him tense beneath her touch. "Adam, I—"

He rose abruptly and stalked away from her. "I'm not in the mood for any teasing tonight."

"I was trying to offer comfort!" Tate retorted.

"Just stay away from me!"

Tate struck back like the scorned woman she felt herself to be. "There are plenty of others who'll welcome my attentions!"

"Like Buck?"

"Like Buck!" That was a lie, but told in a good cause. Saving her pride seemed of utmost importance right now.

"He'll never marry you. He's still in love with Velma."

Since Tate knew he was right, she retorted, "I don't have to marry a man to go to bed with him!"

"Is that so, *little girl?*"

Tate was gasping, she was so furious at the taunting words. But it was clear she could cut her own throat with a sharp tongue. She had certainly dug a hole for herself it was going to be hard to get out of. She took two deep breaths, trying to regain her temper.

Adam didn't give her a chance to speak before he said, "If you're smart, you'll go back home where you belong. Now, before you get hurt."

"Are you firing me?"

Tate held her breath until he said, "No."

"Then I'm staying. If you'll excuse me, I'm tired. I want to go to bed."

Tate had started for the door when Adam quipped, "What, no invitation to join you?"

Tate slowly turned back to face him. She took her time getting from where she was to where he was. She hooked a finger into the opening at the neck of his shirt and looked up into eyes that were both wary and amused.

"I learned at my brothers' knees never to approach a bull from the front, a horse from the rear . . . or a damn fool from any direction. Good night, Adam."

"We'll talk about this again tomorrow," he said to her retreating back.

"Like hell we will!" she replied.

Tate spent a restless night, tossing and turning as her mind grappled with all of Adam's revelations. What she found most disturbing was the possibility that Adam had merely been tolerating her because he felt responsible for her welfare.

Surely she couldn't have been mistaken about his physical reaction to her! More likely, he was attracted to her, but his feelings of responsibility toward her were keeping him from pursuing a relationship. If so, she would soon cure him of that!

Tate felt somewhat cheered by her decision, and she made up her mind to confront Adam at breakfast. Only, when she arrived in the kitchen the next morning, she discovered that he had already eaten and left the house.

"Did he say where he was going, Maria?"

"No, *señorita*."

Tate worked hard all day in the office so she wouldn't have time to worry about where Adam had gone. He was bound to turn up sooner or later. He wasn't going anywhere. And neither was she.

However, by seven o'clock that evening there was still no sign of Adam. He hadn't even called Maria to say he wouldn't be home for dinner. Maria was washing up the dinner dishes, and to keep herself busy, Tate was drying them and putting them away. Maria had tried to start a conversation, but Tate was too distracted to keep track of what she was saying. Finally Maria gave up trying and left Tate to her thoughts.

Tate was worried. Where could Adam have gone? She had already checked once at the bunkhouse, but no one had seen him all day.

When she heard a knock at the kitchen door, Tate leaped to answer it. It wasn't until she opened the door that she realized Adam wouldn't have knocked.

"Buck! You look terrible. What's wrong?"

Buck pulled his hat off his head and wiped the sweat from his brow with his sleeve. "Um, I, um."

She put a hand on his arm and urged him inside the room. "Come in. Sit down."

He resisted her efforts to move him from his spot just inside the kitchen door. "No, I—"

"You what?" Tate asked in exasperation.

"I need your help."

"Of course, anything."

"Maybe you better not say yes until you hear what I

70

have to say." He eyed Maria, but was too polite to ask her to leave.

Aware of the tension in the cowboy, Maria said, "I give you some time alone, so you can talk," and left the room. But she made up her mind she wouldn't be gone for long. The nice *señorita,* she was good for Señor Adam. It would not do to let cowboys like Buck Magnesson take what should not be theirs.

Tate turned a kitchen chair and sat in it like a saddle. "I'm all ears."

Buck fidgeted with the brim of his hat another moment before he said, "I've thought a lot about our conversation last night. You know, about whether or not I could forgive and forget what Velma did? And, well . . . I believe I can."

A smile spread on Tate's face. "I'm so glad, Buck."

"Yeah, well, that's why I need your help. I've decided to go see Velma and tell her how I feel, and I thought maybe if you were along to sort of referee—"

Tate was up and across the room in an instant. She gave the startled cowboy a big hug. "It'll be my pleasure. When would you like to go see her?"

Buck grinned. "Is right now too soon?"

Tate thought about leaving a note for Adam, then rejected the idea. It would do him good to know how it felt to worry about someone who didn't leave a message where he was going!

Maria heard the kitchen door slam closed and came back in to see what Señor Buck had wanted. She frowned and clucked her tongue in dismay when she

71

realized that Señorita Tate had left the house with the handsome cowboy. "Señor Adam will not like this. He will not like this at all."

Maria made up her mind to stay until Señor Adam got back from wherever he had gone and tell him what had happened. Then he could go find the *señorita* and bring her home where she belonged.

Meanwhile, Buck drove Tate to a tiny house with gingerbread trim in a quiet neighborhood off Main Street in Uvalde. She waited anxiously with him to see if Velma was going to answer the doorbell.

Tate saw the light in Velma's green eyes when she saw Buck, and watched it die when she realized Tate was with him.

"I want to talk to you, Velma," Buck said.

"I don't think we have anything to say to each other." She nearly had the door closed when Buck stuck his boot in it.

"I'm not leaving until I say my piece," Buck insisted in a harsh voice.

"I'll call the police if you don't go away," Velma threatened.

"I just want to talk!"

When Velma let go of the door to run for the phone, Buck and Tate took advantage of the opportunity to come inside. Buck caught Velma in the kitchen and pried the phone receiver out of her hand.

"Please, baby, just listen to me," he pleaded.

"Please give him a chance, Velma. I know you're going to want to hear what Buck has to say."

72

Velma froze when she heard Tate's voice. "Why did you come here?" she demanded.

"Buck thought it might make it easier for the two of you to talk if there was someone else here to sort of mediate."

Velma looked at Buck's somber face. She took a deep breath and said, "All right. I'll listen to what you have to say. For five minutes."

Buck set her down, letting her body slide along his as he did. Tate could have lit a fire from the sparks that flew between them. They belonged together, all right. She only hoped Buck would find the right words to convince Velma he meant what he said.

Five minutes later, Velma was still listening, but Tate could see she was torn between the fervent wish to believe Buck, and the awful fear that he would soon regret what he was saying.

"I don't think I'll ever forget what happened, Velma," Buck said. "But I think I can live with it."

That wasn't exactly the same thing as *forgiving* it, Tate realized. Apparently Velma also noticed the distinction.

"That's not good enough, Buck," she said in a quiet voice.

"I love you, Velma," he said.

She choked on a sob. "I know, Buck. I love you, too."

"Then why can't we get back together?"

"It just wouldn't work."

By now Velma was crying in earnest, and Buck

73

would have been heartless indeed if he could have resisted pulling her into his arms to comfort her. In fact, that was just what he did.

Tate suddenly realized another reason why she had been brought along. Her presence provided the only restraint on the sexual explosion that occurred whenever the two of them touched. Even that wasn't sufficient at first.

Buck already had his fingers twined in Velma's red curls, and Velma had her hand on the front of Buck's jeans when Tate cleared her throat loudly to remind them that she was still there. They broke apart like two teenagers caught necking, their faces flushed as much by embarrassment as by passion.

"Uh, sorry," Buck said.

Velma tried rearranging her hair, a hopeless task considering how badly Buck had messed it up.

"You look fine, honey," Buck said, taking a hand at smoothing her tresses himself. But the gesture turned into a caress, which turned into a fervent look of desire, which ended when Buck's lips lowered to Velma's in the gentlest of kisses.

There was no telling where things might have gone from there, except Tate said, "All right, enough is enough! We'll never get anywhere this way. Buck, you go sit over there in that chair. Velma and I will sit on the couch."

Sheepishly, Buck crossed the room and slouched down in the chair Tate had indicated. Tate joined Velma on the couch. She dragged her T-shirt out of her jeans and used it to dab at Velma's tears.

"Now it seems to me," Tate began, "that you both want to give this relationship another try. So I have a suggestion."

Tate outlined for them a plan whereby they would start from scratch. Buck would pick Velma up at her door, they would go out together and he would return her at the end of the evening. Absolutely no sex.

"You have to learn to trust each other again," she said. "That takes time."

Buck's face had taken on a mulish cast. "I'm not sure I can play by those rules. Especially that 'no sex' part."

It wasn't hard to see why. The sexual electricity between them would have killed a normal person.

"No sex," Tate insisted. "If you spend all your time in bed, you won't do as much talking. And you both have a lot you need to talk about."

Tate chewed anxiously on her lower lip while she waited to see whether they would accept her suggestion.

"I think Tate's right," Velma said.

The negotiations didn't end there. In fact it wasn't until the wee hours of the morning that all parties were satisfied. Tate felt as emotionally exhausted as she knew Buck and Velma were. The hug Velma gave her as she was leaving, and the whispered "Thank you" from the other woman, made everything worthwhile.

Tate rubbed the tense muscles in her neck as Buck drove her back to the ranch. She knew Buck was still troubled, but at least now there was some hope that he and his ex-wife might one day end up together again.

When they arrived at the front door to Adam's house, Buck took Tate's hand in his and said, "I don't know how to thank you."

"Just be good to Velma. That'll be thanks enough for me."

He ruffled her hair as an older brother might, then leaned over and kissed her on the cheek. "You're a good friend, Tate. If I can ever do anything for you, just let me know."

"I'll remember that," Tate said. "You don't need to get out. I can let myself in."

Buck waited until she was inside the front door before he drove his truck around to the bunkhouse.

Tate had only taken two steps when the living room lights clicked on. Adam stood at the switch, his face a granite mask of displeasure.

"Where were you?" Tate accused. "I waited for you for hours, but you never came home!"

Adam was taken aback, since he had intended to ask the same question. "Dr. Kowalski had a medical emergency with one of my former patients. Susan asked me to come because Mrs. Daniels was frightened, and she thought the old lady would respond better if I was there."

"I knew it had to be something important," Tate said with a sigh of relief. "Were you able to help?"

"Yes, Mrs. Daniels is out of danger now."

Adam suddenly realized that Tate had completely

distracted him from the confrontation he had planned. His eyes narrowed as he tried to decide whether she had done it on purpose.

"Where have you been all night?" he asked in a cool voice. "Do you realize it's four a.m.?"

"Is it really that late? I mean, that early," Tate said with a laugh. "I was out with Buck. Oh, Adam—"

He cut her off with a snarl of disgust as she confirmed his worst suspicions. "I don't suppose I have to ask what you were doing, *little girl*. If you were that anxious to lose your virginity you should have told me. You didn't have to drag Buck into the picture."

Tate was aghast. "You think Buck and I—"

"What am I supposed to think when you come rolling in at this ungodly hour of the morning with your T-shirt hanging out and your hair mussed up and your lower lip swollen like it's been bitten a dozen times."

"There's a perfectly logical—"

"I don't want to hear any excuses! Do you deny that you spent the night with Buck?"

"No, but something wonderful happened—"

"I don't want to hear the gory details!"

He was shouting by now, and Tate knew that if she had been any closer Adam might not have been able to control the visible anger that shook his body.

"Get out of my sight!" he said in hard, quiet voice. "Before I do something I'll regret."

Tate put her chin up. If this *fool* would give her a chance, she could explain everything! But her pride goaded her to remain silent. Adam was neither father nor brother. Yet he seemed determined to fill the role of protector. She felt the tears that threatened. Why couldn't he see that she only had eyes for one man— and that man was him!

"Some folks can't see any farther than the steam from their own pot of stew." With that pronouncement, she turned and stalked from the room.

Once Tate was gone, Adam swore a blue streak. When he was done, he felt worse instead of better. He had hoped he was wrong about what Tate and Buck had been doing out so late. He had been stunned when Tate hadn't denied losing her virginity to the cowboy. He felt absolute, uncontrollable rage at the thought of some other man touching her in ways he knew she had never been touched. And the thought that she had found it *wonderful* caused an unbearable tightness in his chest.

He tried to tell himself that what had happened was for the best. He was not a whole man. She deserved more. But nothing he said to himself took away the bitter taste in his mouth. She was his. She belonged to him.

And by God, now that her virginity was no longer an impediment, he would have her.

Six

Suddenly it was Adam who became the pursuer and Tate who proved elusive. She gave him the cold shoulder whenever she met him and made a point of smiling and recklessly flirting with Buck. Because of the way Buck's courtship was prospering with Velma, he had the look of a happy, well-satisfied man. Which left Adam seething with jealousy.

Tate suspected she could lift the thundercloud that followed Adam around if she simply told him the truth about what she had been doing the night she had spent with Buck. But she was determined that Adam would be the one to make the first move toward conciliation. All he had done for the past week was glare daggers at her.

However, there was more than anger reflected in his gaze, more than antagonism in his attitude toward her. Tate was beginning to feel frazzled by the unspoken sexual tension that sizzled between them. Something had changed since the night they had argued, and Tate felt the hairs lift on her arms whenever Adam was around. His look was hungry. His body radiated leashed power. His features were harsh with unsatisfied need. She had the uneasy feeling he was stalking her.

Tate escaped into the office by day, and played mediator for Buck and Velma at night. She refused to admit that she was hiding from Adam, but that was the case. His eyes followed her whenever they were in the same room together, and she knew he must be aware of her reaction to his disconcerting gaze.

Exactly one week from the day Tate had accompanied Buck on his pivotal visit to Velma, the cowboy took Tate aside and asked whether she minded staying home that evening instead of joining them as chaperon.

"There are some things I'd like to discuss with Velma alone," Buck said.

"Why sure," Tate replied with a forced smile. "I don't mind at all."

Once Buck was gone, Tate's smile flattened into a somber line. She was more than a little worried about what Adam might do if he found out she was home for the evening. She decided the best plan was to avoid him by staying in her room. It was the coward's way out, but her brothers had taught her that sometimes it was best to play your cards close to your belly.

Tate quickly found herself bored within the confines of her bedroom. She remembered that there was some work she could do in the office—if only she could get there without being detected by Adam. The light was on in his bedroom across the courtyard. Adam often retired early and did his reading—both ranch and medical journals—in bed.

She was already dressed for sleep in a long pink T-shirt, but it covered her practically to the knees. She decided it was modest enough even for Adam should he find her working late in the office. She tiptoed barefoot across the tiled courtyard, which was lit by both moon and stars, slipped into Adam's wing of the house via a door at the far end, and sneaked down the hall to the office.

It could have been an hour later, or two, when Tate suddenly felt the hairs prickle on her arms. She had long since finished working at the computer. Because the chair in front of the desk was more comfortable than the one behind it—which was as straight-backed and rigid as the man who usually sat there—she had plopped down in it to look over the printout of what she had done. She had one ankle balanced on the front of the desk and the other hooked on the opposite knee.

She glanced up and found herself ensnared by the look of desire in Adam's heavy-lidded blue eyes.

"Working late?" he asked in a silky voice.

"I thought I'd finish a few things."

Tate was frozen, unable to move, uncomfortably aware that her long T-shirt had rucked up around her thighs, and that her legs were bare all the way up to yonder. As Adam stared intently at her, she felt her nipples harden into dark buds easily visible beneath the pink cotton.

Adam's chest was bare, revealing dark curls that arrowed down into his Levi's. His jeans seemed to be hanging on his hipbones. His belly was ribbed with muscle, and a faint sheen of perspiration made his skin glow in the light from the single standing lamp.

Adam was no less disconcerted by Tate's appearance. He had come to his office looking for a ranch journal and found a sultry sex kitten instead. His view of Tate's French-cut panties was wreaking havoc with his self-control. Her crow-black hair was tousled, and her whiskey-colored eyes were dark with feminine allure.

"You ought to know better than to come here half dressed," Adam said.

"I wasn't expecting to see you."

One black brow arched disbelievingly. "Weren't you?"

Adam abruptly swept the desk clear of debris with one hand while he reached for Tate with the other. Papers flew in the air, cups shattered, Tate's handful of pebbles pinged as they shot across the tile floor. The last paper hadn't landed, nor the pinging sound faded, when he set her down hard on the edge of the desk facing him.

Tate's frightened protest died on her lips. Adam's fierce blue eyes never left hers as he spread her legs and stepped between them. He yanked her toward him, fitting the thin silk of her panties snugly against the heat and hardness of his arousal.

"Is this what you had in mind?" he demanded.

"Adam, I—"

She gasped as rough hands smoothed the cotton over her breasts, revealing nipples that ached for his touch.

"Adam—"

"You've been teasing me for weeks, *little girl*. Even I have my limits. You're finally going to get what you've been asking for."

"Adam—"

"Shut up, Tate."

He seized both her hands in one of his and thrust his fingers into the hair at her nape to hold her captive for his kiss.

Tate didn't dare breathe as Adam lowered his head to hers. Her body was alive with anticipation. Though she had wanted this ever since she had first laid eyes on Adam, she was still a little afraid of what was to come. She wanted this man, and she was certain now that he wanted her. Tonight she would know what it meant to be a woman, to be Adam's woman. The waiting was over at last.

Adam's anger at finding what he considered a sensual trap in his office made him more forceful with Tate than he had intended. But after all, she was no longer the tender, inexperienced virgin of a week ago.

However, somewhere between the moment he laced his hand into her hair and the instant his lips reached hers, his feelings underwent a violent transformation. Powerful emotions were at work, soothing the savage beast. When they finally kissed, there was nothing in his touch beyond the fierce need for her that thrummed through his body.

Tate was unprepared for the velvety softness of Adam's lips as he slid his mouth across hers. His teeth found her lower lip, and she shivered as he nipped it and then soothed the hurt. His tongue teased her, slipping inside, then retreating until she sought it out and discovered the taste of him. Dark and distinctive and uniquely male.

Tate was lost in sensation as each kiss was answered

by a streak of desire that found its way to her belly. Her breasts felt full and achy, yet she was too inexperienced to ask for the touch that would have satisfied her body's yearning.

Sometime while she was being kissed, Adam had released her hands. Tate wasn't quite sure what to do with them. She sought out his shoulders, then slid her hands down his back, feeling the corded muscle and sinew that made him so different from her.

Her head fell back as Adam's mouth caressed the hollow in her throat. The male hands at her waist slowly slid up under her T-shirt until Adam was cupping her breasts. Tate gasped as his thumbs brushed across the aching crests. Her body seemed alive to the barest touch of his callused fingertips.

"I want to feel you against me," Adam said as he slipped the pink T-shirt off over her head.

Before Tate could feel embarrassed, his arms slid around her.

He sighed with satisfaction as he hugged her to him. "You feel so good," he murmured against her throat.

Tate's breasts were excruciatingly sensitive to the wiry texture of Adam's chest hair. She was intimately aware of his strength, of her own softness.

Adam grasped her thighs and pulled her more snugly against him. She clutched his shoulders and held on as his maleness pressed against her femininity, evoking feelings that were foreign, yet which coaxed an instinctive response.

A guttural groan escaped Adam as Tate arched her

84

body into his. His hands dug into her buttocks, trying to hold her still.

"You're killing me, sweetheart," he said. "Don't move!"

"But it feels good," Tate protested.

Adam half groaned, half laughed. "Too good," he agreed. "Be still. I want to be sure you enjoy this as much as I do."

"Oh, I will," Tate assured him.

Adam chuckled as he slid his mouth down her throat. He captured a nipple in his mouth, sucked on it, teased it with his tongue, then sucked again, until Tate was writhing with pleasure in his arms.

He took one of her hands and slid it along the hard ridge in his jeans, too wrapped up in the pleasure of the moment to notice her virginal reluctance to touch him. "Feel what you do to me," he said. "I only have to look at you, think about you, and I want you!" His chin rested at her temple, and he was aware of the faint scent of lilacs. He would always think of her from now on when he smelled that particular fragrance.

It didn't take Tate long to realize how sensitive Adam was to her barest touch, and she reveled in her newfound feminine power.

When he could stand the pleasure no longer, Adam brought each of Tate's hands to his mouth, kissed her wrists and her palms, then placed her hands flat on his chest. "Lift your hips, sweetheart," Adam murmured as he tucked his thumbs into her bikini panties.

She did as he asked, and an instant later Tate was

naked. She hid her face in his shoulder, suddenly shy with him.

Adam's arms slipped around her. "There's no need to be embarrassed, sweetheart," he teased.

"That's easy to say when you've got clothes on," she retorted.

Adam laughed. "That can be easily remedied."

He reached between them and unsnapped his jeans. The harsh rasp of the zipper filled a silence broken only by the sound of her labored breathing, and his.

Tate grabbed Adam's wrist to keep him from pulling his zipper down any more. "Not yet," she said breathlessly.

She couldn't help the nerves that assailed her. Adam seemed to think she knew what to do, and perhaps she had led him to believe it was so, but she was all too aware of her ignorance—and innocence.

He dragged the zipper back up but left the snap undone. "There's no hurry, sweetheart. We have all night."

Tate shivered—as much from a virgin's qualms as from anticipation—at the thought.

Adam settled her hands at his waist and lifted his own to gently cup her face. He angled her chin so that she was looking up at him. "You're so damn beautiful!" he said.

"Your eyes." He kissed them closed.

"Your nose." He cherished the tip of it.

"Your cheeks." He gave each one an accolade.

"Your chin." He nipped it with his teeth.

"Your mouth."

Tate's eyes had slipped closed as Adam began his reverent seduction. She waited with bated breath for the kiss that didn't come. Suddenly she felt herself being lifted into his arms. Her eyes flashed open in alarm.

"Adam! What are you doing? Where are we going?"

He was already halfway down the hall to his room when he said, "I want the pleasure of making love to you for the first time in my own bed."

Tate had peeked into Adam's bedroom, but she had never been invited inside. It was decorated in warm earth tones, sandy browns and cinnamon. She had remembered being awed by the sheer size of his bed. The antique headboard was an intricately carved masterpiece, and the spindles at head and foot nearly reached to the ten-foot ceiling.

The quilt that covered the bed was an intricate box design Tate had never seen before, but the craftsmanship was exquisite. Tate grabbed Adam around the neck to keep from falling when he reached down to yank the quilt aside, revealing pristine white sheets.

"Now we can relax and enjoy ourselves," he said.

Adam laid her on the bed and in the same motion used his body to mantle hers. He nudged her legs apart with his knees and settled himself against her so that she was left in no doubt as to the reason he had brought her here.

"Where did you get this bed?" Tate asked, postponing the moment of ultimate truth.

"It's a family heirloom. Several generations of my

87

ancestors have been conceived and born here."

But not my own, Adam thought. *Never my own.*

Tate felt the sudden tension in his body. "Adam?"

Adam's features hardened as he recalled what had happened over the past week to cause him to be here now with Tate. She had made her choice. And he had made his. He wanted her, and she was willing. That was all that mattered now.

Adam's kiss was fierce, and Tate was caught up in the roughness of his lovemaking. There was nothing brutal about his caresses, but they were not gentle, either. His kisses were fervent, his passion unbridled, as he drove her ruthlessly toward a goal she could only imagine.

Tate was hardly aware when Adam freed himself of his clothes. She was so lost in new sensations that the feel of his hard naked body against hers was but one of many delights. The feel of his hands . . . *there.* The feel of his lips and tongue . . . *there.*

Tate was in ecstasy bordering on pain. She reached with trembling hands for whatever part of Adam she could find with her hands and her mouth.

"Adam, please!" She didn't know what she wanted, only that she desperately needed . . . *something.* Her body arched toward his, wild with need.

Just as Adam lifted her hips for his thrust, she cried, "Wait!" But it was already too late.

Adam's face paled as he realized what he had done.

Tate's fingernails bit into his shoulder, and she clamped her teeth on her lower lip to keep from crying out. Tears of pain pooled in the corners of her eyes.

Adam felt her muscles clench involuntarily around him and struggled not to move, fearing he would hurt her more. "You didn't sleep with Buck," he said in a flat voice.

"No," she whispered.

"You were still a virgin."

"Yes," she whispered.

"Why did you make me think— Dammit to hell, Tate! I would have done things differently if I'd known. I wouldn't have—"

He started to pull out of her, but she clutched at his shoulders. "Please, Adam. It's done now. Make love to me."

Tate lifted her hips, causing Adam to grunt with pleasure.

Now that he knew how inexperienced she was, Adam tried to be gentle. But Tate took matters out of his hands, touching him in places that sent his pulse through the roof, taunting him with her mouth and hands, until his thrust was almost savage. He brought them both to a climax so powerful that it left them gasping.

Adam slid to Tate's side and folded her in his embrace. He reached down to pull the covers over them and saw the blood on the sheet that testified to her innocence.

It made him angry all over again.

"I hope you're pleased with yourself!"

"Yes, I am."

"Don't expect an offer of marriage, because you're not going to get it," he said bluntly.

Tate fumbled for a sheet to cover herself. She sat up and stared at Adam with wary eyes. "I don't think I expected any such thing."

"No? What about all those dreams of yours— meeting the right man, having a nice home and a gaggle of children playing at your feet?"

"Geese come in a gaggle," she corrected. "And for your information, I don't think my dream is the least bit unreasonable."

"It is if you have me pictured in the role of Prince Charming."

Tate flushed. She toyed with the sheet, arranging it to cover her naked flank.

Adam watched with regret as her tempting flesh disappeared from view. "Well, Tate?"

She looked into eyes still darkened with passion and said with all the tenderness she felt for him, "I love you, Adam."

"That was lust, not love."

Tate winced at the vehemence with which he denied the rightness of what had just happened between them.

"Besides," he added, "I like my women a little more experienced."

Adam did nothing to temper the pain he saw in Tate's face at his brutal rejection of her. He couldn't give her what she wanted, and he refused to risk the pain and humiliation of having her reject what little he could offer.

"If what you want is sex, I'm available," he said. "But I'm not in love with you, Tate. And I won't pretend I am."

Tate fought the tears that threatened. She would be *damned* if she would let him see how devastated she was by his refusal to acknowledge the beautiful experience they had shared.

"It wasn't just sex, Adam," she said. "You're only fooling yourself if you think it was."

His lips curled sardonically. "When you've had a little more experience you'll realize that any man can do the same thing for you."

"Even Buck?" she taunted.

A muscle jumped in Adam's jaw. She knew all the right buttons to push where he was concerned. "You get the hankering for a little sex, you come see *me*," he drawled. "*I'll* make sure you're satisfied, *little girl*."

Tate pulled the sheet free of the mattress and wrapped it around herself as best she could. "Good night, Adam. I think I'll sleep better in my own bed."

He watched her go without saying another word. The instant she was gone he pounded a fist into the mattress.

"Damn you, Tate Whitelaw!"

She had made him wish for something he could never have. She had offered him the moon and the stars. All he had to do was bare his soul to her. And take the heart-wrenching chance that she would reject what little he could offer in return.

Seven

The tears Tate had refused to let Adam see her shed fell with a vengeance once she was alone. But she hadn't been raised to give up or give in. Before long Tate had brushed the tears aside and begun to plan how best to make Adam eat his words.

If Adam hadn't cared for her at least a little, Tate reasoned, he wouldn't have been so upset by her taunt that she would seek out Buck. She was certain that Adam's jealousy could be a powerful weapon in her battle to convince him that they belonged together. Especially since Adam had admitted that he was willing to take extreme measures—even making love to her!—to keep her away from Buck. Tate intended to seek Buck out and let the green-eyed monster eat Adam alive.

It was with some distress and consternation that Tate realized over the next several days that Adam had somehow turned the tables on her. He was the one who found excuses to send her off alone with Buck. And he did it with a smile on his face.

Where was the green-eyed monster? Was it possible Adam really *didn't* care? He was obviously pushing her in Buck's direction. Was this some sort of test? Did he expect her to fall into Buck's arms? Did he *want* her to?

If Tate was unsure of Adam's intentions, he was no less confused himself. He had woken up the morning after making love to Tate and realized that somewhere between the moment she had first flashed that gamine smile at him and the moment he had claimed her with his body, he had fallen in love with her. It was an appalling realization, coming, as it had, after he had insulted and rejected her.

Loving Tate meant being willing to do what was best for her—even if it meant giving her up. He had made the selflessly noble—if absurd—decision that if, after the way he had treated her, she would rather be with Buck, he would not stand in her way. So he had made excuses for them to be alone together. And suffered the agonies of the damned, wondering whether Buck was taking advantage of the time to make love to her.

One or the other of them might have relented and honestly admitted their feelings, but they weren't given the chance before circumstances caused the tension-fraught situation to explode.

Adam had gritted his teeth and nobly sent Tate off with Buck to the Saturday night dance at the Grange Hall in Knippa, not realizing that they were stopping to pick up Velma on the way.

Tate didn't lack for partners at the dance, but she was on her way to a wretchedly lonely evening nonetheless—because the one person she wanted to be with wasn't there. She refused a cowboy the next dance so she could catch her breath. Unfortunately, that gave her time to think.

She found herself admitting that she might as well give up on her plan to make Adam jealous, mainly because it wasn't working. If he truly didn't want her, she would have to leave the Lazy S. Because she couldn't stand to be around him knowing that the love she felt would never be returned.

An altercation on the dance floor dragged Tate from her morose reflections. She was on her feet an instant later when she realized that one of the two men slugging away at each other was Buck Magnesson.

She reached Velma's side and shouted over the ruckus, "What happened? Why are they fighting?"

"All the poor man did was wink at me!" Velma shouted back. "It didn't mean a thing! There was no reason for Buck to take a swing at him."

When Tate looked back to the fight it was all over. The cowboy who had winked at Velma was out cold, and Buck was blowing cool air on his bruised knuckles. He was sporting a black eye and a cut on his chin, but his smile was broad and satisfied.

"Guess he won't be making any more advances to you, honey," Buck said.

"You idiot! You animal! I don't know when I've ever been so humiliated in my entire life!" Velma raged.

"But, honey—"

"How could you?"

"But, honey—"

Tate and Buck were left standing as Velma turned in a huff and headed for the door. Buck threw some money on the table to pay for their drinks and raced outside after her.

Velma was draped across the hood of the pickup, her face hidden in her crossed arms as she sobbed her heart out.

When Buck tried to touch her, she whirled on him. "Stay away from me!"

"What did I do?" he demanded, getting angry now.

"You don't even know, do you?" she sobbed.

"No, I don't, so I'd appreciate it if you'd just spit it out."

"You didn't trust me!" she cried.

"What?"

"You didn't trust me to let that cowboy know I'm not interested. You took it upon yourself to make sure he'd keep his distance.

"You're never going to forget the fact that I strayed once, Buck. You're always going to be watching—waiting to see if I slip up again. And every time you do something to remind me that you don't trust me—like you did tonight—it'll hurt the way it hurts right now.

"I won't be able to stand it, Buck. It'll kill me to love you and know you're watching me every minute from the corner of your eye. Take me home. I never want to see you again!"

Velma sat on the outside edge of the front seat, with Tate in the middle during the long, silent fifteen-minute drive west to Uvalde from Knippa. When they arrived in Velma's driveway, she jumped out and went running into the house before Buck could follow her.

Buck crossed his arms on the steering wheel and

dropped his forehead onto them. "God. I feel awful."

Tate didn't know what to say. So she just waited for him to talk.

"I couldn't help myself," he said. "When I saw that fellow looking at her . . . I don't know, I just went crazy."

"Because you were afraid he would make a move on Velma?"

"Yeah."

"Is Velma right, Buck? Didn't you trust her to say no on her own?"

Buck sighed. It was a defeated sound. "No."

There wasn't anything else to say. Buck had thought he could forgive and forget. But when it came right down to it, he would never trust Velma again. The risk was too great that his trust would prove unfounded.

"I don't want to be alone right now," Buck said. "Would you mind driving up toward the Frio with me? Maybe we can find a comfortable place to sit along the riverbank and lie back and count the stars. Just for a while," he promised. "I won't keep you out too late."

Tate knew Adam might be waiting up for her, but Buck had promised he wouldn't keep her out late. Besides, Adam's behavior over the past few days— throwing her into Buck's company—suggested that he no longer cared one way or the other.

"All right, Buck. Let's go. I could use some time away to think myself."

They found a spot beneath some immense cypress trees, and lay back on the grassy bank and listened to the wind whistling through the boughs. They tried to find the constellations and the North Star in the cloudless blue-black sky. The burble of the water over the rocky streambed was soothing to two wounded souls.

They talked about nothing, and everything. About childhood hopes and dreams. And adult realities. About wishes that never came true. They talked until their eyes drifted closed.

And they fell asleep.

Tate woke first. A mosquito was buzzing in her ear. She slapped at it, and when it came back again she sat up abruptly. And realized where she was. And who was lying beside her. And what time it was.

She shook Buck hard and said, "Wake up! It's dawn already. We must have fallen asleep. We've got to get home!"

Buck was used to rising early, but a night on the cold hard ground—not to mention the events of the previous evening—had left him grumpy. "I'm going, I'm going," he muttered as Tate shoved him toward the truck.

Tate sat on the edge of her seat the whole way home. She only hoped she could sneak into the house before Adam saw her. She could imagine what he would think if he saw her with grass stains on her denim skirt and a blouse that looked as if she had slept in it—which she had. Adam would never believe it had been a totally innocent evening.

When Buck dropped her off, she ran up the steps to the front door—a better choice than the kitchen if she hoped to avoid Adam—and stopped dead when he opened it for her. Adam stood back so she could come inside.

"We fell asleep!" she blurted. "Oh, Lord, that came out all wrong! Look, Adam, I can explain everything. Buck and I did fall asleep, but we weren't sleeping together!"

"I wouldn't have let you sleep, either," he drawled. "Not when there are so many more interesting things to do with the time."

"I mean, we didn't have sex," she said, irritated by his sarcasm.

"Oh, really?" It was obvious he didn't believe her.

"I'm telling you the truth!"

"What makes you think I care who you spent the night with, or what you did?" he said in a voice that could have cut steel.

"I'm telling you that absolutely nothing sexual happened between me and Buck Magnesson last night," she insisted.

Adam wanted to believe her. But he couldn't imagine how Buck could have kept her out all night and not have touched her. He didn't have that kind of willpower himself. His mouth was opened and the words were out before he knew he was going to say them.

"I made you an offer once, *little girl,* and I meant it. If you're looking for more experience in bed, I'll be more than happy to provide it."

Tate's eyes widened as she realized what Adam's

harsh-sounding words really meant. He was *jealous!* He *did* care! If only there was some way of provoking him into admitting how he really felt! Of course, there was something that might work. It was an outrageous idea, but then, as her brother Faron had always preached, "A faint heart never filled a flush."

Tate sat down on the brass-studded leather sofa and pulled off one of her boots. When Adam said nothing, she pulled off the other one. Then she stood up and began releasing the zipper down the side of her skirt.

"What are you doing?" he asked at last.

"I'm taking you up on your offer."

"What? Are you serious?"

"Absolutely! Weren't you?" She looked up at him coyly, batted her lashes, and had the satisfaction of seeing him flush.

"You don't know what you're doing," he said.

"I know exactly what I'm doing," she replied.

Her skirt landed in a pile at her feet, and Tate was left standing in a frilly slip and a peasant blouse that was well on its way to falling off her shoulder.

Adam swallowed hard. He knew he ought to stop her, but was powerless to do so. "Maria will be—"

"You know Maria isn't here. Sunday is her day off."

Tate reached for the hem of her blouse and pulled it up over her head.

Adam gasped. He had never seen her in a bra before—if that's what you called the tiny piece of confection that hugged her breasts and offered them up in lacy cups for a hungry man's palate.

Tate watched Adam's pulse jump when she stepped out of the circle of her skirt and walked toward him. His hand was warm when she took it in her own. "Your bedroom or mine?" she asked.

"Mine," he croaked.

Adam allowed himself to be led to his bedroom as though he had no will of his own. Indeed, he felt as though he were living some sort of fantasy. Since it was one very much to his liking, he wasn't putting up much of a struggle—none, actually—to be free.

"Here we are," Tate said as she closed the door behind her, shutting them into Adam's bedroom alone.

"I've never been made love to in the morning," Tate said. "Is there any special way it should be done?"

What healthy, red-blooded male could resist that kind of invitation?

Adam swept Tate off her feet. From then on she was caught up in a whirlwind of passion that left her breathless and panting. But now he led and she followed.

Lips reached out for lips. Flesh reached out for flesh. She was aware of textures, hard and soft, silky and crisp, rigid and supple, as Adam introduced her to the delights of sex in the warm sunlight.

This time there was no pain, only joy as he joined their bodies and made them one. When it was over, they lay together in the tangled sheets, her head on his shoulder, his hand on her hip, in a way that spoke volumes about the true state of their hearts.

Tate was aware of the fact Adam hadn't said a word

since she had closed the bedroom door behind them. She didn't want to break the magic spell, so she remained silent. But it was plain from the way Adam began moving restlessly, tugging on the sheet, rearranging it to cover and uncover various parts of her body, that there was something he wanted to get off his chest.

"I don't want you to go out with Buck anymore," he said in a quiet voice.

"All right."

"Just like that? All right?"

"I don't want Buck," she said. "I want you."

Adam groaned and pulled her into his arms, holding her so tightly that she protested, "I'm not going anywhere!"

"I can hardly believe that you're here. That you want to be here," Adam said with a boyish grin. "I've been going crazy for the past week."

"Me, too," Tate admitted. "But everything is going to be perfect now, isn't it, Adam? You do love me, don't you?"

She didn't wait for an answer, just kept on talking.

"We can be married and start a family. Oh, how I'd love to have a little boy with your blue eyes and—"

Adam abruptly sat up on the edge of the bed.

Tate put a hand on his back and he shrugged it off. "Adam? What's wrong?"

He looked over his shoulder with eyes as desolate as an endless desert. "I thought I'd made it clear that I wasn't offering marriage."

"But you love me. Don't you?"

Instead of replying to her question, he said, "I was married once before, for eight years. It ended in a bitter divorce. I have no desire to repeat the experience."

Tate couldn't have been more shocked if Adam had said he was a convicted mass murderer. "Why didn't you ever say anything to me about this before?"

"It wasn't any of your business."

"Well, now it is!" she retorted, stung by his bluntness. "You don't have to make the same mistakes this time around, Adam. Just because one marriage failed doesn't mean another will."

He clenched his teeth, trying to dredge up the courage to tell her the truth. But he wasn't willing to risk the possibility that she would choose having children over having him. And he refused to offer marriage while his awful secret lay like a wedge between them.

"I want you in my bed, I won't deny it," Adam said. "But you'll have to settle for what I'm offering."

"What's that?" Tate asked. "An affair?"

Adam shrugged. "If you want to call it that."

"And when you're tired of me, then what?"

I'll never get tired of you. "We'll cross that river when we get to it."

Tate was shaken by the revelation that Adam had been married. She wished she knew more about what had gone wrong to make him sound so bitter. Her pride urged her to leave while she still could. But her heart couldn't face a future that didn't include Adam. With the naïveté of youth, she still believed that love would conquer all, that somehow, everything would work out and that they would live happily ever after.

"All right," she said at last. "An affair it is."

She snuggled up to Adam's back. He took her arms and pulled them around his chest.

"It's a good thing my brothers can't see me now," she teased.

"I'd be a dead man for sure," he said with a groan.

"Just thank your lucky stars that I've been using a false last name. They'll never find me here."

"Let's hope not," Adam muttered.

The conversation ended there, because Adam turned and pulled Tate around onto his lap. He still didn't quite believe that she hadn't stalked out in high dudgeon, that she had chosen to stay. He straightened her legs around his lap and slipped inside her.

Tate learned yet another way to make love in the morning.

It was a mere three weeks later that their idyll came to a shocking and totally unforeseen end.

Eight

Tate was pregnant. At least she thought she was. She was sitting in Dr. Kowalski's office, waiting for her name to be called so she could find out if the results of her home pregnancy test were as accurate as the company claimed. She was only eight days late, but never once had such a phenomenon occurred in the past. Who would have thought you could get pregnant the first time out!

It had to have happened then, because after that first time she had gone to see Dr. Kowalski and been fitted for a diaphragm. She had managed to use it every time she had made love with Adam over the past three weeks—except the time she had seduced him after spending the night at the river with Buck. So maybe it had happened the second time out. That was beginner's luck for you!

"Mrs. Whitelaw? You're next."

Tate sat up, then realized the nurse had said *Mrs.* Whitelaw. Besides, she had given her name as Tate Whatly. So who was this mysterious *Mrs.* Whitelaw?

The tall woman who stood up was very pregnant. The condition obviously agreed with her, because her skin glowed with health. She had curly blond hair that fell to her shoulders and a face that revealed her age and character in smile lines at the edges of her corn-flower-blue eyes and the parentheses bracketing her mouth.

Tate found it hard to believe that it was pure coincidence that this woman had the same unusual last name as she did. Jesse had been gone for so long without any word that Tate immediately began weaving fantasies around the pregnant woman. Maybe this was Jesse's wife. Maybe Jesse would walk in that door in a few minutes and Tate would see him at long last.

Maybe pigs would fly.

Tate watched the woman disappear into an examining room. She was left with little time to speculate because she was called next.

"Ms. Whatly?"

"Uh, yes." She had almost forgotten the phony name she had given the nurse.

"You can come on back now. We'll need a urine specimen, and then I'd like you to strip down and put on this gown. It ties in front. The doctor will be with you in a few minutes."

Tate had had only one pelvic examination in her life—when she had been fitted for the diaphragm—and all the medical hardware attached to the examining table looked as cold and intimidating as she remembered. The wait seemed more like an hour, but actually was only about fifteen minutes. Tate had worked herself into a pretty good case of nerves by the time Dr. Kowalski came into the room.

"Hello, Tate. I understand the rabbit died."

The doctor's teasing smile and her twinkling eyes immediately put Tate at ease. "I'm afraid so," she answered.

The doctor's hands were as warm as her manner. Tate found herself leaving the doctor's office a short time later with a prescription for prenatal vitamins and another appointment in six weeks.

Tate was in the parking lot, still dazed by the confirmation of the fact she was going to have Adam's baby, when she realized that the woman who had been identified as Mrs. Whitelaw was trying to hoist her ungainly body into a pickup.

Tate hurried over to her. "Need a hand?"

"I think I can manage," the woman answered with a friendly smile. "Thanks, anyway."

Tate closed the door behind the pregnant woman, then cupped her hands over the open window frame. "The nurse called you Mrs. Whitelaw. Would you by any chance know a Jesse Whitelaw?"

The woman smiled again. "He's my husband."

Tate's jaw dropped. "No fooling! Really? Jesse's your husband! You've got to be kidding! Why, that means he's going to be a father!"

The woman chuckled at Tate's exuberance. "He sure is. My name's Honey," the woman said. "What's yours?"

"I'm Tate. Wow! This is fantastic! I can't believe this! Wait until I tell Faron and Garth!"

Tate sobered suddenly. She couldn't contact Faron and Garth to tell them she had found Jesse without taking the chance of having them discover her whereabouts. But Jesse wouldn't know she had run away from home. She could see him, and share this joy with him.

With the mention of Tate's name, and then Faron's and Garth's, Honey's gaze had become speculative, and finally troubled. When Honey had first found out she was pregnant, she had urged Jesse to get back in touch with his family. It had taken a little while to convince him, but eventually she had.

When Jesse had called Hawk's Way, he had found his brothers frantic with worry. His little sister Tate had disappeared from the face of the earth, and Faron and Garth feared she had suffered some dire fate.

If Honey wasn't mistaken, she was looking at her husband's little sister—the one who had been missing for a good two and a half months. The prescription for prenatal vitamins that Tate had been waving in her hand suggested that Jesse's little sister had been involved in a few adventures since she had left home.

"I have a confession to make," Tate said, interrupting Honey's thoughts. "Jesse—your husband—is my brother! That makes us sisters, I guess. Gee, I never had a sister. This is great!"

Honey smiled again at Tate's ebullience. "Maybe you'd like to come home with me and see Jesse," she offered.

Tate's brow furrowed as she tried to imagine what Jesse's reaction would be to the fact that she was here on her own. On second thought, it might be safer to meet him on her own ground. "Why don't you and Jesse come over for dinner at my place instead?" Tate said.

"Your place?"

Tate grinned and said, "Well, it's not exactly *mine*. I'm living at the Lazy S and working as a bookkeeper for Adam Philips."

"Horsefeathers," Honey murmured.

"Is something wrong?"

"No. Nothing." Except that Adam Philips was the man she had jilted to marry Jesse Whitelaw.

"Well, do you think you could come?"

If Tate didn't realize the can of worms she was opening, Honey wasn't about to be the one to tell her. Honey was afraid that if she didn't take advantage of Tate's offer, the girl might run into Jesse sometime when Honey wasn't around. From facts Honey knew—that Tate obviously didn't—it was clear the fur was going to fly. Honey wanted to be there to make sure everyone came out with a whole skin.

"Of course we'll come," she said. "What time?"

"About seven. See you then, Honey. Oh, and it was nice meeting you."

"Nice meeting you, too," Honey murmured as Tate turned and hurried away. Honey watched the younger woman yank open the door to the '51 Chevy pickup her brothers claimed she had confiscated when she had run away from home.

"Horsefeathers," she said again. The word didn't do nearly enough to express the foreboding she felt about the evening ahead of her.

Meanwhile, Tate was floating on air. This was going to work out perfectly. She would introduce Adam to

108

her brother and his wife, and later, when they were alone, she would tell Adam that he was going to be a father.

Boy was he going to be surprised!

Tate refused to imagine Adam's reaction as anything other than ecstatic. After all, just as two people didn't have to be married to have sex, they didn't have to be married to have children, either. After all, lots of movie stars were doing it. Why couldn't they?

Long before seven o'clock Tate heard someone pounding on the front door. She knew it couldn't be the company she had invited, and from the sound of things it was an emergency. She ran to open the door and gasped when she realized who was standing there.

"Jesse!"

"So it *is* you!"

Tate launched herself into her brother's arms. He lifted her up and swung her in a circle, just as he had the last time they had seen each other, when she was a child of eight.

Jesse looked so much the same, and yet he was different. His dark eyes were still as fierce as ever, his black hair still as shaggy. But his face was lined, and his body that of a mature man, not the twenty-year-old boy who had gone away when she was just a little girl.

"You look wonderful, Tate," Jesse said.

"So do you," she said with an irrepressible grin. She angled her head around his broad chest, trying to locate Honey. "Where's your wife?"

"I came ahead of her." Actually, he had snuck out

109

behind Honey's back and come running to save his little sister from that sonofabitch Adam Philips. Jesse had never liked the man, and now his feelings had been vindicated. Just look how Philips had taken advantage of his baby sister!

"Faron and Garth have been worried to death about you," Jesse chastised.

"You've been in touch with them? When? How?"

"Honey talked me into calling them when she found out for sure she was pregnant. Is it true what Honey told me? Are you living here with Adam Philips?" Jesse demanded.

"I work here," Tate said, the pride she felt in her job apparent in her voice. "I'm Adam's bookkeeper."

"What else do you do for Adam?"

Tate hissed in a breath of air. "I don't think I like your tone of voice."

"Get your things," Jesse ordered. "You're getting out of here."

Tate's hands fisted and found her hips. "I left home to get away from that kind of high-handedness. I don't intend to let you get away with it, either," she said tartly. "I happen to enjoy my job, and I have no intention of giving it up."

"You don't have any idea what can happen to a young woman living alone with a man!"

"Oh, don't I?"

"Do you mean to say that you and Philips—"

"My relationship with Adam is no concern of yours."

Jesse's dark eyes narrowed speculatively. His little sister glowed from the inside out. He was mentally adding one and one—and getting three. "Honey said she met you in the parking lot of Doc Kowalski's office, but she didn't say what you were doing there. What were you doing there, Tate? Are you sick?"

Jesse was just fishing, Tate thought. He couldn't know anything for sure. But even a blind pig will find an acorn once in a while. She had to do something to distract him.

"Honey's a really beautiful woman, Jesse. How did you meet her?"

"Don't change the subject, Tate."

Jesse had just grabbed Tate by the arm when Adam stepped into the living room from the kitchen. "I thought I heard voices in here." Adam spied Jesse's hold on Tate, and his body tensed. He welcomed the long overdue confrontation with Tate's brother. "Hello, Jesse. Would you mind telling me what's going on?"

"I'm taking my sister home," Jesse said.

Adam searched Tate's face, looking deep into her hazel eyes. "Is that what you want?"

"I want to stay here."

"You heard her, Jesse," Adam said in a steely voice. "Let her go."

"You bastard! It'll be a cold day in hell before I leave my sister in your clutches."

Adam took a step forward, eyes flashing, teeth bared, fists clenched.

111

"Stop it! Both of you!" Tate yanked herself free from Jesse's grasp, but remained between the two men, a human barrier to the violence that threatened to erupt at any moment.

"Get out of the way, Tate," Jesse said.

"Do as he says," Adam ordered.

Tate put a firm, flat palm on each man's chest to keep them apart. "I said stop it, and I meant it!"

"I'm taking you home, Tate," Jesse said. But his words and the challenge were meant for Adam.

"If Tate wants to stay, she stays!" Adam retorted, accepting the summons to battle.

Tate might as well not have been there for as much attention either man paid to her. She was merely the prize to be won. They were intent only on the conflict to come.

There was a loud knocking at the door, but before any of them could move, it opened and Honey stepped inside. "Thank goodness I got here in time!"

Honey stepped between the two men who fell back in deference to her pregnant state. "What are you two doing to this poor girl?" She slipped a comforting arm around Tate's shoulder. "Are you all right, Tate?"

"I'm fine," Tate said. "But these two idiots are about to start pounding on each other!"

"He's got it coming!" Jesse growled. "What kind of low-down hyena seduces an innocent child!"

"Jesse!" Tate cried, mortified as much by his use of the term *child* as by his accusation. Jesse might still remember her as a child, but she was a woman now.

Adam's face had bleached white. "You're way off base, Whitelaw," he snarled.

"Can you say you aren't sleeping with her?" Jesse demanded.

"That's none of your damn business!" Adam snapped back.

Honey stepped back a pace, taking Tate with her, beyond the range of the animosity radiating from the two powerful men.

Tate turned to plead peace with her brother. "I love Adam," she said.

"But I'll bet he hasn't said he loves you," Jesse retorted in a mocking voice.

Tate lowered her eyes and bit her lip.

"I thought not!" he said triumphantly.

Tate's chin lifted and her eyes flashed defiance. "I won't leave him!"

"He's just using you to get back at me," Jesse said. "The reason I know he can't love you, is because *I* stole the woman *he* wanted right out from under his nose."

"What?" Confused, Tate looked from her brother to her lover. Adam's eyes were dark with pain and regret.

Tate whirled her head to look at Honey. The pregnant woman's arms were folded protectively around her unborn child. Her cheeks flamed. She slowly lifted her lids and allowed Tate to see the guilt in her lovely cornflower-blue eyes.

It couldn't be true! Adam wouldn't have done something so heinous as to seduce her to get back at her

113

brother for stealing the woman he loved. But none of the three parties involved was denying it.

Her eyes sought out Adam's face again, looking for some shred of hope that her brother was lying. "Adam?"

Adam's stony features spoke volumes even though he remained mute.

"Oh, God," Tate breathed. "This can't be happening to me!"

Jesse lashed out with his fist at the man who had caused his sister so much pain. Adam instinctively stepped back and Jesse's fist swung through empty air. Before Jesse could swing the other fist, Honey had thrown herself in front of her husband.

"Please don't fight! Please, Jesse!"

It was a tribute to how much Jesse loved his wife that he held himself in check. He circled his wife's shoulder with one hand and held out the other to Tate.

"Are you coming?" he asked.

"I . . . I'm staying." At least until she had a chance to talk with Adam in private and hear his side of this unbelievable story. Then she would decide whether to tell him that she was going to have his child.

Honey saw that her husband was ready to argue further and intervened. "She's a grown woman, Jesse. She has to make her own choices."

"Dammit, this is the wrong one!" Jesse snarled.

"But it is my choice," Tate said in a quiet voice.

Honey slipped her arm around her husband's waist. "Let's go home, Jesse."

"I'm leaving," Jesse said. "But I'll be back with Faron and Garth." He yanked open the door, urged his wife out of the house and quickly followed, slamming the door after him.

Tate felt her stomach fall to her feet. She had been surprised to see Adam stand up to her brother—overjoyed, in fact. But if all three of the Whitelaw brothers showed up, there was no way Adam would be able to endure against them. Her brothers would haul her back home before she had time to say yeah, boo, or "I'm pregnant."

"You might as well say goodbye to me now," she said glumly. "When Faron and Garth find out where I am they'll be coming for me."

"No one—your brothers included—is going to take you from the Lazy S if you don't want to go," Adam said in a hard voice.

"Does that mean you want me to stay?"

Adam nodded curtly.

She didn't want to ask, but she had to. "Is it true, what my brother said? Did you love Honey?"

That same curt nod in response.

Tate felt the constriction in her chest tighten. "Would you have married her if Jesse hadn't come along?"

Adam shoved a hand through his hair in agitation. "I don't know. I wanted to marry her. I'm not so sure she was as anxious to marry me. I asked her. She never said yes."

That was small comfort to Tate, who was appalled to

115

hear how close Adam had come to marrying her brother's wife.

"Is that why you can't love me?" Tate asked. "Because you're still in love with her?"

The tortured look of pain on Adam's face left Tate feeling certain she had hit upon the truth. But she didn't despair. In fact, she felt a great deal of hope. Adam must realize that he could never have Honey Whitelaw now. Time was the best doctor for a wound of the heart. And time was on her side.

She very carefully did not bring up the subject of Jesse's accusation that Adam had made love to her to get revenge on her brother. In her heart she knew Adam would never use her like that. He might not be able to say he loved her—yet—but she was certain that one day he would.

"I need a hug," Tate said.

Adam opened his arms and Tate stepped into them. She snuggled against him, letting the love she felt flow over them both. But his body remained stiff and unyielding.

"Adam, I'm . . ." The word *pregnant* wouldn't come out.

"What is it, Tate?"

His voice sounded harsh in her ear, his tone still as curt as the abrupt nods with which he had acknowledged his love for another woman. Maybe Tate would just wait a little while before she told him she was carrying his child.

"I'm glad you want me to stay," she said.

He hugged her harder, until his hold was almost painful. Tate felt tears pool in the corners of her eyes. She blamed the phenomenon now on the heightened emotions caused by her pregnancy.

But the devil on her shoulder forced her to admit that unsettling seeds of doubt had been planted concerning whether everything would turn out happily ever after.

Nine

Tate spent the night in Adam's arms. He couldn't have been more comforting. But for the first time since they had begun sleeping together, they didn't make love.

When they met across the kitchen table the next morning, an awkwardness existed between them that had not been there in the past.

"You must eat more, *señorita,*" Maria urged. "You will not make it through the day on so little."

"I'm not hungry," Tate said. Actually, she had already snuck in earlier and had a light breakfast to stave off the first symptoms of morning sickness. Under Maria's stern eye, she dutifully applied herself to the bowl of oatmeal in front of her.

Tate's concentration was so complete that she paid no attention to the subsequent conversation Maria conducted with Adam in Spanish.

"The *señorita* has been crying," Maria said.

Adam glanced at Tate's red-rimmed eyes. "Her brother came to visit yesterday, the one she hasn't seen since she was a child."

"This brother made her cry?"

"He wanted her to go away with him."

"Ah. But you did not let her go."

"She chose to stay," Adam corrected.

"Then why was she crying?" Maria asked.

A muscle worked in Adam's jaw. At last he

answered, "Because she's afraid I don't love her."

"Stupid man! Why don't you tell her so and put the smile back on her face?"

Adam sighed disgustedly. "I don't think she'll believe me now."

Maria shook her head and clucked her tongue. "I am going to the store to buy groceries. I will not be coming back for two—no, three hours. Tell her you love her."

Adam's lips curled sardonically. "All right, Maria. I'll give it a try."

Tate had been making shapes with her oatmeal and had only eaten about three bites when Maria whisked the bowl out from in front of her.

"I need to clear the table so I can go shopping," Maria said. She refilled Tate's coffee cup. "You sit here and enjoy another cup of coffee."

She refilled Adam's cup as well and, giving him a suggestive look, said, "You keep the *señorita* company."

Maria took off her apron, picked up her purse and left by the kitchen door a few moments later.

When she was gone, the silence seemed oppressive. Finally Adam said, "What are your plans for today?"

"I guess I'll input some more information on the computer. What about you?"

"I'm moving cattle from one pasture to another."

"Your job sounds like more fun than mine. Can I come along?"

"I don't think that would be a good idea."

"Oh."

Adam saw the look on Tate's face and realized she thought he was rejecting her—again. He swore under his breath. "Look, Tate. I think we'd better have a talk."

Tate rose abruptly. This was where Adam told her that he had thought things over and he wanted her to leave the Lazy S after all. She wasn't going to hang around to let him do it. "I'd better get going. I—"

Adam caught her before she had gone two steps. He took her shoulders in his hands, turning her to face him. She kept her eyes lowered, refusing to look at him.

"Tate," he said in a voice that was tender with the love he felt for her. "Look at me."

Her eyes were more green than gold. He couldn't bear to see the sadness in them. He grasped her nape and pulled her toward him as his mouth lowered to claim hers.

It was a hungry kiss. A kiss of longing for things that ought to be. A kiss fierce with passion. And tender with love.

Adam wanted to be closer. He pulled her T-shirt up and over her head, then yanked the snaps open down the front of his shirt and pulled the tails out of his jeans. He sighed in satisfaction as he closed his arms around her and snuggled her naked breasts tight against his chest.

"Lord, sweetheart. You feel so good!" He cupped her fanny with his hands and lifted her, rubbing him-

120

self against her, letting the layers of denim add to the friction between them.

His mouth found a spot beneath her ear that he knew was sensitive, and he sucked just hard enough to make her moan with pleasure.

Adam froze when he heard the kitchen door being flung open. He whirled to meet whatever threat was there, pulling Tate close and pressing her face against his chest protectively.

Tate felt Adam's body tense, felt his shoulders square and his stance widen. She knew who it was, who it had to be. She turned her head. There in the doorway stood her three brothers, Faron, Jesse and Garth. And Garth was carrying a shotgun.

Tate felt her face flush to the roots of her hair. She was naked from the waist up, and there could be no doubt as to what she had been doing with Adam. Or, from the looks on their faces, how her brothers felt about it. She closed her eyes and clutched Adam, knowing her brothers planned to tear them apart.

"Make yourself decent!" Garth ordered.

Tate reached across to the chair where Adam had slung her T-shirt, and with her back to her brothers, pulled it over her head. When she turned to face them, Adam put an arm around her waist and pulled her snug against his hip.

The three men crowded into the kitchen. It soon became apparent they hadn't come alone. An elderly gentleman wearing a clerical collar and carrying what Tate supposed to be a Bible followed them inside.

"You have a choice," Garth said to Adam. "You can make an honest woman of my sister, or I can kill you."

Adam cocked a brow. "That's murder."

Garth smiled grimly. "It'll be an accidental shooting, of course."

"Of course," Adam said, his lips twisting cynically. "What if Tate and I aren't ready to get married?"

"Man gets a woman pregnant, it's time to marry her," Jesse snarled. "I made a point of seeing Doc Kowalski on the way home last night and told her Tate was my sister. She congratulated me on the fact I'll soon be an *uncle!*"

Adam froze. He turned to stare at Tate, but she refused to meet his gaze. His hand tightened on her waist. "Are you pregnant, Tate?"

She nodded.

Adam's lips flattened and a muscle worked in his jaw. He grabbed hold of her chin and forced it up. "Whose child is it? Buck's?"

"Yours!" Tate cried, jerking her head from his grasp.

"Not mine," he said flatly. "I'm sterile."

Tate sank into a kitchen chair at one end of the table, her eyes never wavering from Adam's granitelike expression.

Meanwhile, Tate's brothers were in a quandary.

"We can't force him to marry Tate if the child's not his," Faron argued.

"But it must be his!" Jesse said. "Look how we found them today!"

Garth handed the shotgun to Faron, then crossed and

sat down beside Tate on the opposite side of the table from Adam. He took Tate's hand from her lap and held it in his for a moment, gently rubbing her knuckles. "I want you to be honest with me, Tate. Have you been with another man besides Adam?"

"No! I'm carrying Adam's child, whether he believes it or not!"

"Adam says he's sterile," Garth persisted.

"I don't care what he says," Tate said through clenched teeth. "I'm telling the truth."

Garth and Faron exchanged a significant glance. Garth stood and confronted Adam. "Can you deny you've made love to my sister?"

"No, I don't deny that."

"Then my original offer still holds," Garth said.

"Given that choice, I suppose I have no choice," Adam conceded with a stony glare.

"What about me?" Tate asked. "Don't I get a choice?"

"You'll do as you're told," Garth commanded. "Or else."

"Or else what?"

"You come home to Hawk's Way."

Tate shuddered. There seemed no escape from the ultimatum Garth had given her. At least if she went through with the wedding, she would still have her freedom. Once her brothers had her safely married they would go back where they had come from—and she could figure out what to do from there.

"All right. Let's get this over with," she said.

"Reverend Wheeler, if you please?" Garth directed the minister to the head of the table, arranged Tate and Adam on one side, and stood on the other side with Faron and Jesse.

He told Adam, "I had to cut a few corners, but I've taken care of getting the license." He gestured to the minister. "Whenever you're ready, Reverend."

If Reverend Wheeler hadn't baptized Tate and presided at her confirmation, he might have had some qualms about what he was about to do. Never had bride and bridegroom looked less happy to be wed. But he firmly believed in the sanctity of home and family. And Garth had promised a large donation to build the new Sunday school wing.

The reverend opened the Bible he had brought along and began to read, "Dearly Beloved . . ."

Tate listened, but she didn't hear what was being said, spoke when called upon, but was unaware of the answers she gave. She had fallen into a deep well of despair.

Tate had never really thought about having a big wedding, but a white T-shirt was a poor substitute for a wedding gown. She wouldn't have minded giving up the festive trappings, if only she were sure the man standing beside her wanted to be her husband.

Adam did not.

How had things gone so wrong? Tate had never meant to trap Adam. It was clear he thought she had slept with Buck, and that the baby wasn't his. She knew from her experience with Buck and Velma that

124

a marriage that lacked trust—on both sides—was in deep trouble. If Adam believed she had lied about the child's father, wouldn't he expect her to lie about other things? Would he, like Buck, overreact from now on if she so much as looked at another man? Of course Buck was jealous because he loved Velma. Tate wasn't so sure about Adam's feelings. He had never once said he loved her.

Tate would have given anything if she had just told Adam about the baby last night. Then, they would have had a chance to discuss things alone. Such as why a man who was obviously able to sire children thought he was sterile.

"Tate?"

"What?"

"Hold out your hand so Adam can put the ring on your finger," Garth said.

What ring? Tate thought.

"With this ring I thee wed," Adam said. He slipped the turquoise ring he usually wore on his little finger on the third finger of Tate's left hand.

Tate was lost. What had happened to the rest of the ceremony? Had she said "I do"?

Reverend Wheeler said, "I now pronounce you man and wife. You may kiss the bride."

When neither of the newlyweds moved, Faron said in a quiet—some might have said gentle—voice, "It's time to kiss your bride now, Adam."

Adam wanted to refuse. It was all a sham, anyway. But when Tate turned her face up to him she looked so

125

bewildered he felt the urge to take her in his arms and protect her.

Garth cleared his throat at the delay.

Adam's jaw tightened. Tate already had three very efficient guardians. She didn't need him. But he found himself unable to resist the temptation of her lips, still swollen from his earlier kisses. Her eyes slid closed as he lowered his head. He touched his lips lightly to hers, taking the barest taste of her with the tip of his tongue.

If this had been a real wedding he would have wanted to cherish this moment. From the shuffling sounds across the table, Adam was reminded that it was real enough. So he took what he wanted from Tate, ravaging her mouth, letting her feel his fury and frustration at what her brothers had robbed them of when they had insisted on this forced marriage.

As soon as he lifted his head Adam saw that Garth had crossed around the table. Instead of the punch in the nose Adam expected, Tate's oldest brother held out his hand to be shaken. To Adam's further surprise, Garth had a grin on his face.

"Welcome to the family," Garth said. He gave Tate a fierce hug. "Be happy!" he whispered in her ear.

Faron was next to shake Adam's hand. "How about a drink to celebrate?" he asked. "I've got champagne on ice outside in the pickup."

"I guess that would be all right," Adam said, still stunned by the abrupt change in attitude of Tate's brothers.

Faron headed outside as Jesse approached Adam. The two men eyed each other warily.

At last Jesse held out his hand. "Truce?"

When Adam hesitated, Jesse said, "Honey will kill me if we don't make peace." When Adam still hesitated, Jesse added, "For Tate's sake?"

Adam shook hands with Tate's middle brother. They would never be good friends. But they were neighbors, and now brothers-in-law. For their wives' sakes, they would tolerate one another.

The wedding celebration was a lively affair. Now that Adam had done the right thing by Tate, her brothers were more than willing to treat him like one of the family.

As the morning wore on and Adam had a few glasses of champagne—and more than a few glasses of whiskey—he began to think maybe things hadn't turned out so badly after all.

Now that he and Tate were married, there was no reason why they couldn't make the best of the situation. He couldn't feel sorry about the baby, even if it meant Tate had lied to him about sleeping with Buck. He had always wanted children, and this one would be especially beloved because it would belong to him and Tate.

After he made love to his wife, Adam would tell her that he loved her. They could forget what had happened in the past. Their lives could begin from there.

Tate's brothers might have stayed longer, except Honey called to make sure everything had turned out all right. When Jesse hung up the phone, he said to his brothers, "I know you don't want to be reminded, but I have work that has to get done today."

Faron guffawed and said, "Tell the truth. What you're really concerned about is getting home to your wife."

The three brothers kidded each other good-naturedly all the way out the door. Once they and the preacher were gone, Tate closed the door and leaned her forehead against the cool wood frame.

"I'm sorry, Adam."

He crossed to her and slipped his arms around her waist from behind. "It's all right, Tate. It wasn't your fault."

"They're *my* brothers."

"They only did what they thought was best for you." Despite the fact he was a victim of their manipulation, Adam could sympathize with her brothers. If Melanie had lived . . . if he had found her in the same circumstances . . . he might have done the same thing. And hoped for the best. As Adam was hoping for the best now with Tate.

He kissed her nape and felt her shiver in his arms. "Come to bed, Tate. It's our wedding day."

She kept her face pressed to the door. She was too intent on giving Adam back his freedom to hear the message of love in his words and his caress. "I can't stand it—knowing you were trapped into marrying me." She felt his body stiffen, and said, "I promise I'll give you a divorce. As soon as the baby is born I—"

Adam grabbed her by the arm and jerked her around to face him. "Is that the reason you agreed to marry me? So you can have a name for your bastard?"

"Please, Adam—"

"Don't beg, Tate, it doesn't become you."

Tate had slapped him before she was aware she had raised her hand. She gasped when she saw the stark imprint her fingers had left on his cheek.

Adam grabbed her wrist. Tate could feel him trembling with rage. She waited to see what form his retaliation would take.

"All right," Adam said in the harshest voice she had ever heard him use. "I'll give you what you want. Your baby will have my name and you can have your divorce. But there's something I want in return, Tate."

"What?" she breathed.

"You. I want you in my bed every night." His grasp on her wrist tightened. "Warm. And willing. Do I make myself understood?"

Oh, she understood, all right. She had offered him the divorce hoping he would refuse. His ultimatum made it clear what he had wanted from her all along. Well, she would just show him what he was so willing to give up!

"Believe me, you're going to get what you're asking for, Adam," she said in a silky voice. *And a whole lot more!*

He started for the bedroom, his hand firmly clamped around her wrist. Tate hurried to catch up, afraid that if she fell, he would simply drag her behind him.

When they arrived in the bedroom he closed the door behind her. Only then did he release her. "Get undressed," he ordered. He crossed his arms and stood there, legs widespread, staring at her.

Tate held herself proudly erect. Sooner or later Adam was going to realize the truth. The child she carried was his. Meanwhile, he was going to get every bit of what he had demanded—and perhaps even more than he had bargained for.

Tate had never stripped to tease a man. She did so now.

The T-shirt came off first. Slowly. She let it hang by one finger for a moment before it dropped to the floor. She looked down at her breasts and saw the aureoles were pink and full. She reached down to brush her fingertips across her nipples, then returned to tease the pink buds until they stood erect.

Adam hissed in a breath of air.

Tate didn't dare look at him, afraid she would lose her nerve. Instead she smoothed her hands over her belly and down across the delta of her thighs, spreading her legs so that her hand could cup the heat there. She glided her hands back up the length of her body, feeling the textures of her skin, aware of the prickles as her flesh responded to the knowledge that Adam was watching every move she made.

She shoved her hands into her hair at the temples and then gathered her hair and lifted it off her nape, knowing that as she raised her arms her breasts would follow. She arched her back in a sensuous curve that thrust breasts and belly toward Adam.

She actually heard him swallow. Then she made the mistake of looking at him—at his bare chest. His nipples were as turgid as hers. As she relaxed her body into a more natural pose, she met blue eyes so dark with passion they were more the hue of a stormy sky.

His nostrils were flared to drink in the scent of her. His body was wired taut as a bowstring, fists clenched at his sides. His manhood was a hard ridge that threatened the seams at the crotch of his jeans. As his tongue reached out to lick at the perspiration on his upper lip, she felt her groin tighten with answering pleasure.

Tate felt exultant. Powerful. And oh, so much a woman. Encouraged by her success, she reached down for the snap of her jeans. Adam's whole body jerked when it popped free. The rasp of her zipper as she slid it down was matched by the harsh sound of Adam's breathing.

She slowly turned down each side of her jeans in front, creating a V through which the white of her panties showed. Then she spread her legs, stuck her thumbs into her panties and let her fingers slide down inside the jeans, pulling her underwear down and slowly exposing a V of flesh on her belly.

Adam swore under his breath. But he didn't move an inch.

Tate took a deep breath and shoved both panties and jeans down low on her hips, revealing her hipbones and belly and a hint of dark curls at the crest of her thighs. She put her hands behind her and rubbed her buttocks, easing the jeans down a little more with each circular motion.

She stuck her thumbs back in the front of the jeans, and met Adam's gaze before skimming her fingers across her pubic arch. A pulse in his temple jumped. His jaw clenched. But otherwise he didn't stir from where he was standing.

Tate smiled, a feminine smile of enjoyment and satisfaction. She gave one last little shove and both panties and jeans began the slide down to her ankles, where she stepped out of jeans, panties and moccasins all at once.

At last Tate stood naked before Adam. Her body felt languid, graceful as it never had. She realized it was because Adam adored her with his eyes. Because he desired her with his body. She made no move to hide herself from him.

It wasn't until she took a step toward him that Adam finally moved.

He glided toward her like a stalking tiger. Tate felt the sexual energy radiating from him long before their bodies met. His kiss was fierce, consuming. His hands seemed to be everywhere, touching, demanding a response. She arched against him, feeling the swollen heat and hardness beneath the denim.

Adam didn't bother taking her to bed. He backed her up against the wall, unsnapped his jeans to free himself, then lifted her legs around him and thrust himself inside.

Tate clung to Adam's neck with her arms and to his

132

hips with her legs. His mouth sought hers, and his tongue thrust in rhythm with his body. His hand slipped between them and sought out the tiny nubbin that was the source of her pleasure. His thumb caressed her until he felt the waves of pleasure tightening her inner muscles around him. He threw his head back in ecstasy as his own powerful orgasm spilled inside her.

Then his head fell forward against her shoulder as he struggled to regain his breath. He finally released her legs so that she could stand, but found he had to hold her to keep her from falling, her knees were so wobbly. He lifted her into his arms and carried her to bed, throwing the sheets back and setting her down gently before joining her there.

He pulled the covers up over them both and found he could barely keep his eyes open. But there was something he wanted to say before he fell asleep.

"Tate? Are you awake?"

"Mmm. I guess so," she murmured against his throat.

"You can admit the truth about sleeping with Buck. It isn't going to make a difference in how I feel about you." *Or the baby,* he thought.

Tate pushed herself upright. The sheet that had covered her fell to her waist. "I'm telling the truth, Adam, when I say I never slept with Buck. Why won't you believe me?"

Adam levered himself up on his elbow and met her gaze with a flinty one of his own. "Because I have the

133

medical tests to prove you wrong."

"Then your tests are mistaken!" Tate retorted. She leaned back against the headboard and yanked the covers up to her neck.

Tate had never looked more beautiful. Adam had to lie back and put his hands behind his head to keep from reaching for her again. The three hours Maria had promised to stay gone were nearly up, and he had no doubt the housekeeper would come looking for him to find out whether he had told Tate that he loved her.

He was glad now that he hadn't. At least he had been spared the humbling experience of confessing his love to a woman who had married him only to have a name for her child. Adam lay there trying to figure out why Tate persisted in lying about the baby.

"Does Buck know about the baby?" he asked.

"He guessed," Tate admitted. Buck had known from the glow on her face that something was different and had confronted her about it. She had told him the truth.

"I suppose he refused to marry you because he's still in love with Velma," Adam said.

Tate lurched out of bed and stomped over to where her clothes lay in a pile on the floor. She kept her back to Adam as she began dressing.

"Where are you going?" he asked.

"Anywhere I can be away from you," she retorted.

"Just so long as you stay away from Buck, I don't care—"

Tate whirled and said, "Buck is my friend. I'll see him when and where and as often as I please."

Adam shoved the covers out of the way and yanked on his jeans. "You took vows to me that I don't intend to see you break," he said.

"You're a fool, Adam. You can't see what's right in front of your face."

"I know a whore when I see one."

Adam was sorry the instant the words were out of his mouth. He would have given anything to take them back. He was jealous, and hurt by her apparent devotion to Buck. He had said the first thing that came into his head that he knew would hurt her.

And he was sorry for it. "Tate, I—"

"Don't say anything, Adam. Just get away from me. Maybe someday I'll be able to forgive you for that."

Adam grabbed his shirt, underwear, socks and boots and left the room, closing the door quietly behind him.

Tate sank onto the bed, fighting sobs that made her chest ache. This was worse than anything she had ever imagined. She had ample evidence in Buck's case of how suspicion and mistrust could make a man act irrationally. She had just never expected to see Adam behave like a jealous jackass.

What was she going to do now?

135

Ten

Adam had ample time all through the day and overnight to regret his outburst. Tate had spent the rest of the day in the office, then retreated to her own bedroom for the night. He had decided it would be best to meet her over the breakfast table and try to mend fences when Maria was there to act as a buffer.

But morning sickness had once again brought Tate to the kitchen early. Instead of waiting to have coffee with Adam, she left the house to go for a walk, hoping it might settle her stomach. Buck waved to her from the loft of the barn, where he was forking down hay. After looking back once at the house, Tate headed toward the barn to talk to him. She had better give him fair warning that Adam was on the war path and looking for scalps.

Adam's mood wasn't improved when he realized, after sitting at the table for half an hour alone, that Tate wasn't coming to breakfast. He had snapped at Maria like a wounded bear when she started asking questions, and now she wasn't talking to him, either. He shoved his hat down on his head and headed out to the barn to work off some steam by cleaning out stalls.

Adam's eyes had barely adjusted to the shadows in the barn when he spied Tate standing next to the ladder that led to the loft. His heart gave a giant leap—then began to pump with adrenaline when he realized that Buck was standing right beside her. And that the

136

lanky cowboy had his arm around Tate's shoulder.

Adam marched over to Buck and ordered, "Get your hands off my wife."

Buck grinned. "Jealous, huh? You've got no reason—"

Adam thought he had damned good reason to be jealous. After all, his wife was carrying Buck's child. His fist swung hard and fast, straight for Buck's nose.

Buck fell like a stone, his nose squirting blood. Tate quickly knelt beside him, grabbing the bandanna out of her back pocket to staunch the bleeding.

"You idiot!" she snapped at Adam. "Go stick your head in a bucket of water and cool off!"

Adam wanted to yank Tate away from the other man's side, but it was plain he would have a fight on his hands if he tried. His pride wouldn't allow him to ask her nicely to come with him. Not that he could have forced the words past the lump in his throat. "Do as you please," he snarled. "You always have."

With that, he turned and marched right back out of the barn. They heard gravel fly in the drive as he gunned his pickup and drove away.

"Who put a burr under his saddle?" Buck asked, dabbing gently at his nose with the bloody bandanna.

"How did you like the way he treated you?" Tate asked.

"Damn near hated it," Buck replied.

"Think about it the next time you see Velma with another man and decide to take a punch at him. Because that's what an unreasonable, mistrustful, paranoid sonofabitch looks like in action."

Buck's lips quirked at the corners. "Are you saying that's the way I act around Velma?"

"Bingo."

Buck tested the bridge of his nose to see if it were broken. "Maybe this bloody nose wasn't such a bad thing after all."

"Oh?"

"Adam might have knocked some sense into me. I know damn well he has no reason to be jealous, even though he thinks he does. He should have trusted you." Buck struggled to his feet. "Maybe I'll just go see Velma again."

"Is there any chance she'll speak to you?"

"If she's been as miserable as I have the past few weeks, she will," Buck said, a determined light in his brown eyes.

"I wish you luck," Tate said.

"I don't think I'm going to need luck," Buck said. "I've got something even better."

"What's that?"

"I think I just might have had some trust pounded into me."

Tate gave Buck a hug, which he was quick to escape with the excuse of dusting the hay off his britches.

"I may have become a trusting soul," he said, "but Adam's still crazy as a loon. No telling when he'll turn right around and come looking for you. I'd feel a mite safer if you go on back to the house."

Tate did as he asked. She hoped Buck's experience with Adam had shown Buck once and for all the folly of being needlessly jealous. Because if Buck could learn to trust Velma, there was some hope that Adam would one day come to trust her.

Meanwhile, Adam had driven north toward Fredericksburg and was almost into the hill country before he calmed down enough to look around and see where he was. He made a U-turn in the middle of the highway and headed back the way he had come.

Jealousy. Adam had never before had to cope with the feeling, and he had been doing a pretty rotten job of it so far. He could spend the little time he and Tate had together before she sought out a divorce condemning her for what was past. Or he could simply enjoy the company of the irrepressible, lively hoyden he had come to know and love. Between those two choices, the latter made a whole lot more sense.

When Adam arrived back at the ranch house he sought Tate out first in the barn. He found Buck working there.

The lanky cowboy leaned on the pitchfork and said, "You finally come to your senses?"

Adam grinned ruefully. "Yeah. About that punch—"

"Forget it." Buck had been working out how he could use his swollen nose to get Velma's sympathy, and then explain to her the lesson it had taught him. "Believe me, I can understand how you must have felt when you saw me with Tate."

"Because of Velma?" Adam remembered how devastated Buck had been when he had found out his wife was cheating on him.

139

"Yeah."

"Uh, have you seen Tate?" Adam asked.

"She went back to the house. Look, Adam, you don't—"

"You don't have to explain, Buck. It doesn't matter." Adam turned and headed back to the house. He found Tate working in his office at the computer.

"Busy?"

Tate jumped at the sound of Adam's voice. She looked over her shoulder and found him leaning negligently against the door frame, one hip cocked, his hat in his hands. The anxious way his fingers were working the brim betrayed his nerves.

"Not too busy to talk," she said. She turned the swivel chair in his direction, leaned back, put her ankles on the desk and crossed her arms behind her head. It was a pose intended to be equally carefree. In Tate's case, her bare toes—which wiggled constantly—gave her away.

In his younger days, Adam had ridden bucking broncs in the rodeo. His stomach felt now as it did when he was on the bronc and the chute was about to open. Like the championship rider he was, he gave himself eight good seconds to make his point and get out.

"I'm sorry. I was out of line—with what I said last night and today with Buck. I'm not asking you to forgive me. I'd just like a chance to start over fresh from here."

Tate sat there stunned. *Adam apologizing?* She had

never thought she would see the day. But like Velma, once burned, twice chary. "Does this mean you're rescinding the bargain we made?"

Adam swallowed hard. "No."

So, he still wanted her, even though he was convinced the baby was Buck's. And he was willing to keep his mouth shut about her supposed indiscretion—and give his name to Buck's child—in return for favors in bed.

A woman had to be out of her mind to accept a bargain like that.

"All right," Tate said. "I accept your apology. And I agree to abide by the bargain we made yesterday."

Adam noticed she hadn't forgiven him. But then he hadn't asked for forgiveness. More to the point, she had agreed that their marriage continue to be consummated.

Tate thought she must be an eternal optimist, because she took Adam's appearance at her door as a good sign. She hadn't given up hope that she could somehow convince him of the truth about the baby, and that they would live happily ever after. It might never happen, but at least now they would be living in amity while they tried to work things out.

"It's beautiful out today," Adam said. "How would you like to take a break and come help me? I still have to move those cattle from one pasture to another." Work that hadn't been done yesterday because they had gotten married instead.

A broad smile appeared on Tate's face. "I'd like that.

Just let me save this material on the computer."

She dropped her feet and swiveled back around to face the computer. She was interrupted when Adam loudly cleared his throat.

"Uh. I didn't think to ask. Did Dr. Kowalski say everything's okay with the baby? There's no medical reason why you can't do strenuous exercise, is there?"

Tate turned and gave him a beatific smile. "I'm fine. The baby will enjoy the ride."

Nevertheless, Adam kept a close eye on Tate. When he saw her eyelids begin to droop late in the afternoon he suggested they take a siesta. He led her to a giant live oak that stood near the banks of a creek on his property. There he spread a blanket he had tied behind the saddle and provided a picnic he had packed in his saddlebags.

Tate pulled off her boots and wiggled her toes. Then she lay back on the blanket with her hands behind her head and stared up at the freckles of sun visible through the gnarled, moss-laden limbs of the live oak. "This is wonderful! A picnic! I had no idea you had this in mind when you asked me to come with you today."

Actually, Maria was responsible for the impromptu picnic. Adam had thought of the blanket himself. The delight on Tate's face was its own reward. Adam sat down cross-legged across from her and passed out ham and cheese sandwiches, deviled eggs and pickles. There was a thermos of iced tea to drink.

"I don't usually care for pickles," Tate said,

crunching into the sweet gherkin in her hand. "But you know, this tastes pretty good."

Adam smiled to himself. In his experience, pregnant women had odd cravings. He had once had a patient who'd eaten liver with peanut butter.

Soon after she had finished her lunch, Tate yawned. "I can't believe how tired I feel lately."

"Your body is going through a lot of changes."

"Is that a medical opinion, Doctor?" Tate asked, eyeing him through half-closed lids. But she didn't hear his answer. The moment she laid her head on her hand and closed her eyes, she fell sound asleep.

Adam cleared away the picnic and lay down beside her to watch her sleep. He had never realized how very long her lashes were, or how very dark. She had a tiny mole beside her ear that he hadn't detected before. And dark circles under her eyes, which he also hadn't noticed.

As a doctor he knew the strain pregnancy put on a woman's body and her emotions. He made a vow to himself to take care of Tate, to make sure that the dark circles disappeared and that the smile stayed on her face.

He knew how she would resent it if she thought he had taken on the role of caretaker. After all, she had fled her brothers because they had been overprotective. He knew he would have to be subtle if he were going to get her to rest. Like the picnic today. He was sure she had no idea she was being manipulated for her own good.

143

When Tate awoke, she stretched languorously, unaware that she had an appreciative audience. When she blinked open her eyes she realized it was nearly dusk. She sat up abruptly and made herself dizzy.

Adam was beside her instantly, his arm around her shoulder to support her. "Are you all right?"

"Just a little woozy. I guess I sat up too quickly. Why did you let me sleep so long?"

"You were tired."

Tate leaned her head on his shoulder. "I guess I was. Hadn't we better head back now?"

He nuzzled her neck, searching out the mole near her ear. "I don't have anything planned for this evening. Do you?"

Tate chuckled. "No, I can't say that I have."

Adam slowly laid her back down and found her mouth with his. He brushed his cheek against her long lashes and slid his hands into her hair, smoothing it back where the breeze had ruffled it into her face.

As the sun slipped from the sky, Adam made sweet love to his wife. They rode home by moonlight, and after they had taken care of the horses, Adam made sure Tate went right to bed. In his room. With his arms around her.

"I'll have Maria move your things to my room," he murmured in her ear. "It'll be more convenient since you'll be sleeping in here."

Tate opened her mouth to object and shut it again. After all, she wanted this marriage to work. It made sense that the more time she spent with Adam, the better chance she had of making that happen. She intended to become absolutely irreplaceable in his life.

But as the days turned into weeks, and the weeks into months, the invisible wall of mistrust between them did not come down. Though she made love with Adam each evening, the words "I love you" stuck in Tate's throat whenever she tried to say them. It was too painful to expose her need to him. Especially since she didn't want to put him in the position of feeling he had to say the words back. Which she was afraid he wouldn't.

Adam was equally aware of how much he had gained when he had moved Tate into his bedroom, and how little things had really changed between them. He found himself enchanted by her constant delight in the baby. He tried to be happy with each stage of her pregnancy. Mostly he was successful.

But he watched her and wondered if she ever thought of Buck. The cowboy hadn't been spending much of his free time around the ranch lately. But Adam was watching. Which meant that he still didn't trust her not to seek Buck out if she got the chance.

Meanwhile, he had waited for Tate to tell him again that she loved him. She hadn't said the words lately. Not once, in fact, since they had gotten married. And he found he wanted—needed—to hear those words.

Tate was in bed with Adam when she felt the baby move for the first time. She grabbed his hand and placed it on her belly. "Can you feel that? Kind of a fluttery feeling."

"No." He tried to remove his hand.

"Wait. Maybe it'll happen again."

"Feel here," Adam said, putting her hand on his arousal. "I think I've got a little fluttery feeling of my own."

Tate couldn't help giggling as Adam's body pulsed beneath her hand. "You've got a one track mind, Dr. Philips."

"Oh, but what a lovely track it is," he murmured, kissing his way down her body. His head lay against her belly when he felt a slight movement against his cheek. He came up off her like a scalded cat.

"I felt it! I felt the baby move!"

Tate smiled triumphantly. "I told you so!"

Adam found himself suddenly uncomfortable. As a doctor he had described the stages of pregnancy to his patients hundreds of times. Yet he found himself overwhelmed by the reality of it. That feather-light touch against his cheek had been an actual human being. Growing inside Tate. A baby that would have his name. A baby that Tate planned to take away with her when she divorced him.

Adam was reminded why he shouldn't let himself care too much about either Tate or the baby. It was going to be bad enough when Tate left him. He wouldn't be able to bear it if he got attached to the child, as well.

Adam didn't say anything about what he was thinking, but from that night onward Tate noticed a distinct difference in his behavior whenever she mentioned the baby. Adam seemed indifferent. Nothing she said got him excited or brought a smile to his face. It was as if the baby had become a burden too heavy for him to bear.

Tate had conveniently forgotten that she had promised Adam a divorce as soon as the baby was born. So she was certain the only possible explanation why Adam wasn't allowing himself to get involved with anything having to do with the baby was because he believed it wasn't his child. She decided to try, once more, to convince him that he was the baby's father.

She chose her moment well. She and Adam had just made love and were lying with their bodies still tangled together. Their breathing had eased and Adam's nose was nuzzled against her throat. The baby was active now, and she pressed her belly against his, knowing Adam couldn't help but feel the movement.

"Adam?"

"Hmm."

"The baby's kicking a lot tonight."

"Hmm."

She threaded her fingers through Adam's hair. "You know, I think he's going to be a lot like his father."

She felt Adam stiffen.

"Like you, Adam. He's going to be a lot like you."

Adam's voice was weary as he said, "You don't have to do this Tate. It's not necessary to try and make me believe the baby's mine. I—" *I'll love it anyway.* Adam bit his lip on that admission. No sense revealing the pain she would be causing him when she took the child away.

"But the baby *is* yours, Adam."

"Tate, we've been through this before. I took tests—"

"What about your wife? Did she take tests, too? Maybe it was her fault and not yours."

"Anne was tested. There was nothing wrong with her."

"Maybe they got your test results mixed up with someone else's," Tate persisted. "I mean, you're a doctor. You know those things happen. Did you see the results yourself?"

"Anne called me from the doctor's office," Adam said.

"You mean you weren't there?"

"I had a medical emergency. I—"

"Then she could have lied!" Tate said.

"Why? She wanted children as much as I did. What earthly reason would she have had to lie?"

"I don't know," Tate said. "All I do know is that a child is growing in my body, and the only man who's put his seed inside me is you!"

For an instant Adam felt a wild surge of hope. Maybe there had been some mistake. Maybe Anne had not lied, but been mistaken. He couldn't believe she would have lied about a thing like that. He had seen her tests himself. The problem did not lie with Anne. So something must have been wrong with him for them to remain childless for eight years.

He felt the hope die as painfully as it had been born. "You're making wishes that can't come true, Tate," he said. "This child isn't mine. I'm sterile."

Tate could have screamed, she was so frustrated. "Is that why you refuse to get involved with anything having to do with the baby?" she demanded. "Because you think it isn't yours?"

"Have you forgotten that you promised me a divorce as soon as it's born?" Adam reminded her.

"What if I said I didn't want a divorce? Would you feel differently about the baby then?" Tate persisted.

"What do you want me to say, Tate? That I'll be a father to your child? I will. What more do you want from me?" The words seemed torn from someplace deep inside him.

Tate felt frozen inside. It was clear Adam wouldn't ever be able to accept the baby she carried as his own. And she wouldn't subject her child to a lifetime of rejection by its father, the one person who should love and protect it above all others. That knowledge, on top of her doubts about whether Adam loved her, made it plain that she would be better off away from here.

She didn't say another word, just allowed Adam to pull her into his embrace and hold her one last time. Once he was asleep, she carefully disentangled herself. She turned and looked at him once before she left the room—and his life—forever.

Eleven

Garth and Faron were shocked—to put it mildly—when Tate showed up on the doorstep at Hawk's Way.

"What happened?" Garth demanded. "What did that bastard do to you?"

"You look awful, Tate," Faron said, putting an arm around her shoulder and leading her inside.

"If that man hurt you I'll—"

"Don't, Garth!" Tate pleaded. "Just leave it alone. Adam and I are both better off this way."

"Do you want to talk about it?" Faron asked.

"I just want to go to bed and sleep for a week," Tate said.

Faron and Garth exchanged a sober look. There were deep shadows under Tate's eyes. Her face looked gaunt and unhappy.

"He'll pay for the way he's treated you," Garth said.

"No! Listen to me!" Tate said, her voice sharp with fatigue and anxiety. "You have to trust me to know what's best." There it was again. That word *trust*. "This marriage was a horrible mistake. I'm going to file for a divorce."

"Don't be hasty," Faron urged.

"You're dead on your feet. You have no idea what you're saying," Garth countered.

"Stop it! Both of you! *I'm a grown woman.*" She laughed hysterically. "Don't you see? I'm going to be a mother myself! Surely it's time for you to admit that

I can manage my own life. You have to love me enough to let go."

Tate didn't wait to hear whether they were willing to concede to her wishes. She was too distressed to deal with them anymore. She ran up the stairs to her bedroom, her rigid bearing defying either one of her brothers to come after her.

"She's changed," Faron said.

"And not for the better," Garth noted.

Faron frowned. "I'm not so sure about that. She's grown up, Garth. She's not a little girl anymore. Six months ago she wouldn't have stood up to you like that. I think she had to be in a lot of pain to leave here in the first place, and a helluva lot more pain to come back. I think maybe we're at least partly responsible."

"I blame the bastard who got her pregnant," Garth said.

"None of this would have happened if she hadn't run away from home. And she wouldn't have run away from home if we hadn't kept such a tight rein on her."

"It was for her own good."

"It doesn't seem that way now, does it?" Faron asked. "I think maybe our little sister grew up in spite of us. And I, for one, am not going to interfere anymore in her life."

Adam had been scowling ever since he had woken up to find Tate gone from his bed—and his life. The first thing he had done was to go hunting Buck. His fury had been boundless when the lanky cowboy was nowhere to be found. Finally, one of the other hands told him Buck had been spending nights with his ex-wife.

That news had confounded Adam. He had doggedly made the trip to Velma's house and knocked on the door in the early hours of the morning. Buck had answered the door wearing low-slung jeans and scratching a head of auburn hair that stood out in all directions.

"Adam! What are you doing here this hour of the morning?"

"Where's Tate?"

"How the hell should I know?" Buck retorted.

By now Velma had joined him, wearing a flashy silk robe, and with her red tresses equally tangled. "What's going on, Adam?"

It was obvious to Adam that Tate wasn't here. But he didn't know where else to look. "Do you mind if I come in?"

"Come on in and I'll make us some coffee," Velma said. "You can tell us what's got you running around at this hour like a chicken with its head cut off."

While Velma was in the kitchen making coffee, Adam put his elbows on the table and wearily rubbed his forehead. Buck waited patiently for Adam to speak his piece.

"Tate's gone. Run away," Adam said at last.

Buck whistled his surprise. "Thought that little filly loved you too much ever to leave you."

152

Adam's head came up out of his hands. "What?"

"Sure. You and that baby of yours was all she ever talked about."

"*My* baby?"

"Sure as hell wasn't mine!" Buck said.

Adam's eyes narrowed. "She spent nearly the whole night with you. Twice."

Buck laughed in Adam's face. "We were here at Velma's house the first night. And we fell asleep on the banks of the Frio after Velma and I had an argument on the second. There's only been one woman for me. And that's my wife."

"You mean your ex-wife."

Buck grinned and held up his left hand, which bore a gold wedding band. "I mean my wife. Velma and I got married again last Sunday."

"Congratulations. I guess." Adam was confused. "But if you're not the father of Tate's baby, then who is?"

Buck pursed his lips and shook his head. "I would think that has to be pretty obvious even to a blind man."

"But I—" Adam swallowed and admitted, "I can't father children."

"Whoever told you that," Buck said, "is a whopping liar."

"But—" Adam shut his mouth over the protest he had been about to make. Was it really possible? Could Anne have lied to him? It was the only answer that would explain everything.

Adam jumped up from his chair just as Velma brought in the coffeepot.

"You're not staying?" she asked.

"I've got to get in touch with someone in San Antonio." He was going to see the doctor who had done those fertility tests and find out the truth for himself.

"When you're ready to go after Tate, I have a suggestion where you might look," Buck said.

"Where?"

"I figure she went home to her brothers. You'll probably find her at Hawk's Way."

"Damn."

Buck laughed. "I'd like to be a fly on the wall when you try to take her out of there."

Adam wasn't able to think that far ahead. Right now he had a doctor to visit in San Antonio.

Early the next afternoon Adam came out of a glass-walled office building feeling like a man who had been poleaxed.

"Your sperm count was low," the doctor had said. "But certainly still within the range that would allow you to father children."

"But why didn't Anne and I ever conceive children?" he had demanded.

The doctor had shrugged. "It was just one of those things that happens with some couples."

Anne had lied to him. Whatever her reasons—maybe she just hadn't wanted to keep on trying—she had lied to him.

154

I'm going to be a father! Tate is pregnant with my child!

The realization was only just hitting him. Adam was floating on air. He had always intended to love the child because it was Tate's, but the knowledge that the baby Tate was carrying was a part of him filled his cup to overflowing.

There was only one problem. Tate was at Hawk's Way. And he was going to have to fight her brothers to get her back.

An hour later, he was in his pickup traveling north.

Adam shouldn't have been surprised when he discovered the vastness of Hawk's Way, but he was. The cliffs and canyons in northwest Texas were a startling contrast to the rolling prairies found on the Lazy S.

The ranch house was an imposing two-story white frame structure that looked a lot like an antebellum mansion with its four, twenty-foot-high fluted columns across the front and its railed first- and second-story porches. The road leading to the house was lined with magnolias, but the house itself was shaded by the branches of a moss-laden live oak.

Adam was glad to see that the barn and outbuildings were a good distance from the house. He was hoping to catch Tate alone and talk with her before he had to confront her brothers. He went around to the kitchen door, knocked softly and let himself inside.

Tate was standing at the sink peeling potatoes. She was wearing an apron, and sweat from the heat of the kitchen made her hair curl damply at her nape.

"Hello, Tate."

Tate dropped both potato and peeler in the sink and turned to face Adam. Once she had wiped her hands dry, she kept them hidden in the folds of the apron so Adam wouldn't see how much they were trembling.

"Hello, Adam," she said at last. "I was just peeling potatoes for tonight's pot roast."

"You look tired," he said.

"I haven't been sleeping much the last couple of days." She swallowed over the ache in her throat and asked, "What are you doing here, Adam?"

"I've come to get you. Go upstairs and pack your things. I'm taking you home with me."

"I am home."

"Like hell you are! This is where you grew up, Tate. It isn't your home. Your home is with me and our child."

Tate felt her heart racing with excitement and with hope. Adam's words now were a far cry from what she had heard a mere forty-eight hours ago. It appeared he intended to be a father to the baby after all.

Before Adam could say more, the kitchen door opened and Tate remembered she had told her brothers to come to the house early for lunch because she wanted to take a long afternoon nap. She quailed at the confrontation she knew was coming.

"What the hell are you doing here?" Garth demanded.

"I've come for my wife."

"Tate's not going anywhere," Garth said.

Adam wasn't about to be said nay. He grabbed Tate by the wrist. "Forget your things," he said. "We can get them later." He dragged her two steps, but could go no farther.

Faron and Garth were blocking the way out.

"Get out of my way," Adam said.

"Look, Adam," Faron began in a reasonable voice. "If you'll just—"

But Adam was in no mood to be reasonable. He twisted around to shove Tate out of the way, then reversed the arc with his fist. Faron was felled by the powerful blow, which caught him completely unprepared to defend himself.

Adam stood spread-legged, facing Tate's eldest brother. "I'm telling you to get out of my way."

"You're welcome to leave," Garth said. "But Tate stays here."

"I'm taking her with me."

"That remains to be seen."

Tate knew her brother's strength. He had at least three inches of height and thirty more pounds of muscle than Adam. "Garth, please don't—"

"Shut up, Tate," Adam ordered. "I can handle this on my own." He was fighting for his life—the right to cherish his wife and raise his child—and he had no intention of losing.

The fight that followed was vicious, but mercifully short. When it was finished, Adam was still standing, but it was a near thing. He grabbed Tate's wrist and helped her step over Garth's body on the way out, letting the screen door slam behind her.

Once Tate and Adam were gone, the two brothers, still sprawled on the floor where Adam had left them, had trouble meeting each other's eyes. Two against one and they were the ones dusting themselves off.

Garth cradled his ribs as he sat up and leaned back against the kitchen cupboards. He pulled his shirttail out and pressed the cloth against a cut over his cheek-bone.

Faron stretched his legs out in front of him as he leaned back against the refrigerator. He rubbed his sore chin, then opened his mouth and moved his jaw around to make sure no bones were broken.

"Guess our little sister is married to a man who loves her after all," Faron said.

"One with a damned fine right hook," Garth agreed, dabbing gently with his shirttail at the bruised skin around his eye.

The two brothers looked at each other and grinned. Garth yelped when his split lip protested.

"Guess that's one suitor you couldn't scare off," Faron said.

"I always said Tate would know the right man when he came along."

"Seems you were the one needed convincing," Faron said, eyeing Garth's battered face.

Garth guffawed, then moaned when his head protested. "By the way, who do you think's going to be godfather to that baby of hers?"

"Me," Faron said, hauling himself off the floor.

"You get to be godfather to Jesse's firstborn."

"Jesse's next oldest. It ought to be him."

"Jesse and Adam don't get along. I'm a better choice," Faron said.

The two brothers headed out to the barn, arguing all the way. Neither of them mentioned the fact that they had been relegated to a new role in Tate's life. Their little sister had found a new protector.

Meanwhile, Tate was aware of every move Adam made, every word he spoke. She had him stop at the first gas station they came to with the excuse she had to use the bathroom. She used the opportunity to clean the blood off his face and bought some bandages in the convenience store to put across the cuts on his cheek and chin.

Once they were back in the car, she said, "You were wonderful, you know. I don't think anybody's ever beaten my brother Garth in a fight."

"I had more at stake than he did," Adam mumbled through his split lips.

Tate's spirits soared at this further evidence that Adam's attitude toward both her and the baby had somehow changed.

It was a long ride back home to the Lazy S, broken frequently by stops to allow Tate to use rest room facilities.

"It's the baby," she explained.

"I know about these things," Adam replied with an understanding smile. "I'm a doctor, remember?"

It was dark by the time they arrived back at the Lazy

S. Maria greeted them both at the door with a big hug.

"It is so good to see you back where you belong, *señora!*"

In Spanish she said to Adam, "I see you have put the smile back on her face. You will tell her now you love her, yes?"

"When the time is right," Adam said.

Maria frowned. "The time, she is *right now*."

Adam refused to be pressed. He excused himself and ushered Tate to his bedroom. He lifted her into his arms and carried her across the threshold.

"Our marriage begins now," he said, looking into her eyes. "The past is past."

Tate could hardly believe this was happening. "I love you, Adam."

She waited for the words she knew he would say back to her. But they didn't come.

There was nothing very difficult about saying those three little words, but Adam felt too vulnerable at the moment to admit the depth of his feelings for Tate. He hadn't really given her a choice about coming back with him. It seemed more appropriate to *show* her that he loved her, rather than to tell her so in words.

He made love to her as though she were the most precious being in the world. He kissed her gently, indifferent to his split lip, tasting her as though he had never done so before, teasing her with his teeth and tongue. Her soft whimper of pleasure rolled through him, tightening his body with need.

His hand slid down to her rounded belly. "My

child," he whispered in her ear. "Our child."

"Yes. Yes, our child," Tate agreed, glad that he was ready to accept the baby as his own.

"I mean, I know it's mine," Adam said.

Tate was jerked abruptly from her euphoria. "What?" She turned to face him, her eyes still wide and dilated with pleasure. "What did you say?"

Adam's thumb caressed her belly as his eyes met hers. "I went back to that doctor in San Antonio. The one who did the fertility tests on Anne and me. I'm not sterile, Tate. Anne lied to me."

Tate's eyes widened in horror as she realized what this meant. No wonder Adam hadn't said he loved her. He hadn't come to Hawk's Way for her at all. He hadn't fought Garth for the purpose of getting her back. He had fought to get back his child!

Twelve

Tate pleaded fatigue from her pregnancy as an excuse not to make love to Adam, and the damned man fell all over himself being understanding. Naturally he wanted to make sure she took good care of herself so *his child* would be born healthy!

But the next morning, when Adam stood blocking her way into the office—because she shouldn't have to work in her delicate condition—Tate let him have it with both barrels.

"I'm just as capable of working with *your* child growing inside me as I was when it was just *my* child!" she snapped.

"But—"

"No buts! I'll eat right, get enough rest and come through this pregnancy with flying colors. Even if it is partly *your* child growing inside me and not just *mine*."

Adam wasn't sure what he had done wrong, but Tate obviously had a bee in her bonnet about something. "What's all this *your* child and *my* child business? What happened to *our* child?"

"That was before you found out you can father as many children as you want. Well, you can go father some other fool woman's kids. This baby's *mine!*"

With that, she shoved him out of the office and slammed the door in his face.

Adam could hear her crying on the other side of the

door. He tried the handle and found it was locked. He pounded on the door. "Tate, let me in!"

"I don't want to talk to you. Go away!"

He pounded on the door again. "If you don't open this door, I'm going to break it down," he threatened.

He had just turned his shoulder toward the door when it opened, and he nearly fell inside. "That's better," he said, walking in and shutting the door behind him. "I think maybe we better talk about this . . . difference of opinion. What's important—"

"I'm not a baby that needs coddling. I'm fully capable of taking care of myself. You have to trust me to—oh, what's the use?" she said, throwing up her hands in disgust. "Trust was never a part of our relationship in the past. I don't suppose that just because you've found out I didn't lie to you about the baby, it's going to change anything between us."

"What does trust have to do with this?"

"Everything!" Tate was quivering she was so upset. "Buck and Velma—"

"Whoa there! What do Buck and Velma have to do with this?" Adam was getting more confused by the minute.

"It doesn't matter," Tate said.

Adam grabbed her by the shoulders. "It obviously *does* matter. Now I want an explanation and I want it now!"

"You sure about that? Food for thought gives some folks indigestion!"

Adam shoved Tate down in the swivel chair and set-

163

tled his hip on the desk in front of her. "Settle down now. This kind of agitation isn't good for the baby. I—"

Tate leaped out of the chair and poked a finger at Adam's chest. *"The baby! The baby!"* she mimicked back at him. "That's all you really care about, isn't it? I'm nothing more than a vessel for your seed. I could be a test tube for all the difference it would make to you! Well, I've got news for you, *buster!* I want more than a father for my child, I want a husband to love me and hold me and—" Tate choked back a sob.

"Tate, I do love—"

"Don't say it! If you really loved me, you've had plenty of opportunities to say so. If you say it now I'll know you're just doing it to calm me down for the sake of the baby."

"I'm telling the truth!"

"So was I! When I told you months ago that this baby was yours and mine—*ours!* But you didn't trust me then. And I don't believe you now! Just like Buck and Velma—"

"Are we back to them again?"

"Yes-s-s!" she hissed. "Because Buck and Velma are a perfect example of what happens when there's no trust in a relationship. You hurt each other, and you're miserable and unhappy together.

"If you love somebody you have to be willing to trust them enough to be honest with them. To lay yourself open to the pain of rejection by admitting how you really feel about them. And you have to trust in their love enough to know that they would never do anything purposely to hurt you. Like lying to you. Or sleeping with another man.

"Without trust, love will just wither and die." Tate swallowed another sob and said, "Like it did with Buck and Velma."

"Are you finished?" Adam asked.

Tate sniffled and wiped her nose with the hem of her T-shirt. "I'm finished."

"First of all, I think you should know that Buck and Velma got remarried on Sunday."

Tate's eyes went wide. "They did?"

"Second of all, whether you believe me or not, I do love you. I've loved you for a long time. I never said anything because . . ."

"Because you didn't trust me," Tate finished in a small voice.

He couldn't deny it, because it was true. "I guess it's my turn to point to Buck and Velma," Adam said ruefully.

"Why?"

"Aren't they proof that people can change? That mistakes aren't irrevocable?"

Tate's brow furrowed. "I suppose."

"Then will you give me a chance to prove how I feel? To prove that I do love you enough to trust you with my heart?"

Tate felt her throat swelling closed with emotion. "I suppose."

"Come here." Adam opened his arms and Tate

walked into them. He tipped her chin up and looked deep into her eyes. "We start from here. Our baby, our marriage—"

"Our trust in each other," Tate finished.

They shared a tender kiss to seal the bargain. But it turned into something much more. Or would have, if Maria hadn't interrupted them.

"Señor Adam, there is a man here with the new rodeo bull he says you must sign for."

"I'm coming, Maria."

Adam gave Tate another quick, hard kiss. "Until tonight."

"Until tonight." Tate managed a smile as he turned and left her. He had given her an awful lot to think about. But it was better to confront these issues now, before the baby came, than later. Garth had always said, "If you have a hill to climb, waiting won't make it smaller."

As Adam began to realize over the next several weeks, it was one thing to believe yourself trustworthy; it was quite another thing to earn someone's trust.

He made love to Tate each night, revering her with words and gestures. But he never told her that he loved her. It was plain from the cautious way she watched him when she thought he wasn't looking, that she wasn't yet ready to hear the words—and believe them.

Maria got thoroughly disgusted watching Señor Adam and Señora Tate tiptoe around each other. She nagged at him in Spanish to tell Señora Tate he loved her and be done with it. "If you say it often enough, she will believe it," Maria advised.

"Do you think so?" Adam asked. "Even if she thinks I'm lying through my teeth?"

"But you would not be lying!" Maria protested. "She will see what is in your eyes. And she will believe."

Adam truly wished it were that simple. He was beginning to despair of ever convincing Tate that he loved her enough to want her both as his wife and the mother of his child.

The situation might have gone on unresolved, with both Adam and Tate less than happy, if Maria hadn't decided to take matters into her own hands.

As far as Maria was concerned, it was as plain as white socks on a sorrel horse that Señor Adam loved the little *señora,* and that she loved him. The problem was getting the two of them to recognize what was right in front of their noses.

So right after lunch one day she sent Señor Adam off to the store to buy some spices she needed for dinner. She waited a half hour, then raced into the office where the *señora* was working.

"Señora Tate, come quick! There's been an accident! Señor Adam—"

By the time Adam's name was out of Maria's mouth, Tate had already left her chair. She grabbed hold of Maria's sleeve and demanded, "How badly is he hurt? What happened? Where is he?"

"It was the new Brahma bull, the one he has penned in the far pasture," Maria said. "He was not watching closely enough and—"

"The bull stomped him? My God! How did you find this out? I never even heard the phone ring! Has somebody called an ambulance? We have to get Adam to a doctor!"

"Señor Buck has already called the doctor. He is with Señor Adam now." Maria smiled inwardly. She hadn't even had to invent an injury for Señor Adam. The *señora* had done that herself. She said, "Señor Buck—"

"Thank God, Buck's with him!" Tate headed for the kitchen to get the keys to her pickup from the peg where she usually left them. But they weren't there.

"Where are my keys? Maria, have you seen my keys?"

Maria closed her hands around the set of keys in her pocket. "No, *señora*. But your horse, she is saddled already for the ride you wished to take this afternoon."

"That'll probably be faster anyway. I can go cross-country. Thanks, Maria. You're a lifesaver!"

Tate had barely been gone ten minutes when Maria heard Señor Adam's pickup pull up in back of the house. She sniffed the onion she had ready and waiting and went running out to the truck, tears streaming, waving her hands frantically to attract his attention.

"Señor Adam! The *señora!* Hurry!" Maria hid her face in her apron and pretended to cry.

"What's wrong, Maria? What happened to Tate? Is

she all right?" He didn't wait for an answer, but bounded up the back steps toward the house.

"She is not there!" Maria cried.

Adam's face bleached white. "She's gone? She left me?"

Maria saw she had made a serious mistake and said, "Oh, no! But she went riding toward the pasture where you are keeping that big-humped bull. Her horse must have been frightened. Señor Buck found her there on the ground."

"She's hurt? Has she been taken to the doctor?"

"She is still there. Señor Buck is with her—"

Adam didn't wait to hear more. He jumped back into his pickup and gunned the motor, heading down the gravel road, hell-bent-for-leather toward the opposite end of the Lazy S.

Maria dabbed with her apron at the corners of her eyes where the onion had done its work. Well, she would soon see the results of her meddling. If she was right, there would be more smiles and laughter around this house in the future. When *el bebé* arrived, Tía Maria would tell the story of the day Papa rescued Mama from the big bad bull and brought her home to live here happily ever after.

Tate managed to get through the gate that led to the new bull's pasture without dismounting, but she still begrudged the time it took the mare to respond to her commands as she opened the metal gate and closed it behind her.

Once she was inside the pasture she kept a sharp lookout for the huge Brahma. She wasn't sure what Buck had done to secure it after it had stomped Adam. The chance that it might still be roaming free in the pasture made her shudder in fear.

Tate hadn't gone far when she heard the sound of a truck spinning gravel somewhere beyond the pasture gate. There was no siren, but she thought it might be the ambulance. Maybe they would know exactly where to find Adam. Tate turned the mare back toward the gate and headed there at a gallop.

She was almost to the gate when she realized the huge Brahma bull, with its thick horns and humped back, was standing there, apparently drawn by the sound of the truck, which usually brought hay and feed.

When the bull heard the horse behind him, he whirled to confront the interloper on his territory. Tate found herself trapped, with no way out. She yanked the mare to a halt, holding her perfectly still, knowing that any movement would make the Brahma charge.

Adam swore loudly and fluently when he realized Tate's predicament. He slammed on the brakes, grabbed a rope from the bed of the truck, and hit the ground running.

"Don't move!" he yelled. "I'm coming."

"Wait!" Tate yelled back. "Don't come in here! It's too dangerous!"

Adam didn't bother with opening the gate, just went over the top and down inside. The rattle of the fence had the bull turning back, certain dinner was about to be served. He stopped, confused when he saw the man on foot inside the fence. He nodded his lowered head from Tate to Adam and back again, uncertain which way he wanted to go.

Adam shook out the lasso and started looking for something he could use as a snubbing post. Not too far away stood a medium-size live oak.

Adam didn't hesitate. He walked slowly toward the Brahma, which began to snort and paw at the ground in agitation. The bull's attention was definitely on Adam now, not Tate.

"Please don't come any closer, Adam," Tate said quietly.

"Don't worry. I've got this all worked out." If he missed his throw, he was going to run like hell and hope he got to the fence before the Brahma got to him.

But Adam's loop sang through the air and landed neatly around the Brahma's horns. He let out the rope as he ran for the live oak. He circled the tree several times, enough to make sure the rope was going to hold when the bull hit the end of it.

By then, Tate had realized what he was doing. She raced her mare to the live oak, took her foot out of the stirrup so Adam could quickly mount behind her, then kicked the mare into a gallop that took them out of harm's way.

The Brahma charged after them, but was brought up short by the rope that held it hog-tied to the tree.

Tate rode the mare back to the gate, where Adam

slipped over the horse's rump, and quickly opened the gate for her. Once she was through, he fastened the gate, and reached up to pull her off the mare.

They clutched each other tightly, well aware of the calamity they had barely escaped. As soon as their initial relief was past, they began talking at the same time, amazed by the fact that they had found each other alive and well and unhurt.

"Maria told me the bull had stomped you!"

"She told me you had been thrown from your horse!"

"I wasn't thrown!"

"I wasn't stomped!"

The realization dawned for both at the same time that they had been manipulated into coming here under false pretenses.

"I'll kill her!" Adam said.

"I think you should give her a raise," Tate said with a laugh.

"Why? She nearly got us both killed!"

"Because she made me realize I've been a fool not to believe what I know in my heart is true."

"I do love you, Tate," Adam said. He pulled her into his arms and kissed her hard. "I do love you."

"I know. And I love you. When I thought you might be dying—or dead—I realized just how much."

"When I thought something might have happened to you, I felt the same," Adam said. "I should have been saying 'I love you' every day. I love you, Tate. I love you. I love you."

Adam punctuated each statement with a kiss that was more fervent than the one before.

Tate was having trouble catching her breath. She managed to say, "Adam, we have to do something about that bull."

"Let him find his own heifer," Adam murmured against her throat.

Tate laughed. "We can't just leave him tied up like that."

"I'll send Buck and the boys back to take care of him and to pick up your mare. We have more important things to do this afternoon."

"Like what?"

"Like plotting how we're going to get even with Maria."

As they drove back toward the ranch house, Adam and Tate plotted imaginative punishments they could wreak on the housekeeper for lying to them. It wasn't an easy job, considering how they had to balance her dubious methods against her very satisfying results.

"I think the best thing we could do is have about five children," Adam said.

Tate gulped. "Five?"

"Sure. That'll fix Maria, all right. She'll have the little devils sitting on her lap and tugging at her skirts for a good long while!"

"Serves her right!" Tate agreed with a grin.

Adam stopped the pickup in front of the ranch house, grabbed Tate's hand and went running inside to find the housekeeper.

"Maria!" he shouted. "Where are you?" He headed for the kitchen, dragging Tate along behind him.

"Here's a note on the refrigerator," Tate said.

"What's it say?"

Tate held the note out to Adam.

Dear Señor Adam,
    Tell her you love her. I'll be gone for two—no, three—hours.

Love, Maria

Adam laughed and pulled Tate into his embrace—where the first of Maria's little devils promptly kicked his father in the stomach.

Center Point Publishing
600 Brooks Road ● PO Box 1
Thorndike ME 04986-0001 USA

(207) 568-3717

US & Canada:
1 800 929-9108